THE BLITZ

By the same author

The History Today *Companion to British History*
(editor, with Neil Wenborn)
From the Bomb to the Beatles
Who's Who in British History (editor)
The Penguin Dictionary of British History (editor)
The 1940s House
The Edwardian Country House
'Over Here': GIs in Wartime Britain
D-Day: Those Who Were There
Wartime: Britain 1939–45
The Children's War: The Second World War Through
the Eyes of the Children of Britain
The Animals' War: Animals in Wartime from
the First World War to the Present Day
War on the Home Front: Experience
Life in Britain During the Second World War
The Thirties: An Intimate History

JULIET GARDINER

The Blitz

The British Under Attack

Harper
Press

HarperPress
An imprint of HarperCollins*Publishers*
77–85 Fulham Palace Road,
Hammersmith, London W6 8JB
www.harpercollins.co.uk

Published by HarperPress in 2010

1

The author asserts the moral right
to be identified as the author of this work

A catalogue record for this book is available from the British Library

ISBN 13 978-0-00-724077-7
ISBN 10 0-00-724077-5

Set in Minion by Palimpsest Book Production Ltd, Falkirk, Stirlingshire

Printed and bound in Great Britain by Clays Ltd, St Ives plc

Mixed Sources
Product group from well-managed
forests and other controlled sources
www.fsc.org Cert no. SW-COC-001806
© 1996 Forest Stewardship Council

FSC is a non-profit international organisation established to promote the
responsible management of the world's forests. Products carrying the FSC
label are independently certified to assure consumers that they come
from forests that are managed to meet the social, economic and
ecological needs of present and future generations.

Find out more about HarperCollins and the environment at
www.harpercollins.co.uk/green

For Martha

CONTENTS

ILLUSTRATIONS

Winston Churchill inspects bomb damage in Battersea, south London. *(© Topfoto)*

Women carrying possessions salvaged from their bombed homes pick their way through the rubble in the East End of London in September 1940. *(Imperial War Museum)*

Firemen play their hoses on the still-burning remains of buildings in Chancery Lane after a raid on the night of 24–25 September 1940. *(© Getty Images/Popperfoto)*

Newborn babies wrapped in an air-raid shelter in Clapton, north-east London, while a nurse instructs their mothers how to knit to pass the time during raids. October 1940. *(© Getty Images/Fox)*

Shelterers spread across the track in the disused Aldwych tube station on 8 October 1940. *(Imperial War Museum)*

A properly-constructed Anderson shelter survives after a house in Croydon is destroyed by a high-explosive bomb in October 1940. *(© Getty Images/Popperfoto)*

Wendell Willkie, the defeated Republican candidate in the 1940 US presidential election, inspects the ruins of Coventry Cathedral after the raid of 14–15 November 1940. *(© Topfoto)*

An elderly couple walk through a devastated Liverpool street after the 'Christmas raids' on Merseyside in 1940. *(© Getty Images)*

King George VI and Queen Elizabeth survey the wreckage at Buckingham Palace caused by a high-explosive bomb on 13 September 1940. *(© Getty Images)*

Much of Holland House, the Jacobean London residence of Lord Ilchester, was destroyed by incendiary bombs on 28 September 1940. *(© Getty Images)*

The artist Ethel Gabain painting a blitzed building in November 1940. *(© Getty Images)*

St Paul's Cathedral after the devastating raid on the City of London on 29 December 1940. *(© Getty Images)*

The water from firemen's hoses froze into long icicles on a fire engine's ladder during a raid on Bristol on 3 January 1941. *(Bristol Evening Post)*

An official taking statements from bombed-out local residents on the morning after a raid on London's East End in September 1940, photographed by Bert Hardy for *Picture Post.* *(© Getty Images)*

Civil Defence workers, including members of the light and heavy rescue squad and demolition workers clearing debris, search for victims trapped beneath a collapsed building. *(© Getty Images/Popperfoto)*

A group of people gather outside a town hall to check the lists of air-raid casualties. Photograph by Humphrey Spender for *Picture Post.* *(© Getty Images)*

Swansea residents queue up for tea and buns from a mobile canteen in February 1941. *(Imperial War Museum)*

Tension erupts in Coventry, with people's possessions scattered in the street after a raid in February 1941. *(© Getty Images/Popperfoto)*

A stream of dispossessed Clydebank residents stumble past a tenement in which a large number of people had been killed after the raids of 13 and 14 March 1941. *(© Getty Images)*

A soldier stands guard in front of a bombed-out grocer's shop in Birkenhead in March 1941 to prevent salvaged stock from being looted. *(Imperial War Museum)*

Members of the WVS working in the open air to prepare soup for those affected by a raid on Liverpool in December 1940. *(© Getty Images/Popperfoto)*

The Dean of Westminster Abbey, Dr Paul de Labillière, inspects the ruins of the abbey's cloisters on the morning after the last raid of the blitz, on 10 May 1940. *(© Getty Images/Popperfoto)*

Hollyhocks, buddleia and willow herb had colonised bombed-out buildings in the City of London's Gresham Street by July 1943. Wildernesses such as this would persist on many urban bombsites for decades. *(© Getty Images/Popperfoto)*

PREFACE

These are the facts, observe them how you will:
Forget for a moment the medals and the glory,
The clean shape of the bomb, designed to kill,
And the proud headlines of the papers' story.

Remember the walls of brick that forty years
Had nursed to make a neat though shabby home;
The impertinence of death, ignoring tears,
That smashed the house and left untouched the Dome.

Bodies in death are not magnificent or stately,
Bones are not elegant that blast has shattered;
This sorry, stained and crumpled rag was lately
A man whose like was made of little things that mattered;

Now he is just a nuisance, liable to stink,
A breeding-ground for flies, a test-tube for disease:
Bury him quickly and never pause to think
What is the future like to men like these?

People are more than places, more than pride;
A million photographs record the works of Wren;
A city remains a city on credit from the tide
That flows among its rocks, a sea of men.

Ruthven Todd, 'These are the Facts'

'Blitz' is an abbreviation of the German word '*Blitzkrieg*', meaning 'lightning war'. It all too accurately describes Hitler's advance through western

Europe in May and June 1940, as Norway, then Holland, Belgium and France fell to the German forces within weeks; but it hardly seems appropriate for the almost continual aerial bombardment of the British Isles that started on 7 September 1940 and continued with little relief until 10 May 1941. Yet 'blitz' is the name by which these eight months were known. It was a German word, and like lightning it came from the sky, and could and did kill. Indeed, an air raid was in many ways like a terrible storm – the sky livid, rent by jagged flashes, obscured by black clouds rolling across it or lit up by the reflected glow of fires, while the noise of bombs and guns echoed like the thunder of Mars, the god of war.

The blitz was the test of war for the British people: it touched everyone's lives, it mobilised the population, and in phrases that have become time-worn but are nevertheless true, put civilians on the front line and made the home front the battlefront. Dunkirk and the Battle of Britain, which preceded it, had essentially been military operations. The blitz was total war. Its intensity and inescapability made it possible to call the Second World War 'the people's war', in which, in the words of the poet Robert Graves, a soldier 'cannot even feel that his rendezvous with death is more certain than that of his Aunt Fanny, the firewatcher'.

The blitz was the war that everyone in Britain had been expecting, and fearing, since that warm Sunday morning in September 1939 when Neville Chamberlain had announced that 'Britain is now at war with Germany'. Although there had been sporadic raids throughout the 'phoney war' that followed, it was not until almost exactly a year after that declaration that the Luftwaffe bombers arrived in force over London. Although England's capital was bombed more heavily and more continuously than anywhere else in the country, the blitz was an attack on the whole United Kingdom: few places escaped its direct effects, none its indirect ones.

In January 1941 George Orwell wrote to the editors of the American journal the *Partisan Review*, to which he would contribute a 'London Letter' throughout the rest of the war: 'On that day in September when the Germans broke through and set the docks on fire, I think few people can have watched those enormous fires without feeling that this was the end of an epoch. One seemed to feel that the immense changes through which our society has got to pass were going to happen there and then.' But he went on to say that these feelings had been erroneous: 'to an astonishing extent things have slipped back to normal . . . When all is said and done one's main impression is the immense solidarity of ordinary people, the widespread yet vague consciousness that things can never be the same again, and yet, together with that, the tendency of life to slip back into the familiar pattern.'

Just a month later, Orwell was demanding that 'either we turn this war into a revolutionary war [against privilege and influence, and for equality and freedom] or we lose it'. Neither happened. The equivocation and ambivalence of wanting change and wanting things to be as they had always been would persist, and politicians consistently declined to define Britain's war aims other than by the simple word 'victory'.

Yet the blitz *was* a defining moment in Britain's history. More than cityscapes were reconfigured in those eight months. The attrition that had been anticipated for over a decade revealed both the incompetence of the authorities, and their misunderstanding of the nature of such warfare and of the needs of the people. But at the same time it demonstrated their sometimes grudging, usually tardy, willingness to accommodate, compromise and innovate. And perhaps, above all, eventually and imperfectly, to listen. To keep the people 'on side' as much as possible, since it was recognised that civilian morale was vital in maintaining full-scale war production and thus Britain's ability to prosecute the war at a time when victory was very far from assured. For this reason, and others, the blitz did prove to be a forcing house, a laboratory, the intense distillation of how an external threat could weld together a nation while at the same time failing to resolve many of its tensions.

The blitz has given the British – politicians in particular – a storehouse of images on which to draw at times of crisis: the symbol of an indomitable nation, united in resolution. The true story is, of course, more nuanced and complicated than that, cross-hatched as it must be by the freight of the pre-war years, of differing experiences and expectations. There were thousands of examples of extreme bravery, fortitude and selflessness. There was also a pervasive sense of exhaustion, uncertainty and anxiety, and acts of selfishness, intransigence and contumely. The words that best sum up the blitz are probably 'endurance' and 'defiance'. And arising out of that, a sense of entitlement: that a nation that had been exhorted to 'take it' could reasonably expect, when the war was finally over, to 'get [some] of it', in terms of greater equality, more employment, better housing, education and life chances in general.

In 1940 the use of the transitive verb 'to blitz' signified 'to destroy by aerial bombardment'. Seventy years later it is sometimes used to mean 'to deal with something energetically; to concentrate a lot of effort on something to get it done'. Both meanings resonate in our understanding of the blitz of 1940–41 and its aftermath.

Juliet Gardiner
June 2010

Before

> I think it is well for the man in the street to realise that there is no power on earth that can prevent him from being bombed. Whatever people may tell him, the bomber will always get through . . . the only defence is in offence, which means that you have to kill more women and children more quickly than the enemy if you want to save yourselves.
>
> Conservative leader Stanley Baldwin, speaking in the House of Commons in 1932

Robert Baltrop was sitting on the roof of a Sainsbury's store in east London on Saturday, 7 September 1940. It was a warm late-summer afternoon, the rays of the sun stretching across the concrete rooftops. The air-raid alert had just sounded, so Baltrop, who worked as a porter in the store, 'humping and cleaning and that sort of thing', had clambered out to take up his post on lookout duty. 'It wasn't bad being a watcher during these daytime warnings, sitting up there in the sunshine and smoking and watching the sky, and looking down at the people going about their business as usual in the streets below. I wasn't really sure what I was watching for, anything dangerous – fires or bombs falling or planes getting near, and I don't really know what I could have done about it. I suppose I should have had to go down the steps and tell them in the shop that a bomb had fallen on them!'

The war was more than a year old by this time. It had been another lovely summer day when Hitler had failed to respond to Britain's ultimatum to withdraw German troops from Poland, and the Prime Minister, Neville Chamberlain, had broadcast to the nation at 11.15 on 3 September 1939 to tell the British people that 'despite all my long struggle to win peace . . . this country is at war with Germany'. Within minutes the air-raid sirens sounded, and Londoners scurried to take shelter. The war that everybody had been expecting had started. Only it hadn't. That first alert was a false alarm, and a metaphor for a long autumn, winter and spring of expectation and fearful anticipation. But until the summer of 1940 there was little sign of the Armageddon that had been feared – except at sea, where the 'Battle of the Atlantic', which would take the lives of more than 30,000 merchant seamen by 1945, had been raging since the outbreak of war as Germany sought to stop supplies reaching Britain to enable her to keep fighting. By the late spring hardly anyone was carrying their gas mask any more, shelters were filling up with water through disuse, a ban had been put on recruiting any more Air Raid Patrol (ARP) wardens, and many volunteers, bored with the endless waiting around, drinking cups of tea and playing darts, had resigned, since there didn't seem to be much for them to do other than act like martinets when any chink showed through the blackout curtains on their patch. Housewives were already beginning to feel fed up with rationing, and the endless queuing and ingenuity in the kitchen that wartime shortages would demand, and more than 60 per cent of the mothers and children who had joined the government's evacuation scheme on the eve of war had drifted back home to the cities by January 1940, no longer convinced that their homes would be bombed, or their children killed, which had been the compelling reason for the exodus. It truly did seem to be a 'bore war' – all the regulations, restrictions and privations of wartime, with few of the dangers on the home front that would make them seem justified.

On 4 April 1940, in what Winston Churchill, recalled to the Cabinet on the outbreak of war as First Lord of the Admiralty, thought was 'a speech of unusual optimism', Chamberlain sanguinely told a Conservative gathering that Hitler had 'missed the bus' in seizing the offensive. Five days later German forces moved to occupy Norway and Denmark, and on 10 May, as Baltrop recalled, 'quite suddenly the Germans invaded the Low Countries; there was the evacuation from Dunkirk [which the British press largely treated as a victory rather than a defeat]; and on 22 June France signed an armistice with Germany. I remember at the Sainsbury's where I worked, somebody coming into the warehouse and almost with satisfaction rubbing his hands together and saying, "Well, we're on our own now" . . . There was a feeling that we were in the war now, and a certain feeling of resolve about it. Dunkirk had its effect. There were Churchill's speeches – "We will fight on the beaches and we will never surrender" – and very quickly daytime air raid warnings started. Again, there was this curious thing just like at the beginning of the war. We expected the worst and it didn't happen like that. We started getting air raid warnings by day and night. [Sainsbury's] agreed with the other shops round about, they would put up the shutters immediately. But nothing happened, and people didn't go home. They stayed in the streets. So the "gentlemen's agreement" between shopkeepers was dropped, and the shops started to open again even when the air raid warnings went, and . . . life went on through the summer. But they were getting nearer.'

Italy had entered the war in support of Germany on 10 June, and six days later the French Prime Minister, Paul Reynaud, resigned and Marshal Philippe Pétain, a military hero of the First World War, took over, and shortly afterwards signed an armistice surrendering northern and western France to the advancing German forces. From across the Channel, Winston Churchill, Prime Minister since Chamberlain had resigned on 10 May, surveyed the defeated British Expeditionary Force evacuated from Dunkirk, and on 18 June, the 125th anniversary of the Battle of Waterloo, he addressed the House of Commons. Whatever had happened in France, he assured MPs, would make 'no difference to the resolve of Britain and the British Empire to fight on if necessary for years, if necessary alone'. He predicted that:

> the Battle of Britain is about to begin. Upon this battle depends the survival of Christian civilization. Upon it depends our own British life, and the long continuity of our institutions and our Empire. The whole fury and might of the enemy must very soon be turned on us. Hitler knows that he will have to break us in this island or lose the war. If we can stand up to him, all Europe may be free and the life of the world may move forward into broad, sunlit uplands. But if we fail, then the whole world, including the United States [he added pointedly, since America was still pursuing an official policy of neutrality] will sink into the abyss of a new Dark Age . . . Let us therefore brace ourselves to our duties and so bear ourselves that if the British Empire and its Commonwealth lasts for a thousand years, men will still say 'This was their finest hour.'

The swift fall of France had not been foreseen by the German high command, and for several weeks they were at something of a loss to know what to do next. In mid-June, as German forces made their final assault on Paris, 120 German bombers attacked eastern England, killing nine in Cambridge,* and the first bomb in the London area fell on Addington near Croydon, though at that time Hitler had expressly placed London off-limits for attack. Throughout June and July there were intermittent random, small-scale daylight raids around the capital and on coastal towns in the south and east, and as far north as the Tyne. South Wales was bombed and shipping in the English Channel attacked, and on 12 July twenty-nine Aberdonians were killed and 103 seriously injured in a raid for which no warning had been given. On 16 July Hitler issued Directive no.16, *Preparations for the Invasion of Britain*, and such an invasion seemed a real possibility to the British. There were rumours from all over the country of sightings of German parachutists (maybe dressed as nuns) floating down, of barges massing in the Channel, of flotillas of gliders conveying troops from occupied France to East Anglia and Kent. On 18 August the *Sunday Express* suggested that 18 September would be a good day for a German invasion: 'The tide would be high, the nights longer than at present, and sea mists and fogs are prevalent at the equinox. Therefore, unless the Nazis come between the eighteenth and twenty-third of next month, they will be wise to postpone their visit until next spring.'

Towns along the Kent and Sussex coasts were evacuated, beaches were mined, piers dismantled and barbed wire uncoiled. An appeal by Anthony Eden, Secretary of State for War, broadcast just after the BBC nine o'clock news on 14 May, for volunteers 'to serve in the defence of their country in its hour of peril' had resulted in a stampede that had reached one and a half million by the end of June. For many months these Local Defence Volunteers (soon to be renamed the Home Guard at Churchill's insistence) had no uniform other than a brassard, and since all military equipment had first to be channelled to re-equip the denuded army, nothing to fight with other than a pitchfork or broomstick, or if they were fortunate, a First World War Lee Enfield rifle. Nevertheless, the band of under-resourced men was evidence of a willingness to 'defend our island whatever the cost may be', as Churchill had demanded.

Hitler hoped that Britain could be persuaded to abandon the fight and

---

* The first civilian British bombing death had in fact come on 16 March 1940, when an Orcadian labourer was killed as he stood by his croft door in the hamlet of Bridge of Waithe. It was presumed that the German plane had lost its way, or had mistaken the hamlet for a nearby airfield.

sue for peace when faced with the success of the blitzkrieg that had swept through the Low Countries and France and now threatened its shores. However, a final peace offer was rejected by the Foreign Secretary, Lord Halifax, on 22 July, and since it was clear that, despite the odds, Britain intended to fight on alone (though of course supported by Empire and dominion forces), various means were considered of bringing the country to its knees, including invasion. But it was obvious that there could be no successful invasion until German planes enjoyed air supremacy, and the aim of what has become known as the 'Battle of Britain' that summer was to wipe out the country's defences. By early July the Luftwaffe was dive-bombing British shipping and ports along the south coast and engaging RAF fighter planes in aerial combat; on 8 August it switched to trying to knock out Britain's fighter defences, with attacks on airfields, radar stations and other targets such as repair sheds and anti-aircraft guns and equipment.

It soon became apparent to Hitler that this strategy on its own was not working. 'The collapse of England in the year 1940 is under present circumstances no longer to be reckoned on,' he told his HQ staff on 20 August. The dogfights over southern England and the bombing raids on RAF targets had not succeeded in putting Britain's air force out of commission. The battle continued, although 15 September 1940 has since been celebrated as Battle of Britain Day, the day on which in retrospect it became clear that against the odds Britain had retained mastery of its skies.

However, Reichsmarschall Hermann Göring, Air Minister and Commander-in-Chief of the German air force since 1935, assumed on the basis of inaccurate intelligence that Fighter Command was all but annihilated, and was anxious to attack London in the hope that this would draw RAF fighter planes to the capital, where they could be picked off. On 24 August, in contravention of Hitler's orders, the Luftwaffe dropped several bombs on London. Although this was most likely an error, it gave Churchill the opportunity to order raids on Berlin, in the expectation that Hitler would retaliate and send his bombers to London, where they would be expected – and supposedly dealt with – thus relieving the pressure on the Western Front in France. On 2 September Göring ordered the Luftwaffe to switch to bombing Britain's industrial and administrative centres and transport and communication links, while the strategy the Kriegsmarine (the German navy) advocated, the blockading of British ports and attacks on her shipping, continued unabated.

So the war entered a new phase. The 'Battle of Britain' was to be carried on by other means. Germany's targets were now industrial installations and transport and communication links around major cities. It was hoped that this would 'cripple' Britain and compel her to seek peace. The home front would become a front-line battlefield for the next five years. And on 7 September 1940, 'Black Saturday', the first day of the war of persistent aerial attack that became known as the blitz, it was the London docks that were in the Luftwaffe's sights.

1

Black Saturday, 7 September 1940

[The British] will understand now, as night after night, we give them the
answer [to RAF bombing raids on Germany] – when they declare they will
attack our towns on a large scale, then we will erase theirs.

Adolf Hitler speaking in the Berlin Sportspalast, 4 September 1940

'The Reichsmarschall is leaving his train and is coming past us. He sees us.
Is this what he was intending? Is he really coming? Yes. He is coming! The
Reichsmarschall is coming from his train and is coming to the radio,' the
German announcer reported excitedly on 7 September. Hermann Göring,
a large, heavy man, clad in a greatcoat, wearing the Grand Cross of the Iron
Cross, which he had been awarded as a result of the French campaign, at
his throat, strode to the microphone to address his fellow countrymen and
women. 'I now want to take this opportunity of speaking to you, to say this
moment is a historic one. As a result of the provocative British attacks on
Berlin on recent nights the Führer has decided to order a mighty blow to
be struck in revenge against the capital of the British Empire. I personally
have assumed the leadership of this attack, and today I hear above me the
roaring of victorious German squadrons which now, for the first time, are
driving towards the heart of the enemy in full daylight, accompanied by
countless fighter squadrons.' So saying, the Commander of the German air
force clambered back into the carriage of his personal train, 'Robinson', and
resumed his journey back from the Channel coast where he had stood on
the cliffs of Cap Gris Nez, binoculars trained on Britain, watching the
German aircraft set out on their mission and maybe hoping to catch a
glimpse of the effects of the havoc their bombs would wreak in their 'major
strike on Target Loge' (the German code name for London).

    Sitting in deckchairs, mowing the lawn or visiting friends that sun-filled
afternoon, people in Kent looked up as the drone of planes grew louder

and louder – 'like the far away thunder of a giant waterfall', thought the American journalist Virginia Cowles. She was having tea in the garden of the Palladian Mereworth Castle, the home of the press baron Esmond Harmsworth, eldest son of Viscount Rothermere, in Kent, forty miles from London. 'We lay on the grass, our eyes strained towards the sky; we made out a batch of tiny white specks, like clouds of insects moving north west in the direction of the capital. Some of them – the bombers – were flying in even formation, while the others – the fighters – swarmed protectively around . . . during the next hour [we] counted over a hundred and fifty planes. They were not meeting any resistance.' To the urbane diplomat turned journalist and author Harold Nicolson, now a Junior Minister at the Ministry of Information, sitting with his wife Vita Sackville-West in their garden at Sissinghurst, also in Kent, the 'wave after wave of enemy aircraft planes looked like silver gnats above us in the air'.

The siren had sounded at 4.43 p.m. that Saturday. Londoners had got used to its ululating note: the sound of 'Wailing Winnie' or 'Moaning Minnie' had been frequent during the last few weeks of constant 'nuisance raids'. 'We are growing accustomed to sudden warnings, and we have developed a quickening of our sense of danger . . . we are not panicky, but we are, at any rate subconsciously, more on the look-out than had hitherto been the case at any time during last year,' the Harley Street psychologist and BBC producer Anthony Weymouth had written in his diary back in August. Harold Nicolson would have agreed. 'People are becoming quite used to these interruptions,' he wrote in his diary as he heard the siren wail on 26 August. 'I do not think that that drone in the sky means death to many people at the moment. It seems so incredible as I sit here at my window, looking out on the fuchsias and zinnias with yellow butterflies playing around each other, that in a few seconds I may see other butterflies circling in the air intent on murdering each other.'

Yet despite the increasing frequency of the alerts, the mournful notes could still send a shiver of dread down people's spines. 'Whoohoo go the goblins, coming back at nightfall/Whoohoo go the witches reaching out their hands for us . . . Are we sure we will be the lucky ones/. . . They have come back, we always knew they would after the story ended,' wrote the author Naomi Mitchison in one of her 'blitz poems'.

The planes droned on. As Robert Baltrop sat on the roof of Sainsbury's, 'all of a sudden on the skyline coming up the Thames were [black specks] like swarms of flies . . . weaving their way through puffs of smoke . . . and my reaction was one of astonishment and . . . well, what's going to happen now? They were flying across my line of vision, and sitting up there on the roof, I had a perfect view of them, watching them fly across the Thames . . . coming in . . . past Dagenham and Rainham and Barking, and they were heading straight for London, and it was going to be the docks that were going to get it . . . I began to hear loud thumps, and those were bombs falling, and clouds of smoke were rising up – clouds of black smoke floating away until you couldn't see anything but a huge bank of smoke, and still they were coming.'

The operational orders issued to 1 Fliegerkorps for that afternoon informed the pilots that 'The purpose of the initial attack is to force English fighters into the air so that they will have reached the end of their endurance at the time of the main attack.' To achieve 'the maximum effect it is essential that units fly as a highly concentrated force . . . The main objective of the operation is to prove that the Luftwaffe can achieve this.'

'We have had many air-raid warnings during the last week, and as soon as the sirens have sounded we have invariably done what we've been told to do – go to a place of safety,' noted Anthony Weymouth, whose 'place of safety' was the hall of his ground-floor flat. 'It is well inside the building, and between us and the blast of bombs are two sitting rooms and the hall of the building. The only windows in the hall have been shuttered and we have been told to leave all the windows open to avoid, so far as possible, broken glass.' So on 7 September Weymouth and his family 'waited for an hour or so, some of us sitting on the mattresses which are now a permanent part of our hall furniture, some squatting on the floor. Audrey [his wife] put on her [ARP warden's] tin hat and went round her sector to see if she was needed. She returned to tell us that a big fire was raging in the City.'

But it wasn't the City of London that three hundred German planes were converging on that late afternoon: it was 'Target G', the docks that lay in the bight of the Thames where it loops around in a U shape like a small child's badly built wooden railway, a lazy-looking attempt to encircle not some pleasant riverside picnic place but Silvertown, a jumble of docks, warehouses and small houses built for workers in the docks and the nearby factories in days when industry and home were hugger-mugger in the poorer parts of towns and cities.

The German pilots had no difficulty in identifying their targets in the clear afternoon light. The first bombs fell on the Ford motor works at

Dagenham, closely followed by a rain of high explosives and fire bombs on Beckton gasworks, the largest in Europe. Below them now lay the great Thames bight at Woolwich Reach, enclosing the three Royal Docks, their warehouses and sheds stacked with foodstuffs and materials vital to the war effort. Within minutes the huge warehouses and factories lining the river on both sides from North Woolwich to Tower Bridge were on fire. Two hundred acres of timber stacks, recently arrived from North America and the Baltic, burned out of control along the Surrey Commercial Docks, the main timber-importing centre in Britain: within twenty-four hours only about a fifth of the two and a half million tons was left. Burning spirits gushed out of the rum quay warehouses at West India Dock, a tar distillery flooded North Woolwich Road with molten pitch, and rats swarmed out of a nearby soapworks. A rubber factory was hit, and the acrid black smoke rolling through the narrow streets of Silvertown mingled with the escaping fumes from the damaged Beckton gasworks and started a rumour that the Germans were dropping canisters of poison gas as well as bombs. Fire burned through the ropes of barges tethered along the quayside and the burning boats drifted downstream, only to return several hours later on the incoming tide, still smouldering, while the intense heat blistered the paint on buildings in areas untouched by the bombs.

A fireman stationed at Pageant's Wharf Fire Station stared in horror as magnesium incendiaries lodged in the wood stacks and oil bombs ignited the timber like kindling on a bone-dry bonfire. It seemed as if 'the whole bloody world's on fire' to Station Officer Gerry Knight as he yelled to the fire station telephonists to call for urgent reinforcements. The regular London firemen were joined by men from the four wartime Auxiliary Fire Service (AFS) substations on the docks, their trailer pumps drawn by vans, taxi cabs – 2,000 had been hired by the start of the war, often with their drivers coming along as part of the deal – or anything that could be pressed into service to get to the blaze.

The AFS, an adjunct of the fire brigade, had started recruiting in March 1938, and had expanded after the Munich crisis, when large posters had appeared on walls and on the sides of fire engines urging: 'Keep the home fires *from* burning'. By the time war broke out, for every regular fireman there were fifteen auxiliaries, and 'it was quite a big job getting them all trained'. AFS members had received sixty hours of basic training, but most had never been called to a major fire before. Now it seemed that all the drill they had carefully learned was for another world: as soon as they trained their hoses on one outbreak, another flared up feet away. Damped down by the water jets, a pile of wood would sizzle in the heat, then burst into flame again. The firemen worked fast to screw together the sections of hose and run them into the river so there was no shortage of water, but soon telegraph poles all around the dock were combusting in the heat, and even the wooden blocks that surfaced the roads were igniting. Grain spilling out of the warehouses made a sticky mess that stuck to the firemen's boots, bogging them down as if they were walking through treacle in some sort of nightmare. Gerry Knight realised that the inferno was burning out of control, impossible to put out, and that if he didn't withdraw his men were in real danger of being trapped by the sheets of flame.

Peter Blackmore was a successful playwright who had become a volunteer fireman after seeing a 'Join the AFS' poster in the London Underground, showing 'a firelit fireman holding the branch of a hose, an exciting picture which stirred the imagination and at the same time in small print set out the glorious benefits of such service, the exceptional wages, the food allowance, the uniform and the leave days'. He had grown used to the sound of the siren, 'more popularly known as the "sighreen". In those days this was the signal for us to rig fully in helmets, boots, leggings, belts, axes and spanners, tear to the appliance-room and man the pumps, there to sit and grumble until the "All Clear" sounded and we could return to an overcooked or cold meal. This seemed to occur many times day and night. We were certainly always ready. Still no blitz came.' But on the night of 7 September 1940 Blackmore was wondering what to make of the 'ominous red glow in the sky, which, had it not been in the east, could have passed for an indifferent sunset' when a colleague came to tell him, 'They're bombing the docks.' 'Down went the bells,' and Blackmore and his colleagues set off eastwards.

As they approached the docks they joined 'an endless queue of appliances, all steadily moving and being detailed to their exact positions. Bombs were falling fast and heavy. We did a great deal of ducking . . . and my heart was in my mouth. The journey towards a blitz, like most apprehension, can be the worst part of it . . . Eventually we came to a standstill at the wharf where we were to spend the endless night. Everything seemed to be on fire in every direction, even some barrage balloons in the sky [winched up in the hope that low-flying enemy aircraft would become entangled in their metal ropes] were exploding. The cinder-laden smoke which drifted all around made us think of the destruction of Pompeii.'

Cyril Demarne, a regular fireman stationed at Abbey Road School in

West Ham in London's East End, was in the school yard when soon after the alert had sounded he heard 'the drone of approaching aircraft rapidly swelling to a roar. Suddenly squadrons of bombers appeared all over the eastern sky, flying very high and escorted by hundreds of fighter planes glinting in the sunlight as they weaved and turned over the bomber formation . . . I dived for the safety of the Control Room, where calls for assistance were already flowing in from Dagenham, Barking, East and West Ham. The electricity mains were damaged in the first minutes of the raid and [as it grew dark] the fire control had to operate by the light of candles set in jam jars.'

'I was frightened out of my life. Bombs coming down, screaming – the row they make, it's a sort of warning saying, "Look out, here comes death." And when they landed they went off with a terrific roar – not one but dozens of them – bang, bang, bang, bang, all the time, everywhere. And then there was the drone of aircraft . . . the noise was the sort of thing that got to me. It . . . dulled the senses . . . you couldn't think clearly.'

'That day stands out like a flaming wound in my memory,' wrote Bernard Kops, a London schoolboy who would grow up to be a playwright.

> Imagine a ground floor flat [in Stepney Green Buildings], crowded with hysterical women, crying babies and great crashes in the sky and the whole earth shaking. Someone rushed in, 'The docks are alight. All the docks are alight.' I could smell burning . . . The men started to play cards and the women tried a little sing song, singing 'I saw the old homestead and faces I loved' or 'Don't go down the mine, Daddy, dreams very often come true' or 'Yiddle mit his fiddle'. But every so often twenty women's fists shook at the ceiling cursing the explosions, Germany, Hitler . . . Yet cursing got my mother and my aunts through those early days. I sat under the table where above the men were playing cards, screwing my eyes up and covering my ears, counting explosions.
>
> 'We're all gonna get killed, we're finished,' one of my aunts became hysterical.
>
> 'Churchill will get us through, he's a friend of the Yiddisher people.' With these words she was soothed.

Len Jones, an eighteen-year-old Poplar resident, went outside when he heard the first German planes overhead. 'It was very exciting because the first formations were coming over without any bombs dropping, but very, very majestic, terrific. And I had no thought that they were actual bombers. Then . . . the bombs began to fall, and shrapnel was going along King Street, dancing off the cobbles. Then the real impetus came . . . the suction and the compression from the high-explosive bombs just pushed you and pulled you, and the whole of the atmosphere was turbulating so hard that, after an explosion of a nearby bomb, you could actually feel your eyeballs being [almost] sucked out . . . and the suction was so vast, it ripped my shirt away, and ripped my trousers. Then I couldn't get my breath, the smoke was like acid and everything round me was black and yellow. And these bombers kept on and on, the whole road was moving, rising and falling.'

By 6.30 the planes – Dornier and Heinkel bombers escorted by Messerschmitt fighters – had turned back and wheeled across the Kent countryside, flying over Romney Marsh and back across the Channel to their bases in France. The All Clear sounded, and East Enders emerged from their homes and public shelters and peered about them at the raging fires, the broken glass, the destroyed and damaged houses, debris everywhere, a pall of greasy black smoke enveloping the scene as firemen desperately tackled massive fires with tangles of hoses snaking across the roads and water sloshing into the gutters.

But this was just a lull. 'Black Saturday' would set the pattern for the next eight harrowing months. First the Luftwaffe would drop showers of incendiary bombs that would start fires. The blazes would both act as a beacon to guide the subsequent formations of bombers with their loads of high-explosive (HE) bombs to their target, and also occupy the Civil Defence services – fire, rescue, medical – so they would not be standing by ready to engage immediately with the crisis when the heavy bombs began to fall.

Just over two hours later, at 8.30 p.m., the siren wailed again. This time the raid would continue relentlessly until dawn, adding further chaos and devastation to the already stricken East End, and widening out to other parts of London. Chelsea and Victoria were hit that night too, but it was the area of the tidal basin around the docks – the Isle of Dogs, Silvertown and Rotherhithe – that took the brunt of the devastation. Bermondsey, Canning Town, Woolwich, Deptford – fanning out to West Ham, Plaistow, Bow, Whitechapel, Stepney and Poplar – also suffered heavy loads of bombs.

Squadrons of Heinkels and Dorniers – 250 in all – came in waves to drop high-explosive bombs onto the still-blazing wharves, the ruined houses, the cratered streets, the terrified east Londoners. AFS despatch riders on motorcycles made their way through the chaos and rubble to report the immensity of the situation to local fire controls. Columns of fire engines raced east, their bells clanging, men called on duty fastening their helmets and doing up their jackets as the engines sped to answer the urgent calls from the East End. When they arrived there was often nobody in charge to be found, and men were simply deployed to fight the nearest fire to hand. Five hundred engines converged on West Ham alone after a request to the London Regional Fire Control Headquarters at Lambeth, where the map of London pinned on the wall, usually dense with markers indicating the availability of fire engines, was ominously clear. There were already nine fires designated as 'conflagrations' (when fires coalesce, burn out of control and spread rapidly), nineteen requiring thirty pumps, forty needing ten, and over a thousand smaller incidents.

By now Surrey Docks was a square mile of fire. The paint on the fireboats attempting to douse the flames blistered in the intense heat, as cranes buckled and crashed into the river. At the Royal Arsenal in Woolwich many of the buildings on fire contained live ammunition and highly flammable nitroglycerine. Water mains had been damaged, and when the hydrants ran dry water had to be pumped from the Thames, reservoirs, even ponds and ditches. At Woolwich a fireman aboard one of six fireboats which had been ordered to return to London from a fire at the Shell-Mex Thameshaven oil refinery on Canvey Island at the mouth of the Thames, its 2,000-ton-capacity tanks ablaze after a bomb attack on 5 September, saw 'an extraordinary spectacle. There was nothing but fire ahead, apparently stretching right across the river and burning on both of its banks. We seemed to be entering a tunnel of fire – no break in it anywhere. All the usual landmarks were obliterated by walls of flame. Burning barges drifted past. For many hours no contact with the shore was possible. We did what we could where we could. At one time we were just getting into position to fight a fire in a large warehouse when the whole of the riverside front collapsed into the water with a mighty splash. The contents of the building, bags of beans, pouring into the river made a sound like a tropical rain storm. Soon after, we were surprised to see two firemen and three firewomen picking their way along the shore in the direction of Southwark Bridge; they told us they had been cut off in a control room for several hours' by the fires.

During the raid, that lasted for over eight hours, 250 German planes had dropped 625 tons of high-explosive bombs and at least eight hundred incendiary bomb canisters, each containing 795 pounds of explosive. A thousand fire pumps were fighting the blaze at the Surrey Docks, with three hundred pumps and over a thousand men trying to contain just one of the largest fires. The firemen wrestled to control their heavy hoses, sending arcs of water through flames that seemed scornful of their efforts, their faces blackened by smoke and soot, their eyes pricking from the heat, their throats and lungs irritated by the smoke and the dust of falling masonry, their uniforms scorched and singed by flying sparks and heavy with the water from the hoses, hungry, thirsty, exhausted.

F.W. Hurd, a member of the AFS stationed at East Ham fire station, was ordered to a fire at Beckton gasworks at nine o'clock that night.

Chaos met our eyes. Gasometers were punctured and were blazing away, a power house had been struck rendering useless the hydraulic hydrant supply (the only source of water there). An overhead gantry bearing lines of trucks communicating with the railway siding was also . . . alight. And then overhead we heard [the German planes], the searchlights searching the sky in a vain effort to locate them. Guns started firing, and then I had my first experience of a bomb explosion. A weird whistling sound and I ducked behind the pump with two other members of the crew. The others, scattered as we were, had thrown themselves down wherever they happened to be. Then a vivid flash of flame, a column of earth and debris flying into the air and the ground heaved. I was thrown violently against the side of the appliance.

. . . After a time things quietened down and we went out again. It was now about 10 o'clock and the fire had been burning unattacked by us for lack of water [when] a local Fire Officer arrived and informed us that he knew where we could obtain a supply! Our 'heavy' was sent about half a mile from the fire to 'pick up' water from three other pumps which were being supplied from hydrants. We relayed the water thro' a chain of pumps to the fire. And then there was nothing to do except watch the hose and guard it where it crossed an arterial road (from being burst by cars proceeding at speed across it), so we had time to look round. What a sight. About a mile to our right was the riverfront. The whole horizon on that side was a sheet of flame. The entire docks were on fire! On all other sides it was much the same. Fire everywhere. The sky was a vivid orange glow . . . And all the time the whole area was being mercilessly bombed. The road shuddered with the explosions. AA [anti-aircraft] shells were bursting overhead. A Royal Navy Destroyer berthed in one of the docks was firing her AA equipment, as were other ships. The shrapnel literally rained down. It was now about midnight and still the racket kept on. It surprised me how quickly one got used to sensing whether a bomb was coming our way or not. At first we all lay flat every time we heard anything, but after an hour or so we only dived for it if one came particularly close . . . At 3am a canteen van arrived and served us tea and sandwiches. It was the first 'bite' any of us had had since mid day the day before, 14½ hours ago.

Just then the bombing became more severe and localised. A brighter glow in the sky immediately over us, then we saw the flames. Another fire had started in the gas works, which by now after 6 hours concentrated work by us, had been got well under control. Then a huge mushroom of flame shot into the air from the docks followed by a dull rolling roar. An oil container had exploded. The whole atmosphere became terrible again with the noise of gunfire. Afterwards when London established its famous [AA] barrage we got used to it, but on that first night it was just Hell.

Water mains had been fractured all over the East End, as had gas pipes and electrical and telephone cables. With no radio communication between the crews and control, messages had to be relayed by AFS and London Fire Brigade messengers, most of them teenaged boys with tin hats, riding motor-bikes or yellow-painted bicycles. Sixteen was the statutory minimum age for such work, but checks were cursory, and many of those undertaking this hazardous and courageous work were younger. They set out to apprise District Control of the situation on the ground, to report the progress of the firefighting and request reinforcements, skidding through wet and cratered streets as the bombs fell, narrowly missing being hit, falling from their machines as girders fell in their path, negotiating piles of rubble, accel-erating away to escape walls of fire, disorientated by the noise, the smoke, the confusion.

One of 'Gillman's Devils', teenaged boys organised by Bill Gillman, Assistant Controller of Operations at West Ham, found himself riding through 'a patch of burning paint on the roadway in Silvertown from the burning paint works on the corner. Paint stuck to my tyres and set them alight but I rode on the pavement until the flames were out.' 'You'd go round a corner and there'd be a great big hole in the road where a bomb had fallen, or half a house had fallen and the debris was blocking the road, or there might be an unexploded bomb,' remembers Stan Durling, an AFS despatch rider. 'But that night when I reported for duty at Millwall, you just didn't know where to look. The chemical works had been hit. Everywhere you looked was fire. Across the water, north, south, east and west, everywhere. It seemed as if the whole East End docks were on fire. It was unbe-lievable.' Sixteen-year-old Stan Hook was in the bath when the bombs started to fall. 'They scream through the air, and then crump, crump, and the bath shook and I thought Christ, bombs. I don't remember drying myself. I don't remember getting dressed. But I was on my bike and back to the [fire] station [on the Isle of Dogs] and that's when I came to. That was the begin-ning at five o'clock and from then until five o'clock the next day I just lived in a daze. A smoke-filled haze covered everything and orders were flying around in all directions, and you were charging around, and bombs were falling and fires were starting, and it wasn't until the next morning that I really thought, well this is war.'

Uncontrollable by any blackout regulations, the river Thames served to guide enemy aircraft to their targets night after night during the blitz. A.P. Herbert, the lawyer, humorist and Independent MP for Oxford University, who had seen active service with the Royal Naval Reserve in France and at Gallipoli in the First World War, joined the River Emergency Service in the Second. This in effect mobilised the Thames as part of London's defences. On the night of 7 September, Herbert was detailed to take his converted canal boat *Water Gipsy* from its mooring at Tower Bridge to pick up some wire from a Port of London Authority wreck lighter and take it to North Woolwich. Rounding Limehouse corner, he and his crew

saw an astonishing picture. Half a mile of Surrey shore . . . was ablaze – ware-houses, wharves, piers, dolphins, barges.

The wind was westerly and there was a wall of smoke and sparks across the river. Burning barges were drifting everywhere but there was not a soul in sight – the small police boat ahead of us had turned back to report – and we had been ordered to Woolwich. [As ours was] a wooden ship and petrol driven, we didn't like the look of it much; but we put wet towels round our faces and steamed at half speed into the torrid cloud. Inside, the scene was like a lake in Hell. We could hear the hiss and roar of the conflagration ashore, but could not see it, only the burning barges and the crimson water that reflected them. It was not as alarming as it had looked outside, the main whirl of sparks and smoke went over us. We took off our towels and felt quite happy. It was something to be the only boat in Hell. We steamed on slowly, using the compass and dodging the barges, and at last the Water Gipsy came out safe, but sooty, the White Ensign [of the Royal Navy] nearly black, the other side. After that, all the other fires we passed seemed no more than night-lights, though there were some brave ones.

I now had the feeling that nothing could touch us – a thing I never felt in a house. At the top of Blackwall Reach a bomb fell fifty yards ahead of us. I ducked down behind the wheel, I know, but truly I felt no fear and this delighted me. We delivered our wire at Woolwich – I hope it was some use – and came back through the smoke to Westminster.

On the shore of North Woolwich adjoining King George V Dock, residents had the terrifying ordeal of being trapped between the dock fires on one side and a row of factories ablaze on the other. Debris spilled from burning buildings, impeding the passage of fire engines and rescue vehicles. There seemed no escape as families rushed through the streets, found their way blocked and agitatedly ran back again. Some sought cover in the public shelter at the Oriental baths – until that was hit by a bomb. The entire population of the area had to be got away as quickly as possible before they were engulfed by the flames. No vehicles could get to them, so, coughing and spluttering in the smoke, and in terror of the fire and the bombs, they groped their way on foot to Woolwich Pier, where they scrambled into small boats and were rowed to safety along the Thames. It was much the same for the inhabitants of Rotherhithe, trapped between walls of flame that were engulfing their houses by the dock walls and the river. While some managed to get to safety by road, others were evacuated by boat.

Kathleen Rylatt was a member of the Women's Voluntary Service (WVS), started by Stella, Marchioness of Reading at the request of the then Prime Minister, Neville Chamberlain, in May 1938. Its original purpose was to recruit more women into the ARP service, but it was now called upon to help in almost any home front situation, no matter how hazardous. On the night of 7 September Rylatt was helping with the evacuation of residents of the flame-engulfed areas around the Surrey Docks. Five people had been found in the midst of the blazing buildings, unable to get out of their shelter as sandbags had fallen in on top of them during the raid. 'The [residents] were horror-struck at the idea of leaving their homes. The road was literally burning and many of them had to be treated for badly-scorched feet.' Rylatt led the terrified people to St Olave's Hospital in Rotherhithe, where those who needed it were given first aid and everyone was comforted with blankets and cups of tea. The leader of a stretcher party who watched the procession streaming out of docklands was 'absolutely amazed. They seemed to come like an army marching and running . . . they looked in a very bad state . . . dirty and dishevelled. Many had superficial cuts and their skin was pitted with tiny slivers of glass from blown out windows . . . and all had a "ghostly pallor" since they were covered in plaster dust from falling walls.'

Bert Purdy, an ambulance driver stationed at Moorgate, was just about to start his meal of tinned salmon and a cup of tea when the raids started. He abandoned his food and set off with the rest of his crew. 'It was chaos, buildings, houses all in a collapsed condition. At times my driving was erratic, I was driving up and down the bomb craters. We saw several mutilated bodies lying in the road. At one point we stopped and moved several limbs and two bodies to a point off the road, covered them with sheets of corrugated iron, intending to remove them later. It was terrible – people trapped, severely injured. People were lying about everywhere. We began to collect the people, render first aid if and when possible; take them to Poplar Hospital. Private cars were waiting outside the hospital for attention. We saw patients with severe head injuries lying on the roof of the cars, blood running down the back window . . . We worked hours; removed patients to Poplar, Mile End and London Hospitals. It was terrible . . . so unexpected and tragic.'

At one point in that terrible night the brother of Gladys Strelitz, who lived in East Ham, urged his sisters, ' "Come on girls, get all the children's clothes in a bag, and we've got to get out of London, there's a lull." And so we got in this bus, and we went to Bow. And when we got to Bow the bombing was going so badly that the conductor pulled the bell and said we wouldn't go any further. So the only place to go was to run into the crypt under this big church. And there the sight that met my eyes, it overcame me. Because there was people praying, and crying and asking God to help us, because there was bombs going on and the crypt . . . was actually shuddering . . . It was too much for me, I just passed out.'

The Communist journalist and typographer Alan Hutt, at the time assistant to the editor of the cooperatively-owned *Reynolds' News* (he later rejoined the *Daily Worker,* which had employed him at its inception in 1930), had been sent down to the shelter at 4.30 that afternoon, as he and his colleagues were arguing about whether the caption to a photograph of roadblocks damaged by an attack in south London the previous day – 'Knocked 'em in the Old Kent Road' – was insensitive. 'Not funny when people've been killed,' one objected. All that night as the journalists were trying to put the paper to bed, they were sent down to the shelter again and again. 'Damned nuisance,' thought Hutt, until he saw the cause of the alarm from the roof.

I can see the fire along the waterfront and a rolling bank of grey smoke twice as high as the barrage balloons. Estimate distance and plot it out on the map which indicates Millwall, Surrey Docks as the beginning (infinite arguments in the office, but it turns out that this is right). Both sides of the river were plastered as far as Woolwich and the fire stretched for miles – eight or nine I shd. say. As dusk fell about 9 o'clock, the sight from our roof was incredible, a fantastic Gustav Doré piece, a gold and grey smoke-canopied flaming glow stretching thickly as far as one cd. see, the skyline silhouetted sharply black against this infernal Technicolor piece. Blackout was dead for the rest of the night and the bombers came back by the light of the fire to blast the East End . . . David has got a magnificent shot of the fire from London Bridge but the censor refuses to pass any pictures – 'nothing that will confirm the enemy's claims' . . . Jenkins goes to the Borough and gets an awe-inspiring view, also seeing the folks trooping to the Southwark tunnel in their thousands. We have to fight to get his stuff in the paper, for the new editor, jittery and helpless as usual says we've no way of getting this to the censor; but then he doesn't want to send anyone out in this – leave it to the agencies – they've got special passes blah blah. O God O Fleet Street . . .

The fire, which has gone down a bit, picks up fiercely and at 1am towards the east there is a leap of flame and . . . clouds of black smoke. A big fire . . . We've all had a scornful sneer over the Private & Confidential Memo to eds [editors] giving a MoI [Ministry of Information] interview with the PM – optimistic stuff . . . 'this has been expected . . . damage may be somewhat serious from a local viewpoint, but seen on the background of our general war effort &c &c . . . '

All Clear at 4.50; a coffee at the milk bar, a taxi to Kentish Town, & a rambling walk home through the dawn, the fire glow melting strangely into the light of day.

A young woman, Ida Naish, was caught in the raid on her way home to East Ham from visiting a friend. When she had arrived at Euston after hours of delays and detours, the station was deserted. 'I came out into the street and there was no sign of [her mother, who was supposed to be meeting her]. The fire was getting steadily brighter, and overhead there were sounds of gunfire with an occasional dull thud in the distance as the bombs dropped. I have never felt so alone in my life.' She managed to get to Aldgate, but

they wouldn't let me book through to East Ham as Bow Road station was no more and Stepney Green had been heavily bombed. I came up to the bus stop and waited with about twenty other people, but it was hopeless. A few taxis came by and we tried hailing them but of course we had no luck . . . I suppose I'd been standing there about forty minutes when providentially my mother walked by right in front of me. She, poor soul, had been turned away from Euston at 8.30 and as the raid was still in progress had started to walk home. She'd already come all that way on foot when I met her but despite that suggested that we should walk on . . . I think if we'd both been feeling hale and hearty, we wouldn't have gone but we seemed so numbed that nothing much mattered.

. . . The whole of Thameside from London Bridge to Woolwich was a raging inferno. You could have seen to read by the light – if you'd felt inclined – and unfortunately for us we had to go by the East India Docks. Commercial Road was the only route open to the East because owing to the damage done to Bow Road, traffic was being diverted . . . And just before we got to Burdett Road, the bombs started falling. The shelters seemed to be absolutely non existent so we just went on . . . At one time we were made to go round back turnings because a delayed action bomb had fallen in the main road and nothing could pass. What was so maddening was the persistent drone of enemy planes which, I might mention, are easily distinguishable from our own. We couldn't get away from it, and felt so completely helpless.

Fires were breaking out everywhere . . . a chapel that lay back about thirty yards from us suddenly burst into flames. It was dreadful. The streets were littered with glass and the pavements pitted with shrapnel from the raid [that afternoon]. Far away down the Barking Road we could see the glare of an incendiary bomb that had landed in the roadway and we decided to take to the back streets. A pale flickering light over towards Barking turned out (so we found later) to be the power station which had been hit. I think something must have hit the gas works, too, because we still haven't got any gas and at the moment [the next day, Sunday, 8 September] our Sunday joint is swinging on an improvised spit in front of the fire.

. . . We were going down one turning when [an ARP] warden stopped us from going on and insisted that we stayed in his house. We were really very grateful and from 11pm to 5am we sat on the stairs in the dark gazing out through the open door to the street which was incessantly lit up with explosions. And how those bombs fell! Canning Town library was hit, Forest Gate got it too, and all around us seemed to be shaking. Dante had nothing on Hitler, believe me.

. . . At last, at 5 o/c, the All Clear went and we finally reached home to find some windows out and the ceiling down in Mummy's room . . .

When I looked from my window I could see that one of the fires on Thames side was still burning and great clouds of black smoke were covering quite a large area.

'Then quite suddenly it ceased,' recalled Fireman Hurd, fighting a fire amidst the noise of screaming bombs and droning aircraft. 'The silence was almost overpowering for a time. At about 5 o/c am the "All Clear" went. We had been subjected, without any real cover, to 8 hours of continual bombing! . . . Relief crews began to arrive (they came from Enfield) . . . we stayed there until 10 o/c on Sunday morning when our Sub Officer handed over to another officer. This officer and his ten pumps . . . had come from Brighton! Our crew proceeded home [then] and what a scene of desolation we passed through. Debris everywhere, confined to the East End though, but I was too tired to care much about what I saw then. We had been on our feet since 6.15 pm on Saturday until 10 am on Sunday, with only one snack in 21 hours.'

The All Clear 'sounded a beautiful symphony' in Bernard Kops' ears:

everyone relaxed, the men arguing politics and the women talking about food, But the younger people wandered out to see the fires and I went with them along the Commercial Road. The closer I got the more black and red it became with flames shooting higher than the cranes along the dockside. Sparks were spitting everywhere and tongues of flames consumed the great warehouses along the black and orange waters of the Thames. Everything was chaos except the fire which was like a living monster with an insatiable appetite. And I was afraid of being devoured . . . so I left and wandered back towards Stepney Green where black smoke covered the sky.

Yet, with all this, there was a feeling of unreality. I couldn't believe it, it was like a film being shown before our eyes, Men were rushing around selling newspapers, screaming about the amount of German planes that were brought down, and there had been a family wiped out where I had been standing . . .

That first night of the blitz, 436 people were killed and 1,600 seriously injured.* Among the dead were seven firemen. Thirteen men were killed when the corporation depot in Abbey Road, West Ham, which was being used as an ARP Cleansing and Ambulance station, received a direct hit. Cyril Demarne, who was nearby, hurried round to find a hand he recognised as that of his friend Wally Turley sticking out from under a huge slab of concrete. Turley, a fireman, had been attempting to put out a fire at the station when it collapsed, burying him, his fellow firefighters and other ARP workers stationed there. It was impossible to move the concrete to free the bodies until heavy lifting gear arrived, so Fireman Turley's arm remained sticking out of the debris, a tragic signpost to one of the many instant burial grounds that night.

Soon after the first raid of the blitz had begun the previous afternoon, the manager of Robert Baltrop's Sainsbury's had decided to close the shop and send all his staff home. Baltrop set out to keep his date with a girl.

> She turned up – it sounds daft but perhaps we all thought it was a bit romantic meeting in an air raid, all this was going on very close to us. We could smell the smoke and hear the bombs, but she had orders to take me home immediately if I turned up so we went to her home and they were all in the Anderson shelter in her back garden, her parents and the lady from upstairs, and we huddled in there, it was pretty awful all squashed in there together with the raid going on and her father talked in gloomy tones about H.G. Wells and how we should all have to live underground, and every time there was a thump her mother screamed . . . The man from upstairs came in straight from work, and he tumbled into the shelter breathless with these stories of roads blocked, streets in ruins, named places that I knew, and it was almost unbelievable to hear someone say, you know this place or that place, well, it's been bombed.

---

* 'Seriously injured' described those who were admitted to and kept in hospital; a person receiving first aid treatment at the time, or subsequently presenting at an outpatients' department or at their doctor's surgery, was categorised as 'slightly injured'. Of course many people sustained minor injuries for which they did not seek medical help, so they do not show up in the figures. Indeed, the Ministry of Home Security was concerned that reporting officers should be clear about what were 'regarded as casualties, or to classify them in some way so that our published figures may represent the true gravity of the situation (i.e. not old ladies removed to hospital from near an incident "for their own comfort")'.

Baltrop finally became 'fed up' with this talk and the confined space, and walked home. His father had been out, 'picking up what news he could about the East End, because we knew it so well, we knew people and places, and he's heard this place had been bombed and that place . . . and we sat and had a cup of tea and he talked grievingly about the East End and the people and how they must be suffering, and then we went to bed and the raid was still going on and we wondered, would we wake up in the morning? What would tomorrow be like? And when I did wake up it was a lovely, sunny Sunday morning, lovely except that I think that four hundred and fifty or more people had been killed in East London, and a huge number injured, terrible, terrible destruction, and the Germans were coming back again that night . . .'

2

'The Most Grim Test in its History . . .'

With our enormous metropolis here, the greatest target in the world, a kind of tremendous fat cow tied up to attract the beasts of prey.

Winston Churchill speaking in 1934 about the prospect of an aerial bombardment of London

Darling Kat, You little know what you say when you tell me to write for the papers. I am not, as you know, made of the stuff Londoners are made of. My instinct is to flee. I cannot report on scenes in shelters. There are hundreds of keen, nerveless people out all night pursuing fires and demolition . . . Still it is endurable and my greatest fear is being forced by Duff [her husband, the Minister of Information] to leave the city. It is so utterly unlike what I imagined the raids on London would be. I thought of a bigger, suddener attack, with the whole population blocking roads, Ministries evacuating to their pre-arranged dispersal stations, frightful dislocation, worse perhaps than this cold-blooded waiting for destruction. Most people don't see it so. They have confidence in a defence being found. 'This is only a phase of war. We'll stick it out all right.' There is not a street that does not show some assault. The curtains flap dismally out of Londonderry House and most of the big Piccadilly houses. I try to avoid the places where the cruellest gashes have been inflicted, but one has to take the way that cut-off streets, encumbered with bombs ticking to explode, allow.

Lady Diana Cooper writing from London to her friend 'Kaetchen' Kommer in New York on 23 September 1940

Around the time the 'big blitz' on London started in September 1940, the War Damage Survey of the Architects' Department of the London County Council (LCC) started to record bomb damage to the capital. Using sheets of Ordnance Survey maps from 1916 that had been updated in 1940 to show boundary changes, new buildings etc., on a scale of 1:2,500 (25.34 inches to the mile), the architects marked incidents of bomb damage across the city's 117 square miles, using different-coloured pencils to indicate degrees of severity. Black denoted those buildings that had been totally destroyed, purple those damaged beyond repair. Those that had sustained 'serious damage, doubtful if repairable' were coloured dark red, while properties 'seriously damaged but repairable at cost' were light red. Orange indicated 'non-structural general blast damage' and those in yellow had escaped all but minor damage – broken windows, or roof tiles dislodged, for example. The architects kept up their meticulous work until the end of the German V-weapon offensive on 27 March 1945 (V-weapon damage was indicated differently), and today their maps make sombre viewing.

The docks consist of little other than large slabs of black, with small infills of purple round the edges. Even more shocking are the narrow streets edging the quays, where dock and factory workers lived in small terraced houses in the shadow of the heavy industries, their lives dominated by their proximity to their work. They often paid the ultimate price for that proximity, as 'collateral damage' to the industrial targets of the Luftwaffe. Most of the Isle of Dogs is black and purple, with the occasional flash of orange. There is not a single house that was untouched, and most were totally destroyed. It is much the same in Stepney, Bermondsey, Wapping, Poplar and Woolwich. East Ham, West Ham, Canning Town, Barking and Beckton are all outside the LCC administrative area, but they suffered grievously too, with people killed, seriously injured, bereaved, made homeless. Although of course not all the damage was done in those nightmare early nights of September 1940, the toll then was chillingly high. In that month 5,730 Londoners were killed, 9,003 were seriously injured, and countless others received minor injuries: the worst totals of the blitz. By November 1940, 2,160 houses in Stepney had been demolished or were beyond repair, while 13,480 were damaged but repairable. A little further north, in Hackney, where the Home Secretary, Minister for Home Security and former leader of the LCC, Herbert Morrison, was an MP, 1,349 homes had been destroyed in the same period and 3,654 badly damaged; in Poplar, eight hundred homes were lost and 13,200 badly damaged. South of the river suffered too, with Lambeth losing 1,758 houses and Lewisham only slightly fewer, though a staggering 23,370 houses there were damaged but just about repairable. There is also a list of those houses 'receiving first aid repairs', with bits of wood, roofing felt and tarpaulin *pro tem*, a roof over the residents' heads, but hardly a home any more. Fourteen thousand nine hundred Lewisham houses had had emergency repairs by November, Poplar, 8,500 and Wandsworth, 9,898.

Len Jones had spent the night of 7 September in a brick and concrete street shelter in Poplar which had 'lifted and moved, rolling almost as if it was a ship in a rough sea. And the suction and the blasts were coming in and out of the steel door, which was smashing backwards and forwards, bashing us against the walls . . . The worst part was the poor little kids; they were so scared, they were screaming and crying, clutching at their parents. The heat was colossal; the steel door was so hot that you couldn't touch it. And everybody was being sick, and people were carrying out their normal bodily needs, and the smell was terrible.'

The next morning, Jones 'went to see how our house was, and when I got there the front door was lying back, and the glass of the windows had fallen in, and you could see the top of the house had virtually disappeared. Inside, everything was blown to pieces, you could see it all by the red glow reflecting from the fires that were raging outside. Then I looked out the back and I suddenly realised that where my father's shed and workshop used to be, was just a pile of rubble, bricks. Then I saw two bodies, two heads sticking up, I recognised one head in particular; it was a Chinese man, Mr Say, he had one eye closed, and I began to realise that he was dead . . . I just convulsed and couldn't get my breath. I was shaking completely. Then I thought, well I must be dead, because they were, so I struck a match, and tried to burn my finger, I kept doing this with a match to see if I was still alive. I could see, but I thought, I cannot be alive. This is the end of the world.'

All that morning the East End was a scene of chaos and despair as people stumbled through the streets searching for family, friends and neighbours in rest centres and hospitals, wondered where to go for food and assistance, scrabbled through the rubble to locate their possessions in houses that had been bombed, attempted to patch up the damage if that was possible – or simply got out. A Thames pleasure steamer was pressed into service to evacuate women and children from the narrow, ruined streets of the Isle of Dogs, where most had lived all their lives and which few had seen any reason to leave – until now. What journalists called 'the mean streets' of the East End were full of what one of them, Hilde Marchant of the *Daily Express*, described as 'a ragged sleepless army whose homes had been smashed'; a 'civilian Dunkirk' fleeing the enemy. 'Little houses, four rooms and a bath tub, eight shillings a week [rent to a private landlord] had taken the attack . . . at daylight [the people] came up [out of the shelters] and many saw the roots of their homes turned to the sky.' Families pushing perambulators or carts, clutching suitcases and bundles crammed with all they could carry – clothes, bedding, household goods, food – 'climbed through streets that had once been two neat rows of houses and were [now] like a ploughed field', either trekking east to the open spaces of Epping Forest or heading 'up West', where it was believed to be safer. Anywhere to get away from the East End before another night of hell.

At midday on Sunday, 8 September, the Prime Minister, Winston Churchill, came to the East End with Duncan Sandys MP, who was married to Churchill's daughter Diana, his brother Jack, and his Chief of Staff, Major-General Hastings Ismay,* to inspect the damage for himself. They found the destruction much more devastating 'than they had imagined . . . Fires were still raging all over the place. Some of the large buildings were mere skeletons, and many of the smaller houses had been reduced to rubble.' Clambering over the debris, Churchill went first to visit an air-raid shelter in Columbia Road, Shoreditch, home of the flower market, where 'about 40 of the inmates had been killed and a very large number wounded. The place was full of people searching for their lost belongings when you arrived,' Ismay reminded his boss later when Churchill wanted to include the poignant occasion in his *History of the Second World War*.

The Columbia Road bomb had been a particularly tragic introduction to the events of the next few months. In what the *Daily Herald* journalist Ritchie Calder called 'a million to one chance', a bomb had crashed directly through a ventilation shaft measuring only three feet by one foot, below which lay a shelter containing more than a thousand people.

Mothers were killed outright before they had a chance to protect their children. Babies were swept from perambulators. Three or four support pillars were torn down and about 50 people lay in stunned heaps . . . Perambulators and corrugated iron lay entangled at the scene.

* Usually known as 'Pug', since, according to Churchill's private secretary John ('Jock') Colville, he 'looked like one, and when he was pleased one could almost imagine he was wagging his tail'.

. . . Although explosions could be heard in all directions and the scene was illuminated by the glow of the East End fires, civil defence workers laboured fearlessly and feverishly among the debris, seeking the wounded, carrying them to safe places, tending their injuries.

Nine doctors answered an S.O.S. and saved lives by improvising tourniquets. They dressed wounds by the dim glow of torches. In one family three children were killed. Their parents escaped. One man, when the smoke and noise had died down, searched for his wife, found her lying on the ground and turned her over. She was dead.

However, as Ismay noted of 'the big crowd, male and female, young and old, all seemingly very poor[, while] one might have expected them to be resentful against the authorities responsible for their protection . . . They stormed [Churchill] as he got out of the car with cries of "It was good of you to come Winnie. We thought you'd come. We can take it. Give it back." ' Or so Ismay remembered. 'It was a very moving scene. You broke down completely and I nearly did, as I was trying to get you through the press of bodies, I heard an old woman say, "You see, he really cares, he's crying . . ." Later we found many pathetic little Union Jacks flying on piles of masonry that had once been the homes of poor people.'

The point of the visit was to boost morale and show the nation that its leader was sympathetic to the East Enders' ordeal, and Churchill was snapped by press photographers as he bounded tirelessly from one bomb site to the next. But the Ministry of Information, anxious that no information on the effects of the raids should be seen by German Intelligence, scratched anything from the negatives that might indicate the location and the full extent of the damage before a select few photographs of the prime ministerial tour appeared in the press.

It was getting dark when Churchill set off back to Downing Street, although the flames of the previous night's fires still illuminated the sky. The Prime Minister's car 'had a long job getting through the narrow streets, many of which were blocked by houses having been blown across them'. While the East End had taken the main impact of the bombs, some had fallen elsewhere – near Victoria station, along the banks of the Thames from Vauxhall Bridge to Putney Bridge (Battersea Power Station was put out of action), and in parts of west London. The seat of government was bound to be a target, although Churchill was extremely reluctant to leave his official London home (he had been obliged to shut his family's country house,

Chartwell in Kent, during the Battle of Britain that summer). But 10 Downing Street was no longer regarded as a safe haven for Britain's inspirational wartime leader, even though, in a flurry of works that had necessitated Churchill moving for a few nights to the Carlton Hotel in nearby Belgravia, a shelter had been built in the garden, and a dining room and sitting room set up in the basement, which Jock Colville thought resembled 'third-class accommodation on a Channel steamer'. The question of where to keep Britain's principal wartime asset led to a tussle that would continue between the obstinate Prime Minister and his staff and advisers throughout the early days of the blitz.

That Sunday, the second night of the blitz, bombs fell again on the docks, reigniting fires that were still smouldering, starting new ones, and stretching the line of fire and destruction along the banks of the Thames: soon twelve conflagrations were lighting up the sky, and testing the resources of the fire services to their limit once again. The two hundred German planes pounded the City too. Every railway line out of London to the south was put out of action, and factories and offices were destroyed, as were more homes. Four hundred and twelve Londoners were killed that night, and 747 seriously injured.

Gerry Knight, who had memorably thought 'the whole bloody world's on fire' the previous night, was on duty again at Pageant's Wharf fire station when the bombs started to drop. One fell on the station killing Knight and a colleague, Auxiliary Fireman Dick Martin. All that could be found to identify the forty-four-year-old Knight were his standard issue thigh-high fireman's boots.

When the photographer Bert Hardy visited the East End two days later, 'he said it was like the end of the world', reported Alan Hutt. 'Whole streets down and gone. East End soldiers deserting to rush home and frantically try to find their folks . . . A man and a woman sitting on a pile of wreckage staring listlessly in front of them without speech . . . Revolting stories of official red tape in dealing with refugees and bereaved survivors . . . climaxing in the hideous affair of the refugees bunged into one East End School on Saturday night to be all bombed to death on Sunday [sic].'

This 'hideous affair' made unbearably raw all the fears and many of the tensions of the blitz just a day after it started. A rest centre had been established at South Hallsville School in Agate Street, Canning Town, and it was there that six hundred men, women and children had been led on Saturday night after it had been decided to evacuate the local area. The refugees were in a state of acute shock. Most had lost their homes; for some, members of their family had been killed or wounded, or were missing; they had few if any possessions; their clothes were torn and dirty, their faces blackened by smoke and soot, often caked with blood, their feet burned and lacerated. They clung to each other, terrified, confused, some hysterical, others racked with uncontrollable anger, others traumatised and unable to speak. Rest centre staff, hopelessly unprepared for such a sudden influx, themselves shocked and anxious, bustled around offering cups of tea – that ubiquitous British panacea – trying to find blankets for the refugees, many of whom were only wearing thin nightclothes, offering reassurance as bombs crashed all around and shrapnel grazed the walls: 'Don't worry, you'll be all right. We'll get you away.'

That day Ritchie Calder had sought out the Reverend Paton, a popular East End priest known locally as 'the Guv'nor', whose dockland church had been bombed the previous night.

> His pulpit still stood, but the roof and front wall had gone . . . I found 'The Guv'nor' at last, he was ashen grey with the anguish of the night. He had been out in the raids, helping his people throughout the night. His lips trembled and his eyes filled with tears when he spoke of his friends who were dead, injured or missing. But his main concern was for the living. He was dashing round the streets seeking out the survivors whose homes had been wrecked.
>
> I went with him. We found many thousands sheltering in a school in the heart of the bombed area. I took a good look at the school. From the first glance it seemed to me ominous of disaster. In the passages and classrooms were mothers nursing their babies. There were blind, crippled and aged people . . . Whole families were sitting in queues perched on pitiful baggage waiting desperately for coaches to take them away from the terror of the bombs which had been raining down on them . . . these unfortunate people had been told to be ready for the coaches at three o'clock. Hours later the coaches had not arrived. 'The Guvnor' and I heard women, the mothers of young children, protesting with violence and with tears about the delay. Men were cursing the officials who only knew that coaches were expected. 'Where are we going?' 'Can't we walk there?' 'We'll take a bus!' 'There's a lorry we can borrow!' The crowds clamoured for help, for information, for reassurance. But the officials knew no answer other than to offer a cup of tea.
>
> One mother complained that her children had been forbidden to play in

the playground . . . [the official showed me why]. In the playground behind
the school was a crater. The school was, in fact, a bulging dangerous ruin.
The bombs which had rendered these people homeless had also struck the
building selected by the authorities as a 'Rest Centre' . . . the school had already
been bombed at the same time as 'the Guv'nor's' church had been bombed.
So had the parish church . . . So had other buildings and streets within a direct
line with it. And then I knew that Sunday afternoon, that as sure as night
would follow day, the bombers would come again with the darkness, and that
the school would be bombed.

And so it was. 'Filled with foreboding', Calder 'hastened back to central
London. Three times I warned the Whitehall authorities during that evening
that the people must be got away before more bombs dropped and certain
disaster overtook them. Local folk back at the school were making equally
frantic efforts to force the local authorities to act.' But the displaced East
Enders were still huddled in the 'shelterless school' at 8 p.m. on Monday
when the alert sounded. At 3.45 on the morning of Tuesday,10 September
'the inevitable bomb' scored a direct hit on South Hallsville School. Half
the building was demolished, and hundreds of tons of masonry crashed
down on its occupants. Rescue workers, frantically digging and scrabbling
in the ruins, tried to free the injured, while a cordon was thrown around
the area to keep people from seeing what was happening, and the censor
warned the press that there were to be no reports or photographs of the
tragedy, so injurious was it feared that it would be to the morale of
the already disquieted city.

The rescue services dug for twelve days, trying to find survivors under
the slabs of concrete and piles of bricks that filled the crater where the
bomb had fallen, before they had to concede defeat. The dead – or parts
of the dead – were carefully transported to an emergency morgue at a
nearby swimming pool. Soon the rumours flew as fast as the fires had taken
hold: hundreds were dead, and the authorities had ordered the site to be
concreted over with bodies still entombed in the wreckage. Calder was
incandescent with rage at the authorities, not only for failing to organise
transport for the refugees, but also for failing to provide what he and others,
including most vociferously the scientist and author of the book *ARP*, J.B.S.
Haldane, had urged was essential for London: sufficient deep shelters to
provide safety for all those in vulnerable areas. Calder went again to the
scene. 'I saw the gaping bomb crater, where stood a school used as a shelter

centre, containing still uncounted bodies – families wiped out while they waited for transport which never came . . . I saw the rescue men descending perilously into it, with ropes around them, saw them pause, every now and then, in a hushed painful silence listening for the sound of the living, saw the tomb of whole families . . . I spoke to the men, fathers of families, who had been cursing on the Sunday. They were speechless and numbed by the horror of it.'

It has never been established why the coaches did not arrive: maybe the address they had been given was inadequate. The George, a well-known pub in the area from which coaches from all over London set off for Essex, had been designated as the rendezvous point – but there are more pubs than one in the capital called The George. Maybe the coaches had been mis-directed to Camden Town, rather than Canning Town. Or maybe the drivers, caught in the raid and seeing the devastation in the East End, simply turned back. Certainly it was a grievous dereliction of duty on the part of the West Ham authorities to leave so many people unprotected in the eye of the raid. And whatever the reason, the result was fatal – 450 dead, Calder claimed in the bitter account that appeared the following year in his admonitory book *The Lesson of London*. West Ham Council announced the death toll as seventy-three, but locals still believe that nearer two hundred people perished in South Hallsville School on the third night of the blitz. Many of the bodies remained unclaimed, despite the fact that the Metropolitan Police circulated photographs in the area of those it was still possible to identify, and were buried in a communal grave in the East London Cemetery at Plaistow.

'They call it crater London now,' read the trenchant journalist Hannen Swaffer's column in the *Daily Herald*. Traffic in the capital was at a stand-still, with streets roped off because of unexploded bombs, fires still smoul-dering and many City businesses closed. It was the King's turn to go to the people on Monday, 9 September. Accompanied by Captain Euan Wallace, Senior Regional Commissioner for Civil Defence, George VI paid a visit to Shoreditch, Bethnal Green, Stepney and Poplar before crossing the river to see the devastation of Bermondsey, Southwark and Lambeth. In places a path had to be hastily cleared through the debris so the royal party could proceed. At one point the King peered down into a crater ringed with 'backless houses, showing bedrooms and sitting rooms with furniture shat-tered, and every curtain hanging in shreds'. Twenty houses had stood there the previous night, but there was now nothing but a hole large enough to hold three or four buses. George VI – not at all displeased to have a clear-cut wartime role at last, as part of the 'morale-boosting' posse – conscientiously insisted on a thorough tour, taking in the docks as well as the devastated streets. Later that day, as he was working in his study at Buckingham Palace, a random bomb fell on the north side of the building, but did not explode until early the next morning, shattering windows and badly damaging the swimming pool. Each night the King and Queen trekked to Windsor Castle in an armoured Daimler. It had been planned that they would go to Worcester in the event of an invasion, and the by-now elderly Queen Mary, the Queen Mother, had decamped the previous year to Badminton, the Gloucestershire residence of her niece, the Duchess of Beaufort.

Monday night's raids lasted for nearly ten hours, killing 370 people and injuring 1,400. But the next night, for the first time, it seemed as if the fightback had begun. 'We had depended on anti-aircraft guns . . . and apart from a solitary salvo loosed at the beginning of the raids, no gun had been shot in our defence . . . we felt like sitting ducks and no mistake,' wrote Violet Regan, wife of an ARP warden, who had sheltered in a Poplar school throughout the raids. 'It was difficult for civilians to understand why there should be no more than spasmodic gunfire [from the anti-aircraft (AA, or 'Ack-Ack', from the staccato noise they made) guns[*]] when hordes of enemy aircraft streamed over London most of the night,' wrote the Commander-in-Chief of Anti-Aircraft Command, General Sir Frederick Pile. 'The intricate and enormous problems of night shooting were unknown to them, and impossible to explain. Londoners wanted to hear the guns shoot back; they wanted to feel that even if aircraft were not being brought down, at least the pilots were being made uncomfortable. It was abundantly apparent,' the C-in-C concluded, 'that every effort must be made to defend the Londoner more effectively, and to uphold his morale in so doing.'

Pile fully appreciated that 'anti-aircraft guns take a little time to become effective after they have been moved to new positions. Telephone lines have to be laid, gun positions levelled, the warning system co-ordinated

---

[*] Most Ack-Ack guns had been deployed to defend factories and airfields during the Battle of Britain, so when the Germans suddenly switched their attention to London, the capital was highly vulnerable, its defence resting on an entirely inadequate total of 264 anti-aircraft guns.

and so on.' But as he lay in bed during those first nights of the blitz, when 'despite the . . . very considerable increase in the number of guns by the second night of the battle, there did not seem to be much more anti-aircraft fire', he became 'both angry and frightened at the same time [much like the rest of the population of London] that our system was no good'. He lay awake 'for the rest of the night thinking how to deal with this business'.

What Pile decided to do, though, had rather more to do with upping British morale than downing German planes. He gathered the senior AA officers together in the Signals Drill Hall in Brompton Road, and instructed them that 'every gun was to fire every possible round. Fire was not to be withheld on any account. Guns were to go to the approximate bearing and elevation and fire. Searchlights were not to expose. R.A.F. fighters were not going to operate over London, and every unseen target must be engaged without waiting to identify the aircraft as hostile.'

The result, Pile found, was

as astonishing to me as it appears to have been to the citizens of London – and, apparently, to the enemy as well. For, although few of the bursts can have got anywhere near the target, the heights of aircraft steadily increased as the night went on, and many of them turned away before entering the artillery zone . . . It was in no sense a barrage, though I think by that name it will always be known.

Anyway, it bucked up people tremendously. The midnight news said some nice things about us, and when I put a call through to my wife the telephone operator said: 'By God this is the stuff. All the girls here are hugging each other.' Next day everyone said they had slept better, and for the first time A.A. Command hit the headlines. Apart from comforting the civilians, it stimulated the gunners, who had been feeling pretty frustrated during the long nights when they had been compelled to hear aircraft flying overhead and dropping their bombs without being engaged.

Although the barrage made sleep impossible in the crypt of the Archbishop of Canterbury's official residence, Lambeth Palace, 'with the noise continuing almost without intermission until 5.40 am', those sheltering there were 'much cheered by this offensive action', which in the view of the Archbishop's chaplain, the Reverend Alan Don, 'had turned back many German planes and fewer bombs were dropped – at any rate in central London'.

The press was enthusiastic too. The *Daily Herald* wrote of 'a curtain of exploding steel', or 'an effective patchwork quilt protecting the capital', with 'London really baring its teeth . . . Londoners sat up in their shelters and listened . . . "Spotters" on London roofs looked at one another and smiled. "That's lovely music," said one of them,' while a nameless man taking shelter felt that it was 'D—d heartening . . . it sounds like the answer to night bombing.'

Not everyone was pleased, of course. Spent shells falling back to the ground were hazardous, and 'some angry voices were raised . . . in the southern and eastern suburbs, upon which the retreating Luftwaffe jettisoned their bombs', while in another suburb the vibrations caused by the Ack-Ack guns were apparently cracking council-house lavatory pans, and 'Would we mind very much moving the barrage elsewhere?'

'The Blitzkrieg Spreads', announced the press on 11 September: 'Hitler's murder squadrons make their most widespread attacks on the London area'. That was how it would be every night until fog and low cloud on 3 November made it impossible for the Luftwaffe to locate their targets, and for one night the capital was silent – no alert, no bombs, no Ack-Ack fire. Fifty-seven nights of continuous raids with no respite. 'What a fantastic life we lead these days,' wrote Phyllis Warner, a teacher who lived at the Mary Ward Settlement Centre in Bloomsbury, in the 'Journal Under the Terror' that she kept during the blitz and sent to the *Washington Post* to give the still neutral America some idea of the quotidian realities of wartime London. 'Every night as the siren goes regularly at eight o'clock we scuttle down into the cellar, and are marooned there until six the next morning. My bedroom has never looked so invitingly comfortable as on these evenings when I hastily dive into a "siren suit" [an all-in-one outfit modelled on a workman's boilersuit and much favoured by the rotund Winston Churchill] and retreat to the basement . . . And here we must spend every evening. Farewell to theatre, films, dances, dinner-parties and such pleasures; we pass our evenings in dugouts trying to read, write, talk or play bridge, so far as the rattle of planes and the crash of bombs will allow. Yet this part of the night is better than the long hours of darkness when we try to sleep through the horrors that surround us. This is the front line, this is the "Journey's End" of this war, and men, women and children, we are trapped in it.'

In shelters much less congenial than the one at Mary Ward House – in domestic cellars, under the stairs, in damp Anderson shelters in back gardens, in public shelters in reinforced basements or on the surface, on tube platforms or in muddy trenches dug in parks or other open spaces, in a margarine warehouse, under bridges and arches – those who remained in London through necessity or choice sat out those long, dark, dangerous nights. By the end of September, the month of the supposed 'knock-out blow' that the Luftwaffe hoped to deliver to Britain, 5,730 people had been killed in the London region. In July the War Cabinet had taken the decision that it would be ill-advised to make casualty figures public, but once the blitz started it became clear that rumours often exaggerated the number of deaths and serious injuries, so stark notices were posted outside town halls giving the number of those killed and injured, but without identifying the location of the 'incidents', and insisting that the information 'must not be published in the press', lest it prove helpful to the Germans by informing them how successful their raids had been.

On some nights that September and October the raids were relatively light, with as few as seven bombers coming over (on 6 October). On others there were as many as 410 (on 15 October), but usually between two hundred and three hundred Heinkels, Dorniers and Junkers filled the sky. The main targets were still the City and the docks, but poor visibility, not entirely reliable navigational aids, and encounters with fighter planes, barrage balloons and searchlights (both of which forced the planes to fly higher) and Ack-Ack fire, meant that it was impossible to be certain of hitting a specific target, particularly by night. By early October Luftwaffe pilots were being issued with maps that indicated a target area – that is, a zone of several square miles within which several targets lay, such as the land within the U loop of the Thames – rather than a specific building or installation, such as Battersea Power Station or the West India Docks, as had previously been the case.

'Indiscriminate bombings' is how Churchill referred to the blitz, declaring that Hitler hoped, 'by killing large numbers of civilians, and women and children, that he will terrorise and cow the people of this mighty Imperial city and make them a burden and anxiety for the Government and thus distract our attention unduly from the ferocious onslaught he is preparing'. But although the bombing did seem indiscriminate, and its intention might have seemed to be to kill and maim civilians, in fact its intention was to devastate the London docks so that the food and matériel essential to the prosecution of the war could not be imported, and to destroy government offices in central London from where the war was being directed.

On 9 September, ninety bombers reached the capital and dropped some of their load on the suburbs: Kingston, Richmond, Malden, Surbiton, Purley, but as the *Daily Express* put it, 'Acacia Avenue clips its hedges beside a crater and carries on.' The first of the many London hospitals that would be devastated by the blitz, Queen Mary, in West Ham, had been bombed on 7 September, killing two nurses and six patients. On the night of 9 September a bomb fell on the London Hospital in Whitechapel Road, and St Thomas's Hospital on the Thames hard by Westminster Bridge, which had been designated as a wartime casualty clearing station, took a direct hit. Three floors of a nurses' home on the north side collapsed, and two nurses and four masseuses were crushed to death under the falling masonry. One of the masseuses, thirty-two-year-old Barbara Mortimer Thomas from Australia, was covered in debris and trapped in her bed forty feet above ground by a steel girder, with only her head and shoulders visible, and the floor supporting her likely to collapse at any minute. Her cries alerted the rescue squad, who started the hazardous task of building a scaffolding tower among the dislodged masonry to reach her, and carefully cut a hole in the wall so that drinks and a hot-water bottle could be passed to her and morphine injected into her one free arm. Mortimer Thomas joked with her rescuers, but just as they were about to free her after sixteen hours, a doctor crawled through the wreckage and found that she had died. The hospital's X-ray department was put out of action, and twenty-five patients were carefully carried to another ward. Seventy others were moved to other hospitals or sent home, while the entire staff repaired to the basement – a 'most incredible sight – one could hardly move without stumbling over a sleeping form'.

The next day, since the water supply had failed, all the remaining patients – except one who had been brought in as an emergency appendicitis case that morning – were evacuated to sector hospitals in the country,[*] with medical students carrying the stretchers to waiting ambu-

---

[*] On 28 August 1939 the Ministry of Health had ordered that since at least 25,000 casualties a day were expected when the blitz started, hospital admissions should be restricted to emergency cases only, and those should be monitored carefully, since the patients might well have to be evacuated. On the day war broke out the Emergency Medical Services came into operation. Under this scheme the capital and its outlying districts were divided into ten sectors, with one or more of the London teaching hospitals at the head of each. St Thomas's, for example, was the key hospital for Sector VIII, which included fifty-one voluntary hospitals and homes and miscellaneous other institutions scattered around south-west London and adjoining parts of Surrey and Hampshire, with the matron of St Thomas's responsible for all the nursing staff in the sector.

lances. St Thomas's was hit again on 13 September and again on the 15th, when two surgeons and a nurse were killed and four were seriously injured, including one in charge of the first aid post who subsequently died. The outpatients ward, the dispensary and the hospital chapel were badly damaged, and the electricity supply was cut off, so doctors and nurses had to tend the patients by candlelight or using the few battery-powered nightlights available. The hospital was hit three more times during the blitz. It was, in the words of its historian, 'for most of the war little more than a heap of ruins; yet it never closed entirely. When things were bad life was carried on in the basement . . . when things were better . . . a semblance of normal life and work miraculously took over in hastily cleared out rooms and wards.'

An air-raid shelter had been established in the basement of Buckingham Palace by appropriating one of the housekeeper's rooms. The ceilings were reinforced with steel girders, the high window protected by steel shutters. The furniture came from all over the palace, while the decoration consisted of valuable Dutch landscapes, many featuring canal bridges and ruminant cows. An axe and an emergency escape ladder lay ready alongside a bottle of smelling salts. Members of the royal household sheltered in an adjacent room with a piano – but the King vetoed its use for rousing singsongs.

'My darling Mama,' Queen Elizabeth wrote to Queen Mary on Friday, 13 September, 'I hardly know how to tell you of the horrible attack on Buckingham Palace this morning. Bertie & I arrived there about ¼ to 11, and he and I went up to our poor windowless rooms to collect a few odds and ends.' As the Queen was removing an eyelash from the eye of the King they heard a plane, which caused them to remark, 'Ah, a German,' as a bomb screamed down. 'I saw a great column of smoke & earth thrown up into the air. And then we all ducked like lightning into the corridor. There was another tremendous explosion, and we & our 2 pages who were outside the door, remained for a moment or two in the corridor away from the staircase, in case of flying glass. It is curious how one's instincts work at these moments of great danger, as quite without thinking, the urge was to get away from the windows. Everybody remained wonderfully calm, and we went down to the shelter . . . I was *so* pleased with the behaviour of our servants. They were really magnificent.' Three of those servants, working below in the chapel, were badly injured, and one subsequently died of his injuries.

That same afternoon, the royal couple toured the East End. 'The damage there is ghastly,' the Queen told her mother-in-law. 'I really felt as if I was walking in a dead city . . . All the houses evacuated and yet through the broken windows one saw all the poor little possessions, photographs, beds, just as they were left. At the end of the street is a school [South Hallsville School] that was hit and collapsed on top of the 500 people waiting to be evacuated – about 200 are still under the ruins [as was believed locally]. It does affect me seeing this terrible and senseless destruction – I think that I mind it much more than being bombed myself. The people are marvellous and so full of fight. One could not imagine that life <u>could</u> become so terrible. We <u>must</u> win in the end . . . . PS Dear old BP is <u>still standing</u> and that is the main thing.'

Harold Nicolson, now working in the Ministry of Information, had been concerned that it would not play well with East Enders if, while they were suffering so grievously, 'the toffs up West' got off lightly. 'There is much bitterness. It is said that even the King and Queen were booed the other day when they visited the destroyed areas . . . Clem[ent Davies, Liberal MP and post-war party leader] says that if the Germans had had the sense not to bomb west of London Bridge there might have been a revolution in this country.' Fortunately (in this context) the Germans displayed remarkably little such sense, and had 'smashed about Bond Street and Park Lane and readjusted the balance' (somewhat) on 9 September. Four days later 'an aircraft was seen coming down the Mall . . . having dived through the clouds and dropped two bombs in the forecourt, 2 in the quadrangle, 1 in the Chapel & the other in the garden. There is no doubt that it was a direct attack on the Palace.'

The attack allowed the press to caption a photograph of the Queen meeting one East Ender: 'Two women whose home has been bombed chat about the experience'. And the King told his mother that in his view, the couple's visits to bombed areas 'helped people who have lost their relations & homes & we have found a new bond with them as Buckingham Palace has been bombed as well as their homes, and nobody is immune"

If nobody was immune – which indeed few were – at least the royals could dress the part for their important role as morale-boosters, as their siren-suited Prime Minister fulfilled that of warrior-leader. George VI chose a series of uniforms, 'wearing in turn the dress of each of the high ranks he bore, as Admiral of the Fleet, a Field Marshal, and Marshal of the Royal Air Force, [making] no further public appearances in mufti [after the outbreak of war] he gave visible notice that he considered himself as continually on duty as any man in the fighting services', in the words of an admiring booklet published after the war.

The Queen had the right to wear a number of uniforms, including those of the WRNS, the WAAF and the St John Ambulance Brigade, and by 1945 her elder daughter Princess Elizabeth was entitled to wear the uniform of the ATS (Auxiliary Territorial Service – the women's branch of the army). Presumably the Queen could also have considered agreeing to don the bottle-green-and-beetroot garb of the Women's Voluntary Service (WVS). But instead the royal dressmaker, Norman Hartnell (who had made her a gown 'especially for air raid nights', and 'a black velvet case for her gas mask'), turned his mind to the problem. He had considered that he 'might perhaps have been useful to the War Office in camouflage, for I had many years of experience in the very antithesis of the art. It had been my special task to make figures stand out in sharp relief to the background, as has to be done in the case of Royalty.' 'What,' he pondered, 'might be appropriate wear for bombed sites and the devastated areas all over the country? How should [the Queen] appear before the distressed women and children whose own kingdom, their small homes, had been shattered and lay crumbled at their feet? In black? Black does not appear in the rainbow of hope. Conscious of tradition, the Queen made the wise decision in adhering to the gentle colours, and even though they became muted into what one might call dusty pink, dusty blue and dusty lilac, she never wore green [presumably for reasons of superstition] and she never wore black. She wished to convey the most comforting, encouraging and sympathetic note possible.' Her hats, 'made by Mr Aage Thaarup', were always 'innocent of veils', so the populace could gaze on this sympathetic countenance without hindrance.

'A sense of invasion,' wrote Virginia Woolf in her diary on 14 September, 'that is lorries of soldiers & machines – like cranes walloping along to Newhaven. A raid is on . . . workmen on the hangar haystack – disguising a gun – said "Wish I was as sure of a thousand pounds as of winning the war."' 15 September 1940 was the day on which it was expected that German forces would invade Britain. 'It may be this weekend,' the *Daily Herald* had warned on the 12th, reporting that Hitler 'has been accumulating shipping in the Channel ports, Hamburg and the Baltic, and obviously does not intend to let them rot. As the Prime Minister said last night, this invasion may never materialise: equally from present indications, it would seem that its attempt will not be long delayed. It may come anywhere in several heads from the coastline which is now in German hands. It is certain that everywhere it will meet with terrific opposition.'

There had already been an invasion scare on the night the blitz started. The previous week barges, motor launches and larger vessels had been photographed massing on the other side of the Channel, to such an extent that, according to the official history, 'by the morning of the 7th there was much evidence from reconnaissance alone to suggest that an early landing might be expected'. In addition, German troops and dive bombers seemed to be moving into position ready for an attack, a rowing boat containing four Germans who confessed (or claimed) to be spies gathering intelligence for an invasion was captured off the English coast, and as the final clincher the moon and tides were in the right conjunction for such a crossing. The Chiefs of Staff were informed that an invasion might be imminent.

At 8.07 p.m. the signal 'Operation Cromwell' went out to all formations in London and the South-East for 'immediate action'. Other commands were also told, but for information only. However, several zealous Home Guard commanders in various parts of Britain summoned their units by ringing church bells. These had been silenced after Dunkirk, and were only to be rung when it was clear that an invasion had started. In the febrile atmosphere of expectancy, heightened by notices flashed on cinema screens recalling soldiers to their barracks at once, rumours rapidly spread that the skies were already full of German parachutists, and flotillas of German motorboats were speeding towards English beaches. Members of the Home Guard hurried to their recruiting stations or carried out their jobs with rifles slung over their shoulders, householders paraded outside their homes with brooms, garden forks and spades, and the challenge 'Who goes there?' rang out throughout the land.

After this panic, General Sir Alan Brooke, Commander-in-Chief of Home Forces since July, tightened up procedures: in future no church bells were to be rung until he had personally counted a minimum of twenty-five German parachutists floating down onto British soil, and communicated that fact.

But the invasion did not come that night, nor any other. It was doubtful if the Germans could have mustered the 20,000 parachutists that the British government feared. The Kriegsmarine did not have any special landing craft at the time, and its commander, Admiral Erich Raeder, did not consider that a seaborne invasion was remotely feasible, while General Alfred Jodl, deputy to Field Marshal Wilhelm Keitel, head of the Oberkommando der Wehrmacht (OBW), the high command of the German armed forces, advised Hitler that invasion should only be contemplated when Britain was paralysed and 'practically incapable of fighting in the air'. On 12 October Hitler postponed 'Operation Sealion', the planned invasion of Britain, and in January 1941 effectively cancelled it. But at the time, of course, no one in Britain could be sure that this was the case, and that the blitz was not the final 'softening up' prior to an invasion. A state of alertness was maintained, and would be reactivated on occasions both as a defence and to encourage the war effort.

London was not alone in those dark days of September and October 1940 in experiencing death, injury and destruction from the air. There were spasmodic raids on the Home Counties, Liverpool had been attacked sixty times by the end of the year, and German bombs had also fallen on the Midlands, Scotland, Wales, the south coast ports Southampton and Portsmouth, the West Country and the North-East. But the capital took the brunt of the Luftwaffe attack, with 27,500 high-explosive bombs and countless incendiaries and parachute mines dropped between 7 September and 13 November.

In those two months London became a city pockmarked with ruins and rubble, its streets assaulted, private spaces ripped open to public gaze, landmarks that had stood for centuries instantly made jagged and fragile, the aftermath of the previous night's onslaught evident in the pall of smoke and dust that hung over the capital, the smell of burning that lingered in the autumn air, roads closed, the snaking coils of fire hoses, the weary, soot-blackened faces of the firemen, the ARP wardens, the heavy rescue squads, the numbing sense of exhaustion. Vere Hodgson, a Birmingham-born woman living and working as a social worker in west London, had come back to the capital 'to face the blitz', as she put it on 10 September 1940. 'This was the night the anti-aircraft barrage took on a formidable tone, and gave Londoners some satisfaction. They had more to listen to than bombs falling one by one. I shall never forget the next fortnight as long as I live . . . sleepless, terrified nights, and days when you could fall off your chair with weariness, and yet somehow held on . . . the tense look on the faces of the inhabitants of Notting Hill Gate – for of course I ventured nowhere else!'

With newspapers forbidden to mention the precise locations of bomb damage, Londoners discovered the topography of destruction for themselves. Anthony Heap, a local government official living with his mother not far from King's Cross station,

> heard of all sorts of places near us which were supposed to have been bombed but on walking round this afternoon, observed that it was the usual pack of false rumours. With one exception Harrington Square where we used to live . . . I could see that two houses on the north side of the square had been completely demolished and a bomb had dropped in the roadway and blown a bus up against them. The bus was still there standing lengthways against the ruins. Furthermore the roofs had been blown off two houses on the corner of Lidlington Place and thirteen houses in Eversholt Street . . . Most of the square's inhabitants had been down the shelter and escaped injury but one or two people had been killed and they were still trying to get out someone buried in the basement.
>
> The volume of gas in our stove very slight today. Presumably some of the borough's supply is being transferred to other districts where the mains have been hit.
>
> I heard that Tussaud's cinema caught a packet last night. So as soon as the All Clear went at 6.25 [on 9 September] I dashed along to see. And by gosh it had too. Only the front of it in Marylebone Road and the proscenium was left standing. The rest was completely demolished as were some buildings behind it as well . . . not a single window in any building in the vicinity remained intact. Huge crowds thronged along the Marylebone Road to see the ruins. It was one of the sights of London today.
>
> 10th Spent entire afternoon going round sightseeing in the raid devastated areas . . . Holborn was easily the worst of the lot. Most of the centre between it and Chancery Lane and Red Lion Square was laid waste . . .

'Only two theatres kept open last night – the Coliseum and the Criterion. The West End and local cinemas kept open but hardly did any business,' reported Heap, who by 16 September had got a job in Finsbury Council's Borough Treasurer's Office, and reported that 'Every time anyone in the office goes out wage paying or rent collecting they come back having witnessed some fresh scene of devastation.' Over the next few weeks he chronicled the damage to central London: St Paul's Cathedral, where

> broken masonry was still piled up in front of the altar and sun streamed in through a hole in the roof; Temple Bar, St Clement Danes Church, the statue

of Richard 1 ('only the sword bent on this') outside the House of Lords . . . the whole area around Cambridge Circus on the south side is in a terrible state now. Practically every street is blocked with debris which the Army Pioneer Corps have now been detailed to clear away. Next week 5,000 of them start work on this all over London . . . Bomb almost demolished 145 Piccadilly the house in which the King and Queen used to live when they were Duke and Duchess of York . . . London Palladium burnt inside nothing visible outside. St James Church, Piccadilly partly demolished. The Fifty Shillings tailor opposite burned down . . . The Carlton Club in Pall Mall stopped a direct hit. Also Carlton House Terrace . . . opposite the former German Embassy . . . Bomb in Blackfriars Bridge Road hit five trams held up by traffic lights during the rush hour. Many casualties . . . Looked at bombed out theatres Brewer Street, Saville Theatre, Drury Lane theatre only just missed a bomb, alleged Queen's Theatre bombed.

But on 10 November Heap was able to report that just a week after London's first raid-free night since 7 September, 'no raids at all today – till evening. Some people inclined to link this with [Neville] Chamberlain's death' – since 'the now-derided champion of peace died today [in fact the previous day] a broken and disappointed man'. Though in Heap's view, 'Whatever the bellicose little upstarts in power today may think of him, history cannot but judge him as a fine statesman and a great gentleman.'

Lambeth Palace, which was perilously close to the river, had received a direct hit on 20 September. Alan Don recorded:

Bomb entered roof just above large drawing room window – drawing room, parlour, little drawing room are wrecked and bedrooms above are a mass of ruins, the pantry etc. a mass of rubble. Four airmen sleeping under a table in the knife room next to the coal hole were only saved by the fact that they had a table over their heads, the contents of the drawing room fell on top of them, but they crawled out unhurt . . . the people in the basement passage were covered with dust and got a severe shaking but were uninjured . . . the crypt was full of people, some 200 of them: had the bomb landed on the other side of Cranmer's Tower they would have received the full force of the explosion. That no one was injured is a miracle. The force of the blast was terrific – the furniture, panelling etc. is reduced to matchwood, the shutters were lying in fragments on the lawn, some of the pieces landed beyond the terrace, the wall of the house is bulging dangerously and great blocks of masonry fell onto the grass . . . a gaping hole in the roof yawns above the landing . . . the whole place is covered in white dust and much of the glass is broken.

The Archbishop of Canterbury was not in residence that night, but when Canterbury Cathedral was bombed for the second time in October, Don began to wonder, 'Are the Germans deliberately trying to kill the Primate? They have had shots at the King and the Prime Minister and they doubtless have no love for CC [Cosmo Cantuar].'

By mid-October 'the Bishop of London reported that between 20–25 of his churches have been put out of action entirely while another 250 have been more or less damaged. St James Piccadilly is a serious loss . . . There is scarcely an historic building in London that remains entirely unscathed and yet we are told that three years of such bombing would be needed to destroy a quarter of London!' wrote Don.

The sight of their ravaged city would imprint itself forever on Londoners who lived through that intense time. On 26 September Phyllis Warner went shopping in Oxford Street: 'I almost wish I hadn't, the sight of that fearful destruction makes me feel so much worse tonight. [It had been severely bombed in the early hours of 18 September.] The less one sees of the result of the bombs the better. The big stores are carrying on gallantly in spite of their troubles. I bought a dress at D.H. Evans, there wasn't a pane of glass in the shop, and the models were all nakedly exposed to the street, but the shop girls, wrapped up in big coats, were models of helpfulness, and I got just what I wanted. John Lewis's great building was bombed and burned until it is only a blackened shell, but it bears the defiant notice "Reopening on October 5th". The other big stores are running "Business as Usual" in such corners as remain.'

Virginia Woolf also observed the destruction of 'that great city', the love of which was, as she wrote to her friend the composer Ethel Smyth, 'my only patriotism': 'to see London all blasted . . . raked my heart'. On the same day that Vere Hodgson returned to London, the Woolfs, Virginia and Leonard, came up from Sussex to spend

perhaps our strangest visit. When we got to Gower St. a barrier with Diversion on it. No sign of damage. But, coming to Doughty St. a crowd . . . Meck Sq. [Mecklenburg Square, where the Woolfs had their London home] roped off. Wardens there, not allowed in. The house about 30 yards from us struck at one this morning by a bomb. Completely ruined. Another bomb in the square unexploded. We walked round the back. Stood by Jane Harrison's house [the classical scholar and anthropologist who died in 1928 had lived at number 11]. The house was still smouldering. That is a great pile of bricks. Underneath all the people who had gone down the shelter. Scraps of cloth hanging to the bare walls at the side still standing. A looking glass I think swinging. Like a tooth knocked out – a clean cut. Our house undamaged. No windows yet broken – perhaps the bomb has now broken them. We saw Sage Bernal [the scientist J.D. Bernal, who worked as Scientific Advisor to the Research and Experiments Department of the Ministry of Home Security during the war] with an arm band jumping on top of the bricks – who lived there? I suppose the casual young men and women I used to see, from my window; the flat dwellers who used to have flower pots and sit on the balcony. All now blown to bits – The garage man at the back – blear eyed & jerky told us he had been blown out of his bed by the explosion; made to take shelter in a church – a hard cold seat, he said, & a small boy lying in my arms. 'I cheered when the all clear sounded. I'm aching all over' . . . we went on to Grays Inn. Left the car & saw Holborn. A vast gap at the top of Chancery Lane. Smoking still. Some great shops entirely destroyed: the hotel opposite like a shell. In a wine shop there were no windows left. People standing at the tables – I think being served. Heaps of blue green glass in the road at Chancery Lane. Men breaking off fragments left in the frames. Glass falling. Then to Lincolns Inn. To the N.S. [*New Statesman*] office: windows broken but house untouched. We went over to it. Deserted. Glass on stairs. Wet passages. Doors locked. So back to the car. A great block of traffic. The Cinema behind Mme Tussaud's torn open: the stage visible. Some decorations swinging. All the R[egent's] Park houses with broken windows, but undamaged. And then miles & miles of orderly ordinary streets – all Bayswater, and Sussex Sqre as usual. Streets empty. Faces set & eyes bleared . . . Then at Wimbledon a raid – people began running. We drove through almost empty streets as fast as possible. Horses taken out of shafts. Cars pulled up. Then the all clear.

'One of the oddest things about our everyday life,' mused Phyllis Warner on 19 September, 'is its mixture of ruthless horror and every-day routine. I pick my way to work past the bomb craters and the shattered glass, and sit at my desk in a room with a large hole in the roof (a block of paving stone came through). Next to a house reduced to matchwood, housewives are giving prosaic orders to the baker and the milkman. Of course, ordinary life must go on, but the effect is fantastic. Nobody seems to mind the day raids, which do little damage. It is the nights which are like a continuous nightmare, from which there is no merciful awakening. Yet people won't move away. I know that I'm a fool to go on sleeping in Central London which gets plastered every night, but I feel that if others can stand it, so can I.'

'Little does [Hitler] know the spirit of the British nation, or the tough fibre of Londoners, whose forebears...have been bred to value freedom far above their lives,' Winston Churchill broadcast in the first week of the blitz. And he purposefully strode off to see the bomb damage for himself, as here in Battersea, south London, and to encourage Londoners to 'hold together and stand firm'.

Women carrying possessions they have salvaged from their bombed homes pick their way through the rubble in an unnamed street in Stepney in the East End of London in September 1940.

'Firemen are busy everywhere, and the place is a bedlam of roaring pumps, hissing water and falling walls. The very air is hot and heavy on the lungs.' Firemen play their hoses on the still-burning remains of buildings in Chancery Lane after a raid on the night of 24–25 September 1940.

Newborn babies wrapped in shawls and placed on a shelf in an air-raid shelter attached to a Salvation Army hospital in Clapton, north-east London, while a nurse instructs their mothers how to knit to pass the time during raids. October 1940.

Shelterers spread across the tube lines in the disused Aldwych station on 8 October 1940. Later the track would be boarded over, the lighting improved and rows of bunks installed.

The efficacy of a properly-constructed and erected Anderson shelter demonstrated by a man whose house in Croydon was destroyed by a high-explosive bomb in October 1940.

3

Sheltering

What a domestic sort of war this is ... it happens in the kitchen, on land-
ings, beside washing-baskets; it comes to us without stirring a yard from our
own doorsteps to meet it. Even its catastrophes are made terrible not by
strangeness but by familiarity. John Strachey, *Post D* (1941)

On the night of 12 September Whitehall was hit during a raid, and the
Ministry of Transport was damaged by high-explosive bombs. Plans had
already been made to move the Cabinet and the chiefs of staff to a citadel
in the basement of the GPO's research centre in Dollis Hill in north-west
London (code-named 'Paddock') if Whitehall were to be bombed out,
though other options had been considered, including various reinforced-
concrete buildings close to Whitehall, such as a rotunda in Horseferry Road.
On 20 September Winston Churchill and his wife Clementine, accompanied by Jock Colville, went to look over what might be their new London
home. They inspected the flats and the 'deep underground rooms safe from
the biggest bomb, where the Cabinet and its satellites (e.g. me) would work
and if necessary sleep', wrote Colville. 'They are impressive but rather forbidding; I suppose if the present intensive bombing continues we must get
used to being troglodytes ("trogs" as the PM puts it). I begin to understand what the early Christians must have felt about living in the Catacombs.'

In fact the PM would prove to be only an occasional and somewhat peri-
patetic 'trog', as in the early days of the blitz he experimented to find what
suited him best, somewhat to the alarm of his staff. One member of his
private office, John Peck, wrote a spoof memo under the Churchillesque
heading 'ACTION THIS DAY':

Pray let six new offices be fitted for my use, in Selfridge's, Lambeth Palace,
Stanmore, Tooting Bec, the Palladium and Mile End Road. I will inform

you at 6 each evening at which offices I shall dine, work and sleep. Accommodation will be required for Mrs Churchill, two shorthand typists, three secretaries and Nelson [the resident black cat at No. 10, of which Churchill had grown fond]. There should be a shelter for all and a place for me to watch air-raids from the roof. This should be completed by Monday. There is to be no hammering during office hours, that is between 7am and 3am. WSC. 31.10.40.

In the event Churchill spent most of his working day at 10 Downing Street, occasionally repairing for the night to the underground Cabinet War Rooms, just off Whitehall, the nerve centre from which, in his words, he 'directed the war', or to London Underground's offices housed in Down Street underground station in Mayfair, on the Piccadilly Line between Dover Street (now Green Park) and Hyde Park Corner stations, which had been closed in 1932 and adapted as offices for the Railway Executive Committee. This was considered to be safe, and boasted a large dining room where the food was reputed to be excellent, though it could be noisy as underground trains rattled past.

In December 1940 the Churchills moved into a ground-floor flat in the No. 10 annexe above the Cabinet War Rooms. It was hardly bomb-proof, but it was more robust than No.10 itself, and was at least fitted with heavy steel shutters that could be closed during an air raid. Apart from Winston's occasional excursions underground, it was in this ex-typing pool that the couple largely saw out the war.

The question of how best to protect the public during air raids was one that had exercised government and civil servants for some time. It had long been estimated that each ton of high-explosives dropped on a congested area would cause as many as fifty casualties, and the RAF had reckoned that on average seven hundred tons of bombs would be dropped daily, although in the first few days in an effort to achieve a 'knock-out blow' the figure was more likely to be nearer 950 tons; or perhaps the Germans would decide on a week-long attrition that would deliver as much as 3,500 tons on London in the first twenty-four hours. An indication of the effects of intense air raids was brought sickeningly home to many British people as they sat in their cinema seats watching newsreels of the bombing of Barcelona and Bilbao during the Spanish Civil War.

A vital matter was to give the public warning of an impending air raid. The country had been divided into 111 warning districts (based on telephone areas rather than local authority boundaries), and messages about approaching enemy aircraft were originated by RAF Fighter Command, which, using direct telephone lines, cascaded the warning to control centres. These would then transmit the message in strict order of priority to those on the warning list: government offices, military establishments, the police, Civil Defence HQs, fire brigades and large industrial concerns in particular areas.

Each stage of alert was distinguished by a different colour code-name. A yellow message was the 'Preliminary Caution', meaning that enemy planes were estimated to be about twenty-two minutes' flying time away. This message was confidential, and the public would not have been aware of its receipt since those receiving it were instructed 'to take the necessary precautions in as unobtrusive way as possible'. A red message, the 'Action Warning', was relayed when the planes were twelve minutes' flying time away. This was the signal for the police to activate the air-raid sirens in their district, which emitted a low, moaning sound that rose to a querulous wail (a 'wailing banshee', in Churchill's phrase), alerting the public to the fact that a raid was imminent and that they should seek shelter. Fighter Command finally sent the green message, 'All Clear', indicating 'Raiders Passed'; for this the sirens sounded a steady two-minute note.

In July 1940 the government shifted the balance from safety first to production first, as the war effort was being disrupted by workers unnecessarily spending unproductive hours in shelters, particularly during daytime raids, when an alert might last for three or four hours. The Home Secretary and Minister for Home Security Sir John Anderson announced that 'Workers engaged in war production should be encouraged . . . to continue at work after a public air-raid warning until it is clear that an enemy attack is actually imminent in their neighbourhood.' This was to be made practicable by the recruitment of roof spotters, who would alert the workers when enemy planes were sufficiently close for them to need to take shelter.

On 25 July another colour was introduced into the spectrum: a purple message would be sent to districts which, although they might be on the raiders' flightpath, were not expected to be a target. On receipt of this, all outside lighting had to be extinguished, but factories were allowed to continue to work at night after the red message had sounded (since there would be no lights to attract raiders). It did have other effects, for example slowing down rail transport and reducing outside work.

Once the blitz started, the duration of the 'alert' and the 'All Clear' warnings was halved from two minutes to one.

In December 1937 the Air Raid Precautions Act had laid on local authorities the responsibility for 'the protection of persons and property from injury and damage in the event of hostile attacks from the air', and required them to submit ARP schemes for approval. There were few guidelines, though a small number of 'model scenes' were circulated. Part of the problem was that no one seemed entirely sure what would be needed, since there was little conclusive evidence of the effect that high-explosive bombs would have, and much more concentration was focused on the effects of poison gas than on what could be done to protect people from bomb splinters, for example. Local authorities received assurances that government funding of around 60 to 75 per cent of the cost (as much as 85 per cent in the case of poor boroughs) of ARP preparations – including shelters – would be forthcoming, providing their schemes were accepted.

In April 1938 Sir John Anderson, who was then Lord Privy Seal, had recognised that the shelter problem was 'probably the most difficult of all the questions with which [local authorities] were confronted'. The government initially acted on two money-saving assumptions: the first was that most towns and cities would have 'a large amount of accommodation which by adaptation and strengthening and by the use of sandbags could be made to give reasonable protection'; the second that all householders needed was advice from local officials, and that they would 'generally do what they could to increase the natural protection of their homes' – though in fact many of the houses in the most vulnerable target areas were poorly and cheaply constructed, and their 'natural protection' was all but non-existent.

Nevertheless, the government's policy for protection of the population during air raids was and would remain one of dispersal: it feared the consequences of hundreds of frightened people sheltering together in one place, and the effect on life and morale if such a shelter received a direct hit. This consideration was inextricably linked to the policy of evacuating 'useless mouths' – that is, women and children who could not materially contribute to the war effort – away from urban and industrial centres as soon as war broke out, and also led to the closing of cinemas on the outbreak of war (though most soon reopened), bans on large crowds at places of entertainment, football matches and other sporting events, and the implementation of a shelter policy.

Local authorities were required to undertake a survey of buildings in their area that could be strengthened to provide shelter accommodation, and to put in place plans to dig shelters in public open spaces. It was, however, considered inadvisable 'to immobilise open spaces during peacetime by turning them into a trench system', which might have been frighteningly reminiscent of the Western Front in the First World War, bearing the suggestion that the home front would indeed become the battlefront.

Meanwhile, householders were advised in a government-issue booklet, *The Protection of Your Home Against Air Raids*, to designate one room as a 'refuge room' against poison gas or bombs – ideally a basement or cellar, but if neither of these was available, 'any room with solid walls is safer than being out in the open'. In the event of an air raid, the 'head of the household' should send all those under his (the male role was assumed) care with their respirators (gas masks) to the refuge room, and keep them there until he heard the 'raiders passed' (or 'All Clear', as it became known), and had satisfied himself that the danger had passed and the neighbourhood was free from gas.

The Munich crisis at the end of September 1938, when Neville Chamberlain desperately parleyed with Adolf Hitler in an attempt to find a solution to German demands for parts of Czechoslovakia, ratcheted up the need to find ways to enable Britain to 'stand the test of imminent war'. On 24 September the Home Office issued directives to local authorities in heavily populated areas to construct deep trench shelters to accommodate 10 per cent of their residents – this work to be completed within an entirely unrealistic three days. The trenches were dug in public spaces such as parks, playing fields and recreation grounds, while householders who had sufficient space were encouraged to get digging in their gardens. A leaflet was circulated setting out how the trenches should be constructed, and owners of private land such as golf courses were approached for permission to slash into their greensward. By early October something like a million feet of trenches had been dug, but these were only ever intended to be used by people caught in a raid, not as somewhere to go to when the alert sounded – a misapprehension that was to endure throughout the blitz. The government constructed or adapted shelters for short-term use: a person's proper place during a raid was considered to be in their home. But for many of the population, their homes offered little or no protection, and they sought refuge in public shelters – or anywhere that they believed was safer than their own usually shelter-less, basement and cellar-less homes.

Although the survey of buildings in London with a view to adapting them as shelters was more or less complete, no structural work at all had been started at the time of Munich, though sandbags started to be piled up around government buildings to protect them. By the time the crisis passed, some unsystematic work had been done in shoring up basements, but there was a general shortage of materials and a lack of precise technical information. Besides which, even if suitable buildings had been identified for shelter use, if they were privately owned the local authorities had no power to requisition them. In the majority of London boroughs, as in towns and cities throughout the country, there were still no public shelters by late September 1938.

But at the end of that year the government finally gave some substance to its policy of dispersal, announcing that 'standard steel shelters' – constructed of corrugated eight-hundredweight curved steel sheets, and soon to be universally known as Anderson shelters – were to be issued to two and a half million households in large towns in the most vulnerable areas. This number of shelters was reckoned to be capable of sheltering ten million people out of a potential vulnerable population of nearly twenty-seven million. The distribution started in February 1939, and anyone earning less than £250 a year could receive their shelter for free. When these had been distributed, it was intended to produce more for sale. Anderson shelters were six feet high, six feet long and four feet six inches wide, and had to be dug two feet into the ground and covered with earth or sand. Each could accommodate up to four or, at a squash, six persons, and they were fairly easy to erect. They were not bomb-proof, as the government pointed out, and would not save their occupants from a direct hit from an HE bomb, but if correctly positioned and well covered, they did offer protection against bomb fragments, blast and falling debris. But of course Anderson shelters were not suitable for everyone: you needed to have a garden.

Trenches dug at the time of Munich were inspected and, if suitably sited, were redug if necessary to four feet deep, lined with concrete or steel and their entrances closed. But they had no sanitary arrangements, or even duckboard flooring, making them unsuitable for night-long occupation – though this often happened – were cold, and apt to become waterlogged. In any case, once the Munich crisis had passed, many local authorities had filled in their trenches and were reluctant to start digging again.

On 15 March 1939 German troops occupied Prague, in direct contra-vention of the Munich Agreement. Civil defence measures in Britain were immediately escalated. A new Civil Defence Bill conferred wide-ranging peacetime powers on local authorities that included the right to designate buildings as public shelters – shops, for example: Dickins & Jones in Regent Street had a much-sought-after basement shelter, as did D.H. Evans in Oxford Street – or clubs or institutes, against the wish of the owner if neces-sary, and to do whatever structural work was required, paying compensa-tion if appropriate. Those people with incomes that entitled them to a government-issue Anderson shelter were supplied free of charge with mate-rials to strengthen their 'refuge room' if they had no space for an external shelter, and the local authority would be reimbursed for the cost of doing the work. New buildings had to incorporate spaces for shelters, and employers with a workforce of fifty or more in a designated target area were obliged to provide shelter accommodation (and to organise ARP services) for their employees; they would receive government funding to help pay for this. Smaller firms in the same areas could apply for funding to safeguard their workforces.

Anderson shelters and reinforced basements were not going to provide protection for all those in vulnerable areas, so in May 1939 money was made available for materials for local authorities to build public outdoor shelters (though they had to foot the bill for the construction costs). For blocks of flats where there was no suitable shelter accommodation for all the residents, and where most were not eligible for free shelters, the land-lord could be compelled to build one if petitioned to do so by more than 50 per cent of the tenants, and could recoup the cost by raising all the rents.

Despite these initiatives, by September 1939 shelter provision was lamen-tably behind schedule. There was a shortfall of about a million of the prom-ised Anderson shelters (those delivered were optimistically pronounced to provide protection for 60,000 people), meaning that even in what were believed to be the most dangerous areas many people had no shelters, and none were offered for sale until the following month. These cost between £6.14s and £10.18s – easy terms available. However, the take-up was limited – by April 1940 fewer than a thousand had been bought, while the base-ment-strengthening programme had hardly started.

In some places the provision of public shelters was more advanced: about three-quarters of the trenches dug at the time of Munich had been reinforced, the City of London reported that its public-shelter-building programme was complete, and on the eve of war most cities exercised their power to requisition suitable sites. Notices proclaiming 'Public Shelter' appeared on various buildings – some more suitable than others. At the end of August 1939, in tardy recognition of this unsatisfactory provision, the government urged local authorities to provide purpose-built public shelters, above-ground 'heavily protected' brick and concrete constructions capable of holding up to fifty people.

Fortunately, the eight-month respite of the 'phoney war', which effectively lasted until May 1940, meant that shelter provision could continue in wartime. However, the materials needed for shelters were now urgently required for military purposes. Smaller Anderson shelters, only four feet five inches long, were now produced and pronounced suitable for four persons, while the original 'standard' Anderson was redesignated as large enough for six people, with an 'extension' tacked on to allow it to accommodate up to ten if necessary. Finally, in April 1940, the production of Anderson shelters was suspended altogether, but by the start of the blitz nearly two and a half million had been distributed, theoretically providing shelter for 12.5 million people. Many gardens, however, were littered with unerected Anderson shelters, now rusting and near to useless. Some enterprising boroughs such as Hackney in east London, under its redoubtable ARP Controller Dr Richard Tee, organised teams of council workmen or volunteers to help householders, and the Bristol Civil Defence Area had taken a similar initiative, but the government decided that sterner measures were needed to compel self-help. From May 1940, under the terms of Defence Regulation 23B, everyone who had been issued with an Anderson shelter had ten days in which to erect it and cover it in the requisite manner, or to report to their local authority that they had not done so. If they did not, and could not show that they were genuinely incapable of doing so, the steel sheets would be collected and issued to another household.

Meanwhile the government was pressing forward with the provision of public communal shelters, intended to accommodate twelve or so families from nearby properties, which it fully funded. After the Russian bombing of Finland in the winter of 1939–40 it was decided that railway stations would be likely targets, so shelters capable of sheltering the equivalent of ten minutes' flow of passengers at peak travel times needed be provided at them. These were started at all London termini, but were far from completion when the blitz started.

By the start of the blitz, of the 27.5 million people living in 'specified areas' (that is, those urban and industrial centres considered particularly likely to be attacked, from which evacuation had been recommended), 17.5 million had been provided with some sort of shelter, domestic or public, at government expense. A few householders had provided themselves with shelters at their own expense, and an additional five million could use shelters at work. These figures were produced by the government when it came under attack – as it had since the mid-1930s – for the slow, patchy and often inadequate shelter provision. There was still an obvious shortfall, and those people not in a 'specified area' were left to their own devices, though issued with a booklet, *Your Home as an Air Raid Shelter*. Moreover, the shelter experience of many was very far from satisfactory.

People with rooms in their homes that they could make as bomb-proof as any domestic arrangement could be were, generally speaking, the most fortunate. BBC producer Anthony Weymouth and his family used the hall of their ground-floor flat in a mansion block in Harley Street in central London: the hall was the most sheltered part of their home, as it had rooms on either side, and its only window, which looked into an inner courtyard, had been fitted with an asbestos shutter. Citizens without such shutters were advised to leave their windows open, to reduce the risk of injury from shattered glass. The Weymouth family spent night after night in their hall, 'lying in the dark on our mattresses for . . . hours listening to the drone of German bombers'. When he worked late at the BBC, Weymouth was obliged to sleep on one of the six hundred mattresses provided at Broadcasting House, 'for the AA barrage besprinkles the street with pieces of shrapnel'.

Patrick Shea, a Northern Irish civil servant who had been put in charge of producing a top secret 'War Book', a manual for senior staff telling them of 'the role and responsibilities assigned to each and every one of them in a great variety of preconceived situations', was living in lodgings in Belfast. The household had a clearly defined 'blitz drill'.

When the alert sounded the more active ones saw to it that the shutters were securely bolted, the bath, hand basins and sinks filled with water in case of fire, candles brought out lest the electricity supply should fail, fires extinguished. The assembly point for the whole household was the large ground-floor living room. Miss Mack, an elderly, socially superior person who normally kept herself to herself in her first floor bedsitter, would make one of her rare appearances amongst us. She would come downstairs draped in her fur coat and carrying her jewel case. Tenderly she would be manoeu-vred into a recumbent position on a mattress under the large dining-room table; for the period of the alert she would lie there, her furs wrapped around her, her jewels clasped to her bosom. The Dublin couple, from whose meal-time conversation one deduced a background of tweedy opulence, would appear carrying two large suitcases colourfully decorated with the stick-on labels of famous shipping lines and faraway hotels. Having chosen their resting-place, they would inflate their two airbeds, settle down on them and with apparent indifference to the sound and fury outside, while away the time scrutinising the pages of out-of-date copies of the Illustrated London News and the Field.

Coffee would be made. Those not lying down or on a fire-watching tour of inspection of the top floor, sat or stood around the empty fireplace. In the tense atmosphere, with so diverse a company, conversation tended to be intermittent and trivial . . . From the darkness beneath the large mahogany table an observation about the brutality of the Germans or the splendid behaviour of the British Royal Family would remind us that Miss Mack was still there.

Phyllis Warner considered that 'We are lucky in having our own shelter [in Mary Ward House in Queen's Square, Holborn, in what would be among the worst-bombed boroughs in London] so that we can have mattresses and even a table or chair or two down there, but even so, with the bare girders and rough planks of its reinforcing, it resembles the worst kind of steerage.'

Those who were supplied with Anderson shelters did not, or could not, always dig them in properly, or failed to cover them with the requisite amount of sand and earth – which was what really gave protection – or to bank up a mound of earth at the entrance to act as a 'baffle wall'. Even those Andersons that were correctly sited were less than ideal. Many filled with water when it rained, and they were cold and cramped, while the noise of bombs and falling shrapnel echoed alarmingly around their tinny walls if they were not properly insulated with soil. The problem, as with all government shelter initiatives, was due to a category error. Air raids had been expected to be sharp and above all short: no one seems to have anticipated that many would last all night. The alert would commonly sound at about 8 p.m., and the All Clear was often not heard until five or six the next morning. So shelters that might have been perfectly acceptable for the half-hour or so that daytime raids often entailed were profoundly unsuitable for an entire night – night after night. The family tensions that must have been engendered by such close and fearful proximity, exacerbated by boredom and exhaustion, are almost too dreadful to dwell on.

On 19 September 1940 *Picture Post* wrote that 'long winter nights are ahead [but] with a little ingenuity you can make them tolerable by fitting your Anderson shelter with home-made bunks'. It showed how Mr Stuart Murray of Croydon had 'turned his shelter into a family bedroom' by nailing a double layer of chicken wire across a wooden frame to provide two upper and two lower bunks, transforming the tin shelter into 'if not a bed of roses, a tolerable resting place'. Other families made several treks each evening before the alert went off, carrying eiderdowns, rugs, deckchairs, pillows and cushions from the house to the shelter. The effect of all this, of course, was to make things even more cramped.

'This going up to the shelter is not as simple as it sounds,' wrote Sidney Chave, a lab technician who lived in Upper Norwood, south London. 'It entails five or six journeys up and down carting the necessary articles, and finally our precious bundle [the Chaves' daughter Jillian, who was just over a year old at the start of the blitz]. As the journeys are made along a wet garden path, in complete darkness accompanied by sporadic bursts of gun fire and with the planes droning overhead, and as one's arms are full up with cushions, blankets and the like – it is not such a jolly affair, this Shelter life!'

Then there were the cold and the dark. A few enterprising handymen ran electric cables to their back-garden shelters so that a bar electric fire could be used, but this could be hazardous. Oil or paraffin heaters were not recommended, since they could start a fire if knocked over, as could a paraffin lamp, and torches were not the answer to the dark, since within weeks of the outbreak of war, batteries had become all but unobtainable. A candle in a flowerpot was suggested, but that carried a fire risk too, and the flickering light was hardly adequate for reading or knitting.

Herbert Brush, a seventy-one-year-old retired Electricity Board inspector, lived in Forest Hill, south London. Clearly something of a handyman, he had managed to fit up some rudimentary bunks in the family Anderson shelter, rig up an electric light for reading, and kept 'half a dozen books on various subjects on a small shelf I have put up'. But it still wasn't entirely satisfactory. 'As usual we spent 12 hours in the shelter last night,' he wrote on 31 October 1940. 'We have got used to hard lying now and go to sleep as easily there as in bed, though I must own up to stiffness in the morning, when I am able to double up on my bed for an hour or so. I can't double up much on two 11 inch boards; that with cushions makes my bed less than 2 feet in width. I can't lie with my face to the wall because if I double up at all my posterior overhangs the bed and that is not a comfortable position: the other way round my knees sometimes overhang but that is not such an uncomfortable position.'

The ever-resourceful Mr Brush continued to try to make sleeping in a tin hut in the garden as acceptable as possible. By December, when it had grown bitterly cold at night, the family lit a paraffin heater in the shelter for an hour or so before the alert was expected, took hot-water bottles in with them, hung a curtain over the entrance and 'fitted shields to keep the draughts off the bunks on either side of the dug out. It is quite a comfortable place now,' Mr Brush conceded, 'when one gets used to the cramped space and the inability to turn over without falling out, for folks of my size.'

Eighteen-year-old Margaret Turpin's family had a brick-built shelter in the garden of their East End home. 'It was so small. My brother was nearly six foot, there was my father, myself, my sister, my mother and a baby, and somehow we were all supposed to be able to sleep in this shelter. But it was impossible. It was only about seven feet long and a few feet wide. We had to sit up all night because there just wasn't room to lie down. I suppose my mother thought my father ought to be the one that lay down [because he had to go to work] and my father thought my mother ought to because she had a little baby. And my brother was tall and had to fit in somehow, and that was the reason that eventually we went to a public shelter, because there was no way we could have slept through a prolonged blitz.'

Others, less in the eye of the storm than East Enders, tried to find somewhere they considered safe in the house, rather than spend the night in an uncomfortable garden shelter. And invariably people would leave their Andersons as soon as the All Clear went, usually in the early hours of the morning, to snatch at least a couple of hours in bed before they had to get up to start the day.

No wonder that as the blitz went on, more and more people declined to use their Anderson shelters at all, even though they proved pretty effective. If correctly sited they were able to withstand the effects of a hundred-pound bomb falling six feet away, or a two-hundred-pound bomb falling twenty feet way, those inside usually suffering little more than shock. Nevertheless, by mid-October 1940, when the raids on London had eased off somewhat, more and more people opted to crouch under their staircase, which was considered to be the safest place in most houses, or drag a mattress under the dining-room table for the night, or even stay in bed and take their chances.

The Prime Minister was the first recipient of a government-issue and much more robust version of the dining-room-table shelter which went into production in January 1941. This was the Morrison shelter, a rectangular mesh steel cage six feet six inches long, four feet wide and about two feet nine inches high, bolted together with a steel 'mattress' and top, named after the then Home Secretary and Minister for Home Security, Herbert Morrison. It proved much more popular than the Anderson, though it was less effective, since it offered no protection from lateral blast. The Morrison was suitable for flats and houses without gardens, it was situated indoors (as in fact had been the original intention for Anderson shelters), it offered protection against falling masonry, could accommodate (snugly) two recumbent adults and two young children, was simple to put up and could be used as a table in the daytime. By this time the minimum income for eligibility for a free shelter had risen to £350 a year, but the distribution of Morrison shelters in London and other cities and large towns did not start until the end of March, just over a month before the 'big blitz' was effectively over.

In theory, local authorities could compel factories and commercial premises to make their shelters available to the general public outside working hours, but in practice this did not happen very often. Employers only had to plead that they did not wish to disrupt war production, which was accepted as paramount. Government departments were also urged to admit the public to their basements, but again this was often resisted on the grounds that the employees might need to sleep on the premises overnight during the blitz. Gradually throughout the winter months more basements were strengthened, but most people who had no suitable refuge at home had few options other than specially constructed public shelters. Again built in the belief that raids would be short and mostly in daytime, most offered no seating, lighting or sanitation, and no facilities even for boiling a kettle for a cup of tea.

Barbara Nixon was a thirty-two-year-old actress and graduate of

Newnham College, Cambridge. When most of the theatres closed during the blitz, she volunteered as an ARP warden in Finsbury, north London, 'which in those days stretched from near Liverpool Street due westwards to Smithfield, covered the area north of King's Cross Road and back along Pentonville and City Roads to include Moorgate and Finsbury Square'. She wrote later: 'During September 1940 the shelter conditions were appalling. In many boroughs there were only flimsy surface shelters, with no light, no seats, no lavatories and insufficient numbers even of these; or railway arches and basements that gave an impression of safety, but only had a few inches of brick overhead, or were rotten shells of buildings with thin roofs and floors.' In Finsbury

we were well provided as regards numbers; there were almost sufficient for the night population, and they were reasonably safe . . . In my [ARP] Post area we had two capacious shelters under business firms which held three or four hundred, also fifteen small sub-surface concrete ones in which fifty people could sit upright on narrow wooden benches along the wall. But they were poorly ventilated, and only two out of the nine that came in my province could pretend to be dry. Some leaked through the roof and umbrellas had to be used; in others the mouth of the sump-hole near the door had been made higher than the floor, and on a rainy night it invariably overflowed to a depth of two inches at one end decreasing to a quarter of an inch at the other, and rheumaticky old ladies had to sit upright on their benches for six to twelve hours on end, with their feet propped up on a couple of bricks. Four or five times during the night we used to go round with saucepan and bucket baling out the stinking water; as soon as Number 9 was reached, Number 1 was full again. It was hard, wet and smelly work . . . There were chemical closets usually partially screened off by a canvas curtain. But even so, the supervision of the cleaning of these was not adequate. Sometimes they would be left untended for days on end and would overflow on to the floor . . . Then there was the question of lights. I have been told by wardens that, for the first two months [of the blitz], shelters in some boroughs had no lights at all. We had one hurricane lamp for about fifty people. How often in the small hours, if the raid had started early, there would be a wail of 'Warden! Warden! The light's gone out!' and children would wake up and howl, women grow nervous and men swear. It was expecting altogether too much of people's nerves to ask them to sit through a raid in the dark. The one paraffin light also provided the only heating that there was in those days. It was bitterly cold that winter, and naturally, therefore, the door was kept shut. Some of the bigger shelters had ventilation pipes, but the smaller ones that held fifty people only had the door. In some, the atmosphere of dank concrete, of stagnant air, of the inevitable smell of bodies, the stench of the chemical closets was indescribable . . . But if conditions in many of our shelters were bad, in some other districts they were incredible. They belonged more properly to the days of a hundred years ago than to the twentieth century.

Joan Veazey, newly married to the vicar of St Mary's Church, Kennington, in south London, went with her husband Christopher to visit a number of local public shelters in September 1940. 'It is amazing what discomfort people will put up with, some on old mattresses, others in deck chairs and some lying on cold concrete floors with a couple of blankets stretched round their tired limbs. In nearly all the shelters the atmosphere is so thick that you could cut it with a knife. And many of the places – actually – stink! I think that I would prefer to risk death in the open to asphyxiation. Mothers were breast feeding their babies, and young couples were making love in full view of anyone who passed down the stairs. In one very large shelter which was made to hold about 300 persons . . . only two buckets as latrines were available . . . and the result was that the whole floor was awash . . . the smell was so awful that we tied hankies around our mouths soaked in "Cologne".'

Not only were such shelters cold, lacking in facilities, damp and malodorous, many were also dangerous. It seems almost beyond belief that a brick box standing out in the open, above ground, could be imagined to offer protection against serious attack. The best that could be said was that it was probably better to be in one of these than to be caught out in the street during an air raid, as you would at least be protected from shrapnel and flying debris. But public shelters had their own hazards. Government instructions for their construction had stipulated that the mortar to bind the bricks should be two parts lime to one part cement, but subsequent directives were more ambiguous, and local authorities bent on saving money, and cowboy builders bent on making money, started to substitute sand for cement – which anyway was in short supply due to the various demands for defence construction – in the mixture. A heavy blast near such an ill-constructed shelter could turn it into a gruesomely named 'Morrison sandwich' when the walls blew out and the heavy roof collapsed on the occupants, trapping and often killing them. In the London area it was found that at least 5,000 such potentially lethal public shelters had been built, while in Bristol 4,000 had to be demolished or radically strengthened for the same reason.

Margaret Turpin's family had started to use a public shelter, along with a number of the families living near their East End home, since the one in the garden had proved unbearably cramped. 'Of course you had to go there early, about seven in the evening, and then come home in the morning.' One night the shelterers had been listening to the wireless when it went off, which 'happened with almost every raid':

The next thing I remember was coming to and trying to move my head, which I couldn't, and as fast as you moved your head, you got a fountain of dust coming down, and it filled your nose and it filled your mouth, and I thought I'm going to die. I tried to shout, but the more I shouted and the more I moved, the more dust I brought down. I must have had lots of periods of unconsciousness, because I remember hearing people, and then a long time after, I remember seeing an ARP helmet, and it was way, way up, a long way away. And then suddenly it was quite near. I do remember the man saying to me, 'We'll soon have you out.' He said, 'All we've got to do is get your arm out.' And I looked at this arm that was sticking out of the debris, and I said, 'That's not my arm,' and he said, 'Yes it is love, it's got the same coat' . . . I don't remember coming out of the shelter. I do remember being in the ambulance, and I think for me that was probably the worst part . . . I felt somebody's blood was dripping on me from above, and I found that awful – mainly I think because I didn't know whose blood it was, whether it was someone I knew and loved or not. And I tried to move my head, but of course it was a narrow space and I couldn't get my head away from the blood. And I heard a long time afterwards that the man was already dead. But it couldn't have been my father because he was taken out of the shelter and he didn't die till two days later . . . He died, my mother died, my baby sister died, my younger sister died. I had two aunts and they died, and an uncle died . . . I knew almost immediately because when I came home from hospital – they sent you home and you were in an awful state really, and you had to find your own way home from hospital and I'd had . . . most of my clothes cut off to be X-rayed and I couldn't use the arm that had been trapped. When I got to the house, there were milk bottles outside and I just knew then that nobody had come home to take them in . . .

The seven were all buried on the same day. My brother said that they put Union Jacks on the coffins. He didn't know who did it . . . I didn't go to the funerals . . . They sent me to Harefield [near Watford] of all places. It was quite a decent place to send me to. But unfortunately the people at Harefield could see the raids on London, and they used to come out to watch, to view it like a spectacle, and I couldn't stand that.

4

Underground

. . . Those first fell raids on the East End
Saw the Victorian order bend
As scores from other districts came
To help douse fires and worked the same
With homeless folks to help them flit
To underground that 'wait-a-bit
In Government, ruled out of bounds.'
But bombs and those sights and sounds
Made common people take the law
Into their own hands. The stress of war
And most of their common sense
Ignored the old 'Sitting-on-the-fence'
They fled to the Tubes, the natural place
Of safety. Whereupon 'save-face'
Made it official. Issued passes,
Being thus instructed by the masses
Folk lived and slept in them in rows
While bombing lasted: through the throes.

From 'In Civvy Street', a long poem by P. Lambah, a medical student, about the
home front in the Second World War

When the alert sounded at about eight o'clock in the evening of Sunday,
13 October 1940, most of the residents of Coronation Avenue, an austere-
looking nineteenth-century block of flats in Stoke Newington, north London,
built by a philanthropic housing company, the Four Per Cent Industrial
Dwellings Society, dutifully trooped down the narrow stone steps to shelter
in the basement. There they were joined by a number of passers-by, since
the basement had been designated as 'Public Shelter no. 5'. The *Daily Express*

journalist Hilde Marchant would call what followed 'the greatest bombing tragedy of the whole of London'. A heavy bomb fell on the centre of the building, penetrated through five floors and detonated in the basement. The entire solid-looking structure collapsed. The floors above caved in, choking smoke and brick dust filled the air, and those who had not been killed by the weight of masonry falling on them found the exits blocked by rubble and debris. The water mains, gas mains and sewerage pipes had been ruptured by the explosion and effluent poured in, drowning and suffocating the shelterers. The rescue squads that rushed to the scene were unable to dislodge the heavy masonry that was trapping the victims.

Screens were erected to keep the gruesome sights from the view of the public, as Civil Defence workers helped by soldiers drafted in from demolition work nearby laboured to rescue any survivors and retrieve the bodies. One member of the Finsbury Rescue Service had persuaded his reluctant wife to take their children to the Coronation Avenue shelter while he was on duty that night. 'For days on end he watched the digging, although there was no hope at all. They tried to persuade him to go away but he only shook his head' as rescuers excavated to find the bodies of his entire entombed family. The rubble was so compacted that it took over a week to extract all the victims. The eventual death toll from that single incident was 154; twenty-six of the bodies could not be identified. There were a large number of Jewish people using the shelter that night: the dead of the Diaspora included a tragic number of husbands and wives or siblings who perished together – the Aurichs, Copersteins, Danzigers and Edelsteins, Hilda Muscovitch and her sister Golda Moscow. The Jewish dead were kept separate from the Gentile, most of whom were interred in a mass burial in nearby Abney Park Cemetery.

So terrible was the incident (as locations where bombs had fallen were blandly called) that an observer from the Ministry of Information arrived the next morning to check on how the borough was coping. She reported that the council was 'rising to the problem in a magnificent way and is acting with breadth of vision and initiative in coping with the endless and acute problems which are being thrown upon it', though the Town Clerk warned her that people's morale was very dependent on how soon homes could be 'patched up', satisfactory billets found or, in the case of older people, they could be evacuated away from the area – though this was proving 'heart breaking', as most of the elderly who desperately wanted to leave had nowhere to go. 'The bill that is being run up for all these extra things [such as transport, food, overnight accommodation, storing the furniture of those bombed out, demolition and repair work] is tremendous, but none of the officials feel that at the moment anything matters except helping people as much as they can, but at the same time preventing their kindness being taken advantage of,' she added in the reproving voice of bureaucracy.

Just over a month after the start of the blitz, the Stoke Newington disaster acutely pinpointed several stark realities of the situation. How well equipped, resourced and prepared were local authorities for major 'incidents' that not only left many dead and injured, but also threatened to confront them with the overwhelming challenge of housing the homeless? How would it be possible to feed the hungry, repair buildings, demolish dangerous structures, get utility and transport systems functioning and ensure that war production was disrupted as little as possible? How would the various Civil Defence organisations – the ARP, the AFS, the rescue and demolition squads, the medical services, plus essential voluntary bodies such as the WVS (Women's Voluntary Service) – cope? And how successful would those in authority – in central government as well as locally – be in tending to the social and emotional needs of the people, to their morale as well as their physical well-being?

But the primary question that preoccupied most Londoners in the early days was: where would they be safe? And the answer seemed to be: nowhere. Anderson shelters were reasonably satisfactory if there was room for one, though they were often damp, cold, cramped and generally uncomfortable, while their metal surfaces magnified the crash and whistle of bombs, and fragments ricocheting off them clattered alarmingly. Moreover, sheltering in a tin 'dog kennel' in the garden could be a terrifyingly lonely experience, and many people preferred the 'safety in numbers' illusion and the camaraderie of communal shelters, where the raid outside could be partly drowned out by talking, singing and playing music. Yet brick-built surface shelters were increasingly distrusted, and shared all the drawbacks of cold, damp Anderson shelters, while adding some of their own when it came to sanitation, general comfort and cleanliness. And, as the Coronation Avenue disaster showed, reinforced basements, the government's cost-saving preferred option, were not necessarily safe – indeed, as onlookers speculated, had the building's residents stayed in their flats rather than going down to the basement to shelter, they might well not have been crushed, and would certainly have been unlikely to be killed by water, effluent and gas seeping into their lungs – an aspect of the tragedy that particularly horrified those who witnessed its aftermath.

In London, and later in the rest of the country, people sheltered where they felt safest – even if this safety was often illusory. As the Ministry of Home Security found, the public showed 'a strong tendency to be irrational in their choice of shelters'. In Shoreditch, residents hurried to the reinforced-concrete hall attached to St Augustine's church, even though it had been refused designation as an official shelter since no part of it was under-ground. The vicar of Haggerston, whose church it was and who had had the hall built himself, felt that since there was not exactly a 'super-abundance' of shelters in Shoreditch, he could not refuse entry to those who wished to shelter there. He displayed a large notice warning, 'THIS IS NOT AN AIR-RAID SHELTER. They who use it as such do so at their own risk,' but still his parishioners and more flocked in.

Molly Fenlon lived in a block of flats near Tower Bridge in Bermondsey. On the first night of the blitz her father, who was a policeman, was on duty in the docks. Her mother, driven frantic by the falling bombs, decided to seek shelter. 'A small party of us from the flats piled our bedding into an old pram and trailed off to 61 Arch, which is a series of arches under London Bridge railway station. It used, in years gone by, to be an ice well, and it felt as though all the ice had been left there, it was so cold. The walls were very damp too, but we were glad enough to go anywhere. Many homeless people, white and shaken, came in from Rotherhithe and the local district.'

The next night Molly's father was off-duty, so the whole family

accordingly, about seven p.m., put its bedding on a pram and marched off. 61 Arch was full, and as it was cold, and damp as well, we decided to go along to the next Arch which is a through road converted into a shelter. That was full too. All the pavement down both sides was taken, so our little party slept in the gutter that night, except me. As there wasn't even room for me in the gutter, I wriggled into the pram. It was a tight fit but I slept . . . Suddenly I woke up to find that a bit of the pram must have grown up and was sticking in my back. Looking at my watch I discovered that it was two a.m. All our party was asleep except Miss N . . ., she was reading a thriller! I found that I ached all over, so struggled out of the pram and spent the rest of the night walking up and down the Arch, smoking and thinking about my fiancé (as he was then) who was . . . in the R.A.F. I remember wondering, a trifle morbidly, if I should live to get married.

We were an assorted lot there: as I walked up and down, I studied the . . . people as they slept. There was a tiny baby, a fortnight old, like a little rosebud in its pram, and an elderly man, bald headed, snoring fit to wake the Seven Sleepers, spread eagled on the ground with no blanket between him and the asphalt . . . Next morning I discovered that I had collected six flea bites on my person, and Miss N . . . was horrified to see a bug crawl across the collar of her raincoat as she was packing up.

After that I struck: told mother that she could please herself but that I would rather be done to death by a German bomb, than bitten to death in an Air Raid shelter. She agreed about that.

From then on the Fenlons slept at home throughout the raids – though they had to move flats when theirs was badly damaged by a twenty-eight-pound AA shell that crashed through the roof. When Molly married her airman fiancé on 17 November, it was in the vestry in the churchyard of St Olave and St John's, since the church had been burnt out in a raid in October.

On 14 October 1940, one of the large trench shelters in Kennington Park received a direct hit. 'They are still digging,' wrote Joan Veazey, wife of the vicar of the nearby St Mary's church, in her diary, 'and there are all sorts of rumours going around as to how many are trapped inside. We know that one of our church families always shelter there . . . So far we can get no news. There is nothing we can do but wait and pray for all those who are listening for the scratch of the rescue shovels.'

The next day the Veazeys 'heard that they have found the Potters who were in the park shelter. If what we are told is true, this family were sitting with their backs to the wall of the shelter, reading and knitting, when there was a sudden blue flash and the earth and concrete started to cave in . . . the blast turned the little daughter upside down and her legs were caught in the concrete of the roof . . . her mother took her whole weight on her shoulders until she was rescued . . . but as they took her out she died of shock and her injuries. Christopher [the vicar] will go to see the others who are badly burned in hospital . . . We do not know how many were killed . . . but the wardens say about 179 persons died in the shelter.'

At Ramsgate on the Kent coast, caves provided natural shelters which the local council had started to improve access to as Hitler marched into Czechoslovakia in the spring of 1939, and which were completed by the outbreak of war. According to *Picture Post*, the three miles of tunnels that lay between fifty and ninety feet underground made Ramsgate and Barcelona 'the only towns in the world that have deep shelters'. There was natural ventilation, and electricity had been run from the town's supply – and there was an emergency generating system if that should fail. Signposts were erected so shelterers would not get lost in the labyrinthine corridors. There was space for 60,000 people (twice the population of Ramsgate), none of whom would be more than five minutes away from one of the complex's twenty-two entrances, and seating for 30,000. Dover strengthened the entrances to its caves too, and bored connecting tunnels and installed bunks, though 'as there was no current of air, you can imagine what it was like when slept in night after night by those with no homes, and little facility for washing. Rather like a rabbit hutch.' Or, as the Inspector General of Civil Defence, E.J. Hodsoll, described the scene in February 1941, 'the equivalent of a gypsy squatters' camp'.

An estimated 15,000 Londoners nightly colonised Chislehurst caves in Kent, which had been used as an ammunition dump in the First World War, with special trains being laid on to convey shelterers there each evening and return them to London in the morning. At first the caves were prim-itive, with bare earth floors and flickering candles or torches the only light, a single water tap and an oildrum filled with creosote for sanitation. But soon electric lighting was organised by two private individuals – one of whom had been renting the caves for the cultivation of mushrooms; donkeys carried away the ash bins that were used as lavatories; the local council provided bunks; and a Red Cross medical centre was opened, complete with emergency operating theatre and canteen. So safe were the Chislehurst caves considered that the children's ward of a local hospital was moved there. At first shelterers were charged a halfpenny a night, but as the facil-ities grew more sophisticated – dances and singsongs were held, and a cinema screen erected; church services were held, with an improvised altar positioned under a 'natural dome', and the congregation joining in the appropriate hymn 'Rock of Ages' – this rose to sixpence, and a team of 'captains' was appointed to oversee things and keep order. By November the local council had taken over responsibility for the caves, but used a light touch for fear of stifling the 'self-help' initiative that had got them organised in the first place.

Existing tunnels below the streets of Luton in Bedfordshire were strength-ened, as was the Ouseburn Culvert in Newcastle upon Tyne, while the Victoria Tunnel in the same city was also used as a shelter. In Runcorn, on Merseyside, where leakage from chlorine gas holders was considered a particular potential hazard in a raid, a network of underground tunnels was constructed. During raids on Plymouth, people trekked across the fields to take shelter inside a tunnel hewn in a quarry. It was cold and dark and water ran down the walls, but it was a haven, and every Sunday the local vicar conducted a service there. In Bristol, an old railway tunnel that had been used to take goods from the port into the city was taken over by 'men, women and children huddled together sleeping on mattresses, planks or straw. Some had corrugated iron sheets or pieces of sacking and canvas placed overhead to catch the water that dripped from the rocky roof of the tunnel. The air was thick with the fumes of oil stoves, oil lamps and various odours of cooking food . . . When the Corporation employees opened the doors in the morning, the stench and fumes came from within like a fog. It was a picture of Dante's Inferno. Many of the people were nervous wrecks. People stayed in the tunnel by day, afraid to lose their places. There was hardly any room between the rough beds. Some performed their natural functions alongside their beds. It was unbelievable that people could be driven by fear to endure such conditions.'

Conditions were as bad, if not worse, in London's most notorious shelter: the Tilbury in Stepney. For the *Daily Herald* journalist Ritchie Calder, it was 'not only the most unhygienic place I have ever seen, it was . . . definitely unsafe . . . yet numbers as high, on some estimates, as 14,000 to 16,000 people crowded into it on those dreadful nights when hell was let loose on East London . . . People of every type and condition, every colour and creed found their way there . . . men from the Levant and Slavs from Eastern Europe; Jew, Gentile, Moslem and Hindu. When ships docked, seamen would come to royster [sic] for a few hours. Scotland Yard knew where to look for criminals bombed out of Hell's Kitchen. Prostitutes paraded there. Hawkers peddled greasy, cold fried fish which cloyed the already foul atmosphere. Free fights had to be broken up by the police. Couples courted. Children slept. Soldiers, sailors and airmen spent part of their leave there.'

'It was an enormous place,' remembered Robert Baltrop. 'I've seen figures like 6,000 sheltering in it every night. It wasn't even properly underground, [much of it] was simply a surface building, and it was almost like a village; people sold things, ladies of the street carried on their business there . . . a whole nightlife went on in the Tilbury, all through the blitz.'

The Tilbury, situated off the Commercial Road, was part of Liverpool Street station goods yard, and was owned by two different bodies. On one side lay vaults and stores; on the other was an underground loading yard, partly below ground, and above it a massive warehouse supported on steel girders. The vaults had been taken over by Stepney Council as a shelter for 3,000 people, but the Home Secretary refused permission for it to requisition the warehouse and the loading bays – by far the larger part. However, the site had been an official shelter in the First World War, and 'It was known to older people as "the place to go".' And that is what happened. When the desperate hour came, they crowded there from all parts of east London, often coming from miles away. The limited capacity of the official section was quickly filled, and thousands overflowed into the rest of the site. There was nothing the owners could do to prevent the torrent of humanity which took possession. The borough council disclaimed responsibility for those who took shelter in the 'unauthorised' areas, on the grounds that it had been refused powers and would be trespassing on private property. Even the police could not at first gain access, except when called in by the harassed policemen of the company concerned.

As long as Calder lived, he wrote, he would

never forget the stampede when the gates were flung open and the swarming multitude careered down the slope, tripping, tumbling, being trodden on, being crushed and fighting and scrambling for the choice of sleeping berths – in the valleys between the gigantic bales of newsprint. Expectant mothers and even children were crushed.

Sanitation barely existed. The only provision was for a handful of workmen usually employed there. The result was that the roadways were ankle deep in filth, which was trodden into blankets on which people were to sleep. Great stacks of London's margarine were stored there. Hundreds of cartons were hopelessly fouled every night. It was over a fortnight before the margarine began to be moved out, by the intervention of the Ministry of Food. People slept among the filth. They slept in the dust between the rails and on the cobblestones of the roadway. They slept on the wooden bays amongst the food. It was appalling.

Hilde Marchant, who visited the Tilbury for the *Daily Express*, was equally appalled: by the sour smell of rancid margarine that pervaded the vaults, by the strong odour of horse in the loading bays, by the 'confused mass of bodies strewn everywhere', but above all when she came to 'the canvas partitions at the end. These were the latrines, twelve chemical lavatories helped by a few buckets for the children. I went into the six latrines reserved for women. They were overflowing, and a woman worker was standing over the door, saying they could not be used any more that night.'

Euan Wallace, Regional Commissioner for the London Civil Defence Region, thought it was 'no use spending a lot of money on things like water closets', as the government lacked the power to requisition the part of the Tilbury owned by the railway company, and in any case, 'It does seem . . . very doubtful whether it is worth putting new wine into such a very old bottle. It can never be anything but a very indifferent shelter and it presents peculiarly difficult health and sanitation problems.' However, by mid-October 'The Prime Minister has been hunting Morrison very hard on the Tilbury shelter question,' reported Wallace, and though 'the City was being unreasonably sticky on providing basements in commercial buildings', accommodation was eventually found so that 4,000 shelterers could be moved from the railway-owned part of the shelter, and conditions improved for those who stayed.

Until then, though, it was largely due to individual unofficial initiatives that things got better. There had not been even a first aid post in the unofficial half of the Tilbury, but a local Jewish doctor volunteered his services and spent his evenings attending to the shelterers' needs, then 'slept the night at his self-appointed post. There were women there – genuine motherly souls with a passion for well-doing – who spent the whole twenty-four hours, for weeks on end, ministering to this vast unruly family. They were self-appointed shelter marshals, without authority and without resources. It was they who brought urns of fresh water into the unofficial shelter, rationing the water as sparingly as though they were the keepers of an oasis in the desert . . . Any minister or official or influential visitor who ventured into that shelter would be button-holed. With evangelical fervour, they would be told of the miseries these people had to endure, of what grand people they were if only they had a chance, and a whole catalogue of all the things that needed to be done.'

It was not only officials who beat a path to the Tilbury shelter: it soon became a tourist attraction for people from 'up West' to gawp at the hellish conditions their fellow Londoners were suffering a few miles away. Rachel Reckitt was in charge of the emergency Citizens Advice Bureau set up at Toynbee Hall in Whitechapel – a 'university settlement' where middle-class workers lived among the poor, hoping to share knowledge and culture, and alleviate the poverty of their neighbours – to offer advice and practical help to East Enders suffering during the blitz. In October 1940 she had a 'night

out with [the distinguished American lawyer] Mrs Goodhart [who] wanted
to see the Tilbury shelter, so, as it was no good early in the evening [when
no shelterers would have arrived] I offered to take her later. She said should
we go and get some dinner at the Savoy, or have it at Toynbee? I believe
she would have liked Toynbee, but saw I wouldn't, so we had a drive round
Wapping and Shadwell and the Isle of Dogs . . . it looked lovely in the fading
light, especially the river. Wapping church and the school have gone . . . all
but the Church tower . . . Then we had a good dinner at the Savoy, with
Leslie Howard [who played Ashley Wilkes in the film *Gone with the Wind*,
which had opened in London a few months previously, and who would be
killed when the plane in which he was a passenger was shot down in June
1943] and Anthony Asquith [the film director 'Puffin' Asquith, son of the
former Liberal Prime Minister] at the next table . . . Afterwards we went
back to Stepney to the Tilbury shelter. Entry there is by pass only as they,
naturally, dislike sightseers (especially those who come East after a good
dinner to see how the poor live!). However, as I know the wardens, I was
able to get Mrs Goodhart in. I especially wanted her to see it in case she
goes to America; as she will be asked to lecture there [and] it would be very
bad if she had to admit she'd never seen a shelter.'

The next month, Rachel Reckitt was taken on

a personally conducted tour of the famous Tilbury shelter, a great honour I
gathered, as Lady Astor [MP for Plymouth Sutton] had been down a few nights
ago and [the District Warden] refused to take her round. He said he was tired
of West-Enders getting an evening's entertainment sightseeing in East End
shelters. I should hardly call it 'amusement' but I could sympathise with him
as he is very busy. Anyway the people resent being exhibited to sightseers.

. . . They have reduced the numbers in Tilbury shelter from 12,000 to about
6,000 and made some improvements, though it is still very bad and many
people sleep on the stones. It is a strange place, vast and very confusing as
there are many parts to it. Most of it is under railway arches and there are
trucks and sidings in it too. People have been known to park their baby's
pram in a truck, and found it gone to Birmingham or somewhere in the
morning!

The District Warden is full of ideas and hopes the war will last long enough
to get hot water laid on and proper feeding. It will have to last a long time
at the present rate!

Ritchie Calder had greatly exaggerated the number of people taking refuge in the Tilbury shelter, as he had inflated the number killed in the bombing of South Hallsville School. He did so because, as a campaigning journalist, he had an urgent agenda. In his view the government was culpably negligent of the safety of its citizens – particularly its poorest citizens, who had not the resources to make their own arrangements. What Londoners (and indeed all those living in vulnerable areas) required were deep shelters. And these the government had consistently refused to provide.

The scientist Professor J.B.S. Haldane had paid three visits to Spain during the Civil War, which had made him something of an authority on defence against air raids – particularly since most British scientists were still using data from the First World War to frame their expectations of Second World War bombing. Haldane had spent weeks in Madrid and Barcelona (where there was 'an extensive system of underground refuges . . . capable of accommodating altogether about 350,000 people', according to the city's mayor) gathering information and making statistical calculations, and what he discovered made him a passionate advocate of deep shelters. While he was not himself a member of the Communist Party – though he was a Marxist, and was the science correspondent for the CP newspaper, the *Daily Worker* – this was a campaign supported, indeed often led, by members of the Communist Party of Great Britain (CPGB), who argued that it would be the working classes living in poorly-built accommodation, clustered around inevitable targets such as docks and factories, who would take the brunt of German aerial attacks. What some might call governmental incompetence in failing to make proper provision, the CPGB regarded as a conspiracy against the workers in a class war that made them in effect the 'poor bloody infantry' of the home front.

Haldane argued that gas was no longer the main danger – he was an expert on poison gas and had designed a gas mask during the First World War – but that the real threat came from high-explosive bombs. He believed that the government policy of dispersing the population into reinforced basements, surface and Anderson shelters, rather than constructing networks of mass underground shelters, was misguided, irresponsible and penny-pinching. In October 1938 he published a paper in the scientific journal *Nature* in which he demonstrated mathematically that there were no grounds for assuming that bombs dropped at random would cause fewer casualties if people were dispersed than if they were concentrated. Later that year his book, called simply *ARP*, was published by Victor Gollancz, founder of the

Left Book Club. It advocated a two-year programme of excavating sixty feet under London to build 780 miles of seven-foot tunnels that could hold the 4.4 million population of the LCC area. These should be built of brick rather than concrete, since in Haldane's view 'The concrete industry is now in the grip of monopoly capitalism, and for this reason prices are likely to be higher relative to brick than would otherwise be the case.' Following the book's publication Haldane stumped the country speaking, usually on CP platforms, and writing articles for the *Daily Worker* demanding better protection for the British public against the blitz. He argued that some of Britain's unemployed – of whom there were still 1,800,000 in the summer of 1939 – could be given work constructing the deep shelters he believed were required, a scheme he costed at an estimated £12 for each person who would be able to take refuge in them.

The *Architect and Building News* had voiced its readers' concerns in October 1938, just after the Munich crisis, about 'sandbagged basements . . . half finished trenches in the parks and squares . . . uncomfortable reminders of the ludicrous inadequacy of the eleventh-hour scramble of three weeks ago', and demanded, 'What is being done?' That same month Finsbury Borough Council, in charge of one of the poorest boroughs in London, provided an ambitious answer. On 4 October Alderman Riley, Chairman of the Finsbury ARP Committee, recommended that the modernist émigré architect Berthold Lubetkin and his firm Tecton, which had designed Finsbury's vanguard Health Centre, opened earlier that year, should be asked to come up with a solution to protecting 'the whole of the population [of Finsbury] in the event of war'. Lubetkin and the civil engineer Ove Arup (who had proved so valuable in solving the construction problems of the Penguin Pool at London Zoo, designed by Tecton in 1934) worked out a 'danger volume' to measure scientifically the comparative protection afforded by different types of shelter, and came up with a plan for fifteen shelters (each housing between 7,600 and 12,700 people) deep underground, approached by spiral staircases that would permit everyone to be safely ensconced within the seven minutes it was reckoned would elapse between the alert sounding and the first bombs falling.

Although Arup greatly exaggerated the night-time population of the borough who would require shelter, it was an elegant solution to stowing the 58,000-odd residents of Finsbury plus essential services deep underground at the cost of ten guineas a head – a sort of Maginot Line of the air war. Finsbury Council organised an exhibition in the Town Hall to show

how it would work, complete with chilling illustrations by Gordon Cullen (whose murals adorned the Health Centre) showing the frailty of other forms of protection, and on 15 February 1939 Lubetkin appeared on the infant medium of television to demonstrate the plan's virtues. But the Home Secretary Sir John Anderson, to whom the plans had to be submitted, prevaricated, waiting for the recommendations of a group of experts including engineers and trade unionists; their White Paper, 'Air Raid Shelters', was finally published in April 1939. Winston Churchill, to whom Tecton had also sent a copy, was not 'favourably impressed . . . it appears to be inspired by the wish to exaggerate the danger of air attack and to emphasise the futility of basement protection in the interest of some particular scheme in which you are associated. The wide circulation of such a book would not be helpful at the present juncture.'

On 18 April 1939 Tecton/Finsbury's scheme was rejected on the grounds of impracticality – experience of building the London Underground indicated that it would take at least two years to build – of cost, shortage of materials, accessibility – it was reckoned that people would need to be within 150 yards of a shelter to get to it through congested streets in sufficient time – and of the fact that the plans were fundamentally opposed to the principle of dispersal. However, in the autumn of 1940 the government changed its mind, ostensibly for technical reasons, since German bombs were getting heavier. Herbert Morrison announced in an upbeat broadcast, 'We Have Won the First Round', that a limited number of deep shelters would be provided in the London region by tunnelling under the tube system at selected stations. But, he insisted, 'It is quite certain that deep shelters cannot play more than a limited part in our plans . . . anything like a universal policy of deep shelters for the whole people or the greater part of it, is beyond the bounds of practical possibility.' Morrison, who had been implacably anti-Communist as leader of the LCC, then launched an astonishing attack on Haldane (without naming him) and other deep-shelter campaigners for being 'political schemers' engaging in 'defeatist agitation'. He accused them of seeking 'to destroy our will to take risks in freedom's cause', and of 'playing Hitler's game': 'These people are not numerous, but they are mischievous; Hitler is no doubt delighted with their manoeuvres. He knows that if our people could be stampeded into putting a narrow personal safety before success, he would win.'

Plans for eight huge shelters, each holding 8,000 people and most constructed beneath existing tube stations, were approved in October 1940.

But the first of three purpose-built deep shelters available to the public (others were used for telecommunications and similar facilities), in Stockwell in south London, was not opened until 10 July 1944 – more than three years after the end of the blitz. One hundred and thirty feet underground, it could accommodate 4,000 people and was equipped with canteens, lavatories and washing facilities, and even arrangements for laundry. By that time Haldane, who had usually taken shelter in a deep trench on Primrose Hill, near where he lived with his journalist wife Charlotte, and after that had been hit, in a shelter below London Zoo at the invitation of his friend Julian Huxley, the Secretary of the Zoological Society, had removed with his laboratory to Harpenden in Hertfordshire.

Even though the government had been resistant to sanction deep shelters, it was a visceral human instinct to seek refuge underground when attacked from above, and that is what many of Britain's urban population sought to do. As well as basements – Anthony Heap and his mother spent the blitz moving from basement to basement near where they lived in Bloomsbury, ending up most nights in the cavernous cellars of the Quaker Friends' Meeting House in the Euston Road – the crypts of churches were popular. At St Peter's church in Walworth in south London, the Reverend J.G. Markham found that his crypt, which had been designated as a public shelter for 230 people, usually housed at least double that number, with shelterers

lying like sardines on a variety of beds, mattresses, blankets or old carpets which they brought down with them. Some sat on deckchairs, some lay on the narrow wooden benches provided by the borough. The stench from the overflowing Elsan closets and unwashed humanity was so great that we had to buy gallons of Pine Fluid . . . the shelter wardens had a whip round among their flock to buy electric fans which did stir the foetid air a trifle, giving an illusion of freshness . . . You can get used to those sort of conditions if you stay in them 12 hours a night, night after night. At least one family stayed there almost 24 hours rather than go home and risk losing their place. Places were as precious, to the regulars, as seats in some theatres, so that queues formed outside hours before the sirens wailed, and I had to provide wardens to regulate the flow of would-be shelterers, some of whom came from some distance, even by taxi.

Lambeth Palace's crypt could accommodate 250 people, and being so close to the Thames and across the road from the thrice-hit St Thomas's Hospital, it was popular with the local community. But not with the Archbishop himself, his chaplain the Reverend Alan Don reported. During the September raids 'sleep was, for most people, out of the question – and even CC [Cosmo Cantuar] descended into the basement for a while. He avoids the crypt – the people there frighten him more than the bombs!'

The Canadian photographer Bill Brandt, who had settled in Britain in 1932 and had established a reputation as a sensitive photo-journalist of English life and mores, was commissioned by the Ministry of Information to photograph London's underground shelters. He spent the week of 4–12 November 1940 capturing the 'drama and strangeness of shelter life' until he caught influenza and had to abandon the project. The most compelling – and also the strangest – of the photographs he took are of people sheltering in the crypt of Christ Church, Spitalfields. Some show people sleeping in stone sarcophagi, while a bewildered-looking Sikh couple and their child huddle in a damp alcove. Ritchie Calder visited the same crypt, taken by the Shelter Marshal 'Mickey the Midget', in civilian life an optician, and he too was struck by the sarcophagi: 'massive stone vaults. In them the bodies of the centuries-old dead had mouldered away. Now their heavy stone lids had been levered off. The bones and dust had been scooped out. The last resting-place of the dead had been claimed by the living.' Others, unable to lever off the lids, lay stretched out on top of the tombs, while more lay in the aisles. There were 'rows of old men and old women sitting bolt upright in paralytic discomfort on narrow benches. Some had "foot muffs" made out of swathes of old newspapers or were hugging hot-water bottles, their heads lolling in sleep. The vaults were bitterly cold. A draught full of menace blew through them – menace because it came from half-submerged windows, not blocked up, just blacked out.'

In the inner vaults, 'stretched on the rough floor was a tall figure of an ex-Bengal Lancer, his magnificent shovel beard draped over a blanket, his head turbaned and looking, in sleep, like a breathing monument to an ancient Crusader . . . Life in this crypt, as in dozens of other crypts . . . in the early days of the "blitz" was worse than primitive. It made the conditions described by Dickens seem like a comedy of manners by Thackeray. The Fleet Prison and the Marshalsea were polite hostelries compared with conditions which existed when the "blitzkrieg" first hit London and drove most [sic] people underground.'

Not all underground people suffered the same discomforts and indignities. Brandt's photographs show a couple coyly snuggling under an eiderdown in the basement of a department store – most West End stores had cleared out their basements to accommodate sleepers. The Savoy Hotel had a commodious basement, though this was often closed when water threatened to flood in if bombs fell on the Thames, which flowed past. On 14 September 1940 a Communist councillor (and later MP) for Stepney and ARP warden, Phil Piratin, who had been active in converting pre-war East End tenants' associations into Shelter Committees to keep up the battle for deep shelters, and to press for better facilities in public surface and tube shelters, led a party of seventy of the borough's residents to the Savoy to demand access to its shelter. 'We decided what was good enough for the Savoy Hotel parasites was reasonably good enough for Stepney workers and their families. We had an idea that the hotel management would not see eye to eye with this, so we organised an "invasion" without their consent. In fact there was no effort to stop us, but it was only a matter of seconds before we were downstairs, and the women and children came streaming in afterwards. While the management and their lackeys were filled with consternation, the visitors from the East End looked round in amazement. "Shelters?" they said. "Why, we'd love to *live* in such places." '

The recently built Dorchester was considered all but bomb-proof with its reinforced concrete structure, but it turned its basement first into Turkish baths and then its basement gymnasium into an air-raid shelter, a 'funk hole' in which the beauteous Lady Diana, wife of Duff Cooper, who had resigned as First Lord of the Admiralty at the time of the Munich crisis, felt 'quite secure' as she lay 'hugger mugger with all that was most distinguished in London society'. 'No one snores. If Papa makes a sound I'm up in a flash to rearrange his position. Perhaps Lady Halifax is doing the same to his Lordship [the Foreign Secretary] . . . They each have a flashlight to find their slippers with, and I see their monstrous forms projected caricaturishly on the ceiling, magic lantern style. Lord Halifax is unmistakable. We never actually meet,' she wrote to her son, John Julius Norwich, evacuated to safety in Canada.

Should a person wish to dance and dine at the Hungaria restaurant in Lower Regent Street, they could book a shelter place in the cellar for the night as well as a table. If the raid lasted all night, breakfast would be served in the morning.

However, the most obvious place in London to shelter underground was the one the government refused to sanction. Although tube stations had been used as shelters during air raids in the First World War, this was forbidden at the start of the Second. The reasons were several: the first was the necessity of keeping people and goods moving during the blitz, of ferrying the injured or homeless away and of bringing essential supplies to the stricken areas. Another was the restricted access to many tube stations: the deep, narrow stairways and escalators would be hazardous if a panicking mass of people converged on them (a fear that was to be realised not during the blitz but in the Bethnal Green tube disaster in March 1943, when 173 people were killed in such a crush). Fear of flooding if the Thames was bombed was another real concern: before the war twenty-five heavy, electrically operated gates were installed at stations on either side of the river at Waterloo, Charing Cross and London Bridge which could be closed within a minute of the order being received from the control room at Leicester Square. And a fourth concern was the fear of a 'shelter mentality' when thousands of people would crowd underground and, feeling safe in their troglodyte existence, would refuse to re-emerge, with disastrous consequences for war production.*

However, on the first night of the blitz East Enders defied official policy and appropriated their own deep shelters by buying a penny-halfpenny ticket for a short journey on the tube, and refusing to come up again, camping in their thousands on the cold stone platforms with no sanitation or refreshment until morning. It was a *fait accompli* which, predictably, the *Daily Worker* celebrated as a people's victory when on 13 September 1940 2,000 people swarmed down the stairs at Holborn station as they had done on previous nights, and 'The LPTB [London Passenger Transport Board] officers seem to have given up on any attempt to keep them out.' Some stayed in stations near to where they lived, others travelled 'up West' until they found less crowded platforms. All felt safer down the tubes, particularly since the sounds of air raids raging overhead were all but blotted out, but in the early days all were uncomfortable, often cold and frequently hungry.

Since so many children were evacuated at this time, some London schools were closed, including ten-year-old Irene Moseley's in the East End. 'So during the day I was sent off with my suitcase to get in the queue for a place on the platform [at Old Street station]. We had to disguise ourselves as travellers, not shelterers, so any bedding that we took down had to be in

---

* In fact the much-feared 'trogs' would be found in the Ramsgate caves; with the approval of Herbert Morrison they were forcibly ejected.

suitcases . . . I used to make a place on the platform for the rest of the family so that when they'd finished work they'd come down and a place was already secured. Otherwise, there would be arguments and quarrels with people who used to push your suitcase or your bedding out of the way, because it was every man for himself down there.'

Whole families arrived bringing blankets, rugs and pillows, bread and cheese or sandwiches and a bottle of tea – or beer – and milk for babies to drink, sweets, and sometimes, hazardously, a small spirit stove to brew up on, though official advice was to keep drinks warm by wrapping the container in layers of newspaper, or constructing a 'hay box'. Some brought playing cards to pass the time, a 'book' (magazine), even a wireless or a wind-up gramophone, and invariably a small box or bag containing their savings, insurance policies, saving cards, ration books and identity cards – their paper wartime lives. Deep underground they were packed like sardines, with no air circulating, nowhere to get food or drink, or wash, and with the only lavatories – if there were any – in the booking hall. Fierce territorial disputes raged over places to sleep, and when every inch of platform space was occupied, latecomers arranged themselves in the corridors and on the escalators, or even in the booking hall, which offered little protection, particularly as many had glass roofs, or large skylights that would have sent shards of glass crashing onto the recumbent forms below in the event of a nearby attack.

A local reporter went to see conditions at Elephant and Castle tube station at the end of September 1940, and what he described sounds as grim as the notorious Tilbury shelter:

> From the platforms to the entrance the whole station was one incumbent mass of humanity . . . it took me a quarter of an hour to get from the station entrance to the platform. Even in the darkened booking hall I stumbled across huddled bodies, bodies which were no safer from bombs than if they had lain in the gutters of the silent streets outside. Going down the stairs I saw mothers feeding infants at the breast. Little girls and boys lay across their parents' bodies because there was no room on the winding stairs. Hundreds of men and women were partially undressed, while small boys and girls slumbered in the foetid atmosphere absolutely naked. Electric lights blazed, but most of this mass of sleeping humanity slept as though they were between silken sheets. On the platform when a train came in, it had to be stopped in the tunnel while police and porters went along pushing in the feet and arms

which overhung the line. The sleepers hardly stirred as the train rumbled slowly in. On the train I sat opposite a pilot on leave. 'It's the same all the way along,' was all he said.

The Reverend Christopher Veazey and his wife Joan visited the same Elephant and Castle tube station, where some of their parishioners were settling down for the night. 'I had not realised just how many people were sheltering there,' wrote Joan Veazey after their visit on 17 September 1940. 'They were lying closely packed like sardines all along the draughty corridors and on the old platforms, so that people who wanted to get on the trains had to step over mattresses and sleeping bodies. There was a picnic feeling about the whole set-up, families were eating chips and some had some fish . . . others were singing loudly. Tiny babies were tucked up in battered suitcases, and small children were toddling around making friends with everyone. We tried to chat with some of the folk, but there were too many to be able to help very much. The noise was terrific . . . both of trains running to a standstill and of people shouting above the noise.'

Families would usually stay in the tube until the All Clear went (not that they could hear it), and they were usually cleared out by station staff at around six in the morning, to allow cleaners in to prepare for the day's activity. 'It was frightening . . . because you never knew what to expect, whether you had a home or not to go to. Sometimes the fires were still raging, the fire engines were there, you were picking your way across rubble and lots of water in the streets from the hoses, and all the time you were wondering "have I still got a home?",' remembers Irene Moseley. 'When you did get home, there was probably no gas or water. So I was almost reluctant to leave the Tube, it was a home to me . . . there were a lot of other children down there and we'd play hide and seek along the platform and up the escalators. It was a haven, you felt safe down there.'

Barbara Betts (later Castle, the Labour Cabinet Minister), who was trying to scratch a living as a journalist – writing mainly for *Picture Post*, which rarely paid, and trade papers such as the *Tobacconist*, which paid, but not much – and was also an ARP warden in St Pancras, joined one of these 'troglodyte communities one night to see what it was like. It was not a way of life I wanted for myself but I could see what an important safety valve it was. Without it, London life could not have carried on the way that it did.'

Since the blitz, the picture of a mass of humanity sleeping in the tube, as portrayed by Henry Moore in his chalk drawings of underground shelters, has become one of its most iconic images, along with the dome of St Paul's Cathedral wreathed in smoke during the raid on the City on 29 December 1940. Some accounts seem to suggest that the entire East End was nightly crammed into the underground. In reality a 'shelter census' of London's central area at the height of the blitz showed that there were 177,000 people sheltering there – that is, around 4 per cent of London's population, which compares with 9 per cent in public shelters and 27 per cent in Anderson shelters. One hundred and seventy-seven thousand is still a large number of people, but despite this large-scale colonisation, the government retained an equivocal attitude towards the tube being used for shelter.

In mid-September 1940 the Home Secretary, Sir John Anderson, accompanied by the Minister for Aircraft Production and newspaper magnate Lord Beaverbrook, and Lord Ashfield, chairman of the LPTB (who had previously expressed a preference for closing down the entire underground system) had visited Holborn tube station. They had talked to shelterers, many of whom from the East End were literally living down there, having been bombed out of their homes in the first raids. It was by now obvious that it was simply not possible to enforce a ban on the tube being used as shelters unless the authorities were prepared to risk a collapse of home-front morale and very ugly confrontations, with the police reinforced by the military barring station entrances and keeping angry and fearful people in the streets during a raid. The government grudgingly changed its policy, though it insisted that the underground was primarily for transport, and that shelterers must not interfere with that. But gradually some order and regulation – and some facilities – were introduced.

At the beginning of October 1940 Herbert Morrison replaced Sir John Anderson as Home Secretary and Minister of Home Security. The Home Secretary, the senior Secretary of State, was essentially responsible for law and order, whereas Home Security, a ministry canvassed at the time of Munich as a wartime essential and attached to the Home Office when war broke out, was in charge of all civil defence against air attack. This included responsibility for air-raid wardens, the firefighting services, first aid, decontamination and rescue squads, as well as facilities such as civil defence equipment and shelters, and arrangements concerned with blackout and air-raid warnings. Moreover, the Minister had to coordinate all those ministries that would be affected by air raids and their aftermath: Transport, Food and

Health, among others. And soon Morrison would also be Chairman of what a Labour Party pamphlet described as 'the Blitz Team', the official title of which was the Civil Defence Committee of the War Cabinet, taking on an absolutely pivotal role in the prosecution of the war on the home front and the well-being of the people in acutely testing and hazardous times.

He was well placed to do so. The son of a Lambeth policeman, Morrison had left school at fourteen, and had been active first in the ILP (Independent Labour Party) and then the Labour Party. He had been a conscientious objector in the First World War, and in 1920 became Mayor of Hackney in east London, at thirty-two the youngest in London. Two years later he was elected to the London County Council (LCC), and in 1923 as Labour MP for South Hackney. Appointed Minister for Transport in the second Labour government from 1929 to 1931, he also led the LCC from 1934 until 1940, though he effectively abandoned this role when he was appointed Minister of Supply in May 1940. Morrison had a deep commitment to and knowledge of his native city – and undoubtedly more of a common touch than the rather grand and austere Anderson – and his time as an MP in Hackney had coincided with the borough's notably energetic ARP activities. Before the war he had been a member of the ARP (Policy) Committee, and he would have seen the papers relating to the problems of future air raids.

Ritchie Calder was ecstatic at the appointment. In an open letter published in the *Daily Herald* he wrote:

> Dear Herbert Morrison, When I heard you had been appointed Home Secretary I went home and slept soundly . . . I have seen men and women, these tough London workers of whom you and I are proud, whose homes have gone but whose courage is unbroken by the Nazi bombers, goaded by neglect and seething with resentment and furious reproach. THEY LOOK TO YOU . . . Much of the breakdown which has occurred in the last month could have been foreseen and avoided; or having arisen could have been mastered by anyone who understood the human problem of the Londoners and the complications of local government . . . you have a task as great as your abilities. Go to it Herbert . . .

Improving the shelters was only part of Morrison's task: there were many other pressing administrative problems that needed urgent attention, but he made shelters a priority, though some changes were already in hand, with local authorities empowered to provide bunks, sanitation, drinking water and first aid, and to enrol voluntary shelter marshals, while a paid ARP warden would be assigned to each occupied tube station.

In the afternoon of 3 October 1940 the new Minister went to Buckingham Palace to kiss hands with the King and receive his seals of office. That done, Morrison set off to inspect shelters in south London, starting at Southwark tube station, where a raid was in progress and Ack-Ack guns were firing constantly as he and the inevitable retinue of journalists toured the non-facilities and spoke to shelterers. The next day it was the East End, where, accompanied by Admiral Sir Edward Evans in full dress uniform and wearing his medals and white gloves (Evans had been second in command to Captain Scott on his Antarctic expedition in 1910, but was always known as 'Evans of the *Broke*', after the ship he had commanded in the First World War), one of the two Regional Commissioners for London, he headed straight for the notorious Tilbury shelter. After a quick tour of that wartime Hades, Morrison ordered structural improvements that would cost £5,000. 'What does money matter?' he exclaimed. 'There are thousands of lives involved! Get it done at once!' He had called in on the unfinished Bethnal Green tube station on the way, and on hearing that 'at least 4,000 slept there nightly', declared it an official 'deep shelter' sixty feet below the street.

Morrison immediately appointed the diminutive Labour MP 'Red' Ellen Wilkinson – so named for her ginger hair and her radical politics, which included leading hunger marchers from her shipbuilding constituency, Jarrow, to London in 1936, and who may have been Morrison's mistress at one time – as one of his three Parliamentary Secretaries, and gave her direct responsibility for shelters. The appointment of this 'dumpy, energetic little woman' as Morrison's 'liaison between the shelters and his Whitehall desk' pleased another critical journalist, Hilde Marchant of the *Daily Express*, who was now described as one of the newspaper's two 'Commissioners for the East End'. 'I met [Wilkinson] several times in the shelters and Whitehall and liked her. She is direct and decisive, a busy vigorous woman who has impressed the men she works with, and she has got her practical hands firmly on the subject.' Harold Nicolson, currently ensconced at the Ministry of Information, would also become a fan of Wilkinson's 'realism'. 'She said to me: "You deal with ideas and one can never see how an idea works out. I deal in water closets and one can always see whether it works or not." I do so like the little spitfire. I should so like to see [her and Florence Horsbrugh at the Ministry of Health] made Cabinet Ministers.' Wilkinson turned out not only to have 'nerves of fire and steel' as she toured shelters all over

Britain during the first months of the blitz, but a personal empathy with the shelterers: she had been bombed out of her flat in Guilford Street, not far from King's Cross, in October 1940.

Every day a straggling queue could be seen outside most underground stations from mid-morning, with people clutching their cushions, blankets and other night-time necessities, waiting for the gates to open for them at 4 p.m. The government, concerned that this could have a serious impact on war production as well as the regular life of the capital, was anxious that the concession, as it saw it, to use the tube as shelters should be regarded as that, and not as a right. The underground should not be depicted as a destination of choice, and the Home Office issued memos to newspaper editors requesting them to be circumspect in their coverage of people sheltering there. Articles such as one in the *Sunday Dispatch* on 22 September, which reported that 'by 6pm there seemed no vacant space from St Paul's to Notting Hill, from Hampstead to Leicester Square . . . types varied much from the trousered, lipsticked Kensington girls to the cockneys of Camden Town; but all were alike in their uncomplaining, patient cheerfulness', could only fuel the overwhelming desire for platform space that the government feared. Representing the underground as a sanctuary only for those unable to deal with the raids in any other way might limit the numbers. The Ministries of Transport and Home Security issued a joint appeal to 'the good sense of the public and particularly to able-bodied men to refrain from using tube stations as air raid shelters, except in cases of urgent necessity' – though presumably an air raid was an urgent necessity. The notion of it being 'unmanly' to use the tube was reiterated by notices on the platforms urging: 'Trains must run and get people to their work and homes. Space at the Tube stations is limited. Women and children and the infirm need it most. Leave it to them!' The *Daily Express* reported that on the night of 28–29 September 1940 twenty unattached young men were directed by police and station staff at South Kensington to find somewhere else to shelter. But men – some of whom might have been troops on leave – needed safety and sleep too. 'I am 29 and though I am not in the army yet I am just as much in the frontline as any soldier in this country,' complained a twenty-nine-year-old working man. 'It really is unreasonable to abuse chaps who are waiting to be called up.'

Grudging recognition may have been forthcoming, but since there was so little official enthusiasm for tube sheltering, improvements lagged. On 24 September it was announced that a million bunks would be fitted in

London's shelters, so that 'whatever type of shelter is used, whether private or public, the aim is now that all the people of London shall have a definite space allocated in which they can sleep at night . . . when the [large basements, street and trench] shelters are fitted with bunks they will look something like American sleeping cars . . . Families would be allocated a specific space with [two- or three-tiered] bunks and sanitation . . . and encouraged to think of it as their own property and make it as comfortable as possible.' However, 'no bunks are to be fitted into the underground stations, although the use of the stations for night shelters has been recognised and they are now being used under police supervision'. There were reports that 'police supervision' included quizzing would-be tube shelterers and turning them away if they were considered to have other options – even if they were mothers with babies or small children in tow.

But on 4 October 1940, after a three-hour tour of underground stations, Admiral Evans announced that he intended to introduce a system of ticketing so that regular users could be allocated a space, which would obviate the need for hours of queuing – and also wipe out the thriving black market operated by 'droppers'. These racketeers would 'persuade' a sympathetic tube worker to let them in ahead of the patient queue waiting until 4 p.m., on account of their supposed poor health, and would then 'bag' the best pitches by placing bits of bedding on them, and charge unfortunate shelterers the exorbitant sum of 2s.6d for them – at a time when the average wage was around £3 a week. Evans also promised that bunks *would* be provided, and that 'the problem of sanitation has been solved in most cases' – though this was disputable, since 'sanitation' usually meant a few overflowing chemical toilets, or people using the rail lines as a public convenience.

The first of the three-tier metal bunks were installed at Lambeth North station on 25 November 1940; by early March 1941, 7,600 had been erected in seventy-six stations. Most of them were allocated to regular shelterers, though 10 per cent were to be left free for those caught out in a raid. There were still, however, people who had to sit up all night, as they did in some public shelters. Latecomers had to cram in wherever they could – in corridors or the booking hall, or on escalators (switched off). The two platforms at Holland Park station would be almost full by 5 p.m.: by 7 p.m. the only space left was at the bottom of the emergency stairs. That same spring local councils were authorised to provide water-borne sanitation in place of the easily-knocked-over chemical toilets, and that reduced the stench a bit. At Old Street station, Shoreditch Council provided a laundry and disinfecting service for bedding free of charge to the 'tubeites'. Washing facilities other than the occasional small handbasin were not provided: people either had to go home to spruce up before a day's work, or use a nearby public bath (though many of those had been taken over by the Civil Defence services, often to be used as mortuaries). 'We didn't have bathrooms and facilities like that in our houses. We were used to going to the public baths, and when they were taken over, you just had to go home and if the water was still on, you'd just have a quick wash and off to work. But if the water was off, then you had to get it from a standpipe in a jug . . . It was very hard to wash your hair or anything like that. Personal hygiene rather went out of the window, but you just got used to it.' In West Ham, Lever Bros equipped a van named 'Lifebuoy Boys', after one of its soaps, that toured the shelters offering people a chance to have a shower as they came out.

Local authorities, private caterers and voluntary organisations such as the WVS and the Salvation Army organised platform canteens in larger stations where shelterers could buy tea and buns, and sometimes hot soup, pies or sausage rolls, and cigarette-vending machines were installed in some stations. The LPTB equipped six tube trains to carry buns, cakes, biscuits, chocolate and urns of tea and cocoa around the network, served by staff wearing red armbands bearing the letters 'TR' (Tube Refreshments). Robert Boothby, Parliamentary Secretary to the Ministry of Food, who had been 'astonished' by seeing 'at least 700 people' disgorging from one tube station at the end of the night to begin what could be a long trek home, commandeered coffee stalls and vans and had them positioned to sell tea, cocoa and soup to shelterers as they emerged blinking into the light of early morning.

'It was better after that,' concedes Irene Moseley. 'The bunks weren't comfortable by any means, but it was better than sleeping on the platform. Things became a bit more organised . . . a lady used to come round with biscuits and buns, and down one end of the platform were portable toilets. It wasn't perfect by any means, but it was an improvement. And the best thing was that you were entitled to be there, and that made you feel a lot better . . . it gave you a sense of belonging really.'

A week after the start of the blitz, the King's physician, Lord Horder, had been appointed to head a committee to look into shelter conditions both above and below ground. Father John Groser, the 'turbulent priest' of Stepney, was one of the members, as were the elegant Rose Henriques, wife of Basil Henriques, Warden of a Jewish settlement in the East End, and Alderman Charlie Key, MP for Bromley and Bow, who was soon to play a key role in the defence of London. The committee reported informally within four days and more formally at the end of September, though MPs complained that there was no full written record of its findings that they could consult. This, the Parliamentary Secretary to the Minister of Health, Florence Horsbrugh, intimated, was because it was highly undesirable that the enemy might find out what dreadful conditions Londoners were suffering as a result of its attacks.

Horder's recommendations to reduce overcrowding, and various other measures, were largely followed – but slowly. They included providing a first aid post with a nurse in eighty-six shelters, the appointment of Shelter Marshals in the larger ones, prohibiting smoking in public shelters unless a separate section for smokers could be provided, the issue of masks to guard against infection, improved sanitation and lots of scrubbing with disinfectant, and using blowtorches on crevices to kill bugs – and regular inspections by Medical Officers of Health and their staffs to make sure all was as it should be. The greatest fear must have been of a diphtheria, measles or whooping cough epidemic, but fortunately this never happened; the main health hazards were impetigo, lice and scabies: most shelters were soon regularly sprayed with sodium hypochlorite or paraffin to try to deal with this, and any wooden bunks were replaced by metal ones, as wood was hospitable to lice. Hilde Marchant, in her unofficial role as 'East End Commissioner', was all for people being required to pass through a 'Health Ministry hut' at the entrance to every shelter, with disinfectant liberally used, and any unfit person being weeded out and sent to hospital, while bunks would be disinfected daily too, and bedding inspected and carted off to be fumigated if necessary.

Bedding was a touchy subject, since obviously it was likely to harbour bed bugs and worse. The Ministry of Home Security advised that it should be 'aired daily so it keeps sweet and fresh'. The *Swiss Cottager*, a news-sheet produced by and for those who sheltered at that particular Bakerloo Line station, urged shelterers to 'PLEASE stop the evil habit of shaking out blankets, mattresses etc., over the track each morning. The spreading of dust and germs over people, many of whom suffer from coughs and colds and "shelter throat" is little more than criminal. One of the gravest dangers we face is the spread of infection. Take your bedding home and do the shaking in your own back yard.'

While shelterers were being warned that 'Coughs and Sneezes Spread Diseases', and that they should always use a handkerchief, the chemist Sidney

Chave, who had been drafted into the Emergency Public Health Laboratory Service, 'set up primarily to protect the health of the civilian population under the stresses of war' at the London School of Hygiene and Tropical Medicine, was trying to produce 'a simple snuff which could be widely distributed to prevent the spread of diseases among the people who crowd into the underground . . . each night'. In December a mosquito prevention squad started work, since in the warm, damp atmosphere these were a constant irritation, and experiments started with disinfectant sprays incorporated into ventilation systems in case an epidemic did take hold.

Getting people to and from work was regarded as a wartime priority, and police patrolled the tube stations to ensure that no one took up residence before the official entry time of 4 p.m. There were two white lines painted on the platform: until 7.30 p.m. shelterers were obliged to stay behind the first one, eight feet back from the platform edge, so passengers could get on and off the trains. After that they could spread out to the second line, four feet from the edge of the platform, and also occupy corridors and stairways. Although most people were sympathetic to the plight of the tube troglodytes, some found it a 'terrible hindrance . . . it is practically an impossibility to get anywhere quickly these days'.

Behind those white lines, a great deal went on between 4 p.m. and 11 p.m., when most adult shelterers retired for the night. Some entertainment was generated by the shelterers themselves: sedentary pleasures such as reading, writing letters, knitting, playing cards or board games, gossiping, playing the mouth organ or wind-up gramophone, having a communal singsong or dancing. Parties, quizzes and play readings were organised to pass the long air-raid hours. Bermondsey held a weekly discussion group at which the topics included travel, unemployment and 'Should women have equal pay for equal work?' The introduction of bunks was rather regretted by some, since it reduced the space available, but gramophones fitted with loudspeakers donated by the American Committee for Air Raid Relief to five of the largest shelters could make an evening spent in them seem more like a concert. Collections were taken for first aid equipment or towards a Christmas party, or presents for the children at Christmas.

Some shelters produced monthly news-sheets, including Holborn, Belsize Park, Goodge Street and the Oval, as well as the *Swiss Cottager*. There was also the *Subway Companion*, which was short-lived in its ambition to be distributed to all tube stations being used as shelters. 'Greetings to our nightly companions, our temporary cave dwellers, our sleeping companions, somnambulists, snorers, chatterers and all who inhabit the Swiss Cottage Station from dusk to dawn,' ran the *Swiss Cottager*'s first instalment. Each issue offered information and advice: 'a Committee of Shelter Marshals has been formed. It hopes to act as a bridge between you and the London Passenger Transport Board, and also do what it can for each and every person using this station at night. If you have any suggestion or complaint – if you think something should be installed, provided or remedied, please let us know and we shall do our best to meet your wishes.' 'To guard against colds and infection . . . a face mask can be made with a few inches of surgical gauze, or even butter muslin. Sprinkle it with a little oil of eucalyptus and tie over the face with a strip of tape at bedtime. We understand the government intends to do something about face masks. Unfortunately, intentions are a poor medicine and instructions a useless preventive.' Exhortations: 'there is still far too much litter in the station at the "All Clear". It is the prime duty of each and every one to leave the station in a clean and decent condition. Dustbins are provided in the station for refuse.' 'Do not bring camp beds into the station. Three camp beds occupy as much space as four blankets or a single mattress, so the available space is reduced by one fourth. YOU might be that fourth person turned away for lack of room.' 'Don't expect home comforts or plenty of elbow room. Suffer a little inconvenience to make room for the next person.' 'Vibration due to heavy gunfire or other causes will be much less felt if you do not lie with your head against the wall.' 'Please do not contribute to any unauthorised collection. Members of the Committee may be recognised by their carrying a yellow armlet with the letter "C" in black.' 'It is your duty to report anyone spitting to a member of the Committee or a Warden.' Jokes: 'Our morning paper tells us that one person in every eight snores. This station seems full of eighth persons.' (Government-issue earplugs were supplied at stations: proof against the noise of Ack-Ack guns, perhaps, but maybe not snorers.)

Aldwych station, on a branch of the Piccadilly Line, was closed at the end of September and converted into an underground shelter. It had been reckoned that it would be able to accommodate 7,500, but although this was over-optimistic, once the walls had been painted, the rails removed and the track covered over with sleepers, and two hundred bunks and lighting installed, some 2,000 people were able to shelter in the tunnel that ran from Aldwych to Holborn. The space was extended in the spring of 1941, taking over part of the tunnel where the Elgin Marbles and other treasures from the British Museum were being stored. Westminster Council donated 2,000 books from the borough's libraries for the shelterers' use, educational lectures were arranged to pass the time, the left-wing Unity Theatre put on the lighter sketches in its repertoire, and ENSA (the Entertainments National Service Association, or 'Every Night Something Awful', depending on your point of view) imported entertainers such as George Formby, as well as Shakespearean plays and a projector for films underground. A local vicar conducted a regular service at the Aldwych shelter, and a play centre was provided for small children at Elephant and Castle, with a qualified teacher to provide handicraft lessons. Such diversions spread to other shelters during that long winter underground (soon fifty-two stations had a library), and at the request of the Mayor of Bermondsey, one of the most-bombed boroughs in London, the LCC sent instructors to the shelters to teach drama, dressmaking, handicrafts and first aid, while children were provided with paper and paints, and produced 'violent masterpieces in which Spitfires bring down Heinkels amid sheets of flame'.

But there was one thing that no one could provide: any guarantee of safety. On 7 October 1940 seven shelterers were killed and thirty-three injured at Trafalgar Square station when an explosion caused the concrete and steel casing over an escalator to collapse, bringing down an avalanche of wet earth. The next day nineteen were killed and fifty-two injured – most of them refugees from Belgium – at Bounds Green station in the northern suburbs, when a house next to the station was hit by a bomb and toppled over, causing a tunnel to collapse and bury the victims in masonry and debris.

On 14 October a heavy bomb fell on Balham High Road in south London just above a point where underground tunnels intersected. It caused a sixty-foot crater to open, and immediately a double-decker bus fell into it. Below ground a deluge of ballast and sludge, dislodged by the explosion, engulfed the platforms where six hundred people were sleeping, and gas from fractured pipes seeped in. Sixty-eight were killed, including the stationmaster, the ticket-office clerk and two porters. Many drowned as water and sewage from burst mains poured in, soon reaching a depth of three feet. The toll would have been even higher had not two LPTB staff wrenched open the floodgates. Seven million gallons of water and sewage had to be pumped out before salvage work could begin. For weeks afterwards those sheltering in nearby stations along the Northern Line were aware of a 'ghost' train that slipped quietly along the track around midnight clearing the debris of the Balham disaster, a tragic cargo that included shoes, bits of clothing, handbags, toys and other heart-stopping possessions.

At a minute to eight in the evening of 11 January 1941 a bomb fell on the booking hall of Bank station in the City, and a massive explosion tore through the station. It blew a massive two-hundred-foot crater in the road, which was so large that a bridge had to be built over it to get traffic flowing again. Many passers-by were killed, but in attending to them the rescue services did not realise at first that there was even greater carnage underground. The blast from the bomb 'travelled through the various underground passages, and in particular forced its way with extreme violence down the escalator killing those sleeping at the foot of it at the time, and killing and injuring others sheltering on the platform opposite the entrances', while some people were hurled into the path of an incoming train. A total of 111 people were killed at Bank, including fifty-three shelterers and four underground staff. An inquiry into the disaster opened on 10 February 1941. 'It is difficult to convince people that even when they are 60 or 70 feet underground, they are not safe,' remarked the chair. It had been alleged that inadequate sanitation was a key factor, as there were only a few chemical toilets in the station, and since these were soon overflowing, many declined to use them, and were queuing to use the conveniences in the booking hall when the bomb fell. The inquiry found that in fact no deaths and only a few minor injuries could be attributed to this. There was no first aid post on the platform, and there was no emergency lighting. There had been other recent 'incidents' in the area (notably on 29 December 1940), so roads were closed and access to the station was difficult, while fallen debris cut off access to the Central Line (both the Central and Northern Lines pass through Bank), meaning that it had taken doctors and stretcher parties more than an hour to reach it. While the injured waited for the medical services to arrive, a Hungarian refugee doctor, Dr Z.A. Leitner, who had himself been injured in the blast, gave more than forty morphia injections as he ministered to the injured single-handed in the gloom and choking dust. At the inquiry the hero doctor paid tribute to those he had helped. 'I should like to make a remark. You English people cannot appreciate the discipline of your own people. I want to tell you, I have not found one hysterical, shouting patient. I think this very important, that you should not take such things as given – because it does not happen in other countries. If Hitler could have been there for five minutes with me, he would have finished the war. He would have realised that he has got to take every Englishman and twist him by the neck – otherwise he cannot win this war.'

5

Front Line

The Warden. For some time before the blitz he was regarded by most of his charges with anything from cool indifference to active suspicion as a Nosey Parker.

> But it's 'Saviour of 'is country'
> When the guns began to shoot.

Front Line 1940–1941: The Official Story of the CIVIL DEFENCE of Britain (1942)

I detect in myself a certain area of claustrophobia. I do not mind being blown up. What I dread is being buried under huge piles of masonry and hearing the water drip slowly, smelling gas creeping towards me and hearing the faint cries of colleagues condemned to a slow and ungainly death.

Harold Nicolson's diary for 24 September 1940

'There is no public record of the labours of the inter-departmental Committees, of the Boards of Inquiry, of the Treasury minute, of the final Cabinet minute, which settled upon the word "incident" as the designation of what takes place when a bomb falls on a street,' wrote John Strachey. 'Yet how important it was to select such a word . . . So when the time came, Whitehall had a word for it . . . "Incident" cannot be held to convey very graphically the consequences of a bomb. Just the contrary. The word is wonderfully colourless, dry and remote: it touches nothing which it does not minimise. And this, it may be supposed, was what recommended it conclusively to the authorities. It formed an important part of their policy of reassurance. For while anyone might be frightened of a bomb, who could be frightened of an incident?'

Strachey, the son of the owner and editor of the *Spectator*, was an old Etonian, highly intelligent and with a chequered political past. In February 1931 he and his fellow Labour MP Oswald Mosley had resigned from the

Parliamentary Labour Party when Mosley's expansionist plans to end unemployment were rejected, but by July, repelled by Mosley's growing fascism, Strachey had left Mosley's New Party. The following year his application to join the Communist Party of Great Britain was rejected, probably because he was regarded as an unreliable intellectual, but he called himself a Communist and wrote as one throughout the thirties. His extremely influential (and best-selling) book *The Theory and Practice of Socialism*, for Victor Gollancz's Left Book Club (of which he was one of the founders), was published in 1936. By April 1940, disillusioned by the Nazi–Soviet Pact, Strachey broke with the CP, and on the eve of the blitz he signed up as an ARP warden, an experience he would lightly fictionalise in his book *Post D*, published while the blitz was still raging. It is a detached, controlled, probing account, infused with what W.H. Auden called 'the surgeon's view of pain', and the *New Statesman* thought it so good that it 'killed anything else in range'. In his ARP role Strachey attended many 'incidents'. Ford, his alter ego in the novel, had got into 'this ARP business' by doing a few night-time watches at the suggestion of his formidable Chelsea landlady, herself an ARP warden.

> At first he took part in watches and patrols on the next night and on subsequent nights. At first his equipment consisted in a borrowed tin hat – the one real necessity. But gradually other pieces of equipment came his way: a badge, an armlet; a borrowed torch. At a certain point in this development he was duly enrolled. Later it was suggested that he should become a full-time paid warden (wages £3.5s a week for men, £2 for women). This involved being on duty every night but one a week, and being available for duty in the event of a raid ('on call for sirens') all day. At that period raiding was continuous every night, and there were usually three or more raids each day. Hence full-time wardens could not do anything else. As Ford had several other activities which he was loth [sic] to abandon, he decided to become an unpaid warden, on duty four nights out of five, but not on duty during the day. After enrolment he was duly provided with uniform and full equipment. In his borough, this consisted of a suit of overalls, a webbing belt carrying on it a message pad and a couple of bandages for first aid purposes; a torch hung round his neck by a strap; a steel helmet; a civilian duty gas mask.

He had taken this decision largely because

the main trouble of being a pure civilian during a prolonged air bombardment is that as such one's only duty is to seek and to maintain one's own and one's companions' safety. And this is inevitably demoralising. The instant that an individual is given even the simplest objective function, and becomes a member of an organised (and uniformed, this is notoriously important) group, the whole burden of deciding whether or not on any particular occasion to seek his or her safety is automatically removed. While one is functionless one is continually irritated by such questions as 'Isn't it really very silly to stay upstairs (or to go out) in this degree of Blitz?' The instant the individual has become a warden, ambulance driver, member of the auxiliary fire service, rescue and demolition squads or stretcher bearer, this question is, nine times out of ten, settled for him or her . . . the enrolment of tens of thousands of men and women in the various Civil Defence Services would have been fully justified for psychological reasons alone, even if, as was by no means the case, their functions had been objectively useless.

The motivation of Barbara Nixon, who was married to the distinguished Communist Cambridge economist Maurice Dobb, was much the same when in May 1940 she became a voluntary (part-time) warden. 'I wanted an active job; I particularly wanted to avoid being in the position of many women in the First World War – of urging other people to do the work they wouldn't think of doing themselves. At that time the ATS seemed to be mainly a matter of cooking and cleaning, for neither of which was I either competent or inclined; I found that the AFS entailed mainly switch-room work [for women], and First Aid Posts seemed to me to be too reminiscent of Job waiting patiently for troubles to be brought to him.'

The government had made its first appeal for ARP wardens in January 1937. In some places fully-worked-out Civil Defence schemes, including the recruitment of ARP wardens, were put in place within months; in others virtually nothing happened, either through inefficiency, a distaste for 'warmongering', or because there was no clarification about who would foot the bill. Herbert Morrison himself had been the spokesman for the Local Authorities Association in demanding that the government should pay 90 per cent, if not the whole cost, of these measures. On 1 January 1938 the ARP Act came into force, compelling local authorities to set up ARP schemes including recruiting wardens and expanding their fire services by forming and equipping the AFS. The Act committed the government to contribute between 60 and 75 per cent of the money to pay for these services.

But recruitment was sluggish: a radio appeal for a million men and women ARP volunteers in March 1938 largely fell on deaf ears. The Munich crisis in September changed everything: suddenly war seemed a threatening reality, and by the following March over a million people had volunteered. This still fell short of what was needed, and training in things such as gas detection and treatment, blackout regulation enforcement, first aid and various other air-raid practices was slow to be provided, as was equipment.

The wardens' service attracted most volunteers, but during the phoney war there had been an alarming falling away of personnel (which was not helped by the government's ban on recruitment) as disheartened citizens either transferred to the Local Defence Volunteers after it was set up in May 1940, or drifted away, wondering what their wartime role actually was, other than often being roundly abused and called a 'little 'itler' when they tried to reinforce blackout regulations. The blitz would decisively show them.

The ARP was a locally embedded service: it was essential that wardens knew their area well, so that when there was a raid they knew how many people lived in a particular house, whether any had been evacuated or might be away, were infirm or had small children, whether there was an Anderson shelter in the garden, or if the occupants regularly used a public shelter. All this detailed knowledge of local residents and their habits would be invaluable in ascertaining where people were likely to be when a bomb fell, so that ambulance services could be directed efficiently and rescue parties shown where there might be survivors buried in the rubble.

Districts varied in the ratio of wardens they could muster, but in general in large towns and cities the norm was ten wardens' posts to the square mile. The posts might be located in a shop, a hall or a basement, or even sometimes in a warden's front room. There would be a Post Warden, and usually a deputy, and the area would be divided into sectors, each covering a few streets with around five hundred residents. There would be between three and six wardens for each sector, reporting to a Senior Warden. Some posts might have sub-posts too. In the country the posts would have to cover a much larger area, maybe encompassing several villages, and the wardens would have to assume more all-round responsibilities and competencies as the support services would take longer to arrive.

In Fulham, in south-west London, then a largely working-class district, some two hundred volunteers had enrolled by April 1939. The majority of them were middle-aged, and one in six was a woman: single women were more likely to join, since they generally had more time on their hands than married women with homes to run. In Fulham the volunteers came from a wide range of occupations, from the manual to the professional to the 'artistic', including a number of retired (mainly middle-class) men. This was not surprising, since the National Service handbook issued in January 1939 (that is, before the call for LDV – Home Guard – volunteers) had made it clear that ARP was the only job in Civil Defence open to older men. Some of the recruits were too old to fight, others had been turned down on medical grounds or were in reserved occupations, while others were waiting to be called up. When asked why they had enrolled, most replied in terms of 'wanting to do my bit', though some had come under pressure from employers and friends, and one twenty-six-year-old middle-class woman supposed that she 'must have been drunk. It was New Year after all.' Almost all would come to feel disillusionment with poor organisation, lack of relevant training, hanging around with nothing much to do and not having a 'clue what to do in case of an emergency'.

Frederick Bodley and his wife Kath had enrolled as ARP wardens at Stoneleigh in Surrey within a fortnight of the outbreak of war in September 1939, and persuaded their neighbour Joan to do so too. Around 90 per cent of ARP wardens were part-timers who would come on duty at the end of a working day. The Bodleys' first post had been in a private house, but it was soon moved to a smallish concrete building, which was 'very comfortable for we have a radio, shove ha'penny board, playing cards and an electric kettle. The heating is supplied by two electric radiators.' There was also a foot-wide bench that served as a bed, though this was soon 'considerably widened and made very comfortable with the addition of a horse hair seat', while layers of newspaper were spread over another couple of benches so that games of dominoes could be played.

The post to which Barbara Nixon was first attached was in the basement of an old house. It was equipped with a camp bed and chairs, tea-making facilities and a dartboard to help wardens while away the time between patrolling the streets and responding to an alert. She was issued with a tin hat, a whistle and a respirator, and taken on a tour of the seventeen public shelters in the area. Her fellow wardens were 'railway workers, post-office sorters, lawyers, newspaper men, garage hands, to a few of no definable profession'. When in December 1940 she decided to become a full-time warden (after overcoming considerable Town Hall resistance to the appointment of married women), paid 'the magnificent sum of £2 5s a week', Nixon was transferred to a post in the north of Finsbury, where the raids had been heavier. 'Nothing was left. The heart of the largest city in the world was a wilderness. Here and there desultory trails of smoke curled up; the pigeons had deserted it, no gulls circled over it, the only inhabitants were occasional scurrying rats . . . The silence was almost tangible – literally a dead silence in which there was no life. It was difficult to believe that this was London.' Her companions were 'the toughest set of wardens in the borough'. It was 'unwise' to ask what people had done before the war, because 'owing to the fact that race tracks, boxing rings and similar chancy means of livelihood closed down at the outbreak of war, there was a considerable percentage of bookies' touts and even more parasitic professions in the CD [Civil Defence] services, together with a collection of workers in light industry, "intellectuals", opera singers, street traders, dog fanciers etc. In the early days the Control Rooms were crowded with chorus girls. There was also an ex-burglar, a trade unionist, and two men who hoped that joining the ARP would defer their call-up papers; the post warden was an ex-electrician.' And all, except Nixon, 'had been to the local school, though at different times, and they knew the family history of nearly everybody in the neighbourhood'; this urban community was as tight-knit as any Cotswold village.

From October 1939 until September 1940 the Bodleys received training in anti-gas procedures, learned how to use a stirrup pump to put out incendiary bombs, took part in 'smoke drills' in which they learned how to enter a burning building (on their stomachs, with their mouths as near the floor as possible), fire drill and putting out an incendiary bomb that was already blazing, and had mock exercises to teach them how to deal with an 'incident', complete with 'bodies' with labels attached detailing their imaginary injuries. They listened to a series of lectures on the correct way to load a stretcher, make a splint, bandage limbs, disinfect a gas mask and encourage the public to use theirs.

Nixon received some rudimentary instruction too, though it was on the job that her real training began. The Home Office recognised that 'training can never be finished', and she became aware of 'the multitudinous things a warden needed to know, from the names of the residents in each house, and which shelter they used, hydrants, cul-de-sacs, danger points in the area, to the whereabouts of the old and the infirm who would need help in getting to the shelter, telephone numbers and the addresses of rest centres etc.'.

Full-time wardens had one day off a week, and part-time wardens were expected to turn up three nights a week; but in the blitz most put in many more nights. When the 'yellow alert' – bombers within twenty-two minutes' flying time – was received in the wardens' post, they would stop their game of cards or darts, or wake up from a snooze, don a tin hat and set off with a fellow warden to patrol their sector.

When the 'red alert' was received – indicating that planes were twelve minutes' flying time away – the public sirens – the 'Wailing Winnies' (or Willies) or 'Moaning Minnies' – would sound, and people would start hurrying to the shelters, encouraged by the wardens who would be 'ticking off the names of the residents in their area as they arrived, then back they went to hurry and chivvy the laggards and see that those who chose to stay in their houses were all right . . . They carried children, old people, bundles of blankets, and the odd personal possessions which some eccentrics insisted on taking with them to the shelters.'

The ARP wardens' role was partly to look out for bombs falling, incendiaries alight or other incidents, acting as the 'eyes and ears of the Control Centre in the field' as the Ministry of Home Security's account of the blitz put it, and partly to be 'the chartered "good neighbour" of the blitz', giving reassurance that there was someone out there in the dark streets, lit suddenly with blinding flashes of whiteish-green incandescent light as chandeliers of incendiaries fell, made violent by the drone of the bombers. ('Where are you? Where are you?' the novelist Graham Greene imagined them saying), the 'sickly familiar swish of bombs' falling with a thud, the crash of falling shrapnel and masonry, the deafening rat-tat-tat of the AA guns which 'rose and fell in intensity', each sounding subtly different. John Strachey called one near his Chelsea post the 'tennis racket' for the 'staccato, yet plangent, wang, wang, wang; not unlike a sharp exchange of volleying at the net' it made. For the journalist M.E.A. ('Mea') Allan, some of the AA guns on Hampstead Heath 'just crashed, others sounded as if 50 people in the upstairs flat were playing tig around a billiard table, others as if 50 equally noisy children had collected tin trays and were banging them with hammers'.

Eight out of every ten heavy bombs dropped by German planes on Britain during the Second World War were high-explosive (HE) bombs – Sprengbombe-Cylindrisch (SC) general-purpose bombs – though tens of thousands of incendiary bombs fell during the blitz. The bombs were of various weights, ranging from 112 pounds (the bomb most generally dropped during the blitz, though by the beginning of 1941 heavier bombs were being used) to the 2,400-pound 'Hermanns' (named after the portly Göring, Commander-in-Chief of the Luftwaffe), the 4,000-pound 'Satan' (which could produce a crater large enough to accommodate two double-decker buses), and the largest bomb ever dropped on Britain, the 5,500-pound 'Max' (both names self-explanatory). The bomb's thin metal casing was filled with amatol (TNT, ammonium nitrate and sometimes aluminium powder), and there was an electrical fuse in its side to detonate and ignite the explosive material, forming a ball of expanding, blazing gas while sharp shards of metal casing flew out with deadly penetrative power.

Around 10 per cent of HE bombs did not explode on impact – by the end of September 1940 there were 3,759 UXBs (unexploded bombs) in London. Sometimes this was because they had a faulty mechanism, but as the blitz went on it could be because a variety of sophisticated time-delay mechanisms had replaced the simple impact fuse. This was to ensure that the bombs would cause maximum havoc in the area where they fell, with premises evacuated and roads closed until they could be defused *in situ* or moved and exploded in a safe 'bomb graveyard' such as Hackney Marshes, White City or Richmond Park. London and Birmingham in particular suffered major inconvenience from UXBs. Before the blitz it had been imagined that bomb disposal could be left to Civil Defence workers, with ARP wardens throwing UXBs into baskets or onto handcarts and getting rid of them, and in the early days this did indeed happen. But it was technical, skilful, and often life-threateningly dangerous, work, so Bomb Disposal Parties were formed of Royal Engineers – an officer and a number of 'sappers' – initially working with hammers and chisels, though more refined tools were later developed to extract the fuse.

Sometimes a UXB might embed itself a few feet in the ground, or fall into a static water tank (dotted around as reserve water supplies for firemen) or a gasometer, but many penetrated deep below the surface and were difficult to get at. The defusers' survival depended on staying one step ahead of German technology, since as soon as they learned how one time-delay mechanism worked, it would be replaced by another. By the end of 1940, 123 officers and men of the Bomb Disposal Squads had been killed and sixty-seven wounded. The deaths did not cease with the end of the war, as UXBs continued to be uncovered. By 1947, 490 had been killed in the battle to extract those 'great, torpid, iron pigs from their holes' and render them harmless.

Another hazard of the blitz was the so-called 'land mine', or parachute bomb. In fact these were magnetic sea mines that had probably demonstrated their usefulness as land missiles when they were accidentally dropped on coastal towns. They were impossible to target accurately, and floated to earth supported by green or khaki-coloured artificial silk parachutes, causing widespread damage: land-mine bombs proved particularly effective in smashing through modern pre-stressed concrete buildings.

Incendiary bombs were small, but they could be deadly too, starting fierce fires where they fell unless they were extinguished immediately with sand or water. The most commonly used thermite magnesium incendiaries were about eighteen inches long and only weighed around two pounds each, so thousands could be carried by a single plane. Some would be dropped singly, others packed tight into a canister which would burst above the ground, scattering its contents over a wide area. When ignited by a small impact fuse, the magnesium alloy would burn for ten minutes at a temperature that would melt steel, and metal particles would be thrown as far as fifty feet. There were also oil bombs, roughly the size and shape of a dustbin and packed with oil and other explosive materials which again would burn furiously over a wide area. Like HE bombs, the simple impact fuse in incendiaries was progressively replaced by delay mechanism fuses, which by 1942 had increased to six minutes, while the bombs became heavier, so that they could penetrate straight through the roofs of buildings to the floors below rather than smouldering among the tiles and rafters.

For months the shortage of wardens had meant that his wife Kath had been Frederick Bodley's ARP partner, which had worried him as they trudged the streets, he with a balaclava and she with a woollen scarf under their tin hats, dodging shrapnel and falling masonry, looking in on all the public shelters in their sector to see that everything was all right, and to offer reassurance and a running report on the night's activities.

When a bomb fell while they were on patrol, the nearest wardens would hurry over to assess the situation and what help was needed. In those days before mobile phones or pagers, one of them would then speed back to their post to ring the Control Centre to make a report, and also the fire services if there was a fire, before returning to the incident. If the phone lines had been cut in the blast, a despatch rider would be sent off on what could be a dangerous journey with information and requests for help from the other services. 'I go into a house, decide who's alive and who's dead, tot up the number of victims and what is necessary in the way of fire services, ambulances, demolition etc.,' wrote an ARP warden in Kent who thought that 'women are better [as wardens] than men in most cases . . . They can see in a moment who is in a house because they know what to look for. If the kettle is on the stove they know that the occupants are probably downstairs and have not gone to bed; if there is a cot, they know that there is a baby about somewhere.'

The wardens would deal with as much as they could without summoning help – putting out incendiaries with sand or a stirrup pump before a fire took hold, administering first aid to anyone with minor injuries, directing people whose homes had been made uninhabitable to the nearest rest centre, making notes of the incident.

It was the responsibility of the Control Centre to act on reports from its 'eyes and ears in the field', decide how the incident should be dealt with and what Civil Defence services despatched. In theory, the police were in charge of all bomb incidents, though after complaints from various London boroughs, including Hackney and Finsbury, the recruiting and training of ARP wardens was left to the local authorities, and any constable trying to assert his authority was likely to be firmly rebuffed by the warden in charge, who felt he or she knew the procedures, the area and the people.

An ARP 'incident officer' would direct the services at an incident and tell the firefighters, who would have arrived with pumps appropriate to the estimated size of the blaze at the ready, if there were any dangerous substances stored nearby. The Heavy Rescue Squad (the 'ragged trouser brigade', as they were called), wearing overalls, tin hats with the letter 'R' stencilled on them, thick gloves to protect against glass, stout rubber boots – not waders like firemen wore, although they were often thigh-deep in water and sewage – would use jacks, blocks and tackles, and sometimes later in the blitz oxyacetylene cutting equipment, to try to lift masonry out of the way so they could get to the victims. First they would cut off the supplies of water, electricity and gas – gas masks offered no protection against domestic gas – since it all too often happened that people survived the collapse of their homes, only to be gassed or drowned before they could be rescued. What the rescue squad really needed were cranes – ideally on the back of their lorries – to lift the heavy beams and lumps of rubble, but there was a shortage of these, so it was a matter of crowbars and hands – and there was always the danger of a building collapsing.

If it was thought that a building had been occupied, a first aid party would arrive (known as 'stretcher parties' in London, identified by the letters 'SP' on their helmets). They would treat minor injuries on the spot and carefully lift the more badly injured onto a stretcher – or anything that would serve as a stretcher if there wasn't one available: a door or plank perhaps. Casualties were labelled at the incident, using an indelible pencil and a luggage label, or lipstick scrawled on the victim's forehead *in extremis*: 'X' for internal injury, 'T' for tourniquet applied, etc. If the injuries were not critical the patient would be taken to a first aid post for assessment, rather than overwhelming the hospitals with cases that did not require operations or bed nursing. These posts were staffed round the clock by a doctor and nurse ready to clean wounds, stitch up cuts, remove splinters of glass or metal and strap up fractured limbs. If the injuries were more serious, the patient would be loaded into an ambulance (usually with 'M' for morphia added to the litany on the luggage label or forehead). This might be a regular peacetime one camouflaged with dark grey paint, or it might be any half-suitable vehicle, such as a baker's or a greengrocer's van, many of which led a double life during the blitz: delivering goods during the day (if they could get the petrol), lent for transporting the injured at night. Or even a taxi or private car adapted with a roof rack on top to carry a stretcher.

Finally, the mortuary vans would arrive to take away the bodies laid out on the ground, with a makeshift shroud of a torn curtain, bloodsoaked sheet or bit of sacking to provide some semblance of dignity in death. Again these vehicles were usually requisitioned peacetime ones, and sometimes great anguish could be caused to relatives when they realised that their loved ones were being taken away in an ill-disguised dustcart or butcher's van. As well as bodies, the vans would collect the dreadful jigsaws of blitz death – legs, arms, indefinable lumps of flesh collected in baskets to be taken to the mortuary, where attempts were made to assemble sufficient parts to represent a body that could be placed in a coffin for the family to bury and to mourn. 'Some of the mortuaries had been blitzed. Those that remained were overcrowded,' wrote the Mayor of Stepney, Frank Lewey. 'Every effort had to be made to identify bits of ashy intestines, hands, legs, limbless and headless trunks. One such trunk, which was never identified, was clad in burned corsets, which were stuffed with 950 one-pound notes.' 'It was a terrible task,' wrote Frances Faviell, who had studied art at the Slade and was thought therefore to have a good grasp of anatomy. 'The stench was the worst thing about it – that and having to realise that these frightful pieces of flesh had once been living, breathing people . . . if one was too lavish in making one body almost whole, then another would have sad gaps. There were always odd members which did not seem to fit, and there were always too many legs.'

When Neville Chamberlain had first approached Stella, Marchioness of

Reading, about organising a Women's Voluntary Service (WVS), he had envisaged it as a way of attracting more women to sign up as ARP wardens. But by the time of the blitz the WVS, which had started as a small group of women whose names Lady Reading had taken from her address book, and would grow to over a million during the course of the war, had become an essential auxiliary service in its own right. In their bottle-green and beetroot uniform, with sensible felt hats squashed on their heads, the ladies of the WVS were as welcome a sight at an incident as the ARP warden in his or her tin hat was in a public shelter. They would drive up in a mobile canteen to serve tea and buns to parched and weary rescue workers. They very quickly learned ingenious ways of making tea when the water pipes had been severed and there was no gas or electricity to be had. They would pore over lists of local residents with the wardens to make sure everyone was accounted for, take shaken and confused 'bombees' (as those who had been bombed out of their homes were known) to a Rest Centre, and lend a hand in any other way they could. Later in the blitz the WVS set up Information Points (IPs) at each major incident, and took upon themselves the grim task of breaking the devastating news to those whose homes or workplaces had been destroyed, and accompanying the shocked and grieving to hospitals or mortuaries to try to find or identify their loved ones.

Explained as a series of procedures – even diagrammatically, as the Ministry of Home Security's *Front Line** did – dealing with an incident sounds very organised, a smooth operation, tasks allocated, command chains clear. But of course it wasn't. There was often chaos and confusion in those unrelentingly grim and dangerous nights. 'In theory the warden reported an incident from his Post telephone, the Heavy Rescue Service did the digging and releasing, the Stretcher Party put the victim on a stretcher, the Ambulance loaded and conveyed that stretcher to hospital. At practice exercises this arrangement worked excellently, but in an actual raid, when it was general[ly] pitch dark, when there were incidents in all directions, when the telephones often broke down, there were frequently a waste both of personnel and time.' Barbara Nixon felt that while she had been taught a lot about gas – which kind smelt of geraniums, which of mustard – three ways of dealing with an incendiary device and about the blast from high-explosives, there were a lot

---

* Written by Clem Leslie, Herbert Morrison's public-relations adviser when he had been at the LCC, creator of the gas companies' 'Mr Therm'.

of important things, such as what exactly were the responsibilities of an ARP warden in a raid, how an incident should be controlled, what the rules were in public shelters, that no one seemed too sure about – or failed to pass on. 'No amount of training can teach you everything,' she concluded, 'but there should be sufficient to assure that you know what you ought to do in an emergency. An incident hardly ever goes according to the book; but if you have a thorough knowledge of what you are supposed to do, you are much quicker at thinking of something else that you can do. My own case is typical of many. I was extremely anxious to be as helpful as possible, but I had hardly any idea of what, officially, I was supposed to do.'

Even if a Civil Defence worker (as ARP workers came to be called by the spring of 1941, in recognition of their wide competencies) had been buffed to a peak of efficiency by training sessions, lectures and increasingly realistic mock incidents, the reality could prove uniquely challenging. As they attended to an incident, raids would continue, with bombs falling all around. The workers would be deafened by the crump of falling missiles, at risk from bomb blast, falling shrapnel and the ever-present danger that the masonry they were trying to excavate would crash down and bury them as well as the victims they were trying to release. Acrid smoke would swirl around, and brick dust clog their throats and lungs. The smell of an incident was 'unmistakable, indescribable . . . it is more than a smell really; it is an acute irritation of the nasal passages from the powdered rubble of dissolved houses; it is a raw, brutal smell . . . it was the smell of violent death itself. It was as if death was a toad that had come and squatted down at the bottom of the bomb craters of London.'

It was often very dark, with rescuers stumbling blindly around trying to discern what had happened: when an alert was on, no lights were allowed. The incident officer might have a small, shaded blue light to mark his position as he tried to coordinate the other services – the rescue squads, stretcher parties, ambulance men and AFS units. Some controllers might allow a shaded torch, but others would not, in the mistaken belief that among all the flashes from bombs and flares, German planes flying 25,000 feet up would be able to see the feeble glow from a torch bulb and unload their deadly cargo straight onto it. Moreover, the streetscape would often have been dramatically changed by a bomb explosion: houses jostled into each other, familiar landmarks gone, with only piles of rubble where they had once stood. It was confusing, anxious work, exhausting, taxing work, and it could be profoundly disturbing too.

John Strachey/'Ford' watched with grim fascination as the Heavy Rescue Squad worked after an incident on the Chelsea Embankment where five houses had been destroyed, leaving a crater with two mounds on either side of it, one fifteen feet high, the other twenty-five.

They had evidently been at work for some hours . . . apparently moving the debris with their hands. When the baskets were filled they took them to other parts of the mound and emptied them. It looked aimless. Ford climbed on the debris to try to see what they were at. As soon as he got onto the mound he found that it was made up of an extraordinary texture . . . the rescue squad . . . were sinking a small shaft vertically downwards through the mound . . . of brick and plaster rubble, more or less shattered lengths of floor joists and beams, pieces of broken furniture, rugs, carpets, linoleum, curtains, pieces of crockery, often unbroken, all made into a homogeneous, tight-pressed pudding . . . They worked in much the same way as archaeologists open up the debris of millennia; but this was the debris of seconds . . . They seemed to him to be working in an incredibly primitive and inefficient way – with their bare hands, and without any tools even, let alone any mechanical appliances.

One of them began to let himself down into the shaft, which was encumbered by ragged ends of floor boards and beams. He got to the bottom and then wormed his body round till he was lying in a knot with his head down by a crack, where some tattered rubble was held up an inch or so by a joist end . . . The rescue men stood still, and one of them called down to be quiet . . . The rescue man down the shaft put his mouth to the crack and said 'Are you there chum?' Everybody kept really still . . . The rescue man at the top said 'Can't you hear him any more, Smith?' Smith said, 'Yes but he's getting very faint.' Ford had not realised before that there were people alive under them in the mound . . . He could now see that their apparently primitive method of work with their hands was in fact the only way . . . They began to smell gas – not poison gas, but ordinary domestic gas. As the shaft progressively opened up the mound, the shattered pipes of the house permeated it with gas. 'Nobody must strike a match,' said Frank. But the rescue men went on smoking just the same.

Every now and then Ford was called over

to take charge of some bit of personal property that had been unearthed . . . several pots and pans, a china dish, unchipped even, two ration books . . .

and a lady's handbag, undamaged, full of its owner's make up . . . When he had collected a small heap of these he took them over the road to . . . where a small dump of miscellaneous and trivial possessions had been established. A man, a boy in his teens, and a girl who was crying a little, stood in a doorway . . . As Ford put down his handful of dust-encrusted possessions, the man said: 'Don't matter about those. What I want is you to get my boy.' Ford didn't say anything. 'Is there any hope – for him?' . . . 'I don't know,' Ford said, shaking his head . . . 'Is there a boy under there?' he said to one of the rescue men. 'Lad of about fifteen, we're told. Some say there's two, some say there's three of them,' he replied.

So the painstaking excavation went on, filling basket after basket.

The shaft was about ten feet deep now. The atmosphere of the group working round it began to change. Everyone began peering at the bottom of the shaft . . . There seemed nothing new there except one more greyish yellow joint, which ended in a curious grooved knob. After looking at it for some time Ford saw that it was a rubber-coated fist and an arm bare to the elbow. It seemed far too big for a boy of fifteen. The rescue men filled more baskets with rubble . . . They uncovered a large, untorn and apparently new, though intensely grimy blanket . . . 'How are they lying?' asked a smallish man in brown plus fours, with no uniform nor badge [who] the rescue men called 'Sir'. 'Directly at the bottom here, sir,' said Frank. 'Well, get them out then; what are you waiting for?' said the man in the plus fours, sharply. But the rescue men did not want to pull the blanket off at once. They moved about, collected their saws, took off their gloves, wiped their faces . . . Then Smith came back from the canteen and got down the shaft again, and pulled off the blanket. Ford could not instantly see anything underneath it except a good deal of white and red, and a good deal of white and blue material. Then he realised these were the pyjamas of two bodies, lying face down on top of each other, or, rather, with their arms and legs intermingled both with each other, and with the network of boards, joists, bits of bedsteads and the omnipresent rubble . . . The bodies had been driven, whether by the blast itself or by the falling debris, not only into the material of the houses, but into each other. They were locked in a reluctant intercourse . . . There was no blood or gross mutilation. But the bodies had become part of the debris; they had become one constituent of many constituents of the mound. They had been crushed and pressed into the decomposed raw material of the five houses [that had been bombed]. Like the clay of the London sub-soil, their clay had lost its individual existence and become an indissoluble part of its environment.

Leonard Whitlock was an ambulance driver in Southwark, south London. 'A huge bomb had fallen on Guinness's buildings [a block of flats] in Pages Walk. I was supposed to stay in the lorry but I went in and there was a woman sitting by the fire with a little baby, she was looking at it. I said, "Come on lady, you can come out now, it's more or less clear." But she was dead. They were both dead. The shock. Just like that. And her husband . . . he was embedded in the wall. The blast had [pushed] him right into the wall. And when they pulled him out, all his flesh and his clothes were left on the wall.'

Stanley Rothwell, an artists' model, joined Lambeth ARP service in southeast London. 'A motley crew we were from all walks of life – stage actors, jugglers, acrobats, a musician and one-time lion tamer, necromancers, wrestlers, boxers, shop assistants, scholars, old lags, barrow boys etc., all thrown together by the misdeeds, miscalculations of power greedy statesmen of this imperfect, chaotic world of ours.' One night Rothwell's team was called out to Thorne Road, south Lambeth, where three Anderson shelters had been hit. There seemed to be only minor injuries in the first two, but the third had been blown out of the ground.

I looked up at the wall of the house, as I lifted my torch (which I had been shielding and keeping trained on the ground because of enemy observation from above) I could see what looked like treacle sliding down the wall. I realised what it was, and seeing that nothing could be done in the darkness, I took my squad back to the depot to report what I had seen and to prepare to come back at daybreak with shrouds and the death wagon to do the unsavoury job of picking up the bits and pieces. This macabre business was to be my lot for the rest of the war. During training I had instructed my men to treat the dead with reverence and respect, but I did not think we would have to shovel them up. Now this job had to be done with a stiff yard broom, a garden rake and shovel. We had to throw buckets of water up the wall to wash it down. The only tangible things were a man's hand with a bent ring on a finger, a woman's foot in a shoe on a window sill. In one corner of the garden was a bundle of something held together with a leather strap, as I disturbed it it fell to pieces steaming. It was part of a torso. The stench was

112

something awful and it clung to my nostrils for some time after; in fact I never lost that smell until some time after the war was over. We gathered about six bags of bits and pieces; one pathetic little bundle, shapeless now, tied with bits of lace and ribbon, had been a baby. As we loaded the death wagon two dogs came along, sniffing in the dust and rubble. I threw a clod of earth at them to chase them off . . . It takes more than blind courage to face this task and handle these gruesome bundles, it takes guts of an unusual order, or else one has a callous nature that cares for nothing. If you are sensitive you carry the scars for the rest of your life . . .

My old soldiers, seasoned campaigners in battle, worked with tears streaming down their faces. Jock Weir crossed himself and dropped onto his knees to pray; many times I had to excuse myself to go along and vomit after these gruesome jobs.

The next nine or ten weeks was a continuous nightmare, the enemy visited us every night. Casualties got heavier, we were saturated with blood, dirt and stinking sweat. Our uniforms were now stiffened with clotted blood, we were impregnated with the acrid fumes of cordite and explosives and old brick dust. The only sleep I had been able to snatch was an occasional nap between raids in a chair in the depot on the alert ready for the next call out, gas mask at the ready and tin helmet ready to be snatched up and put on.

This is a side of warfare that is unglorious, that someone has to face, a side that is rarely mentioned, a side of war that gets no medals, a side of war that if the bemedalled glory boys who wield the power, if they had to face it, would change their tunes.

But in fact there were medals for this 'unglorious' side of war. Four of Rothwell's colleagues

went to Buckingham Palace to be decorated . . . by the King for the work they did after Morley College was hit [in October 1940]. Young children were staying there waiting to be evacuated the next morning, they had a direct hit and many were killed. Directly opposite was a working men's hostel which also received a direct hit in the same raid, the whole building collapsed sandwiching them between the floors. It was difficult to get to them, the rescuers had to cut through bed mattresses and move girders and work upwards from underneath, blood dripping on them as they worked while doctors stood by to administer morphia. It was one of the worst incidents to date, the casu-

113

alty list was heavy. But in other incidents and on other occasions of great heroism many an heroic deed passed unnoticed; many a hero went and remains unsung.

But some were sung. On 23 September 1940, George VI, speaking from Buckingham Palace, which was by then bearing 'honourable scars' of the blitz, announced that 'in order that they should be worthily and promptly recognised, I have decided to create, at once, a new mark of honour for men and women in all walks of civilian life' for valour on the home front, as there were medals for those at the battlefront. The George Cross (named for England's patron saint as well as its king) was intended to be the civilian equivalent of the Victoria Cross, which was awarded for 'acts of the greatest heroism or of the most conspicuous courage in circumstances of extreme danger'– though during the blitz so many soldiers were involved in hazardous work such as defusing unexploded bombs that of the first hundred recipients of the George Cross, seventy-six were military personnel. Another award was announced: the George Medal, which Churchill intended should be handed out to Civil Defence workers in their thousands – though to his chagrin this didn't happen. By the end of 1940 only seventy-one had been awarded, but this rapidly increased to 535 by the end of 1941. However, Rothwell was right: thousands of grimy, exhausted, courageous men and women did remain unberibboned and largely unsung.

6

The Test of War

I have no wish – though I have been accused of having one – to make political capital out of our national misfortunes, but on the other hand it is impossible to win a war without facing hard facts.

And these are that our ruling and official classes proved themselves incapable of dealing adequately with the world as it was before the war, and when the war came they showed precisely the same lack of energy, courage and insight . . .

But when the . . . crisis came and it began to be realised that this was the people's war (and not You doing it for Us) it was as if vast new springs of courage, energy, power had suddenly been tapped.

J.B. Priestley, *Daily Herald*, 3 September 1940

For many of the poor it had been a disaster comparable with the loss of life. For many of the wives, their home had been their life's work. All their energy, all their attention, for more than thirty years had gone into polishing, patching and scrubbing; they went without luxuries to get the furniture, they spent years paying for it, and now that furniture which was almost part of them is a pile of splinters. The face of one woman was purple with crying, and the tears streamed down her cheeks but she made no noise.

Barbara Nixon, *Raiders Overhead: A Diary of the London Blitz* (1943)

Although 6,945 people had been killed and 10,615 injured as a result of enemy action by air raids on the home front in September 1940, and a further 6,334 lost their lives, and 8,695 were injured the following month, the carnage was on nothing like the scale that had been feared and planned for. Thankfully most of the rows of waxed cardboard or papier-mâché coffins stacked up in requisitioned swimming pools and public baths had not been called for.

But what this meant was that provision for the living was grossly inadequate, since little thought had been given to those who might not lose their lives, but would lose their homes and all their possessions. Rest centres were not equipped to offer much more than a cup of tea and a slice of bread, or possibly a bully-beef sandwich, and maybe a chair to sit on. And those who went to them were supposed to move on within twenty-four hours, just like tramps in the casual ward of a workhouse. Yet, with nowhere else to go in the early days of the blitz, people were having to stay for days on end in desperately overcrowded halls. During September and October 1940 some 40,000 houses were destroyed or badly damaged each week; by the end of May 1941, 2.25 million people had been made homeless, and almost two-thirds of these lived in London. In effect, one person in every six in London was without a home. And with the loss of a home went the loss of the means of sustenance: no food, no cooking facilities, only the clothes the victims stood up in – and those would often be filthy, soot- and brick-dust-stained, wet and torn, and smelling of cordite and charred wood. And often the places that suffered the most in the blitz were working-class areas clustered around docks and factories, where people had little money or resources, or opportunity to leave.

Kingsley Martin, the editor of the *New Statesman and Nation*, admittedly a left-wing journal, primed to criticise the government's lack of foresight whenever possible, went to the East End at the beginning of October 1940. He spoke to a number of people who after a raid had 'wandered about for thirteen hours, having lost every possession in the world except what they stood up in, and were directed to a series of addresses which involved as much as eight miles walking before they were cared for. I suggest that they should be treated as casualties and that some of the idle ambulances and casualty staff should be used to aid them. One of the crying needs in all such cases is for some person who knows what facilities exist for relief, food, clothing, evacuation etc., to be stationed in each area, and to have the duty of looking after these people at once and giving them the information they need.'

Martin suggested that what underlay this paucity of provision – and forethought – was the assumption that if people were bombed out, they could just go around the corner and put up at a hotel, or to the country to stay with friends. Neither of these options was remotely realistic in places such as Canning Town or East Ham.

The responsibility for those bombed out of their homes was given to the poor law authorities. Although that term, with its connotations of charity and the workhouse, had been officially changed in 1929, it was still how most of those who had dealings with its public face thought of it. Public Assistance Committees (PACs) – those bodies to which those without work in the 'hungry thirties' had had to apply when their unemployment benefit entitlement ran out, and which had administered the hated Means Test to ascertain how much benefit an unemployed man might receive, had been given the task of providing financial assistance ('cash aid') in wartime. This had initially been envisaged as being required by those who were temporarily unemployed as a result of bomb damage to factories or other places of work, and general wartime industrial dislocation and distress, and by women who had evacuated with their children and were in need of help since they were temporarily separated from their husbands.

But by 1935 it had begun to dawn on the government that in the event of war there would be other calls on the public purse, such as rehousing, feeding and clothing the victims of air raids: a report by the Air Raid Precautions Department (established in April that year as part of the Home Office) suggested that for every house razed to the ground, as many as a hundred might suffer damage, and that if all went well with the provision of shelter, even people in bombed-out houses might easily escape with their lives – though the lack of detailed research into the effects of bombs made this prediction rather uncertain.

The poor law principles of 'less eligibility' – making sure that the poor were not more comfortable in the workhouse than in the harsh world outside – and of ensuring that the indigent did not become a charge on the parish, dogged planning for the needs of victims of the blitz. As in the case of all wartime exigencies, the government proposed, and expected local authorities to dispose – but did not provide the money for them to do so. It was, the Treasury insisted, the responsibility of local authorities to relieve the destitute, and in wartime this would mean those who were in need as the result of war. This led to a tragically ridiculous situation whereby local authorities were supposed to provide for their own ratepayers, but if air-raid victims abandoned their bombed homes and fled a few streets away to the next borough, they would be classed as evacuees, and central government would take responsibility for them.

Unsurprisingly, local authorities were not happy with this arrangement: they would have to find money from the rates – and in poor boroughs this was onerous – and work out how many blankets, how much furniture, crockery and other necessities their own 'native' population might need, and how much 'refugees' might consume. They would also have to seek government sanction to spend money on would-be refugees/evacuees – if they could be distinguished – and make fiddly bookkeeping calculations to see who should foot the bill for each cup or blanket. In further evidence (if it were needed) of a poor law mentality permeating high places, the LCC was refused permission to buy blankets, on the grounds that they would tempt people to stay in rest centres for longer than strictly necessary. The Council was, however, grudgingly permitted to spend £4,000 for other equipment, with some conditions attached, while the Scottish Department of Health was allowed to spend just £1,000 on equipment for rest centres.

This persistence of 'localism', the system by which a borough had certain responsibilities for the welfare of its citizens, but not for those from other boroughs, had generated an excessive amount of bureaucracy and time-consuming accountancy since the outbreak of war. There had been endless disputes about which authority should pay for the travel expenses of those evacuated from danger to safe areas, their sick care, vermin control, school milk, the burying of the dead and myriad other expenses. Was it the receiving authority, or the despatching authority? And during the blitz this question of responsibility only grew more acute, as a second wave of evacuees left the bombed cities for the country, and thousands who lost their homes in one part of a city sought sanctuary in another: the ebb and flow of people moving from one authority to another in 1940 totalled 7,693,467 and in 1941 it was 6,736,338, which brought almost unimaginable administrative consequences.

Although in theory local authorities had the power to provide billets for those who no longer had a home, they were not allowed to do so 'in advance of the property being required'. When the blitz came no such arrangements had been made, and schemes for repairing houses that could be made habitable were completely knotted up in red tape and form-filling. Three weeks after the start of the blitz, around 25,000 people were still crammed into rest centres in the London area. Many of them had been there for days, fed on bread and margarine, biscuits and tea, and just possibly soup (soon known as 'blitz broth') if a tin opener had been provided: none had in Bethnal Green. The bombees would be caked with dust and dirt, and maybe had blood-matted hair: a forgotten feature of the blitz is how filthy people got in those nights of falling masonry, swirling debris and soot. But there were likely to be only a few bowls that could be used for washing, and no soap, flannels or towels. A social worker in east London in those early days was shocked by the 'unforgettable picture . . . of dim figures in dejected heaps on unwashed floors in total darkness: harassed, bustling but determinedly cheerful helpers distributing eternal corned beef sandwiches and tea – the London County Council panacea for hunger, shock, misery and illness . . . Dishevelled, half-dressed people wandering between bombed houses and the rest centres salvaging bits and pieces or trying to keep in touch with a scattered family . . . a clergyman appeared and wandered about aimlessly, and someone played the piano.'

The rest centres were usually in schools (which were empty since their pupils had, again in theory, been evacuated), or if there was no suitable school in the area, a church hall or some similar place. Local authorities had only been permitted to spend £20 converting premises into rest centres, so it is hardly surprising that they were dreary, uncomfortable, inhospitable places. And most had had no structural work done on them to make them safer from raids. So in effect the government's policy of dispersal was breached by its non-policy of rehousing – and thousands who had already lost their homes, or were 'time bombed' – moved out because of a UXB – spent days in vulnerable, overcrowded, ill-equipped rest centres. If they could find them, that is, for local authorities seemed almost coy in revealing where their rest centres were, and often Shelter Marshals hadn't been told either. One of the exceptions was Hackney, which claimed that it had been fully prepared for war at the time of the Munich crisis, and where Dr Richard Tee was the far-sighted ARP Controller. The borough was plastered with notices directing residents to the nearest rest centres as soon as the air raids started.

A family bombed out of its home had immediate needs: shelter, food, maybe money, most likely clothing, and certainly information. Later would come the question of housing – either the possibility of making their damaged home habitable, or finding somewhere else to live. The emergency rest shelters were overcrowded, food was inadequate, the small reserves of clothes that had accumulated were soon dispersed, and information was hard to come by: notices did go up in some places, but they were usually written in officialese with words such as 'incapacitated' and 'household effects', baffling to those with low rates of literacy who were already tired, confused and distressed. And, unlike ARP notices, they were rarely translated into Yiddish, the only language of many in the East End who needed to read them. The harassed workers at rest centres were often unable to answer such pressing questions as where victims could get clothing, apply for emergency cash grants if they had no money, replace their ration books, without which they couldn't buy food, and identity cards, and claim for their lost possessions. How could they get their house repaired, or if that wasn't possible, were they eligible for rehousing? And if so, how would they go about finding somewhere to live?

In late September 1940 Mass-Observation compiled a report on conditions in the East End. They followed the (mis)fortunes of the emblematic Smith family, who had been bombed out of their Anderson shelter (though as M-O admitted, a typical family would have been much more likely to have been sheltering in a public shelter or the tube).

When they come out they ask the air raid warden what they should do. He advises them to go to the nearest rest centre organised by the Public Assistance Board of the LCC, probably in a local school. There they find a much over-worked poor law officer, who has already been on duty for 18 hours and is not going off for another six. He sees that they are provided with food . . . blankets, and if necessary some extra clothing. If they have a definite address to go to in the country or elsewhere in London, he can provide them with money for fares. If not they must wait until a billet can be found for them. Some time during the day, an officer of the Assistance Board comes round, to register claims for advances on compensation for clothing or furniture destroyed. For this it is necessary to have obtained form V.O.W. from the Town Hall and sent it to the District Valuer, but as the supply of these forms was very limited, this formality was often waived. If any member of the family was insured under the Unemployment Insurance Acts and had been put out of work by the failure of the gas supply, he would go round to the Labour Exchange, but as likely as not be unable to sign on because the exchange kept on shutting during air raid warnings. If any member of the family had been seriously wounded, an application would have to be made to the Assistance Board for an injury allowance, and the possibility of a further application to the Ministry of Pensions for a disablement pension kept in mind. After a day or two, if they were lucky, an offer of a billet in another part of London would arrive. An official at County Hall would ring up the rest centre and say, 'I have arranged billets for 250 people in Clapton, or Westminster or Wandsworth,' or wherever it might be. 'How many have you got that want to go there?' Then, assuming that Clapton or Westminster or Wandsworth had not got a bad name in that particular rest centre for lousy or dangerous billets, they would go. When they had got into their billets, and been issued with a billeting certificate, they would, if they were in need of money, go along to the nearest employment exchange and get an emergency allowance . . . Another family might want to evacuate yet be unable to because their house was not completely ruined and they had no address to go to, or might have an address to go to, but be unable to get there because of an aged or infirm parent. Yet another family might decide to go off into the blue to Oxford in the hope (usually unfounded) of finding billets there.

Thus, people had to trail round a depressing number of agencies to try to get their lives together again to some degree. Half a dozen different over-lapping government departments were involved in dealing with what was essentially one problem: the homeless family. And on the ground, the response of the agencies could leave much to be desired: for example, while the Ministry of Food could advise local authorities on setting up communal feeding schemes, it had no powers to compel them to do so, or to fund them. People were unable to get any money from the Assistance Board until they had an address, delays were lengthy, and application forms ran out. Few East Enders had any idea that they might be eligible for an allowance from the Ministry of Pensions if they had been disabled in a raid. Labour exchanges 'let the public down badly', being closed more often than they were open. There was considerable confusion about who was, and who was not, eligible for help with evacuation. In sum, the authorities were charged with being ill-prepared to deal with the physical effects of raids, and to have almost entirely neglected the psychological ones, and most officials were inflexible and extremely poor at communicating essential information.

Various powerful individuals and charitable organisations had moved into this maelstrom of paralysis and confusion, which the official historian of the home front called 'the crisis of London'. The Quaker Society of Friends sent workers and supplies to the East End; the Canadian Red Cross provided 50,000 blankets, 100,000 items of warm clothing and 50,000 tins of food which were distributed by the Charity Organisation Society to shelters and rest centres in the East End; the American Red Cross sent over bundles of clothing; the WVS, 'a kind of maid of all work to established authorities', did 'excellent auxiliary work' in supplying warm clothing, bringing in mobile canteens, helping evacuate those who wanted to leave and organising round-the-clock additional staffing for rest centres, as did local social workers. Individuals did their notable bit too. The indomitable 'Mrs B' was a market trader who sold beetroots by day, but by night effectively took charge of the Ritchie Street rest centre in Islington, finding bedding, milk powder and mysterious soporific powders for the dozens of babies and small children who huddled there nightly with their mothers.

The churches did what they could to help, setting up rest centres of their own – two hundred people were cared for in a Roman Catholic school off the Commercial Road, and a convent in nearby Artillery Lane had been turned into a rest centre – and the Catholic, Anglican and Methodist Churches all worked to arrange the evacuation of homeless people or those who wanted to get away but failed to meet the requirements of official schemes, ran clothing depots and generally tried to alleviate conditions in the shelters and rest centres.

In the East End clergymen were frequently recognised figures of authority, respected by those whose children they had baptised and whose dead they had buried, and those who never went inside a church, or did not share their religious persuasion. Having lived among the poor, such priests were acutely aware of the people's needs, and were more than a match for any petty official. It was said that in the early days of the blitz Father John Groser was 'the real government of Stepney'. In the 1930s Father Groser, who described himself as 'a Socialist of a very advanced type though I belong to no political party', had come to Stepney after being unable to find a parish following his support for the General Strike in 1926. He had been offered the living of Christ Church, Watney Street, off the Commercial Road, a derelict building that was scheduled for demolition, but he built up the congregation to such an extent that the church was reprieved. He was an active anti-fascist in the days when Oswald Mosley and his British Union of Fascists were trying to mobilise anti-Semitism in the East End, and he took on the presidency of the Stepney Tenants' Defence League, which in an area of appalling housing had many bitter battles with slum landlords.

When the blitz came, Groser took decisive action. Told that no blankets could be issued in a school where people were sheltering, he simply forced the locks on cupboards and handed them round. He broke into food stores to get provisions, and lit a bonfire in his vicarage drive to cook meals. Throughout the next nine months the tall, angular priest could be seen marching round his parish, his cassock flying out behind him, and wearing a kerchief rather than a dog collar. He organised a mobile canteen staffed by 'conchies' (conscientious objectors), to be parked outside the Watney Street shelter every night, and teams of helpers (including the film director

Paul Rotha) would wheel bathchairs around the railway arches where people sheltered with large enamel jugs of cocoa made by Mrs Groser, which they sold for 2d a cup. Groser helped the ARP services dig for the injured at incidents, and, like his fellow priests, every night he would tour the district offering help, support and reassurance to his parishioners, and praying with the injured and the dying. From September until December 1940 he pestered Whitehall until doors were put on some of the railway arches, and sanitation, bunks and feeding facilities installed. He organised play centres for the children there, youth clubs, discussion groups, play readings and Saturday-night dances to a wind-up gramophone, all to keep up the morale of those under nightly attack. The Reverend Lex Miller was a Presbyterian clergyman who worked ceaselessly to help the blitz homeless in the East End, and the Reverend William Paton was another tireless worker and inspiring agitator for better conditions for his West Ham flock; before the blitz was over he abandoned his pulpit and took over the job as ARP Controller for his beleaguered borough.

Dr Jimmy Mallon, Warden of Toynbee Hall (and a former governor of the BBC), was another 'leader's leader . . . a man they all turn to to get things done when the normal channels are clogged with red tape . . . Indeed . . . they often expected him to work miracles.' He sometimes almost did, personally accepting a donation of a thousand beds from a furniture manufacturer for rest centres when the local authorities considered it would be too difficult to organise. Toynbee Hall also housed a Citizens Advice Bureau, among the first in the country, which offered advice to all affected by the raids, and the nearby Bernhard Baron settlement, started in memory of Jewish soldiers who fought for Britain in the First World War and run by Basil and Rose Henriques, together with the Jewish Youth club, organised communal feeding and a clothing depot. Though Clement Attlee was one of the MPs for Stepney (his seat was Limehouse), he was also leader of the Labour Party and a member of Churchill's War Cabinet, so was 'naturally a very distant figure', but he had been helpful when direct appeals were made to him for assistance, as was the Member for Whitechapel, Jimmy Hall. As well as being a forceful voice in the Commons with his demands for better shelter facilities for his constituents, Hall was often to be found out on the beat at night with Father Groser, looking after their welfare. 'Gradually, the machinery of Government was unclogged of its peacetime entanglements, and geared to a wartime tempo, where it is more important to get things done than to worry about who ought to pay for them – for the cause of much of the red tape is to make sure that the Treasury of the X County Council or Y Borough Council does not pay more than what it considers its fair share of the costs.'

Lord Woolton, the Minister of Food, decreed that since so many ration books had been lost in the raids, and shops where people had been registered had been bombed, rationing would be suspended in badly affected areas, and the LCC was authorised to provide blankets, camp beds and, almost the most important thing, hot meals. Since after a raid in October, 20 per cent of Londoners were without gas, or their gas pressure was too low to cook by, and water supplies could be cut off for days at a time, the problem of feeding was not confined to those in rest centres. The initial solution was mobile kitchens, provided first by voluntary organisations such as the WVS, the Salvation Army or the YMCA, and finally by the Ministry of Food, with the LCC being permitted to deliver hot food and drinks to rest centres. But providing sustenance for a blitzed population would be a long-term problem, and it wasn't just civilians affected by bombing who needed hot meals, but Civil Defence workers on long shifts and those who could not get home for a midday meal as had been their custom, because of transport difficulties.

The answer was communal feeding facilities, though the writer and broadcaster J.B. Priestley didn't like the term: it sounded, he thought, as if people were expected to 'trough it together' as well as 'rough it together'. Flora Solomon, Chief Welfare Officer at Marks & Spencer, had, with the support of Simon Marks, started a communal feeding centre on a housing estate in Kilburn before the blitz, providing hot, reasonably priced meals for anyone who needed them. This was to be the model for the Londoners' Meal Service, organised for the LCC largely by Valentine Bell, the retired head of Battersea Polytechnic, using army field kitchens he had collected from Aldershot. By Christmas 1940 there were 104 such centres (sometimes called 'Citizens' Kitchens'), serving meals at the rate of 10,000 a day, as well as nearly two hundred SOS mobile canteens run by the LCC and various voluntary organisations, and a 'food convoy' consisting of two lorries containing cooking facilities and cooks, a water trailer, three mobile canteens and two vans with stores ready to be despatched anywhere in the capital that they were needed, accompanied by four despatch riders.

'Blitz meals' would become standard fare in air-raided towns and cities, though 'common sense variations' were permitted if stocks allowed. The menu would consist of a thick vegetable soup (with the addition of meat if it was available) plus a cup of tea for adults and milk for children, and the meals were served throughout the day in most places, and around the clock 'where blackout permits and circumstances require'. They were free only to those in need, and the caterers were reimbursed by the Ministry of Food.

Housing the victims of air raids was a more difficult and more sensitive problem. As rest centres gradually ceased to be administered like the casual wards of workhouses, their numbers expanded. By May 1941 there were 780 in London, with room for around 105,000 people, their funding became more generous (or rather, more realistic), their facilities more comfortable and their staff more humane. But they could only ever be a staging post on the way to rehabilitating the homeless. Henry Willink, the MP for Croydon, was appointed one of the two special Commissioners for London on 26 September 1940, charged with coordinating services for the homeless. The other Commissioner was Sir Warren Fisher, former Head of the Home Civil Service, whose responsibilities were the clearance of debris and the repair of roads and utilities. Willink declared that his first intention was to empty the rest centres in order that they could assume their proper function as casualty clearing stations on the battleground that was now the home front. But where were the occupants to go?

By late October 1940 there were supposed to be almost 25,000 requisitioned properties available for homeless people all over London, and over 12,000 billets outside the capital, yet in that time only 7,000 people had been rehoused from the 101 boroughs covered by the London Civil Defence Region.* Requisitioning empty properties and evacuating the homeless was bogged down in a morass of confusion and crossed lines of responsibility between the LCC and the boroughs. Moreover, relocating human beings is not a simple matter of moving pieces around a board: it takes understanding, tact and time. All things in short supply in those chaotic weeks.

Many people refused to move. Rachel Reckitt reported that in Stepney, 'people are still living in houses which were the only one left standing in the street. Some refuse to leave even if they are alone in the building.' The elderly in particular, attached to their homes, devastated by the loss of their possessions, afraid that they would not be able to draw their pensions if they moved away from the post office where they did so every week, often

---

* By February 1941 a total of 278,623 Londoners had been billeted away from their homes, while 56,985 had been rehoused.

insisted on staying where they had always lived. Others needed to remain in the area since it was where their work was, and travel was expensive. Many women refused to leave if their husband stayed, seeing it as their duty to stay to look after him, or, bruised by the experience of evacuation at the start of the war, refused to let their children go. In a world of loss and desperate uncertainty, people clung to the communities they had always known, reluctant to move to strange areas – even if it was only 'up West' – where they knew no one, where things in the shops were dearer, where they entirely logically reckoned they might not be any safer anyway. 'The East End people now refuse to be sent to the West End, especially anywhere near Buckingham Palace,' noted Harold Nicolson.

Although the transfer of people from one part of London to another was never successful, and by November was done only as a last resort, some did take advantage of the opportunity. A week after 'Black Saturday' the Ministry of Health had asked thirteen London boroughs, including Westminster, Kensington, Chelsea and Hampstead, to requisition as many empty properties as they could and prepare them for families to live in, and apparently several thousand East Enders did traverse the capital to set up home a few boroughs distant. M.E.A. Allan reported on East End families ensconced in grand Belgravia addresses, knitting wool squares for a baby's quilt in Lord Linlithgow's drawing room in Chesham Place. 'They looked rather lost, like commercial travellers who had missed their train, doing crossword puzzles in the hotel lounge. They said they were very happy.' Fifty homeless Jewish people had been accommodated at the surprising invitation of Lord Redesdale, father of the pro-fascist Unity Mitford, close friend of Hitler, and Diana, the interned wife of Oswald Mosley, at his large house in Rutland Gate.

'Trekking', picking up what you could carry and trudging out of the city, the age-old image of refugees in war-torn countries, poignantly vivid in the 'exode' in France clogging the roads as German troops advanced earlier that summer, would happen all over Britain after a particularly heavy raid. In early September 1940, Londoners streamed from the East End to Epping Forest. Others set off west or north, walking, cadging lifts, sleeping in ditches or haystacks on the way, ending up in Reading or Oxford, where hundreds lived for several weeks in appallingly squalid conditions in the Majestic Cinema, bedding down between the aisles or in the orchestra pit, since Oxford, which had a large number of 'official' evacuees, refused to billet those who had turned up on the off-chance.

The reception the refugees received varied. Some thought of them as 'spongers', while others urged that 'people should make allowance for them. They've had a bad time. You've got to take that into account.' Windsor would not accept 'Jews or children', Baldock in Hertfordshire was reputed to be very unwelcoming, and word got around among those fleeing London that it was to be avoided. Much depended on the organisation in the town. Basingstoke was reported to have a very energetic WVS organiser who dispensed with red tape in finding billets, but in other places there were many stories of refugees going along the streets knocking on doors in an unsuccessful attempt to find someone to take them. The people of Stevenage in Hertfordshire, however, showed 'zeal' in coming forward to offer billets to those who had managed to find their way to the town. Local authorities did have the power to compel those with the space to take in evacuees, but billeting officers were, on the whole, loath to force evacuees on those who resisted – though in Hatfield action was taken against a couple who lived alone in a £2,000 house yet refused to accept bombed-out, or just frightened, lodgers.

When the raids began there was no help for those who wanted to leave London, other than 'assisted private' schemes by which mothers who found their own accommodation could obtain travel vouchers, while those who took them in would receive a small allowance. The Mayor of Stepney, Frank Lewey, arranged transport for women and babies by commandeering council dustcarts and cleansing lorries and piling the evacuees onto them. But he and his staff were 'far too busy to keep records of the evacuees. It was all we could do to get them out of London fast enough. We did not know where they had all gone or who had gone there, except that one hundred and fifty had gone to Ealing, two hundred and thirty to Richmond, and so on. Then, of course, we began to be besieged by relatives who had no idea where their dear ones had vanished to; and we could not tell them! We could not even tell if they were evacuated or buried under the local rubble by some bomb explosion . . . I recall vividly a very old Jewish woman who came to me [in tears]. "Vere is my Solly?" she kept saying, hardly above a whisper. "My only one. My boy. I have not got anyone else . . . Sir, only my Solly. You will find him won't you?" I did my best. I found he had gone to Glasgow. I wrote to the mayor of Glasgow. Search was made. Solly was never found. Was he perhaps an unidentified victim in a Glasgow raid? We shall never know.'

The problem remained that despite these mass, muddled, undocumented exports and arrangements with other boroughs, many of those who did want to leave had nowhere to go. Rachel Reckitt, working at Toynbee Hall in Whitechapel, was 'kept busy all day with mothers and children waiting to evacuate, but nothing can be done unless they have friends to go to . . . Lots are wandering, homeless, towards the City this morning with suitcases, all they had saved . . . There was one terribly pathetic girl of 19 with a baby of 2 weeks and another of 17 months – a soldier's wife – absolutely exhausted. We tried every institution in London and couldn't get her in anywhere. She collapsed in the end, and I got her into a Convent Rest Shelter for the night. The MP's wife promises to fetch her to-morrow and get her away by hook or by crook. She only came out of hospital on Saturday . . . the arrangements are hopelessly inadequate. I can't imagine what the authorities have been doing as they must have foreseen all this. Naturally I came across the people most whose homes have gone, but the fact that three out of four Toynbee maids and cleaners have lost their homes shows the percentage.' The Warden of the settlement, Dr Mallon, agreed that Reckitt could have 'up to £30 to use for travelling expenses of intending evacuees who have an address to go to but don't come under any scheme. So I have got one or two off this way to-day. Generally when they ask to be evacuated, I ask "Has your house been demolished yet?" and if it hasn't I have to tell them to wait until it has, as then we can do something. So later they come in with broad grins to announce that now it has been blown up and they can get away.'

The only help available was from similar voluntary agencies which would somehow, though they had no official powers, whistle up accommodation, equip it with basic necessities and provide travel vouchers. The scheme to get children out of London was speeded up, and for the first time the introduction of compulsion was very seriously canvassed. Yet only 20,500 of the 520,000 children in London left the city in September, including 2,000 under-fives sent by the Waifs and Strays Society to houses in the country leased and equipped partly by donations from the American Junior Red Cross. By December the number had dropped to 760 unaccompanied children.

Anxious about a growing chorus of criticism in the press, and fearing that the thousands of Londoners squatting in rest centres, shelters and other unsuitable places wouldn't be prepared to 'take it' for much longer, the government announced that funds would be available for mothers who wished to evacuate with their children from certain East End boroughs. Yet despite an escalating campaign to 'get the children away' and Willink's initiative in providing hostels for men whose families had left but who needed to remain in London themselves, the response was poor. So poor that far from applicants swamping the reception areas, it was possible to extend the offer to the whole of London.

Despite a concerted propaganda effort, only 2,600 'useless mouths' had left London by the end of September, and each month fewer and fewer left. And some, despite the air raids, were flooding back. Traditionally thousands of East Enders took an 'oppin' 'oliday each September, enjoying a dose of open air while working picking hops on Kentish farms. So when the raids started, such hoppers were out of London, and there was pressure that they should be encouraged to stay away. Negotiations dragged on, and finally Kent's local authorities agreed to billet those hop-pickers who wanted to stay, though in many cases the father was obliged to return, since he was likely to be either in the forces or in a reserved occupation employed on war production.

The solution wasn't just finding an empty house: people needed furniture, cooking equipment, bedding, clothing – and money too. Again, the voluntary organisations stepped in in the first instance: the Lord Mayor's Air Raid Relief Fund, which by the end of the war stood at nearly £5 million, paid for the WVS to provide warm clothing and bedding. It had made £1,000 available to the Mayor of Stepney for relief work, 'with no questions asked. He gives it to everyone who applies – chits to his friends' shops to allow them to buy up to a specified amount with no receipts asked for and no enquiry as to the genuineness of the applicant. This is a complete contrast to the local officials who make it so tiresome and difficult for anyone to get a penny that they usually give up trying! There seems to be no happy medium,' bemoaned Rachel Reckitt.

When Henry Willink was appointed as Commissioner, he made clear where responsibilities lay. Local authorities were tasked with resettling homeless people in fresh accommodation. Social workers and housing officers were detailed to help in the process, and those who dealt with the public were reminded what traumas they had been through and encouraged to lose their 'hungry thirties' inquisitorial and punitive rigidity, and to be as helpful and flexible as they could. Welfare advisers were appointed at rest shelters to give advice and information, and staff from the Assistance Boards went into the shelters and rest centres (rather than expecting the bombees to trail round half a dozen offices) to tell people what they were entitled to, handing out hardship money there and then if necessary. The Ministry of Information printed 50,000 leaflets that were distributed to all blitzed towns in January 1941, giving such essential information as

> *You can get drinking water at . . .*
> *Drink only boiled water and milk*
> *Rest Centres are at . . .*
> *Transport for . . . will leave at . . .*
> *For help and information go to . . .*

The Assistance Board also kitted out a number of vehicles as mobile information centres, complete with loudspeakers, that could be sent to an 'incident' to broadcast important information. By late October 1940, various 'one-stop shops' had extended the work of the Citizens Advice Bureaux, and by the end of the blitz, where there had been none at all in September, there were seventy-eight information centres and twenty-one administrative centres, pulling together a range of services and information that unfortunate air-raid victims had had to trudge miles on fruitless quests to obtain previously. But the work of the CABs was still essential in dealing with a wide variety of problems, such as the effects of wartime legislation, compassionate leave for members of the forces, making sure that servicemen overseas knew what had happened to their families, people's pension entitlements and a myriad other things. From two hundred CABs just after the outbreak of war, by 1942 there were over a thousand dotted all over the country, housed in village halls, schools, cafés, anywhere there was room for a table and a telephone.

Most people had no wish to leave their local areas: they wanted their homes repaired, and to be able to move back in as soon as possible. But materials were short, labour was short, and it was often many weeks before anything was done – during which the condition of the property deteriorated further, with rain pouring in. At one time 6,000 roof tilers were required in London alone – more than existed in the whole country. Priority had been given to getting utilities fixed, roads clear and railways running, but with winter fast approaching, the need to make houses weatherproof became more urgent. As usual, Stepney suffered more than most: by 11 November 1940, about 40 per cent of its houses had been damaged. Many of these were so shoddily built that they were not worth repairing, and there was no billeting or rehousing officer in the borough. The War Office was persuaded to second 5,000 men of the Pioneer Corps, most with some experience of the building trade, while more building workers were included on the register of reserved occupations, and 3,000 sappers were drafted to help repair public utilities. Squads of these men would be ready to move anywhere in the country where heavy raids had made their services necessary. Repairs could be little more than rudimentary, costing on average £8 or £9 per house – tacking on roofing felt, stretching tarpaulins, boarding up windows with 'opaque material' – but these could at least make buildings just about habitable.

Insurance companies had made it clear before hostilities broke out that their policies did not include war damage. The government made equally clear its intention to give compensation for such damage 'at the end of the war but not before'. Money would only be paid to reimburse actual physical losses and the essential repair of damage, not contingent ones such as loss of trade. The amount would be calculated as the cost of 'reasonably reinstating the property to its former condition in line with building costs in March 1939'. Although the processing of claims was speeded up during the blitz, many people had to wait until years after 1945 to get payment.

The responsibility of repairing the property fell on the owner or the landlord, who would foot the bill and reclaim the costs after the war, although the council would carry out the work 'if there was a housing shortage or the owner or the landlord was unwilling or unable to do so'. If a badly damaged house was rented from a private landlord (and at the start of the war around 60 per cent of the residential property in Britain was rented from private landlords) the tenant could decline to pay rent, but if he or she wanted to hold on to the lease, they had to do the repairs (or have them done) as soon as possible, though they would not have to pay rent until the property was habitable again. A landlord who refused to release the tenant from his or her lease had to complete the repairs as soon as possible. If only part of the house was habitable, the rent was to be adjusted accordingly – the amount to be decided by the courts if necessary.

If the house was being bought on a mortgage, there was no legal obligation on the building society to make good the damage, but it was hoped that it would behave like a responsible landlord and do so. The mortgagee was not, however, released from the liability to pay the mortgage: if the property was beyond repair and he or she had nowhere to live or carry on their business, an £800 grant could be claimed, part of which was intended to be used to pay off the mortgage.

Local authorities were empowered to requisition halls, warehouses or garages to store furniture salvaged from people's bombed-out houses, so they could claim it when they had somewhere to put it. This had been a matter of some difficulty. 'The big problem is what to do with the furniture that might be salvaged from bombed houses, if anyone would do it. The owners have to watch it rapidly deteriorate in the bad weather,' worried Rachel Reckitt. There simply weren't enough removal vans to transport all the furniture that needed moving, and people were reluctant to leave it in their uninhabitable homes, for fear of looting. Some unscrupulous firms were profiting from the shortfall by hiking up their prices to levels most East Enders could not contemplate. Now local authorities started to provide or rent their own removal vans.

If a householder needed to put furniture into storage, grants were available to cover that cost, but nothing could be paid out on furniture that had deteriorated as the result of being left in a bombed-out property. Claims could be made for lost possessions – cars, clothes, jewellery, ornaments and suchlike – valued at market or repair value 'at the date of damage'. This would not be paid until after the war, but for those with an annual income of less than £400 it was possible to get an advance: more than that and it was considered that you had a sufficient financial cushion not to need state help.

Thus, slowly and falteringly, the gross deficiencies of the early days of the blitz – honestly and disarmingly admitted by the Minister of Health Malcolm MacDonald, son of Ramsay – were largely rectified. It was hardly surprising that many local authorities had seemed paralysed by the magnitude of the problems they faced in those first days. As Ritchie Calder put it crisply, 'To leave local officials to deal with the . . . situation was like leaving the mayor of Dunkirk to evacuate the British Expeditionary Force.'

At the outbreak of war, another layer of administration had been inserted between Whitehall and the local authorities. Britain had been divided into Civil Defence regions, each with an unelected Regional Commissioner. These 'miniature governments' were intended to be capable of acting autonomously, taking full control of their regions should communication links with Whitehall be severed as a result of invasion, bombardment or some other act of war. The then Home Secretary, Sir John Anderson, was quick to assure local authorities that this was a wartime measure only: the regional government structure would be disbanded as soon as peace came.

Exceptionally, the London region had two Regional Commissioners working under the Senior Commissioner, Captain Euan Wallace, until

January 1941, and after his resignation on health grounds Sir Ernest Gowers was promoted to the post. A senior civil servant, Gowers concentrated on 'indoors' administration, while the more charismatic Admiral Sir Edward Evans concentrated on being outdoors and particularly in liaising with the local authorities in the region. Sir Harold Scott was Chief Administrative Officer of Number Five (London) Civil Defence Region, which comprised approximately 720 square miles of the Metropolitan Police District. Operating out of his HQ in the steel-framed Geographical Survey and Museum in South Kensington, Scott divided the region into nine groups, each containing a number of boroughs and each under a Group Control Officer. This imposed reorganisation was not entirely popular. After October 1940 Evans, and on occasion Gowers, started to hold regular meetings with the Town Clerk of each borough, who was usually also the ARP Controller – though many declined to attend: on 23 October only sixteen Town Clerks, out of ninety-five boroughs in the London region, turned up.

Group Number Three, which comprised the City of London, Holborn, Finsbury and the East End, with its HQ in a 'dingy Weights and Measures office behind Shoreditch Parish Church', was to be the hardest hit and most tautly stretched of all the groups. It was also the most disputatious, and in at least two cases the most disastrously incompetent. In Stepney, one of the worst-hit East End boroughs in the first days of the blitz and thereafter, the ARP Controller was not the Town Clerk but the leader of the council, Councillor M.H. (Morry) Davis, an appointment that was contrary to government advice that a council official, rather than an elected representative, should take the post. He incurred the anger of both the government and the Regional Commissioners as stories of the appalling state of the Tilbury shelter in particular, and other shelters and rest centres in Stepney, were splashed across the press (usually in reports by Ritchie Calder). Though some Stepney residents thought Davis was a 'great guy', to others he was 'a swine'. The opinion of one local man was trenchant. 'Davis is responsible for all this,' he said, gesturing to the devastated streets. 'Davis. Bloody lot of matchboxes he gives us. There ain't a shelter in the whole fucking place, there ain't one. Matchboxes, that's what he gives us. Blow on them and they'll go to pieces. That blasted Davis, I'd like to lay me hands on him.'

Winston Churchill insisted that Davis must be 'superseded' (that is, sacked), and he was succeeded as ARP Controller by E. Arnold James, the Town Clerk. But James, perpetually torn between the instructions from the Ministry of Home Security and the 'views and policies of the Council', which it was his job to serve, fared no better, and after two months in the job he resigned in anticipation of being dismissed.

In this war within the war, the Minister of Home Security, Herbert Morrison, acted decisively, parachuting in someone from outside the borough as ARP Controller. Eric Adams, Town Clerk of Islington, was a 'civil dictator', *The Times* charged. Predictably, the skirmishes continued, but within six months, operating out of the People's Palace theatre on the Mile End Road, since Stepney Council's offices at Wapping, adjacent to the docks, had been destroyed on the first night of the blitz, Adams had improved the situation sufficiently for him to be able to go back to Islington (with an OBE). However, Morrison refused to return the control of Stepney Civil Defence to the borough until almost the end of the war, by which time Davis was in prison for an unrelated offence (travelling on the tube without a ticket, and some shady dealings over a false identity card), and James had been removed from his post over a scandal about surcharging while he had been Town Clerk of Finsbury at the time of the proposals to build deep shelters.

West Ham's was a sorry saga too. Silvertown, Canning Town and the docks had been battered by bombs. Shops were boarded up, the borough's thirty-five cinemas reduced to two by the end of 1940, pubs – 'formerly so numerous' – reduced to rubble, drab terraced houses destroyed or exposed to the elements as if a giant tin opener had wrenched them open, showing the peeling paint and faded wallpaper within. It was a fractured and desolate place. Now the territory largely of the old, and of scavenging cats and vermin, it was badly served by those with a duty to care. Although West Ham could boast Britain's first (Independent) Labour MP, Keir Hardie, elected in 1892, by 1939 its local politics were in a parlous state. There were sixty-four councillors: at the outbreak of war, fifty-seven of these were Labour; the opposition totalled only seven. And the councillors were getting on a bit – most were around sixty and had lost their vigour and drive, while many of the younger, more energetic, better-educated men of the borough worked for the local authority, and were therefore debarred from seeking election. And in wartime the challenges were, to say the least, 'quite novel and could not be carried out by reference to precedence'.

In West Ham, the profoundly taxing problems of providing air-raid shelters, coordinating ARP activities, clothing and feeding the bombees and housing the homeless, proved beyond the council's capabilities. The situation had not been helped by the government prevaricating so long before laying the responsibilities of Civil Defence provision on a deprived borough.

It was also exacerbated by the fact that West Ham had a strong pacifist tradition, and the council was therefore reluctant to undertake activities and spend ratepayers' money in ways that could be regarded as provocatively warmongering before hostilities started. In addition, West Ham was still repaying £4,400 a year on a Goschen loan, extended to boroughs after the First World War to undertake projects intended to relieve unemployment in their area. Pleas by local MPs to have this remitted had fallen on deaf ears in Whitehall.

West Ham would get through four ARP Controllers in quick succession. Despite the scale of its problems, the borough councillors objected to 'interference in their household' by Whitehall, and thought it would be humiliating for the Mayor-Elect to be subservient to the ARP Controller. A compromise had been reached whereby the Deputy Town Clerk was appointed Controller, and the Mayor Chairman of the Emergency Committee. But in March 1941, after a few relatively quiet weeks during which the Controller had gone off to visit his daughter, who had been evacuated to the country, there was a very heavy raid on West Ham. The Controller's absence, and the general fiasco that ensued, led to Herbert Morrison threatening to take responsibility for Civil Defence away from West Ham and put it in the hands of the Regional Commissioner. In the event, and with the unfortunate example of Stepney fresh in everyone's minds, this was averted, and instead a greatly respected local Presbyterian minister, the Reverend W.W. Paton (a friend of Ritchie Calder, and known throughout the area as 'The Guv'nor'), was appointed ARP Controller despite his youth and relative inexperience as a councillor. Things improved, but as the Regional Commissioner reported to Morrison in August, 'The task of getting an efficient machine set up in West Ham seems almost hopeless, and we may ask for the supersession of the Council' – though again they didn't.

When Southampton was bombed at the end of November 1940, the ARP Controller (and Town Clerk) was found to be 'entirely unsuited to coping with emergencies', the Mayor was adjudged 'a poor creature', and the Chief Constable went sick after the second night of bombing. A group of RAF officers temporarily assumed control of the city's Civil Defence, until Robert Bernays, MP for Bristol North and a Deputy Regional Commissioner, was appointed by the Commissioners of the Southern Region to take charge. Liverpool too had its problems, as did Plymouth and Coventry, whose Town Clerk was considered 'a joke and nonentity and no one takes any notice of him' by the Regional Commissioner.

Although the Regional Commissioners were always presented as a wartime expedient that would fade away when democratic politics were reasserted after the war, the not infrequent chaos, the crossed lines, the lack of administrative competence and the general second-rateness of some local politicians did cause many people to wonder if one of the lessons of the war might be that politics needed radical restructuring.

Enthusiasm for a greater role for the state and more central control had been a recurring theme of the left throughout the thirties. National public works initiatives had seemed the answer to intractably high rates of unemployment, and nationalisation had been proposed as the solution to the inefficiencies, underinvestment and poor labour relations in industries such as coal mining and the railways. As it was increasingly clear that the network of panel doctors, local and voluntary hospitals was not answering the needs of the sick (there had been considerable debate as to the degree to which voluntary hospitals could be conscripted into the war effort during the blitz and how they would be compensated), blueprints had been produced and schemes canvassed for a state-funded national health service. Now it seemed that the war in general and the blitz in particular had thrown these deficiencies into sharp relief and provided a compelling need, a possible model and rather unusual laboratory conditions for testing a new way of governing Britain.

For Ritchie Calder the 'lesson of London' – by this he meant the way the capital had dealt with the social consequences of the blitz – urgently needed to be learned by those in authority in the rest of the country. His idea, endlessly plugged, was for a Welfare Board for London, 'embracing the whole local authority system and coordinating the work of the various ministries', and presumably extended throughout the country. This would not be a simple matter: nor would the fanciful call of Tom Harrisson of Mass-Observation for a Ministry of the Everyday, a special branch of government to deal with the whole human problem, 'a wide-awake unit composed of ordinary people . . . to foresee the difficulties caused by the human factor'.

There was a long way to go. The War Office, which might have been expected to have some idea of how to deal with bomb damage efficiently, was reported to have been unable to organise clearing up the shattered glass from its own corridors for a fortnight after the windows had been blown out by bomb blast. When the Borough Engineer of Stockton-on-Tees suggested that it might be useful to organise a party of his colleagues from other northern towns to come to London to see how the capital was managing, the Minister of Home Security brusquely rejected the idea.

But for Calder, the lesson was bigger than picking up some useful tips. After all, an epoch had come 'crashing down in the angry brown dust of crumbling property. The ruins of the Victorian town houses in the West End and of the slums of the East End were apocalyptic; they were symbolic of the catastrophic End of an Age . . . Profound administrative lessons have been taught by London's experience. Drastic reorganization of local government is necessary, not only in terms of war needs, but of peace-time reconstruction. It has been shown that the present system of artificially defined boroughs is just as inadequate to the needs of the day as the Vestries – parish units – were at the end of the last century.'

The campaigning journalist Calder would doubtless have been less than enthusiastic about keeping in post the unelected Regional Commissioners such as Lord Geddes for the South-East, Lord Dudley in the Midlands (regarded by William Mabane at the Ministry of Home Security as 'the least successful Regional Commissioner') and the financier Lord Harlech ('the best', according to Mabane) in their wartime form. At the start of the war, such Commissioners tended to be county worthies, landowners and gentry, ex-military men and Indian Civil Servants who had proved their administrative competence in the Empire, though Geddes had been a professor of anatomy, Director of Recruiting at the War Office in the First World War and an MP. Later in the war Herbert Morrison appointed several Labour men as Deputy Commissioners, including William Asbury, a trade unionist and Chairman of the Sheffield Emergency Committee throughout the blitz, who took up the post in the Southern Region in September 1942, and went on to fulfil a similar administrative role in the British Zone in Germany after the war. Rather Calder sought structural democratic change, wanting to retain the Regional Councils, set up Regional Welfare Boards, and consolidate communal feeding arrangements as the first step towards 'a sensible food-economy and . . . post war nutritional service'. And since evacuation had taken city dwellers into the countryside, they would act like 'Trojan horses invad[ing] the strongholds of Toryism' to bring about this essentially socialist state.

Barbara Nixon had absorbed the 'Lesson of Finsbury', and come up with similar conclusions. She had applauded the idea of local control in principle, but in practice had realised that it depended on a cadre of competent local leaders which she had not found, and this lack had led to overlapping responsibilities, territorial stand-offs, confusingly different ways of doing things in different boroughs, unproductive conflict between the boroughs and the LCC, and insufficient democracy on the ground, since 'Far too many people think that democracy means the maximum of non-interference by the State in their affairs, instead of the maximum interest and interference by them in State affairs.'

William Robson, in 1930 founder with Leonard Woolf of the journal *Political Quarterly*, and a longstanding advocate of local government reform, seized the wartime moment, and in February 1941 wrote an article for *Picture Post*, a pithier version of one he had contributed to his own journal under the byline 'Regionaliter', reminding readers that 'Regional Government has been demanded by every competent expert and innumerable Royal Commissions and committees. Unfortunately vested municipal interests . . . resolutely set their faces against any far reaching reform . . . the Regional Commissioners . . . are an experiment of the highest interest and impor-tance . . . when peace comes [we must ensure] that the Regional Commissioners are replaced by directly elected regional councils above a tier of local councils.'

But the notion of such reform was aborted even before the war was over. By 1943 various committees had in effect concluded that while regional bodies were 'absolutely justified' in wartime, there was not 'a sufficient case for adopting any similar system as a permanent administrative organisa-tion in time of peace'. And in 1945, as the various Civil Defence functions were wound up and personnel discharged, the newly elected Labour govern-ment accepted the recommendations of the White Paper on Local Government Reform, and congratulated local authorities on their wartime work, and, while recognising that the discrepancy in size between some metropolitan boroughs was problematic, stated that it could see no case for prolonging the life of a wartime expediency. In the case of local govern-ment the status quo was – and pretty much remains – the option. But there were other lessons learned in the laboratory that was the blitz, that would be tested and in some cases put into practice in the post-war years.

7

Guernicaed

Well, workers, it's hard luck on Coventry and, of course, it's hard luck on the workers and we're going to tell you something you may have cause to remember. It's this. Coventry is the first place to be attacked in this way, outside of London and Liverpool, but we are bloody sure it's not going to be the last . . . Most people thought it wouldn't be too easy to smash up one of the biggest production bases in the country, but it was . . . There has never been such a bombardment before, either in this country or anywhere else in the world, relative to the size of the town . . . and the main question now is 'What's next on the list?'

A broadcast at 9.10 p.m. on Saturday, 16 November 1940 by Workers' Challenge, a 'black' radio station broadcasting from Nazi Germany, but purportedly run by dissident British workers

The raids on London that had been continuous throughout September and October 1940 seemed to have begun to tail off. The night of 3–4 November was the first since the blitz had begun on 7 September that the alert had not sounded. But on Friday, 15 November Anthony Heap's diary recorded, 'Terrific raid on Coventry last night. Cathedral among buildings destroyed. Not a particularly attractive town architecturally but important commercially.' It wasn't Coventry's first attack: besides the IRA bombs that had ripped through the city in the summer of 1939, killing five people and injuring many more, it had suffered intermittent raids since August 1940. In September sixteen people had been killed in a raid, a few days later the Standard Motor works at Canley had been badly damaged and several people injured, the Rex Cinema was hit, and in mid-October several elderly residents and the matron had been killed when Ford's Hospital, an old people's home, was bombed. By 14 November, 448 people had been killed or seriously injured in Coventry as a result of enemy action. Moreover, every time it looked as if the bombers were making for nearby Birmingham, the sirens would sound in Coventry too.

Anthony Heap may have considered Coventry to have few redeeming architectural features, but the city could trace its origins back three centuries before Leofric, the Saxon Earl of Mercia, established a Benedictine monastery there in 1043 and his wife Godiva, according to legend, rode naked on horseback (or maybe it was the horse that was naked, i.e. unsaddled) through the streets to 'free the town of Coventry from heavy bondage'. A cloth town since the Middle Ages, and always an important commercial centre, Coventry had boasted some important Tudor buildings, including Ford's Hospital, founded in 1509, which had been so badly damaged by the Luftwaffe, and St Mary's Hall (formerly the Guildhall), a fifteenth-century building that had served as the city's seat of government for a time. But most prized of all were the churches that gave Coventry its epithet 'The City of Three Spires': the fourteenth-century Christ Church, Holy Trinity and St Michael's, described as 'one of the largest and most beautiful of all those churches built in England 600 years ago in the new style [Perpendicular] in which English builders had broken away from the lavish continental style to something peculiarly English in form'.

By the 1930s clothmaking and later ribbon-making had largely given way to the manufacture of synthetic fabrics (Courtaulds had built a vast modern factory) and engineering. Known as the 'bicycle capital of the world', Coventry was tightly packed with small factories and workshops manufacturing machine tools and car parts, cheek by jowl with ancient buildings, shops and houses. This industrial modernism meant that the city had managed to escape the worst of the Depression, and had benefited greatly from the government's rearmament programme. Its population had more than doubled since the start of the twentieth century, and in 1940 it stood at nearly a quarter of a million.

Coventry was in the front line of Britain's 'battle for production': many of the small workshops in the city had turned to making components vital to the war effort, such as the watchmaking firm Fred Lee, that by 1940 was producing industrial jewels for compass bearings instead of timepieces. Three-quarters of all the gauges used in the nation's armaments were made in Coventry, Dunlop put aside most of its car- and cycle-tyre manufacture work to turn out tyres for aircraft and barrage balloons, and anti-gas clothing, while GEC was producing VHF radio sets to be used in fighter defence and Courtaulds was making up its synthetic fabrics, including nylon, into parachutes. Vickers Armstrong and Hawker Siddeley were turning out engines and frames for Blenheim light bombers, Avro Ansons and soon Stirlings and Lancasters too. The Rolls-Royce factory was stripping and recondi-tioning its engines, including the famous Merlin, to power Spitfire and Hurricane fighter planes. In addition, at the request of the Air Ministry, by 1940 Coventry was ringed by a belt of so-called shadow factories that could take over manufacture should the original ones be knocked out of action by a raid. It was front-line stuff, and it made the Midlands city a target in Germany's campaign to defeat Britain by crippling its capacity to wage war. Indeed, Coventry had been assigned as a 'key target' in pre-war air defence exercises, second only to London.

Against the dates 14 and 15 November on the calendar for 1940 was an empty circle, the symbol for a full moon. A hunter's or a poacher's moon, as it had been called in peacetime, now renamed a 'bomber's moon', some-thing to be dreaded for the bright light that would make it easier for the German bombers to home in on their targets. The Air Ministry fully expected a heavy raid that night. But where?

On 11 November the code-breakers at Bletchley Park had revealed that the Luftwaffe was planning a major attack imminently; and overheard boast-ings by a German prisoner of war, coupled with intelligence about the posi-tioning of X-Gerat, the device that threw intersected beams over a target to guide German bombers, which then released their bombs, indicated that the attack was likely to be on the Midlands: Wolverhampton, Birmingham and Coventry were all in the frame for 'Moonlight Sonata', as the operation was code-named. If it was clear which was the target, then as well as massing fighter planes above it, and training the full panoply of AA guns, a brilliant device invented by Dr (later Professor) R.V. Jones could, by means of radio transmission, 'bend' the beam guiding the bombers and throw the pilots off target. But that was only possible if the target had been definitively iden-tified – which it hadn't.

At 5 p.m. on 14 November the crews of Kampfgruppe 100 were being briefed at their base near Saint-Nazaire, on France's Atlantic coast. 'Our task is to repay the raid [on Munich] of the English during the night of 8 November [the anniversary of the 1923 Beer Hall Putsch],' they were told. 'We shall not repay it in the same manner by smashing up harmless dwelling houses, but we shall do it in such a way that those over there will be completely stunned. Even though the raid on Munich by the "gentlemen" of the Royal Air Force was a complete failure, neither the Führer nor our Commander-in-Chief, Reichsmarschall Göring, is willing to let even an attempt to carry out an attack on the capital of the [Nazi] movement go unpunished, and we have therefore received orders to destroy the industries of Coventry tonight. You know what this means, comrades . . . If we can paralyse the armament centre tonight, we shall have dealt another heavy blow to Herr Churchill's war production . . . tomorrow morning the factories there must lie in smoke and ruins. We rest till 7.30. Then we get ready for take off . . . comrades, good luck!'

At 7.07 p.m. on the day that the former Prime Minister Neville Chamberlain was cremated in London, and on which at a service in Birmingham, his native city, the Bishop pointed out that while Chamberlain had not succeeded in his 'valiant efforts for peace', he had 'failed greatly', the 'Air Raid Message Yellow', 'Raiders Approaching Your Area', was received at the ARP control room in Coventry's Council House. Three minutes later the signal changed to 'Air Raid Message Red', 'Raiders Overhead', and as the ululating, mournful notes of the siren hung in the dark, the first bombs began to fall.

An incessant shower of incendiary bombs rained down, many suspended in the air like chandeliers before they lodged on rooftops or fell to the ground. The last bus leaving Coventry for Leamington nosed its way out of the city, its lights turned off, but they weren't needed: the glare from the burning incendiaries made it light enough for commuters to read their evening papers. Owen Owen, Coventry's department store, was soon ablaze, and within an hour there were already 240 fires plotted on the map in the Central Fire Station; it became a pointless enterprise to stick in any more pins, as the whole of the city centre seemed alight. Then, following the incendiaries, high-explosive bombs and land mines came crashing down. A five-hundred-pound bomb went straight through the roof of Sir Alfred Herbert's works in Canal Lane two and a half miles from the city centre; the main Daimler factory was struck by two land mines, several HE bombs and dozens of incendiaries; and the 'shadow factory' was hit too.

By 9.30 'a halo of red flames' could be clearly seen from Warwick, seven miles away, and Birmingham, eighteen miles to the west, and both sent convoys of fire engines and men clanging through the country lanes to help fight the conflagration, though many of the phone lines were down, and it was difficult to communicate directly with the Coventry authorities to find out exactly what was required. Herbert Morrison was on one of his first tours of the provinces as Minister of Home Security, and that night he was dining with the Regional Commissioner of the West Midlands, Lord Dudley, at Himley Hall, thirty miles away, as was Wing Commander John Hodsoll, Inspector General of Civil Defence. As they were sitting down to a champagne supper, news came through of the attack. The party hurried outside, and could see 'flames already lighting the clear sky over Coventry'.

The *Daily Express* journalist Hilde Marchant was in Birmingham 'the night they Guernicaed Coventry'. She was sitting in a hotel lounge drinking black coffee and talking to some Midlanders who felt aggrieved that though they too had been bombed, the newspapers took little notice: it was all London, London, London. That night the balance would be redressed. 'Looks Coventry way,' ventured a porter as wave after wave of planes droned overhead.

Winston Churchill had been apprised of the situation, and after dining 'excellently and in great comfort' in 'the burrow' (Down Street underground station), he spent an anxious night on the Air Ministry roof watching the situation develop.

The raid lasted for eleven hours. By 8.30 p.m. 'Coventry appeared to be ablaze from end to end . . . The smell of smoke and ceiling plaster was stifling . . . Fire engines and ambulances were screaming past. People were streaming out of the alleys and courts, panic stricken, and it was obvious that that terribly crowded district was suffering.' The Coventry and Warwickshire Hospital, near the ordnance factory, displayed a lighted red cross on its roof to indicate its status. But to no avail that night: a bomb crashed onto the men's ward. Dr Harry Winter watched 'the whole wall of the building fall slowly outward and crash across the open ground where we'd been a few seconds before'.

We put patients on stretchers and blankets along the main floor corridors, which were already so crowded that I had to tread carefully from one end of the hospital to the other. Then the casualties started to come in from outside.

We had made elaborate preparations about classifying the patients as they came in but they began to arrive so fast that we didn't have time for detailed examinations. All we could do was divide them roughly into resuscitation cases and those requiring immediate surgery. The resuscitation cases were whisked into beds and given electric blankets and oxygen to help them recover from the shock of their wounds. The immediate surgery cases were divided among the three theatres. I suppose I did about fifteen operations throughout the night . . . The other theatres handled about forty . . .

We couldn't work very rapidly. The majority of cases were lacerations or injuries to limbs. The complication with bomb lacerations . . . is that you get a small wound on the surface but extensive disruption underneath. Everything is pulped together. It's no good fixing the surface wound without doing a major cutting job on the inside . . .

Every few minutes the theatre shook with the thud of a nearby bomb. About midnight the electric power went off but I continued with the operations I was on by the light of two small bulbs run by our own emergency lighting system. Every few minutes, the nurses and the anaesthetist threw themselves under the operating table as the bombs roared down. I didn't like to follow them, but every time one whisked uncomfortably close I instinctively pulled the knife away and ducked sideways . . .

Up on the top floor of the Gynaecological Ward we had fifteen women whom we couldn't move. They stayed in their beds through it all without a complaint, although the bomb that smashed the staff quarters next door covered them in glass . . . and plaster. In another wing we had to leave a dozen fracture cases. All night long they lay on their backs, unable to move, hung up on their frames, and watched the Jerry planes cruising about the firelit sky through a huge hole that had been blown out of the wall of their ward.

A young woman recovering from an operation in the hospital was

carried down a large curving staircase in my bed by soldiers to the basement . . . As they left me, a bomb screamed and I screamed with it. One soldier ran back, folded me in his arms and rocked me. Other patients then joined me and all night the noise of screaming bombs was terrible . . . Twenty high-explosive bombs fell on the hospital, five were direct hits and all but around a hundred of the 1,600 windows were blown out . . .

[In the morning] my father turned up looking haggard and afraid. Where my bed had stood in the ward was a large hole, so he thought the worst. My family had watched from the village [where we lived], fearing for me, their eldest, helpless in the hell that was Coventry. My father helped to carry me out to a waiting ambulance, pulling the blanket over my face because he said it was cold, but really so that I should not see the rows of bodies lying there.

It was much the same for a student nurse at Gulson Road Hospital.

Wendell Willkie, the defeated Republican candidate in the 1940 US presidential election, toured the Midlands, determined to 'see things for himself' in Britain's blitzed towns and cities. On 3 February 1941, accompanied by the Bishop of Coventry and the city's Mayor, Willkie inspected Coventry Cathedral, which had been all but razed in the raid of 14–15 November 1940.

Merseyside was second only to London in the continuous bomb damage it sustained: 70,000 people were left homeless. Here, an elderly couple walk through a devastated Liverpool street after the so-called 'Christmas raids' on the area in 1940.

King George VI and Queen Elizabeth survey the wreckage at Buckingham Palace caused by a high-explosive bomb on 13 September 1940. They are seen here talking to one of the palace's ARP wardens.

A Molotov 'breadbasket' of incendiary bombs fell on Holland House, the Jacobean London residence of Lord Ilchester and the great centre of Whig society in the eighteenth and early nineteenth centuries, on 28 September 1940. Firemen managed to save parts of the east wing, but much of the rest of the house was destroyed. The famous library, designed by the architect John Thorpe, was gutted.

Ethel Gabain looking *soignée* while perched on rubble and debris, painting a blitzed building in November 1940. Gabain, best known as a portraitist, was employed by the War Artists' Advisory Committee to record the war on the home front. In May 1941 hers were among the works sent for the exhibition 'Britain at War' at the Museum of Modern Art in New York.

St Paul's Cathedral, surrounded by ruins, but a survivor of the devastating raid on the City of London on 29 December 1940.

The beds began to fill up very quickly. The operating theatres began their tasks. Sometimes we would have to clear away thick dirt before seeing the patient: they seemed to have been dug out of the ground . . . We were using emergency supplies and hurricane lamps. The casualties then became a never-ending stream . . . we were conscious of the very heavy bombing that was going on around us . . . but most of the nurses felt secure hearing the guns on the factory roof. At one time two floors of the factory were on fire, but the men manning the gun never moved. We heard later that they had promised to protect 'their nurses' at all costs . . .

Everyone was working as a member of a team . . . even the consultants, who were normally treated like little gods . . . became human. During the course of my training, I had always the fear of being left with the limb of a patient in my hand after amputation . . . the blitz on Coventry changed all that for me. I didn't have the time to be squeamish . . . Thousands of patients passed through the hospital that night. If a patient died, he was just taken out of the bed and it was remade to take the next patient.

All night, huddled in public shelters, frightened Coventarians would hear snatches of news from ARP wardens who poked their heads in: 'The Birmingham Road's blocked,' 'Woolworth's gone,' 'The cathedral's on fire.' A child, sheltering with her sister in their nightclothes, was driven from under the stairs when their house north-west of the city centre was hit. Running along the street to the public shelter she found that 'although it was November . . . the air was hot and acrid. It was brilliant moonlight and with all the fires it was as bright as day and the sky was red, "just like blood", I remember thinking, and then suddenly I was deadly frightened. And so we ran down that road, which reminded me vividly of a film I had seen, *The Last Days of Pompeii*, with the buildings on fire and dropping into the road as we ran. It seemed we ran miles and miles until we got to the public shelter, which was crammed with people, who were packed further in to make room for us. Children were crying and screaming, women were weeping, and everybody scared stiff.'

Just before midnight, a further wave of bombers swept across Coventry. They had no need of navigational aids now: the burning city was a beacon, their targets illuminated as clear as day. Since 8.47 p.m. all the telephones at the Central Fire Station except one private line to the control centre had been out of order for outgoing calls, and only two incoming lines were working spasmodically. Any calls that did get through were used to transmit requests for additional help. Birmingham Fire Service signalled to London, 'FIRE SITUATION AT COVENTRY EXTREMELY SERIOUS. CITY ALIGHT'. The canal bank had been breached by a bomb, and valuable water that could have helped to fight the fires flowed wastefully into the ground. Mobile water carriers, hose lorries and heavy pumps set off, the vehicles having to negotiate craters in the road as they approached the inferno that was Coventry.

By 1 a.m. the windows in the operating theatre at the Coventry and Warwickshire Hospital had all been blown out, and Dr Winter decided that since

> a bitter cold wind was blowing through the room it was too cold to uncover the patients and too cold to operate, for I was shivering from head to foot. The windows of the second floor theatre had also been blown out, so we were forced to move into the ground floor theatre where the windows were protected by a brick wall. We decided to take turns doing the operations, but since one theatre could not cope with the large number of cases, we could only take the more urgent ones. When I had a few minutes off between turns, I went along the corridor for a cigarette. It was an amazing scene . . . far worse than the descriptions I've heard of the front-line casualty clearing stations in the First World War. Patients were lying head to toe on every inch of space. The nurses were marvellous. With hurricane lamps and hand torches, they moved among the patients comforting them and giving them little sips of water . . . Near the entrance lobby I noticed the hospital superintendent. He was kneeling beside the patients lying on the floor, and as I passed along I could hear a few words of their prayer . . .
>
> Although we have only 440 beds, we had 275 patients when the raid started and I estimate that at least 300 more were admitted during the night. New patients were put on top of the beds while the old patients sheltered underneath them.
>
> By 4 a.m. I couldn't keep a steady hand any longer . . . Then our emergency light failed just as I was in the middle of an operation. We quickly rigged up an automatic headlamp to a battery set and I finished the job. Bombs were still crashing down, and every few minutes hunks of earth and debris crashed against the brick wall outside the theatre. By this time no one bothered to duck.

Terrified people were leaving the city, most on foot, many in their nightclothes. An aircraftsman was told to take an aircraft transporter and run a shuttle service, taking as many people as he could on each trip to a hangar on the outskirts of Coventry. Other drivers did the same, and soon there were more than a thousand people crammed into an empty hangar next to one housing five or six Wellington bombers.

The 'White Message', 'All Clear – Raiders Passed' signal did not reach Coventry until 6.16 a.m., and since the cables to the siren system had been severed in the raid, few people heard the eerie wail of a single siren echoing across the fields from outside the town, and did not emerge until they heard an ARP warden or a policeman yelling, 'It's all over, you can come out now.' In the drizzle and grey mist of that November morning, a truly terrible sight met their eyes. 'Hardly a building remained intact. It was impossible to see where the central streets . . . had been. Fires were still raging in all directions and from time to time there was the crash of a fallen roof or wall.' 'It was like an earthquake,' reported a senior regional officer in a censored memo.

The medieval and Tudor centre had suffered the worst in the raid – 'picturesque and fine for visitors, but the firemen cursed the [wood framed buildings]. The rickety roofs and floors fell into the cobbled streets, blocking the way for the fire engines.' A third of the city centre had been completely destroyed, mainly by fire, and at least another third would require extensive rebuilding, a Ministry of Home Security inspector who arrived in the city on the morning of Saturday, 16 November reported. The six-hundred-year-old cathedral was still smouldering, molten lead dripping from its roof. Coventry's would be the only cathedral in Britain destroyed during the war. It had no pillars or roof, just ruined aisles and piles of rubble, 'shattered cherubs, and twinkling stained glass . . . and a crumpled heap of brocade identified the altar', but its three-hundred-foot spire was still intact, pointing to the sky from whence its destruction had come. One in twelve of Coventry's houses and flats had been destroyed or rendered uninhabitable, and two-thirds of those remaining had been damaged. Thirty-five per cent of shops had been destroyed, from the large department store Owen Owen to small corner shops. At a 'very rough estimate' the Ministry of Home Security inspector ventured that two-thirds of Coventry's factories had been destroyed or put out of commission, including the Daimler factory (which had been hit by twenty-two HE bombs), the Humber Hillman works, the GEC factory and Sir Alfred Herbert Ltd's forty-acre factory site – all key participants in the 'Battle for Production'. Bombs blocked every railway line out of the city, and the stations, many of which were damaged, had to be closed. Water mains had been fractured, and one of the city's two gas holders had 'gone up like a giant firework', depriving households and factories of gas. The city's streets were impassable with debris and UXBs, huge craters yawned everywhere, a pall of greasy smoke hung over the streets, glass crunched underfoot, bodies lay tossed at grotesque angles, severed limbs and torsos an obscene and sickening sight. A woman watched soldiers in the street 'picking up bits of arms and legs and putting them in potato sacks as if they were working in a harvest field'. 'Coventry is a city of the dead,' wrote one resident to her daughter in London.

> We have no gas, electric light, and in most cases, no water. We have no milk or bread at the moment. Mobile vans are going round the town with bread and water. Loud speakers are going round telling the homeless where to meet to be taken out of the city . . . next door have completely vanished and the whole family buried underneath . . . Many land mines must have been used, as whole streets have vanished. There is nothing left of Broadgate, the Cathedral is in ruins, only the spire is left and that doesn't look safe. The Central Library has gone, the Market Hall has gone, in fact, I think it would be easier to say what hasn't gone.
>
> The centre of the town is roped off, no one is allowed within half a mile of it. There are so many unexploded bombs about that they are talking of blasting the town because none of the buildings seem safe . . . one can't get near the Council House for people waiting for death certificates and there are many thousands buried underneath Market Hall, Owen Owen, and other shelters. None of the factories is working. Everyone seems bewildered . . . Well, Beryl, we are safe so far and I don't see why we should be afraid now, for there is nothing left for them to bomb.

A 'major raid' was classified by both German and British authorities as one in which more than a hundred tons of high-explosive bombs were dropped. Five hundred tons of high-explosive bombs and 30,000 incendiaries had fallen on Coventry that night. Five hundred and sixty-eight people had been killed and 1,256 injured, many seriously. The dead included nine police, reservists and messengers, and eleven ARP wardens, one a woman. The toll would have been even heavier had not earlier raids driven people to seek shelter outside the city. And shelter provision in Coventry had been generally quite good – many of the factories had huge underground shelters, and there were seventy-nine public shelters, with room enough for 33,000 people.

Most, though not all, had stood up well to the raids. Nevertheless, in a city with a population of 238,400, it was certain that almost everyone in Coventry would know someone who had been killed or grievously injured during the eleven-hour attrition.

The next morning Hilde Marchant, sceptical of reports from 'the chambermaid, the waiter, the hall porter [that the Coventry raid] had been worse than anything before', set off from her Birmingham hotel to see for herself. Most cars were stopped and turned around, not allowed to enter the devastated city, but Marchant showed her press pass and was waved through the barrier, where she found 'a familiar sight – one I had seen in Spain and Finland . . . the people of Coventry were trekking out – not sure where they were going, what they would do, but just moving to try to get away from the sounds of the night . . . lorries were packed with women and children sitting on suitcases and bedding', others were on foot, pushing perambulators or handcarts. 'Five miles outside the town we had picked up the first thin smell of smoke, but as we went nearer the air thickened and carried charred bits of wood in through the car window. It was a heavy, stifling smell that bit into your throat and lungs . . . as we came to the edge of the city, the air became as warm as a spring day. Though it was noon, the city was darkened by the black fog that darkened the sky and the thick banks of soot that were suspended over the streets. The people who walked the streets had grimy faces and their eyes were reddened with the heat and smoke. They were walking slowly and without direction over the broken road and pavement.'

Most stayed in the city, 'even if it meant sitting among the rubble, boiling a battered kettle on a fire made of wood from the rafters, searching for lost possessions among the bricks, shattered wardrobes and smashed cupboards, huddled in a torn blanket or dusty best coat in a roofless kitchen . . . the shops and banks defiantly opened. The staff of Barclays stood on bricks to avoid the pools of water around them, with no heating or light, and with all the windows out. But before they opened they had to dig through the rubble to get to their strongrooms. Marks & Spencer opened, proudly proclaiming "Messrs Marks and Spencer of Smithford Street are playing their part in defying the activities of the Hun but opening in Whitefriars Street." That day too, the papers were back on the streets, sometimes inaccurate, occasionally hiding or distorting the depressed mood of the city . . . but describing the full horror of the previous night.'

As loudspeaker vans toured Coventry warning people to boil all water for fear of typhoid, and urging them to be inoculated, exhausted Civil Defence workers continued to dig in the rubble for survivors, and medical staff stood by to give injections of morphia. Marchant climbed through the window frame of a house next to the central police station, in the worst-bombed area. 'Stretching for about half a mile in front of the window was a bumpy, open plain broken only by an occasional girder that poked through the ruins like an open rib. There was no form or tracing left in the earth of the streets and houses that had been there. The foundations had been smashed into the ground. There were no bedsteads or tables to identify a home. No chimney pots or tattered roofs to define the shape of a house. Just a dead, dusty, petrified plain. That night the German High Command phrased it more sharply . . . "Our airmen used the technique of destruction which they have mastered." They invented the word "Coventrated" though I am a pedant and prefer the earlier version of "Guernicaed", where the technique was first rehearsed [in April 1937 during the Spanish Civil War].'

Herbert Morrison also arrived in Coventry the morning after the raid, accompanied by Lord Beaverbrook, who as Minister for Aircraft Production was concerned to see how badly factories had been damaged – some twenty-seven had been hit – and how quickly they could be back in production, and Ernest Brown, the Minister of Health. They had a very sticky encounter with the Mayor, J.A. Mosley, an ex-railwayman who with his wife had been rescued from their garden shelter to find their house wrecked, the Town Clerk and the Chairman of the city council's Emergency Committee, while the totally exhausted, unwashed and unshaven Chief Fire Officer fell asleep halfway through the meeting. The local officials demanded to know why the Luftwaffe had been allowed to fly over the city hour after hour, unchecked by RAF fighter planes or anti-aircraft defences – not that this was Morrison's responsibility. They also insisted that Civil Defence should be made compulsory, and that men should be exempted from military service to serve on the home front. To emphasise Coventry's plight, the Mayor offered the Minister a glass of whisky, apologising for the fact that there was no water in the city to go with it. For his part, Morrison was concerned at what he thought was an air of 'defeatism' in Coventry, and initially threatened to put the city under martial law. He dropped that idea, and left the Emergency Committee in charge, but 'gave orders right and left' to get things moving, arranging for the army to be brought in to help clear up – a few of the soldiers were armed, since there were fears that riots might break out.

Morrison was reasonably satisfied that the regional structure had worked well, with assistance coming to Coventry's aid from outside the city, but he was disturbed by the fact that when fire brigades from elsewhere arrived at stricken cities in the Midlands and the North, their hoses often would not fit the local hydrants, while some procedures varied so much between different brigades that 'they literally had to have interpreters on duty to explain to the visiting fire services what were meant by the words of some orders' – a potential disaster in a blitz situation. It was not the first time that Morrison had been made aware of these problems, but the Coventry blitz rammed them home, and he would work on fundamental changes to the Civil Defence services over the following weeks and months, trying to negotiate the many minefields in the delicate relations between local autonomy and central direction and organisation at a time of national emergency.

Beaverbrook confined his intervention to a metaphor-laden speech that irritated his listeners, who wanted reassurance and practical advice. What they got were high-flown references to the RAF having its roots deep in Coventry's aircraft industry, and the need for the city to rise from the ashes so that the 'tree' would 'burgeon, putting forth fresh leaves and branches'. However, despite the lack of power and water, the freezing conditions with windows blasted out and some buildings unstable, by December 1940 production had resumed in most of the damaged factories, if not at full output, and 80 per cent of the workforce were back on the shop floor.

Ritchie Calder, usually hot on the case of officials failing the people, was surprisingly upbeat after his visit to Coventry, reporting that the WVS had established rest centres at Kenilworth, and soon others opened in nearby towns. Florence Horsbrugh at the Ministry of Health had sent out an SOS to her Ministry's inspectors all over England, and they converged on Coventry to help sort out its catastrophe. By midday on Saturday the 16th, all the casualties had been moved out of the city. Twenty thousand blankets were sent into the area, as were 'loaves by the hundred thousands'. The Ministry of Food organised emergency supplies 'for a city that was almost destitute of food', and rationing was suspended, since so many people had lost their ration books, though shopkeepers instituted their own rough-and-ready system to make sure stocks would go round. The most acute need was for water: dozen of churns of milk arrived, brought by the Co-operative Dairies, and the WVS was even washing up in milk since the water pressure was so low. But soon water carts and flexible piping arrived. Soldiers cooked meals and staffed rest centres, and 'with experience of barrack room hygiene' advised people 'not to sleep with their heads close together but top to toe to avoid the spread of infection'. Calder was particularly impressed to witness men returning to their places of work to see if it was still standing – and to collect their pay – and women grubbing around in the debris to find bits of broken furniture with which to light a fire to cook their husbands' dinner.

Tom Harrisson had been in Birmingham on the night of the raid – a Mass-Observation team had been in Coventry for six weeks preparing a survey on war savings – and he drove straight over to Coventry the next morning. That evening three M-O investigators arrived to report on the situation. Their findings, which were not made public at the time, were rather different from those of Ritchie Calder.

The investigators found an unprecedented dislocation and depression in Coventry on Friday. There were more open signs of hysteria, terror, neurosis, observed in one evening than during the whole of the past two months together in all areas. Women were seen to cry, to scream, to tremble all over, to faint in the street, to attack a fireman, and so on.

The overwhelmingly dominant feeling on Friday was the feeling of utter helplessness. The tremendous impact of the previous night had left people practically speechless in many cases. And it made them feel impotent. There was no role for the civilian. Ordinary people had no idea what they should do . . . On Friday night there were several signs of suppressed panic as darkness approached. In two cases people were seen fighting to get on to cars, which they thought would take them out into the country, though in fact, the drivers insisted, the cars were just going up the road to the garage. If there had been another attack on Friday night, the effect in terms of human behaviour would have been much more striking and terrible. As it was, a quiet night, followed by a fine morning, changed the atmosphere for the better. This was not due to official activities which were centred almost entirely on the fires and debris.

The investigators saw 'no signs of any official mobile canteens, there was no use of loud speaker vans, of Information Committee notices, special announcements, or anything of that sort, though voluntary organisations did great work with individual families'. However, 'It should be stressed that *no sign whatever* was found of anti-war feeling, and there were very few grumbles. People were full of admiration for the A.R.P. and A.F.S. services, and no one was blamed for the alleged running out of water at about 2a.m.'

In sum, M-O concluded that the same shortcomings applied in the provinces as they had in the capital: plenty of forethought given to the material damage caused by an attack – casualties, dealing with fires, clearing up debris, etc. – but woefully little to the social and psychological effects, to how the homeless could be accommodated, or their houses repaired.

Although Churchill's private secretary John Colville wondered if the 'violent bombardment of Coventry [was] possibly the First Movement of the Sonata which may continue throughout the moon period', the bombers did not return on the Friday night. Since the railway into Coventry was so disrupted, the King motored from Windsor, arriving on Saturday morning. He offered to bring his own sandwiches so that the royal visit would not strain Coventry's limited resources, but that wasn't necessary: Lord Dudley sent his butler over with a cold lunch from Himley Hall, which was eaten in the Mayor's parlour in the company of Herbert Morrison, by the light of candles stuck in beer bottles on the table. Not very many Coventarians actually saw the King as he 'walked among the devastation' (more saw the newsreel later), but the monarch thought that 'they liked my coming to see them in their adversity', and Lord Dudley reported seeing people's faces 'light up when they recognised' him. However, the formidable WVS organiser Pearl Hyde, then a councillor, later mayor, declined to meet him, saying she was too busy, too dirty and wearing trousers. For his part, the King felt that Coventry was 'in a very sorry state . . . the old part & the centre of the town looks just like Ypres after the last war. The people were all dazed from the shock of it,' he wrote to his mother, Queen Mary, in the pink of health herself, but getting bored at Badminton. Harold Nicolson was amused by Morrison's 'almost sobbing reference to the King's visit' when he made his report to the Civil Defence Cabinet Committee the following Wednesday. 'He spoke about the King as Goebbels might have spoken about Hitler. I admit that the King does his job well. But why should Morrison speak as if he were a phenomenon? How odd these Labour people are!'

There was a grim and tragic coda to the raid. After Coventry's swimming pool, originally requisitioned as a mortuary, had been damaged in an earlier raid, a corrugated-iron-roofed building near the gasworks was designated to replace it. It had space for five hundred bodies. Luggage labels would be tied to each corpse with details of where it had been found, the identity if known, and the number of the ambulance that had taken it to the mortuary, written in indelible pencil. But during the raid, the bomb that hit the gasometer had also taken off the roof of the mortuary, and when it rained heavily a couple of nights later, the writing on the labels was almost washed off, making it near to impossible to identify the bodies. Relatives often had great difficulty in doing so, particularly if the person was a victim of bomb blast: as many as four people might claim the same body as that of their loved one.

The solution decided on was to strip each body of all its clothing and possessions: the body was then put in a coffin, and the possessions into a sandbag. Both were given the same number, which was entered into a register. Relatives were then invited to identify clothing or jewellery rather than the body. The system worked well, and most bodies were identified, but 'it was gruesome work which was done by the stretcher party personnel. A bottle of brandy was very useful.'

Since an unprecedented number of people had been killed on the same night, in a relatively small area, the Emergency Committee decided that individual private funerals would simply prolong the agony, and that a mass funeral would be less painful (it would also fudge any remaining problems of identification), although this was a new departure for blitz victims. Grieving relatives were 'persuaded' that a communal burial would be a fitting tribute, and were encouraged to remember the dead as they had been in life. The council would bear the cost of the public funeral, but the grant of £7.10s payable for the private burial of an air-raid victim, would only be paid for those who had lived outside the city, and only then if they had been Civil Defence workers, children under fifteen, or had been 'gainfully employed', that is not housewives or the elderly.

The first civic funeral was held on Wednesday, 20 November, though bodies were still being recovered from the ruins. Two long trenches were dug by mechanical diggers, and the coffins, two deep, draped at intervals with Union Jacks, were laid in them under the cover of darkness. The seemingly endless line of mourners stretched far into the distance on that dreary, damp day when 172 people were buried; the mass funeral of a further 250 was held the following Saturday. A few of the bereaved were in uniform, some carried wreaths or bunches of flowers, some held children by the hand. The solemn, heartbreaking ceremony was conducted by the Bishop of Coventry, a Roman Catholic priest and a Nonconformist minister. Then the mourners filed past the two long, narrow graves, dropping their flowers on top of a coffin – any coffin, for no one could know in which of the plain oak caskets the remains of their father, mother, husband, wife, sibling or child lay.

A Spitfire wheeled overhead below the grey, scudding clouds as the Bishop of Coventry gave the address on 20 November. 'Let us vow before God,' he prayed, 'to be better friends and neighbours in the future, because we have suffered this together, and stood here today.'

8

Britain Can (Probably) Take It

We all refuse to face the fact that unless we can invent an antidote to night-bombing, London will suffer very severely and the spirit of our people may be broken. Already the Communists are getting people in shelters to sign a peace-petition to Churchill. One cannot expect the population of a great city to sit up all night in the shelters week after week without losing their spirit. The only solution I can see at present are reprisals, which we are both unwilling and unable to exert. If we are saved, we shall be saved by our optimism.

Harold Nicolson's diary for 24 September 1940

James [Pope-Hennessy] is writing a book called History Under Fire for which I am doing the photographs. Besides the vandalistic damage, we must show the tenacity and courage of the people, and we do not have to look far.

Cecil Beaton's diary for 12 October 1940

Bombing stiffens people's morale. It has the opposite effect from the one intended. It makes you hate the enemy. But you have a fatalistic attitude. My little daughter used to get worried about me, because I'd sent her away to the country. And I'd take a map and I'd give her a pin and I'd say, 'now drop that pin on the map, and see if you can make it drop on my house'. And of course she couldn't . . . And you have this feeling, like soldiers in battle, they think they'll be the ones that escape . . . Morale was high in the blitz – I really don't know why it was so high. I think it was something to do with the fact that we were all working together for the same thing. We were all in it together.

Jill Craigie, film-maker

The destruction of Coventry's cathedral became a 'voiceless symbol of the insane, the fathomless barbarity which has been released on civilisation', as

St Paul's Cathedral in London would later become an equally potent symbol of Britain's will to resist.

John Piper, who would later be described by Kenneth Clark, the Director of the National Gallery who headed the War Artists Advisory Committee (WAAC), as 'the ideal recorder of bomb damage', was sent to do just that in Coventry the morning after the raid. He was horrified by what he saw: bodies still being pulled out of the rubble, charred fragments of wood in the air, 'a thin fog of smoke and steam like a concentration of the blighted November weather with that strange new smell that this war has produced – mixture of the smells of saturated burnt timber and brick dust with the emanation from cellars and hidden places'. He stood around, at a loss what to do, feeling it would be insensitive to pull out a pad and start sketching among the misery and desolation all around him. When he spotted the open door to a solicitor's office he thankfully went inside, explained his mission, and a typist moved out of the way so he could sit in the window and draw what he saw. His work was hurried back to London by the poet John Betjeman, who was working for the Ministry of Information, and within a short time had been printed as a postcard: it was not an entirely accurate portrayal, as Piper had used a certain amount of artistic licence, but it sold widely, becoming 'for Britain what Picasso's *Guernica* had been for Spain' – though without the same depiction of tortured human suffering.

Before the war, Piper, an artist of the romantic school, had driven around the country painting ivy-clad ruins that had crumbled through the gradual effects of centuries of weather and neglect; now his subjects were 'instant ruins'. Other artists found similar wartime continuities. The aim of Kenneth Clark in persuading the MoI to set up WAAC (there had been a similar scheme in the First World War, and Clark had also been much impressed by the work of the Canadian war artists' scheme), though 'of course I did not disclose it, was simply to keep artists at work on any pretext, and as far as possible, stop them from being killed'. Determined that the art produced should show not just battlefields, but the experiences of civilians 'taking it' on the home front too, Clark recruited a number of artists, several of whom were initially profoundly unsure about how to translate their peacetime art into the idiom of war. The blitz provided the answer for Graham Sutherland, who 'transferred his feelings for the menacing forms of roots and trees to twisted girders and burnt out bales of paper'.

For Henry Moore, who had fought in the First World War but found it hard 'to get my attitude to war clear and satisfactory, even to myself' in the

Second, the epiphany came one night in Belsize Park underground station, where he and his wife were caught for an hour during a raid. All around lay rows of reclining figures, similar to those he had been painting and sculpting for years: 'Even the holes out of which the trains were coming seemed to me like the holes in my sculptures.' The WAAC commissioned Moore to represent 'the group sense of communion in apprehension . . . in a world peopled by figures at once monumental and ghostly' through the medium of pen and ink, watercolour, chalk and wax crayon. Clark rhapsodised about the results: 'The tube shelters gave Henry Moore a subject that humanised his classical feeling for the recumbent figure, and led to a series of drawings which will, I am certain, always be considered the greatest works of art inspired by the war.'

Not all agreed. Keith Vaughan, a fellow painter and a conscientious objector, anonymously reviewing some of Moore's shelter paintings in an exhibition of war artists' work early in 1943, found it tragic but 'understandable, that so many Londoners confronted with these drawings feel baffled and insulted. Here is a whole new underground world from which they find themselves totally excluded, though the elements were so familiar.' Vaughan felt that the subjects, turned into sculptural forms by Moore, may have found the shelter drawings of another war artist, Edward Ardizzone, more empathetic. They depicted 'a steaming human throng. Here is the familiar moment, the bustling crowd, the burdened mothers, with their endlessly tiresome children. The friendly voices, the smells, the chips, the newspaper. The easy-going, cheerful society which was certainly part of shelter life.' Moore soon grew bored with working in the tube when regimented bunks were installed and the occupants no longer appeared like 'a white-grub race of troglodytes swathed in blankets', and turned his attention to depicting miners in their drive for coal production.

None of John Piper's paintings of Coventry ravaged by bombs showed human figures. Some criticised them as being little but elaborate stage sets, the backdrops of tragedies that absented and nullified the suffering caused by such devastation: they 'move towards abstraction and fail to involve us in the horror itself'. Piper's biographer Frances Spalding defends him against the charges, while admitting that his chief concern 'was not the human ordeal endured during the night of the raid but the architectural ordeal and the anguish associated with it'. The paintings, she says, show that 'the ruined cathedral becomes a stage on which history has walked . . . they recreate a feeling of desolation and destruction'. Moreover, she adds practically, the censors would certainly have vetoed material that showed the human suffering caused by the raid.

The role of the censor during the blitz was a particularly sensitive one. There were two objectives: to deny information to the enemy, and to maintain the morale of the civilian population. And the former was sometimes used in justification of the latter.

The Ministry of Information was not flying particularly high at the start of the blitz. Discussed in principle since 1935, it was established (or rather re-established, since there had been a similar organisation at the end of the First World War) the day after war broke out, 4 September 1939. It was housed in the neo-brutalist London University Senate House in Bloomsbury, and reputedly employed 999 of Britain's most creative communicators (in fact 954: 827 at HQ and 127 in the regional offices). John Betjeman and Harold Nicolson worked there, as did Graham Greene for a bit, the *belle lettrist* Peter Quennell, the urbane cartoonist Osbert Lancaster, the film producer Sidney Bernstein, P.L. Travers (the creator of Mary Poppins) and another writer, E. Arnot Robertson. Alongside assorted civil servants, lawyers and academics also worked one Joan Hunter Dunn, a member of the catering staff of London University, which the MoI had taken over. Her healthy, sporty Home Counties looks greatly took the fancy of Betjeman, who immortalised her in verse: 'Miss J. Hunter Dunn, Miss J. Hunter Dunn/Furnish'd and burnish'd by Aldershot sun/ . . . I am weak from your loveliness, Joan Hunter Dunn.'

Disliked by the press, mistrusted by the public, ridiculed by Tommy Handley on the wireless – *ITMA* referred to it as 'the Ministry of Aggravation and Mysteries', while to others it was 'the Ministry of Disinformation' – the MoI had got through two unsatisfactory Ministers by May 1940. 'Hush, hush, chuckle who dares/Another new Minister's fallen downstairs,' chanted the lower ranks. The second was Sir John Reith, former Director General of the BBC and known by Churchill as 'old Wuthering Heights'. The MoI would not properly find its feet until Churchill's protégé Brendan Bracken took charge in July 1941. During the blitz Duff Cooper, who had resigned as First Lord of the Admiralty in disgust over the Munich Agreement, a socialite and *bon viveur* of considerable ability, was at the helm – not terribly successfully either. 'Duds at the top and all the good people are in the most subordinate positions,' was the opinion of Harold Nicolson, who as Cooper's deputy was somewhat mid-stratum himself, until dismissed by Churchill in July 1941.

The blitz made the MoI's job more problematic – though in fact the Ministry had lost its role as censor in October 1939 when a Press and Censorship Bureau was established under Sir Walter Monckton, who was directly responsible to the Minister of Home Security. In principle, the press was like any other citizen in wartime: under Defence Regulation 3, it was prohibited from 'obtaining, recording, communicating to any other person or publishing information that might be useful to an enemy'. In theory this only affected the reporting of news: comment was supposedly free. Every editor had been issued with 'Defence Notices', a document which listed subjects about which it was considered that no information should be published without advice from the censorship department. Throughout the war this was supplemented by an endless stream of memoranda and letters to editors – 5,000 in all, one editor claimed. Editors were also sent background briefings that in effect told them the facts which they must not publish, so at least they knew what they were leaving out, and frequently proffered advice on how they might handle a particular subject in their pages. Of course there were a lot of hard-to-call areas: an armaments factory might not be mentioned, but what if it had a football team? Could its matches not be reported? It might be all right to print a story about a little old lady rescuing her cat from her bombed-out house, but not that a vicar had done something similar in the ruins of his named church.

But since Britain was a democracy, and was fighting the war in defence of democracy against totalitarianism, censorship of the press was voluntary (in theory, at least: Morrison summarily closed down the Communist *Daily Worker* in January 1941, and threatened similar action against the *Daily Mirror* in March 1942). It was up to newspaper editors to submit reports to the censor which might have security implications, and while these might be cut, delayed or banned altogether, they would not be rewritten by the MoI. On the whole, and perhaps rather surprisingly given his affiliation, the chief press censor, Rear Admiral George Thomson, was generally given to supporting Fleet Street (and its provincial colleagues) against the service chiefs when it came to the suppression of news, though reports of parliamentary debates in Hansard were frequently scored through by the censor's blue pencil.

It had been one thing to minimise bad news from overseas, or about the continuing disastrous losses at sea; it was rather different when bombs were falling on Britain, and people could see perfectly well what was happening in their locality. In such circumstances, downplaying or glossing over bad news and exaggerating good did not lead to feelings of reassurance and optimism, but rather to suspicion, distrust and scepticism. It had been left to Churchill to point out soberly after Dunkirk that 'Wars are not won by evacuations.' The British public had been shielded from reports of the dejected and demoralised troops who had limped back across the Channel, leaving behind almost all of their equipment and weapons, many of their fellow soldiers dead, seriously injured or taken prisoner, and a defeated and occupied France. As far as the British press was concerned, Dunkirk was all about brave glory boys, who just couldn't wait to get 'another crack at Jerry', and who were accorded a hero's welcome by wildly cheering crowds on their return.

The following month the press was apt to treat the Battle of Britain rather like an exciting cricket match, chalking up the score of downed German planes; even the Air Ministry exaggerated RAF successes and played down its losses – by 55 per cent, it was calculated after the war. So when the blitz came the groove had already been etched for reporting that fire and rescue squads invariably arrived 'promptly on the scene', while shelterers and the bombed out were always cheerful and defiant, waving an angry fist at 'itler as they emerged, and cheering the royal couple whenever they appeared on the scene (though Harold Nicolson noted that they had been booed in the East End on 17 September 1940).

The MoI's publicity material had patronised and infantilised the population in the early months of the year. The most exasperating example was the well-known poster '*Your* Courage, *Your* Cheerfulness, *Your* Resolution WILL BRING US VICTORY', though the use of such made-up characters as 'Miss Leaky Mouth', 'Miss Teacup Whisper' and 'Mr Glumpot' to warn against spreading defeatist rumours was almost equally infuriating. During the early days of the blitz this attitude persisted, despite wiser counsel that adults were capable of hearing some bad news without falling into a panic, and that it was lack of information that induced anxiety and suspicion: 'Details kill the public distrust of vague announcements,' as a former editor of the *News Chronicle*, Tom Clarke, himself now working for the MoI, put it. It was equally important to acknowledge that constant murderous air raids *were* frightening and depressing, and that people would be justified in losing confidence in their government if they felt that important information was being deliberately withheld from them, or that some official pronouncement was intended to jolly them out of their legitimate feelings, rather than recognising and respecting what hell they were going through.

In December 1940 the MoI quietly dropped its slogan 'Britain Can Take It' after intelligence reports showed that the public resented the image of the wisecracking Cockney emerging from the ruins whistling 'There'll Always be an England', and were 'irritated by propaganda which represented their grim experience as a sort of particularly torrid Rugby match'. Almost a year after the blitz ended, Brendan Bracken put the position bluntly: 'This is a people's war, and the people must be told the news about the war because without them and their spirit, we can't achieve victory.'

The delicate balance between maintaining security and upholding morale was played out over the questions of identifying where major air raids had taken place, and how many casualties there had been. On the one hand the Ministry of Information urged that news about air-raid damage and the number of casualties should be released as quickly as possible. The public did not like being kept in the dark, and in the absence of authoritative information, often grossly exaggerated rumours spread rapidly, and were hard to quash. On the other hand, the Air Ministry was opposed to such openness, arguing that any information about air raids would help the enemy assess their accuracy and effectiveness. Finally, in February 1940 it was agreed that Regional Information Officers should be permitted to release lists of casualties sustained in their areas, displayed outside the Town Hall (but without addresses, if they might provide evidence of where bombs had fallen, for example on a vicarage, a solicitor's office or a doctor's surgery), and it was recommended that an estimate of the number of casualties should be reported nationally as soon as this was clear. That idea was vetoed by the Cabinet in July 1940: casualties were not to be counted, but to be described as 'slight', 'considerable' or 'heavy'.

There were further limitations. An indefinite ban was put on mentioning the names and locations of buildings essential to the war effort – aerodromes, dockyards, factories, etc. – known as 'military objectives', that had been hit. A list of these was kept by the Technical Censorship Section, since it wasn't always obvious what factories were involved in war production: for example, one whisky distillery was producing alcohol for war purposes. It was equally important that no names of military objectives that had *not* been hit should be mentioned, as that could be construed as an open invitation to have a go next time. Moreover, it was vital that the enemy should not know if power installations, main railway lines and suchlike had been damaged, and there was particular sensitivity about any references to water mains being put out of action, which might suggest that this had interfered with the firefighters' ability to tackle a conflagration. When this happened in Bristol, the censor immediately came down on the *Bristol Evening News*, and the information was removed from later editions of the paper. Identification of the precise area bombed should not be revealed lest it helped the Germans perfect their navigational techniques. As Rear Admiral Thomson explained, 'To have told the enemy pilots they hit Madame Tussaud's on the previous night might well have given them the information they required to bomb Baker Street station on the following night. They might, for example, work out that pilot Johann Schmidt who had been over that district of London, had let his bomb go forty yards too much to the right' (though this presumed a precision of aim that was rarely achieved).

There were also strictures issued to local newspapers to stagger obituary notices, so that no one could work out from them if a particular street had been hit, and not to specify addresses or precise dates of death, just the month. Businesses that had been bombed and had moved to new premises could publicise the fact ten days later, or sooner if the advertisement was drafted with care, but without giving their former address. 'If clients of Messrs John Smith have enquiries to make, will they please call at No. 10 Church Street,' was Rear Admiral Thomson's suggestion. He did, however, recognise that while 'it was a fairly good assumption that the premises of Messrs. John Smith had been hit (the address could easily be found by the enemy in a telephone directory or other book of reference) it wasn't a certainty. In any event . . . a certain amount of risk had to be taken to enable the economic life of the country to continue without interruption.'

The restrictions went further than this. Except for very large cities such as London or Liverpool, the name of a town that had been bombed was not given until twenty-eight days later, and then the precise date of the raid would not be mentioned, though the attack on Coventry was an exception. The eight o'clock BBC news bulletin on the morning after the raid mentioned that 'Enemy attacks were mainly directed against the Midlands where a very heavy attack was made on one town in particular. It is feared that casualties were heavy.' Although the one o'clock lunchtime news did not give the raid priority, the second item reported that 'The city of Coventry was heavily attacked last night, the scale of the raid being comparable with those of the largest night attacks on London.' At 6 p.m. the raid was being described as 'very severe' and 'particularly vicious', and that afternoon an emergency four-page edition of the Coventry evening paper, the *Midland Evening Telegraph*, was on sale, proclaiming (erroneously) 'Coventry Bombed.

Casualties 1,000'. In this instance the MoI decided there was more morale-boosting potential in revealing the extent of the damage, thus giving the impression of the enemy as a brutal bully – which is where the Guernica analogy, though inaccurate, was very potent – and also that London was not the only city in the front line. The image of a ravaged but courageous Coventry sped around the world; indeed, the MoI allowed photographs of bombed churches, schools and hospitals to be issued to the American press, as evidence of German brutality.

However, there were limits. Tom Harrisson was invited to give a talk on the radio about his visit to Coventry with his M-O team. It was a chillingly vivid description of 'people walking blankly round the city looking at the mess . . . the commonest sound was the scraping of shovels and the shifting of rubble . . . I've been chasing air raids in this country ever since they began: often I've heard awful stories of the damage and arrived to find them grossly exaggerated. But about Coventry there hasn't been much exaggeration: in fact the centre of the town reminded me more than anything of photos of Ypres in the last war.'

The matter was discussed by the War Cabinet. The Secretary of State for War considered it to have been 'a most depressing broadcast, [which] would have a deplorable effect on Warwickshire morale. Other Ministers confirmed this view.' Winston Churchill was more conciliatory, doubting if it had done much harm, but he did request that the procedures of the BBC should be 'considered'. This resulted in a proposal at the end of the year that the Ministry of Information should appoint two advisers, one on foreign and one on home affairs, who would have the ear of the Minister in the event of a dispute. As it happened, this implied threat to the BBC's independence did not materialise, since neither adviser ever interfered.

The same month as the Coventry raid, Harold Nicolson complained on behalf of the Cabinet Home Policy Committee that there had been a report in the *News Chronicle* that over a hundred schools had been hit in the London area. He 'wanted assurance that publication of statistics or catalogues of air raid damage would be strictly controlled in future'. The MoI responded with some suggested vaguenesses: Northern Ireland was to be treated as a single area; but Scotland was to be divided into thirteen areas which included the Western Islands, the Highlands, North-Central, South-West etc.; while England was to comprise the Bristol Channel, the Thames Estuary, the Home Counties, the Channel Coast, the North, etc. And 'great care must be taken to have an assurance that these places will not be further qualified by the Press. For instance, it might be most dangerous to have uncensored reports of incidents, say, in the Southern part of the Home Counties, or near the North of the Lake District.'

Then one of the Air Ministry's own blew it. Air Marshal Sir Philip Joubert de la Ferté (the de la Ferté was usually ignored), in charge of the practical application of radar in the RAF, was recognised as the Air Ministry's official spokesman. At 1 p.m. on 27 November, during a broadcast on the BBC, he not only mentioned the Coventry raid but went on to say that:

Since this raid there have been several repeat performances, only two of which have approached the Coventry raid in effectiveness. On that Friday night London got a pretty severe bombing but no vital damage was done. On Saturday and Sunday bad weather intervened and the German effort was a complete failure. A relatively small number of their aircraft wandered round the south of England for some hours and then jettisoned their bombs, mostly into open fields, and went home. On last Monday it was Birmingham's turn. Almost as many aircraft as were directed against Coventry crossed our shores. But the result of the attack from the German point of view was not very good, and the effort seems to have been largely scattered. Since then there has been a further heavy attack on Birmingham, and two smaller raids on Southampton and Bristol.

Morrison was icily furious, raising this as 'an example of grave inconsistency in policy', for which the press might have ample grounds for complaint. He requested a meeting. The MoI acknowledged that the broadcast had been in breach of the guidelines, but pointed out that the press was adopting

the unsatisfactory and rather discreditable expedient of using German communiqués to indicate, more or less, the actual sites of the attack. This raised the American correspondents to something like fury and was made the pretext for an attack on censorship, which, to say the least, is unfortunate having regard to our present relations with the USA. None of this, of course, was felt to matter so long as an important point of security was being safeguarded and the Censorship lent all its efforts to persuading Editors and correspondents that it was essential to co-operate with the Air Minister's wishes in matters of this sort, even though to the lay mind they might seem absurd. Then 'without any sort of preliminary warning' along comes Joubert . . .

It seems plain that we cannot go on in this way if the public inside and outside this country are to retain any respect for the official attitude towards news.

The MoI demanded that since the principle had been breached, 'the A[ir] M[inistry] will recognise the necessity of naming or permitting the naming of large towns which have been subject to deliberate and concentrated attacks, even at night'.

Joubert admitted to 'a lapse', and said he was 'very sorry that owing to pressure of work he had not submitted his talk to the Air Ministry's censorship staff', promising that in future he would always do so.

The transgressions continued. Lady Astor was reported to have given an 'unfortunate' interview to the *Daily Herald* after the bombing of Plymouth in April 1941, and the *Evening Standard* published a 'dilatarious [sic] article' on the same subject. On 5 May a 'Strictly Confidential' memo was issued to the editors of morning and evening newspapers: 'The Minister of Home Security . . . asks Editors to pay particular attention to the need for depriving the enemy of information about the effects of repeated nightly bombing raids of a particular town. Reports indicating marked disorganisation of civil defence, health or local government services, or large scale evacuation, or great disturbance of any aspect of normal life in a town, are a direct invitation to the enemy to renew and continue his attacks . . . If criticism of the Government is thought necessary, let it be printed by all means, but in such a way as not to connect the grounds of criticism with a particular place, or a particular series of raids.'

The Conservative MP Leo Amery put the other side of the problem. Birmingham had been badly bombed on 19 November 1940, with fifty-three workers killed at the BSA factory, and other areas had been devastated by land mines and HE bombs. There were further heavy raids on the city throughout November in which at least 682 people were killed, 1,087 seriously injured and over 2,000 houses demolished or rendered uninhabitable. On 11 December Birmingham suffered another raid, this time lasting for over thirteen hours, in which 263 people were killed and 243 badly injured. Amery, who was the Member for Birmingham Sparkbrook, one of the worst-affected areas in the city, had gone to take a look around for himself. He found that 'everything seems to have been done to resume work with the minimum of delay'. Plant from the BSA factory was being dispersed to other factories – something like a hundred lorries a day were leaving with machinery and equipment – and

> the General Manager told me that . . . the spirit of the working men is excellent. I went into a good few small shops and found them everywhere cheery and with only one mind and that was winning the war. Nor did I come across any complaints . . . as to the inadequacy of anti-aircraft guns or fighters* . . . There is, however, one matter which Birmingham has felt very deeply and that is while Coventry and Bristol were mentioned by name [presumably in the Joubert broadcast] they were referred to simply as a West Midlands town. They don't mind how much they are knocked about, but they like their fellow countrymen to know it! They think it out of the question that the Germans should not know when they are over Birmingham and I had it pointed out to me that the BSA works as such have been definitely located and attacked three times by the enemy, who obviously knew precisely the target he was going for.

Hull would be another town that would suffer the neglect of anonymity in the spring of 1941, being referred to as 'a northern coastal town' rather than by name. Aggrieved citizens felt that the singular nature of their suffering was not given due acknowledgement: they just became part of the aggregate of incidents. People in Bristol, Liverpool, even Ramsgate, felt that it was invariably the London blitz that was given most attention by the media, with an occasional exception such as the high-profile raid on Coventry, while the rest of the nation took the usual back seat. This was clearly not good for morale.

Civilian morale had been on the mind of the government since the mid-1930s, but the blitz made the concern acute. How would the people of Britain react when they were subjected to severe raids night after night? Would morale crack? Panic set in? War production grind to a halt as hordes fled from the affected areas? Would there be a mass pressure to surrender, to sue for peace, from a nation that couldn't 'take it' any more?

But what exactly was 'morale'? 'The woolliest concept of the war', thought

---

* This was not a general perception: many considered that Birmingham's Civil Defence had been 'leaderless' that night, and the Chief Officer of the Fire Brigade 'resigned' two days after the raid, to be replaced by a Home Office appointee.

the people-watcher Tom Harrisson. And how could it be measured? It was a word frequently bandied around in MoI reports of the home front, but rarely defined, though Stephen Taylor, the Ministry's Director of Home Intelligence, came up with a useful suggestion: 'Ultimately morale must be measured not by what a person thinks or says, but what he does and how he does it.' From the official perspective, 'low morale' would be indicated by 'panic, hysteria, grumbling about those in authority, scapegoating, refusing to leave shelters, absenteeism, apathy'; while 'high morale' was characterised by 'calmness, cheerfulness, co-operation, high productivity, volunteering'.

Collecting information on civilian morale could be a sensitive subject, since it carried more than a whiff of a totalitarian thought-police force. The Ministry of Information had established a Department of Home Intelligence in December 1939, and Mary Adams, a BBC producer who had lost her job when the infant television service closed down at the outbreak of war, was appointed its director. The department was not universally welcomed in Whitehall. A number of politicians found the whole notion of 'intelligence-gathering' somewhat sinister, and were confident that MPs themselves would be perfectly adequate conduits and interpreters of the public mind in wartime.

After the fall of France in June 1940, Home Intelligence was required to report daily on the state of morale in the country, and the reports were circulated within the MoI and to other ministries such as Home Security, Food, Labour, Supply, the War Office and the Air Ministry – a circulation list of around a hundred in total. All the reports were of course highly confidential. Three weeks after the start of the blitz, the daily reports began to be collected into a weekly digest.

Adams used a network of information-gathering sources for these reports. The most 'scientific' and quantitative of these was the Wartime Social Survey, organised by the Professor of Commerce at the London School of Economics, Arnold Plant, under the auspices of the National Institute of Social and Economic Research, which also carried out surveys for a number of Whitehall departments. The Social Survey investigators acted as conventional market researchers, using questionnaires to interview members of the public and collating the information as statistical data. Its activities were kept secret, but in July 1940 the truffling journalist Ritchie Calder had uncovered the Survey's existence. The Minister of Information, Duff Cooper, was obliged to defend the use of 'Cooper's snoopers', as the press dubbed the investigators, in the House of Commons from charges of 'throwing the shadow of the Gestapo over honest and loyal creatures'.

MoI's Regional Information Officers (RIOs) throughout the country were expected to call in each day between noon and 2.30 p.m. to inform about morale in their region. They would have gathered their information 'partly by discussions with their own staff, partly by casual conversations initiated or overheard on the way to work, and partly by a hurried series of visits to public houses and other places where the public foregathered'. The RIOs would also have garnered information from Chief Constables and passed that on to Home Intelligence, while various organisations and companies such as the London Passenger Transport Board, Citizens Advice Bureaux, W.H. Smith and the Brewers' Society were also sent questionnaires regularly. The BBC's *Listener* research surveys were scrutinised, and naturally political parties were asked for their impressions. In a rather more clandestine way, Special Branch reports were made available to Home Intelligence, and the postal censors submitted anything they thought bore on morale in the country.

Then there was Mass-Observation. Despite the obvious appropriateness of using an organisation that had been taking the nation's pulse since 1937, the MoI, regardless of its near-obsession with wanting to measure civilian morale, was reluctant to employ M-O, and certainly to be seen to do so: initially it wondered about paying for its reports out of Secret Service funds. But Mary Adams was favourably inclined towards it, thinking that M-O was more in touch with the people's real feelings than the more official channels ever would be, and was determined to employ the organisation to undertake surveys on a fairly regular basis. Although she recognised that its methods were hardly scientific (M-O's practice was to eavesdrop on conversations in cafés, pubs, shops, the street), and its findings needed to be interpreted with care, she defended the organisation against the charge that its members were a bunch of dangerous pinkos. 'What does one mean by "subversive"?' she queried. 'The results of Mass-Observation are, not unnaturally, critical of certain social happenings and I do not think that criticism is subversive. The use to which criticisms may be put may lead to subversive actions. But it is our business to acquaint ourselves with criticisms and direct the attention of those in authority to the causes of discontent.'

Mass-Observation set the bar rather high, defining morale as not only 'the determination to carry on, but also the determination to carry on with the utmost energy, a determination based on the realisation of the facts of life and with it a readiness for many minor and some major sacrifices, including, if necessary, the sacrifice of life itself'. This would have been hard to quantify, but throughout the blitz M-O was in the forefront of trying to do so.

Undoubtedly Mass-Observation's reports were less gung-ho than some others submitted to Home Intelligence. They noted depression, and sometimes incidences of panic, in the East End, Coventry, Liverpool, Manchester, Portsmouth and Southampton. Some in authority regarded their reports as in themselves deleterious to morale, and suggested that M-O had a vested interest in engendering a volatile situation, since if all was calm and cheerful there would be less need for close scrutiny, and thus less work for M-O. But, as Mary Adams insisted, 'Morale should never be overplayed. A raid will have made many people frightened and far from "heroic". They will resent a standard being set which they know to be impossible.' M-O reported that negative feelings, even panic and an uncontrollable desire to get away, were not irrational, and usually passed within a few days, to be replaced by a re-emergence of stoicism and defiance. In any case, traumatised feelings should not be equated with defeatism. Indeed, it is striking that in all the Home Intelligence reports throughout the blitz, the term 'defeatism' occurs only twice. There was clearly a difference between people feeling frightened, violated and angry with 'the authorities', and wanting to throw in the towel and bring an end to the bombing on any terms.

The BBC played a particularly key role in the morale stakes. With thirty-four million listeners, the wireless was a vital source of wartime communication. But for some months the Corporation struggled to find its place in the war machine. *The Listener* was clear what this was: 'The first and most obvious function of broadcasting . . . is the dissemination of news, of pronouncements by our leaders, and of instructions to citizens on the many problems that confront them . . . But the maintenance of morale is of the first importance . . . If a dose of light entertainment helps us to forget our troubles even momentarily, there is no need to begrudge ourselves that pleasure: refreshment of this kind strengthens us to face the grimmer tasks.' Yet at the start of the war, what the Home Service broadcast was regarded by most listeners as deeply unsatisfactory. And since the regional services had been closed down on 1 September 1939, and the Forces Programme, transmitting largely music and light entertainment to lighten the boredom of the troops, did not begin until February 1940, that was all that was available. Hours of music, much of it provided by Sandy MacPherson at the BBC theatre organ, interspersed by war bulletins and leavened by the very occasional talk, or *Children's Hour*, was all there was to listen to. Thirty-five per cent of listeners were reported to be 'fed up' with the BBC by October 1939, while 10 per cent had stopped listening altogether.

Gradually things improved, and by the time the blitz started news, entertainment and music had found a more satisfactory balance. The catchphrases of the characters from Tommy Handley's *ITMA* (*It's That Man Again*) – Mrs Mopp's 'Can I do you now, sir?; 'This is Funf' ('the enemy agent with the feet of sauerkraut'); Colonel Chinstrap; 'Ta-Ta for now' (or 'TTFN'); 'After you, Claude,' 'No, after *you*, Cecil' – had entered the nation's lexicon, while the *Brains Trust*, with five men (and sometimes a woman such as Marghanita Laski) discussing philosophy, art and science, which started transmission in the middle of the blitz on 1 January 1941, was a surprise hit, drawing ten million listeners by 1944.

Such entertaining, informative and uplifting programmes certainly fitted the BBC's remit as morale-raiser, but news broadcasts remained problematic. Air Marshal Joubert notwithstanding, the BBC was subject to the same restraints as the press, and came in for the same criticism for revealing too much or too little. And there were other sources of news about the progress of the war. A clutch of Continental stations could be picked up on most British sets: the most popular programmes were those of Lord Haw Haw (William Joyce), the former Propaganda Director of Oswald Mosley's British Union of Fascists who had fled to Berlin on the eve of war, and his 'Jairmany Calling' broadcast nightly from Radio Hamburg. Thirty per cent of adult Britons with radios were reported to listen to Lord Haw Haw regularly by January 1940, although his appeal had begun to wane by the time the blitz started, and of the sixteen million who tuned in to the BBC's main nine o'clock news bulletin, six million turned over to Radio Hamburg afterwards. This was partly due to fascination at the unerring inside knowledge of Britain in wartime that Joyce seemed to possess, but also to the feeling that the BBC was too much under the thumb of government, that what it told the people was propaganda rather than an accurate account of the situation.

At first the BBC ignored its Nazi propaganda competition; but then it tried various strategies to counteract the appeal of Haw Haw, including moving the popular variety programme *Band Waggon*, with Richard 'Stinker' Murdoch and Arthur Askey, into the same time slot. By the spring of 1940 the fightback had begun, with speakers pointing out that it was unpatriotic to listen to Haw Haw, and the introduction of a topical comment programme, *Postscripts*, after the nine o'clock news on Sundays. At first featuring the barrister Norman Birkett KC, then the blunt-speaking Yorkshire playwright and novelist J.B. Priestley, these broadcasts flattered listeners that there were debates to be had even in wartime and that they were sufficiently mature to understand them. In any case, by this time Haw Haw had begun to seem less well-informed about British life, and more contemptible, than previously, though he could be chilling with his threats that 'The Jews will get it tonight,' or 'The bombers will be over the Morris works in Oxford,' and his boasts that the Germans were pulverising British towns and cities.

As ever, the only truly effective riposte to misinformation was full disclosure, but the BBC was caught in the same security-versus-morale conundrum as any other channel of information dissemination. Even more so in fact, since 90 per cent of British homes had a radio – though wartime shortages and the fact that about a third of all households had no mains electricity supply, and therefore relied on hard-to-get batteries, probably meant that at least 10 per cent of these sets were out of order. The main news bulletin at nine o'clock every evening was a fixed feature of most people's wartime lives, with the family gathering round the solid Bakelite set in the lounge. The BBC was regarded as twice as authoritative as any other medium when it came to relaying important information, which gave it an added responsibility. Moreover, it was deeply embedded in the blitz, as the fading of the radio was usually an early sign of an impending attack, since programmes went off air during raids. One live interview programme, *Standing on the Corner*, with Michael Standing, was renamed *Standing in the Shelter* in November 1940, with radio lines installed in some public shelters in London. As well as reporting on raids, the BBC experienced one on 15 October, when a five-hundred-pound bomb fell on Broadcasting House in Portland Place. The crash could be heard by listeners, but after a brief pause, Bruce Belfrage 'kept calm and carried on' reading the news. On the night of 8–9 December a land mine exploded in Portland Place, killing a policeman, injuring several BBC staff and putting Broadcasting House temporarily out of action.

On the whole, the BBC did not go in for what Mary Adams called 'overplaying morale', though there were unfortunate exceptions: a report in February 1941 on the high spirits of bombed-out families in Swansea was one, as was a cringe-makingly upbeat documentary, *They Went To It!*, broadcast on 24 November 1940, presumably as a corrective to – or penance for – Harrisson's 'most depressing broadcast'. Sometimes it seemed the BBC could never get it right: if, at the behest of the MoI, it failed to mention a raid, or suggested that it had been light when it fact it had been heavy, it would be accused by those involved of belittling their suffering. If, on the other hand, a raid on a rural area was reported, the BBC was likely to be accused of needlessly scaring parents whose children had been evacuated.

Even though the MoI had tactfully shelved 'Britain Can Take It' as slogan for its own people, it proved an invaluable export. On 3 September 1939, the day Britain declared war on Germany, the US President, Franklin Delano Roosevelt, had broadcast one of his 'fireside chats' to his countrymen and women. 'When peace has been broken anywhere in the world, the peace of countries everywhere is in danger,' he said, but concluded: 'I have said, not once, but many times, that as long as it remains within my power to prevent it, there will be no blackout of peace in the US.' America would remain neutral, would refuse to get involved in another of Europe's 'civil wars'. Isolationist feeling was strong in Congress and the country: a poll in 1939 showed that 67 per cent of the population believed that the USA should maintain its neutrality, only 12 per cent were prepared to give aid to Britain while remaining neutral, and a mere 2 per cent were in favour of declaring war on Germany. While Britain needed US aid – including matériel, heavy bombers in particular – it was still in debt to the United States from the First World War, and had no way of paying for it.

On 29 December 1940 Roosevelt announced a new policy of aid to Britain, which would come to be known as Lend Lease. The production of ships, tanks and other war supplies would be accelerated, and these would be lent, rather than sold, to Britain. 'If your neighbour's house is on fire you lend him your hose and you don't ask for money – what you want is your hose back when the fire has been put out,' the President explained in another homely fireside chat. But despite Harold Nicolson's welcome that this was 'the decisive act of the war', what Britain needed, as *The Times* put it, was not to be thrown a line as it battled to 'save our drowning civilisation', but for America 'to wade in, at least up to her waist'.

In fact America was doing a great deal more than holding the towel: Roosevelt had promised that the country would be the 'great arsenal of democracy', and had compromised its neutral status to a remarkable degree, but he had to exercise great caution in moving towards actual war, for which his country had no appetite. America would be generous with matériel and comforts (the American Red Cross supplied immense amounts of clothing, bedding and food throughout the blitz, as did other organisations and individuals), but there remained the unresolved question of war debts; there was a perception that Britain was an imperial power, fighting to maintain its Empire; and there was a suspicion, fostered by the outgoing Ambassador to London Joseph Kennedy, that Britain would collapse under the Nazi onslaught (even Roosevelt only reckoned Britain's chance of victory as one in three in the summer of 1940), and that all the resources America poured into the fight would be lost or appropriated by the Germans. But the lesson Britain had learned by 1940 was that the war could not be won without US participation.

The radio broadcasts and newspaper reports of American correspondents such as Ed Murrow, Quentin Reynolds, Dorothy Thompson, Eric Sevareid, Vincent Sheean and Ben Robertson became another weapon in Britain's arsenal, convincing the folks back home that the country had shaken off her old imperial ways and was fighting a 'people's war', that she was suffering greatly but that her people were proving brave and resilient, and would win through. A new Britain had been forged at Dunkirk, according to Dorothy Thompson, or as Ed Murrow more bluntly put it, 'Britain is still ruled by class,' but the country would hang together.

Roger Eckersley, the BBC's chief censor, was anxious to give the American journalists all the help they needed, since their reports constituted 'the finest form of propaganda of which we can avail ourselves'. He wanted them to be given unrestricted access to downed German planes and scenes of air-raid damage, believing that their reports had the unique potential to 'impinge on the American consciousness what air raids really mean'. Herbert Morrison agreed to allow accredited US correspondents to visit all sites of bomb damage, except those of military significance.

What the American journalists really wanted to do was to 'chill the spines' of their listeners back home by broadcasting eye-witness accounts of air raids in progress. Finally, after much shilly-shallying, permission was granted for an unscripted broadcast, and on 21 September 1940 Ed Murrow stepped out onto the roof of Broadcasting House with his microphone. Although on that particular night the raiders were not overhead for long, the Ack-Ack fire sounded dramatic enough for the US press to report 'Murrow Ducks Bombs in London' next morning.

When Buckingham Palace was hit on 13 September, the US press were invited round so they could report that the King 'stands with his people in the Front Line'. They were also taken to Coventry on the morning after the raid. Murrow's tin hat was dented by shrapnel as he was 'dodging in doorways', and the London offices of CBS were bombed out in October.

On the whole, what was relayed to the American public was an uncritical portrait of Britain's united and steadfast defiance, what would become the foundation of the post-war 'myth of the blitz', though James Reston drew the attention of *New York Times* readers to the plight of London's blitz homeless. British commentators joined in: J.B. Priestley broadcast regularly to the US, though he avoided the most lurid descriptions of 'the hell that was London' and the society photographer Cecil Beaton was commissioned by the MoI to take pictures of the home front, and later of the war overseas. His poignant picture of a small child injured in the blitz appeared on the front cover of *Life* magazine on 23 September 1940, and was reproduced on a pro-intervention poster issued by the Committee to Defend America by Aiding the Allies, which had been set up in May 1940.

On 20 October 1940 the film-maker Humphrey Jennings (one of the original founders of Mass-Observation) wrote from the Adelphi Hotel, Liverpool, to his wife Cicely in America:

> We have begun work on film-reporting of the blitz and are now up to our eyes in it – first pic *London Can Take It* specially for you in the States! . . . Some of the damage in London is pretty heart-breaking – but what an effect it has had on the people! What warmth – what courage! What determination. People sternly encouraging each other by explaining that when you hear a bomb whistle it means it has missed you! People in the north singing in public shelters: 'One man went to mow – went to mow a meadow'. WVS girls serving hot drinks to firefighters during raids explaining that really they are 'terribly afraid all the time!' People going back to London for a night or two to remind themselves what it's like.
>
> Everybody absolutely determined: secretly delighted with the privilege of holding up Hitler. Certain of beating him: a certainty which no amount of bombing can weaken: only strengthen. A kind of slow-burning white heat of hatred for the Jerries and a glowing warmth of red flame of love and comradeship for each other which cannot be defeated: which has ceased to think of anything else but attack.

With its maker possessed of such a fiercely beating patriotic heart, it was hardly surprising that Jennings' ten-minute film, made under the auspices of the MoI Film Division, was perfect propaganda for the British cause, and 'a success in the States', as he wrote to his wife in November. Warner Brothers distributed *London Can Take It* (which was subsequently edited for the home market and tactfully retitled *Britain Can Take It*), donating all profits to the British War Relief Fund. It played in eight New York cinemas simultaneously, and had soon been watched by an estimated sixty million Americans.

The commentary, by the booming-voiced American journalist Quentin Reynolds, was recorded in the bar of the Savoy Hotel, which Reynolds was reluctant to leave, as was another short propaganda film also made by Jennings, *Christmas Under Fire*. This was filmed largely among the tube shelterers, and closed with a lump-in-the-throat-inducing shot of scrubbed-faced choirboys praising 'the prince of peace', with Reynolds growling an implicit indictment of American foreign policy: 'There is no reason for America to feel sorry for England this Christmas [1940]. England doesn't feel sorry for herself... Destiny gave her the torch of liberty to hold, and she has not dropped it... she is thankful that when the test came she had the high courage to meet it, and today England stands unbeaten, unconquered, unafraid.'

'You burned the city of London in our houses and we felt the flames that burnt it,' wrote the poet and Assistant Director of the US Office of War Information, Archibald MacLeish, to Ed Murrow. 'You laid the dead of London at our doors and we knew the dead were our dead – were all men's dead – were mankind's dead and ours.' In October 1940 the British Ambassador to Washington, Lord Lothian, noted an 'almost miraculous change of opinion in the United States after it had become clear that the country was effectively resisting the German air attack', and by December, 60 per cent of those polled were now prepared to risk war.

But it wasn't harrowing reports and images of the blitz, nor the sterling resolve of the British people under German fire, that brought America into the war on the Allied side: it was the bombing of the US naval base at Pearl Harbor by the Japanese on 7 December 1941.

9

The Fear of Fear

The whole atmosphere of modern war is likely to revive those unreasonable
fears that the human race has inherited from its remotest ancestors: gas masks
that make us look like strange animals; underground shelters; rumours and
suspicions; enemies overhead and unseen, wailing sirens; screaming air bombs
and vast explosions in the night. Small wonder, then, that we are afraid lest
in the face of real danger our first impulse should be to behave like little children . . . We are afraid of being afraid.

Edward Glover, Chairman of the British Psycho-Analytical Society, writing in 1940

It wasn't the raids themselves that frightened me, it was death . . . Am I going
to be blown to pieces, am I going to die in agony, different things like that
go through your mind. If I'd been killed outright I wouldn't know nothing
about it. You've always got that fear . . . a lot of people said to me 'you must
be a brave man'. No one's brave. People just have different ways of looking
at the world.   Thomas Tapfield

A month after the start of the blitz, George Springett, a writer and conscientious objector, went into his local chemist's shop in Bromley in Kent on
the outskirts of London, and asked the manager, 'How's trade these days?'
'Oh, fair,' the manager replied, 'but people aren't taking anything like the
amount of medicine they did before the war – especially nerve tonics and
the like. Now, there are customers of mine who in peacetime had a bottle
of tonic every few weeks. You'd think that in these strained times they would
want three times the amount of nerve mixtures. Never believe it, they don't.
These nervous people positively revel in raids.'

Like this Kentish chemist, the government had anticipated that the war
would result in serious problems with the nation's 'nervy types'. A committee
of psychiatrists from London teaching hospitals and clinics was set up in

1938 to consider the possibility of widespread civilian panic and an 'epidemic of shell shock [similar] to that observed during the war of 1914–18'. In addition, the government was advised by a psychiatrist and a neurologist, both of whom had worked with the army in the First World War and who, as a result, tended to regard the civilian population as an army division 'strung out in battle formation'.

The recommendations to the Ministry of Health were sombre. The experts reckoned that psychiatric casualties were likely to exceed physical ones by three to one. On the basis of the government's estimate of those likely to be killed or wounded, this meant there would be three to four million cases of acute panic, hysteria and other neurotic conditions in the first six months of the war – a terrifying prospect of bedlam incarnate. To deal with this, it was proposed that treatment centres would have to be set up in the suburbs, the outpatient departments of hospitals on the outskirts of towns and cities would be required to work around the clock, and mobile teams of psychiatrists and child-guidance experts should be on hand to go wherever required at speed. The committee considered that the civilian population, which was not trained in military discipline and organisation, and did not normally live with the possibility of facing violent and imminent death, was likely to be infected with 'an impotent fretfulness', and to be unable to function. But, the Ministry was warned, there were 'not enough trained psychiatrists in London to deal with more than a few teaspoonfuls of the casualties that would doubtless occur'. The prediction was terrifying: not enough psychiatrists, insufficient police and an understrength army, the top brass of which would be most reluctant to allow their men to undertake panic control of the civilian population when there was a war to be fought.

The Ministry of Health did not set up such an elaborate system as the psychiatrists recommended, but as a precaution the major London psychiatric hospitals were cleared as much as was possible by restricting admissions, accelerating discharges and transferring either the patients, or in many cases the entire organisation, out of London and other vulnerable cities. Since studies from the First World War indicated that the further a shell-shocked soldier was evacuated from the trenches before treatment, the less likely he was to recover, specialist hospitals (termed 'Neurosis Centres') to treat the expected epidemic of psychiatric casualties were set up within easy proximity of London and other cities. For example, the staff of the Maudsley psychiatric hospital in south London relocated either to Belmont Hospital in Sutton, or to the converted premises of Mill Hill public school in Barnet, both on the outskirts of London. The patients sent to either would be away from the danger zone, but still within hearing distance of bombs and gunfire, in the hope that this acclimatisation would wean them back to their normal lives as soon as possible.

In the event, all this proved largely unnecessary. 'The blitz, when it did come, fell far short of the dimensions anticipated, and it was soon apparent that waves of war neurosis [both acute and chronic] were merely figments of the psychologists' own imagination,' wrote Edward Glover, a follower of Freud and collaborator of Ernest Jones. As director of the British Pyscho-Analytical Society, Glover had offered advice to the government, but it had been 'rejected without ceremony'. The wards of the 'Neurosis Centres' remained empty, and in 1941 were turned over to military purposes, while a 'War Emergency Clinic' set up at 96 Gloucester Place in London by Glover and other psychoanalysts to treat traumatised air-raid victims closed, since it had no patients. Although there was an increase in the number of neurotic patients seen in the 216 psychiatric clinics in England and Wales between 1938 and 1941, Dr C.P. Blacker, who was invited by the Minister of Health to do a 'stock taking' of psychiatric facilities and usage in wartime Britain, concluded that this was due 'in large part or entirely to a growing use of the country's psychiatric services by general practitioners, and might have occurred in the absence of war. There are no grounds for supposing that the war has caused an increase in the more serious forms of mental disorder requiring admission to hospital.' Moreover, Blacker concluded, 'cases of neurosis attributed by psychiatrists to air raids, are astonishingly few. About one new case in thirty seen at outpatients clinics in 1940, 1941 and 1942 was a psychiatric air raid casualty. Over a third of these patients had previously suffered from some psychiatric disability.'

A survey of the number of psychological disorders presenting to a Willesden GP's practice in north London from September 1940 to May 1941, compared with the equivalent figures for 1937, as well as to GPs and psychiatric outpatient departments in Merseyside, which experienced heavy raids in 1941, found only an insignificant increase. Another survey, based on war pension data gathered in Bristol and London, came to the same conclusion: 'After intensive raids there is a slight increase in the total amount of neurotic illness in the affected area, occurring chiefly in those who have been neurotically ill before.' And Edward Glover admitted that only one case referred to his clinic could be classified as 'war neurosis'.

Those who suffered traumatic experiences in the blitz, but were generally in robust mental health, appeared to recover quickly without significant psychiatric intervention. Glover described the case of Mrs A, an elderly woman who had customarily sat on the settee in the lounge with her husband during a raid, but one night, feeling tired, had retired to bed, leaving her husband on the settee. That evening a bomb fell on their flat, pinning Mrs A to her bed under piles of debris. She managed to struggle free, calling to her husband. He had been killed, but she did not know he was dead. Neighbours proved unwelcoming, so she was taken in her nightdress, wrapped in an ARP blanket, but without her dentures, which had been lost in the debris, to a first aid post. There she was given an aspirin and told she must be quiet or she would wake other patients, and that she would probably hear news of her husband in the morning. Predictably she spent a sleepless night, and by morning was becoming very agitated. She was then taken to a rest centre, but kept in isolation because she was agitated. Fifteen hours after the incident she was finally told that her husband was dead – which she had obviously suspected must be the case. By this time she was in 'emotional distress', crying, shaking, talking incessantly and bemoaning the fact that she had left her husband's side and not been killed with him. Dr Glover went to see her, let her talk, tried to keep her warm and comfortable, and eventually a doctor arrived and administered a large dose of bromide. All that day she was agitated, and was found wandering round the ruins of her flat. She questioned Dr Glover in great detail about his life, 'as if she must at all costs escape from her own difficult life and lead mine instead'. When a raid started the following night she panicked, imagining herself back in her bed and about to be buried again. Glover stayed with her, and eventually she fell asleep. When she woke the next morning, 'her appearance had completely changed. She looked refreshed and years younger. She spoke with confidence and was prepared to face whatever was before her. She was prepared if necessary to identify her husband's body. (This was not allowed by the authorities, as he was not in a condition to be seen by her.)' A relative came to collect Mrs A, who was 'appreciative of the kindness shown to her [though not as much as might have been hoped initially], and in a fit condition to tackle the future'. A few weeks later Dr Glover received a letter from her, saying she was making plans to come back to London from the country and intended to undertake some war work, probably helping in a mobile canteen.

Glover compared the case of Mrs A, a case of 'transitory' shock, with that of a 'war neurotic' whose wife had been killed in a raid. He remained in a state of agitated depression long afterwards, was unable to work, had no powers of concentration, his memory was 'grossly disturbed and his social reactions completely changed. He lived a solitary life and could not bear contact with his former associates. He brought his small son back from [evacuation in] the country, but was unable to care for him.' This unfortunate man, Glover discovered, had 'marked anxiety and [an] obsessional disposition'; moreover, 'his psycho-sexual history was not entirely satisfactory'.

Such differences could be observed in people who had suffered exactly the same experience. A husband and wife were dug out after an incident in which another couple had been killed: both were injured, though not seriously. The wife remained in a state of acute anxiety, refusing to undress and go to bed, even though she had been evacuated to the country, whereas the husband insisted on staying in London and carrying on with his job as normal, despite his injuries. Again, investigation revealed that while the husband had shown 'no sign of a neurotic disposition, the wife's past history indicated that from childhood she had shown many signs of a neurotic character, a fact confirmed by questioning the husband as to their domestic life'.

The wildly exaggerated pre-blitz predictions had been based on the 'casual assumption that there could be little to distinguish the life of civilians living under air raid conditions from that of soldiers living under front-line conditions such as existed in the Great War', but in fact they were different in a number of ways. There were some similarities on the home front to a battle-front during the first days of continuous bombardment of London's East End, in Coventry, and later on Merseyside, Clydebank and in Plymouth, and this is where signs of panic and hysteria were noted – though they were generally short lived. The writer Celia Fremlin, who worked as an ARP warden and also for M-O, recalled an East End shelter: 'At the beginning, when nobody was used to it, the women got absolutely hysterical. They were screaming and saying "I can't stand it, I'm going to die, I can't stand it." And there would usually be one who was saying "Calm down, calm down." Sometimes the women would be really hysterical, crying and falling on the floor. I only once saw it as bad as that, in a shelter. The next time I went there, four nights later, they were all much calmer, they'd bought stools to sit on, and there was even a bit of community singing. Because once you've been through three nights of bombing, you can't help feeling safe the fourth time. So the only real panic I saw was then.'

In general, raids were not relentlessly continuous, and even in London, which was blitzed continuously for fifty-seven nights, the bombs fell all over the capital, so while some boroughs, notably Holborn, Stepney and the City of London, were attacked with the largest number of bombs, there were nights when no bombs fell on them, even as other parts of London were being blitzed, and there were some streets in those boroughs that were not hit. The same was true of other places that suffered grievously – Merseyside, Glasgow, Coventry, Swansea, Plymouth, Hull.

Melitta Schmideberg, the psychoanalyst daughter of Melanie Klein (to whose views she was implacably opposed) who worked with Edward Glover, Donald Winnicott, John Bowlby and others monitoring reactions to the war among their own patients, noted how intensely parochial people became in wartime. 'Life took on a more medieval colouring. At dusk some of the big streets looked almost like a village street: at night they were dark and deserted. One became district, even street conscious. What happened in one's own street was of vital importance, while other districts seemed very remote. They were, of course, actually further off owing to the disturbances of traffic.' Schmideberg recalled a conversation with her greengrocer in late September 1940 during which she confessed that she was only really interested in whether a UXB near *her* house had been exploded, whereas the greengrocer was only interested in one a street away because it lay behind *his* shop. This localism was reinforced by the fact that large numbers of people had left London, either because they had been bombed out or because they had opted to evacuate. Those left behind for economic or other reasons felt a sense of siege, but also of pride, of 'sticking it out', of 'taking it', and this engendered a sense of community. 'Neighbours became more important. Everybody needed one another's help or comfort, and since so many had left London, those who remained felt they had more in common. Many neighbours spoke to each other for the first time in their lives, often having made each other's acquaintance in the small hours of the morning.' Communities were formed in shelters, which gradually took on the atmosphere of a club or a (mostly) dry pub, and there were people who would look back on the blitz less as a period of fear than with a certain sense of loss for the camaraderie engendered by those extraordinary times. Londoners in particular felt that their experience was unique (this of course infuriated people in provincial cities which were suffering acutely too – though not for anything like such a prolonged period as the capital), and could find letters from friends or relatives in the country, telling of a bomb that had fallen on the village green and shattered five panes of glass in a nearby house, hilarious.

Unlike soldiers in battle, for civilians ordinary life in familiar surroundings went on in the intervals between raids. Lord Woolton, the Minister of Food, remarked with some truth that egg rationing produced more emotion than the blitz – and probably as many letters to the press. Melitta Schmideberg was amazed to find that in the midst of the worst period of the blitz, the usual preparations for spring continued in the London parks, and 'one would have a lengthy correspondence with one's laundry over a lost handkerchief, seriously conducted by both sides. It would not occur to either party, that if either the laundry or one's own house were hit, more would be lost than the handkerchief.' The investment in normality became crucial. Schmideberg noticed that her patients, including some from the badly bombed East End, would make a considerable effort to keep their appointments, despite acute travel problems, since making a subsequent appointment suggested confidence that both analyst and patient would still be there next week.

While soldiers could 'benefit' from shell shock, in that they would be invalided away from the source of danger, civilians gained nothing from such a breakdown, particularly as hospitals had the reputation of being particular targets for bombers. Shops often served as local beacons of survival, making a point of staying open even when their windows were blasted out and their roofs sagging, with defiant slogans such as 'More Open Than Usual'. Defiance was an important component of wartime morale. There were surprisingly few calls for retaliation on Germany, most people declined to adopt Churchill's nomenclature of the 'Hun', instead usually referring to the Germans as the less threatening 'Jerries', and jokes were of a belittling kind. 'I see the decorator's boys were over again last night,' people might say, a reference to Hitler's supposed past as a painter/decorator. Or a bus conductor would apologise to his passengers for the endless detours during a raid by explaining: 'There's a nasty old man in the sky dropping stones.' People would decline to move from a bombed area, arguing, 'Why should I oblige Hitler and leave?' (The wartime equivalent of today's politicians' 'We must not let the terrorists win.') When there was no raid, they might joke, 'Jerry's caught short tonight,' and so on. People would tend to exaggerate their 'bomb stories', claiming greater damage or greater proximity to an incident than was in fact the case, with what appeared to be pride rather than fear. They would indulge in 'jaunty behaviour . . . inclined to pop in and out in order to keep an eye on the progress of an attack, rather like passengers in a liner taking a turn on deck to inspect the weather'. Though this could suggest a 'defence through defiance', a psychoanalyst, Dr George Franklin, noted other examples of what might be termed 'jaunty behaviour' occasioned by heightened anxiety and the bravado required to mask it. 'Apparently normal people drank more alcohol. Sexual desire, especially in women, was much intensified during the blitz. A number of men complained to me about their wives making excessive demands, and I know of very many who were unfaithful to their husbands.' This phenomenon was explored by Marghanita Laski, writing under a pseudonym, in her wartime novel *To Bed With Grand Music*.

The doughty blitz spirit should not be exaggerated, however. 'I have met many conscientious citizens who are afraid of being afraid,' wrote 'A Psychiatrist' in the *Daily Herald* in early October 1940. 'I tell them it is natural to feel fear in air raids and human to show fear. And it is honest to admit it. What your country has a right to ask of you is that you conquer fear to such a degree that you don't cause panic in others ... Courage consists in admitting fear and controlling it for the sense of duty and to strengthen others.' Those people who stayed in heavily bombed areas did develop a degree of fatalism after their initial moments of fear (otherwise they could hardly have stayed), adopting comforting mantras about a bomb having your name on it, and if it did, you were doomed, if it didn't, you'd be all right – there was nothing you could do either way. The majority of people were never directly affected by a bomb, and while they would undoubtedly have seen much bomb damage if they lived in or visited London, Liverpool, Glasgow or other target cities, they were unlikely to see many gruesome sights: dead bodies or parts of bodies. That did not apply to Civil Defence workers – ARP wardens, stretcher bearers, members of the heavy rescue squads, ambulance drivers, volunteers such as the WVS. But their work gave them some protection: they had a role, something neces-sary and important to do in a raid, rather than just sit there listening and waiting. They were working with other people in the same position, and could talk about their experiences afterwards with mates who had had similar ones. They had a uniform (and in wartime a uniform felt right), and an authority that they might well not have had in peacetime. And having to be brave, many found, actually made them brave.

But there undoubtedly was fear, evidenced by the numbers who left London and other cities, who 'trekked' into the countryside after heavy raids without any clear destination. It was entirely rational to be afraid: bombs and shrapnel were lethal. People were vulnerable, and ultimately, as Stanley Baldwin had said back in 1932, 'The bomber will always get through,' and kill men, women and children, with shrapnel, by bomb blast or by being buried by falling masonry, or drowned or gassed as a result of fractured pipes – terrible deaths, and in 1940–41 there were 43,685 of them.

Yet, as Dr Glover insisted, by the end of the blitz the 'Mass Neurosis Myth' was being replaced by a 'No Neurosis Myth'. It was a question of defi-nition, of lack of research, of no uniformity of diagnostic approach or data, of the fact that so many possible cases of neurosis never showed up at hospital, that records were lost – if they were kept at all. People were evac-uated and no record was kept of them. Many might show no obvious symp-toms at the time of their blitz experience, but might have a delayed reaction, perhaps as much as a year later, which would not be tracked. In any case, the question of how psychological symptoms presented was problematic. Most GPs in the 1940s had scant knowledge of psychiatry, and were unlikely to probe somatic symptoms to see if there were underlying psychological causes. Even if a patient did complain of depression or confusion, unless these were demonstrably acute, he or she was more likely to be given a 'tonic' than to be referred to a psychiatrist or the psychiatric outpatients department of a hospital, and certainly to a psychoanalyst. As George Orwell wrote, 'Doctors in wartime tend to develop a rather ruthless attitude towards psychological disturbances' – on the home front as on the battlefront.

Despite the setting up of the London Psycho-Analytical Society by Ernest Jones in 1913, and the arrival in London from Vienna of Sigmund Freud with his psychoanalyst daughter Anna in the summer of 1938, psycho-analysis was not a major concern of the majority of British medical prac-titioners, the subconscious not something much probed. And probably most people who might have benefited from psychological help didn't even get as far as consulting a doctor (which would have cost money, unless they were covered by some form of insurance), but would be described by their family as 'nervy', or as having had a 'bad time' in the blitz, and coped with at home.

There are many accounts in interviews and letters of people suffering considerable mental anguish during the blitz, but seeking or receiving profes-sional help is rarely mentioned. Priority at the time had to be given to phys-ical injuries: on the whole psychological damage, which was imagined to right itself with rest and something useful to do, slipped through the net. 'You were just going backwards and forwards to work, and when you were out, you didn't know what was happening to your mum, or your sisters. You didn't even know if you had a home. I felt at the time that it was hopeless. To me as a young person, the whole world seemed hopeless. I couldn't see an end to it. Everywhere was getting flattened and burned,' recalled firewoman Emily Eary. Viola Bawtree, who lived in Sutton, Surrey, wrote on 10 November 1940, 'I've not heard a warning for weeks, but today I heard almost every one and each time it gave me a horrible heave inside. I don't know how to describe it, like you might get if you heard a sudden wail of someone in distress, or a shriek of pain.' A young civil servant noticed that her hair was beginning to fall out. 'We started talking about hair – I told [a colleague] about my bald patch and she said immediately "That's nerves." I am very much inclined to agree with her. I know I have often felt very strained and tired, and at one time travelling in those tubes was just a hideous nightmare to me.' Doctors noticed an increase in peptic ulcers, and advertisements for diarrhoea remedies increased: people spoke of feeling fear in the pit of their stomach, in their guts.

Those caught in air raids might feel particularly helpless: unlike soldiers under fire, they had no means of fighting back, though conversely they were not required to kill. Civil Defence workers had the advantages of action, involvement, routine and camaraderie, but at a terrible cost. Not only were they in the front line, out in raids with only a tin hat to protect them, but they had to deal with truly awful situations. Not just the injured and the dead, but the completely dismembered. And because they were by design a local service, they had often known the people whose remains they were having to excavate, to toss into a basket. They also lost colleagues, men and women with whom they had shared literally unspeakable experiences over months, sometimes years. Like the Home Guard, many were 'twice citizens', working at their ordinary jobs by day, undertaking exhausting and hazardous work by night, usually with minimal training, and certainly with no understanding of 'post-traumatic stress' either on their own part or that of their superiors.

Irene Haslewood was a driver for stretcher bearers in Chelsea, but 'in an incident, I become fifth stretcher bearer or general dog's body'. Her old sixteen-horsepower Hillman saloon was stacked with four stretchers on the roof, and herself, four men and 'all our first aid paraphernalia' crammed inside. 'Our official job is to be first out on any incident, to sort out the living from the dead.' Haslewood was off duty when at 10.15 p.m. on 19 November, Sloane Square tube station suffered a direct hit from a 2,000-

pound bomb, 'just as a train was leaving the station, so the bomb caught the last two coaches and all of the passengers who had disembarked from the train. It also caught the big underground canteen which is kept open at night for bus drivers etc. I believe the utter carnage of the disaster beggared description. Some of the men who had been working on the job tried to tell me about it. They hardly got anyone out alive. Most of the poor bodies had been stripped of their clothing from the blast. Two stark naked and mutilated bodies of young girls hung high up in the twisted steel girders – trapped by their feet hanging head downwards. The men could not get them released for days and had to work under this ghastly spectacle. They never found out how many dead they collected, because there were so many small bits and pieces of bodies they could not reckon things out. The men collected these gruesome pieces in dustpans – and then of course the question arose of what to do with them? They did not know whether to send them to the mortuary or to Durhams Wharf – where all the refuse is taken away in barges down the river. I am glad to say they decided on the latter.'

William Regan, an ARP warden on the Isle of Dogs, recalled the tension he and his colleagues were under. After South Hallsville School had been hit, 'the school playground shed had been screened off for cleaning and shrouding bodies. I never saw them coffined. It was fine, warm weather, and the shed was wide open, with the bodies lying on the asphalt: soon, by order and example, [the chief officer at Poplar mortuary] had his men stripping off what clothing remained on the corpses. "Now, wash 'em off," he says, and the first one to try had a water bucket and a sponge, and began gently to wash the face of one corpse with a sponge. The expert soon stopped that: he wasn't going to have a four-hour job. He ordered two of his men to keep the buckets of water coming, and with a long-handled, well wetted mop, gave the first corpse a good wash, back and front, and showed the men how to wrap them in shrouds, label them, and stow them ready for final disposal. Each one took about three to four minutes, and, as he said, "That's how it's done. You'll get the hang of it soon enough." I don't think they ever did.'

A week later, Regan went to investigate another incident. 'We gathered three bushel baskets of remains. I picked up two left feet. One of the men saw a body perched on the rooftop. Nobby Clark climbed up and recovered it. It was badly mutilated and it was some time before we were able to identify it as female. I had picked up two left feet, and with a right foot, Major Brown thought the three feet accounted for three people. Some of the men were feeling queasy, so rum was dished out. I was TT [teetotal] so I gave mine away, and eventually we found enough evidence to account for three people, so we came away.'

Regan had volunteered for duty over Christmas 1940, and was called to a bombed Poplar school, the layout of which he knew well because he had worked to build it.

There were no survivors after all this time [three months] so systematic clearance was called for. After an hour or so George [Jillings, a fellow warden who had been in the building trade with Regan] called me to help him with a doormat he had found, but could not pull clear. It was black, and of a thick, curly texture, so I fished around for a while loosening the packed rubble, then George came back with a length of iron rod to prise it out. I told him it was a bloke, and I knew who it was, Herbie Martin.

Meanwhile, everyone else had gathered in one spot. We went over to find out why. They had found two bodies and sent for Light Rescue to come and take them away, and while I watched two more bodies were being uncovered. I know none of us are very happy about handling corpses and it shows. They had uncovered two young girls, about 18 years of age, quite unmarked, and looked as if they were asleep. I looked around at the other men, and most of them looked shocked, and a bit sick: we had usually found bodies mutilated, and they were usually lifted out by hands and feet and quickly got away. Major Brown sees one man being sick, so he fishes out a bottle of rum to be handed round.

By now, I am feeling a bit angry at the prospect of these two girls being lugged by their arms and legs, so I got down beside them, and they have obviously been in bed for the night. They both have only their knickers and short petticoats on, and the dry weather we have had, and the rubble packed round them had preserved them. Their limbs were not even rigid. They were life-like. I could not let them be handled like the usual corpses. I would have belted the first one who handled them with disrespect, but nobody makes a move to shift them, they just stand there, gawping.

I looked at George, and I said 'Stretcher, blanket.' Then I put my right arm under her shoulders with her head resting against me, and my left arm under her knees, and so carried her up. 'You'll be comfortable now, my dear.' I did exactly the same with the other one. I stood and waited for some smart Alec to make a snide remark, but nobody did. I cooled down a bit after I had smoked a cigarette. I wonder why I had been so angry?

Civil Defence workers' families were granted a modest pension if they were killed, and there were disablement payments for those injured, although these were lower for women than men. As the *Lancet* pointed out, for the purposes of 'injury allowances' and pensions, a war service injury was defined as 'a physical injury to a volunteer arising out of and in the course of the performance of his duties as a member of the civil defence organisation . . . the definition does not cover neurasthenia or similar sickness in which the symptoms are induced merely by apprehension and fears of enemy action'. Later, trade unions lobbied for pensions to be awarded to their members whose psychological injuries made them unable to continue working.

However, Lord Horder, the King's physician, who had chaired the committee on the use of public air-raid shelters, reminded *Times* readers on 15 October 1940 that 'The shock troops of this great [civilian front-line] army are the various A.R.P. services, especially in the big cities . . . If we believe that the nation which is most resilient establishes thereby a sound basis for ultimate victory we must learn to treat our A.R.P. workers as we treat our fighting forces. A primary need of our frontline fighters, whatever their service, is the rest pause. To remain within the vulnerable areas and to be deprived of sleep invites both physical and moral collapse.' He instanced a 'small scale experiment undertaken by a single-handed Red Cross transport officer who transported personally as many of her colleagues as she could to hospitable quarters within reach of London for one night. This private venture succeeded beyond all our hopes. Tired, bomb-haunted women returned in new heart and better health as the result of the leeway of sleep being made up, the memory of one night's rest between sheets, one day's food in quiet, and a sight of the English scene instead of bricks and rubble.' The scheme should be undertaken, Horder urged, 'by those responsible for every unit of civil defences services, petrol rations should be allowed, and a register of willing hosts and hostesses should be kept'.

The Red Cross worker mentioned was Joan Woollcombe, and as a result of Lord Horder's letter, readers sent in money to extend the scheme. A voluntary part-time ARP worker in Sevenoaks in Kent suggested that there were many like her living in the Home Counties who would be happy to be 'lent' to badly affected London districts on a regular basis, to take the place of exhausted London workers, and the Londoners might like to stay in the homes of their substitutes while they were taking over for a bit in London.

In May 1941 *The Times* was able to report that as an extension of Mrs Woollcombe's scheme, Mr and Mrs Raymond Dumas had moved into their gardener's cottage, and their own house in the 'blissfully quiet spot' of Great Missenden in Buckinghamshire, had been turned into a place of respite for fifty ARP (or 'Civil Defence', as they were known by then) workers, twenty-five men and twenty-five women. The first to arrive spoke with gratitude of 'the restfulness of the place and the solace it affords to overtaxed nerves, minds and bodies'. By 1942 the scheme had spread across England and Wales, with forty Civil Defence workers a month leaving London alone for various rest homes (often in private houses) or to take up beds in convalescent homes. By March 1944 over 30,000 had had a spell in such places, either to recover from illness or injury, or simply to enjoy some 'recuperative rest' so they could carry on with their gruelling war work.

Rest alone was seen as the cure for the ills and traumas of the blitz. There were no counselling or psychiatric services on offer, unless an individual was severely traumatised and unable to return to work, or sought help privately. Mostly people repressed their experiences, did not talk about them, and got on with the job. There is little follow-up evidence of whether this worked in the long term. But Lyndsey Stonebridge and others have pointed out that there are many examples of wartime anxieties expressed in literature by those who had seen the blitz at close quarters. Graham Greene worked at the Ministry of Information and was an ARP warden until he took up espionage, as was his wartime lover. His 1943 novel *The Ministry of Fear* is a dark work of intrigue and madness set in the blitz. Greene's house on Clapham Common received a direct hit, a scene re-envisaged in *The End of the Affair* (1951), a novel suffused with war guilt and anxiety. Henry Green (Henry Yorke) replayed his anxieties in his novel *Caught* (1943), about the AFS, of which he was a member. Rose Macaulay, who was bombed out of her flat, reprised the threatening strangeness of blitzed London in *The World My Wilderness* (1950), as did Elizabeth Bowen in her disturbing reiterations of wartime anxieties, most particularly in her novel *The Heat of the Day* (1949) and her short story 'The Demon Lover' (1945).

Tom Harrisson, who, as he said, 'was not a medical man, though trained as a biologist', took issue with the 'surprisingly low degree of nervous and shock responses' in April 1941. On the basis of the 'exceptional facilities' afforded by his work for Mass-Observation 'for the observation of ordinary people during the past seven months of heavy raids . . . in widely separated areas from Plymouth to Liverpool, from Coventry to Clydeside', he claimed to have found several cases of people who had left heavily bombed areas, 'found a billet . . . and then caved in. In some cases they have simply taken to bed and stayed in bed for weeks at a time. They have not shown the marked trembling of hysteria, but an extreme desire to retreat into sleep and be looked after, as if chronically ill. We have found such cases mainly among women but also among men and children . . . Gradually, over the months we have become impressed with the possibility that there may be quite a large number of them . . . Certainly, such cases . . . are not likely to be reported to or to reach a psychiatrist. Yet they may be serious and even recurring reactions.'

Harrisson argued from the work of Mass-Observation in the 'morale field', visiting 'all the "blitztowns" except Belfast that . . . it is often those not so directly or physically affected by air raids who are most upset by them'. He suspected that 'the most upsetting factor is *uncertainty* . . . First, you never know what night the raid is going to come. Secondly, you never know which 'plane noise or other noise is the noise which may mean your end.' The psychologist Charles Berg agreed with this, reporting a conversation with a soldier on leave who had sought treatment for his anxiety state: 'Sitting in an Anderson shelter waiting for the bomb to come is the worst. I have a phantasy that a great bomb will come down through the opening of the shelter, and then come up and get me . . . It seems to me that I would not mind being bumped off, but I cannot bear waiting for it . . . there is so much tension that something has *got* to be done. If I sit in an Anderson shelter, I feel it is going to be done *to* me, whereas if I fight it would be much better. Then I would be doing it to somebody.'

As far as Harrisson was concerned, 'Too many generalisations have been made from a purely London experience. London is a different story: it is so huge and anonymous. I know from personal experience that it is ten times more unpleasant to be bombed in a place like Coventry, or Bristol, where every bomb is personal, and every piece of damage is a disaster to one's own town, instead of this great aggregation called London. In London, moreover, those with nervous tendencies have had an invaluable line of retreat, lacking in practically every other city. They have been able to bury themselves in the Tubes. The Tubes have provided a safety valve for those who otherwise might have behaved badly.' By implication, deep shelters would have helped this problem in provincial cities as well as in the capital. However, Edward Glover had seen cause for concern here too. Some people had adopted what he characterised as a 'shelter slug' mentality, a patholog-ical reluctance to leave the underground stations when the All Clear went, even in daytime.

One consequence of heavy and continual bombardment that Harrisson did not mention was exhaustion. This had been especially noticeable in the early days of the blitz, when Londoners were reported to be going about their business looking 'drawn and white' or 'ashen grey with tiredness'. At the end of September 1940, Mass-Observation produced a report on how much sleep people were managing to snatch. On 12 September, 31 per cent of those polled claimed not to have slept at all, 32 per cent for less than four hours, 22 per cent between four and six hours, and only 15 per cent managed six hours or more. Respondents claimed to be 'fagged out', 'dread-fully tired'. Worst affected of all were those living near AA gun sites. Seventy per cent of those living near a large gun at Wormwood Scrubs claimed to have had no sleep at all, although they maintained that 'Though the noise was awful, we were glad to hear it.' Women were reported to get less sleep than men, and the working classes less than the middle classes – probably because the walls of their houses tended to be thinner, more slept in public shelters, and in September 1940 it tended to be the East End that was pummelled worst. Earplugs were recommended, and were eventually distrib-uted to a limited number of boroughs, where they proved popular. Alderman Key told the Commons on 9 October that in Poplar 140,000 pairs had been handed out. Earplugs did 'require training so the user gradually becomes accustomed to not being able to hear, and so not listening for the sound of bombs and planes'. M-O also recommended that 'the importance of sleep in daytime for those who *could* make the time but are unwilling to shirk their duties, should be stressed. These are mainly housewives.' It noted, but did not recommend, that 'aspirins and alcohol were other methods tried to induce sleep'.

Gradually things improved somewhat, and people became more immured to the noise of the raids, but certainly most Londoners were tired out until at least the end of 1940, and then through the spring of 1941. It was the sounds of war, the discomforts of war – damp, crowded Anderson shelters, fetid public shelters and tube platforms, with a cacophony of snoring and grunting, hard benches or bunks to sleep on. Soon the greatest luxury was a good night's sleep: it was the thing the London teacher Phyllis Warner most enjoyed when she spent a weekend in Oxford in October 1940. Advertisements offering remedies proliferated – Horlicks claimed that its malted drink helped to achieve the 'third level' of sleep that was necessary to provide the energy to face the coming day. Lack of sleep meant that people increasingly took risks, reckoning that they would rather dice with death by staying in their own bed at night than drag themselves down to another sleepless night in the shelter.

The effect of air raids on children was of particular concern. The magazine *Housewife* offered counsel: 'First there is the question of waking children during night raids in order to take them to a place of greater safety. Safety is certainly important but so is sleep. There is all the difference in the world between the mental stability of a child who is constantly woken at night (from whatever cause) to one who is allowed to sleep from, say 8pm to 7am undisturbed.' What children needed, the magazine prescribed, was 'unbroken sleep . . . on the other hand, peaceful slumbers which are terminated by wounding or disablement are too dearly bought, so it is obviously unwise to leave children in the bedroom of a bungalow or upper storey of a small house when some better shelter is available . . . in an area where continuous raids are to be feared . . . permanent sleeping quarters should be prepared which are themselves a shelter and where the children and one adult can sleep every night in as much safety as it is possible to provide. The one adult is important because even sleeping children must never be left alone during a raid. It is true that many will become accustomed to sleep through the most terrific noise, but an extra loud explosion may wake them and then they will find much comfort in a sleepy, indifferent murmur from a trusted "grown up" saying that it is only a fight and that the English are winning.'

But was that really sufficient? Should children be in 'blitztowns' at all? The government had not thought so: the official evacuation scheme which started on 1 September 1939 had encouraged that all children – either with their school or with their mother or carer if they were under school age – along with any other '*bouches inutiles*', or 'useless mouths', should be removed from 'danger zones', and much propaganda was expended to encourage parents to leave their offspring in safe areas during the phoney war when none of the threatened bombs fell. It was not a very successful campaign: by December 1940 more than 60 per cent of those who had left London had returned. When the blitz started some parents did either take or send their children into the country, but in September 1940 there were still an estimated half a million schoolchildren in London, and many pre-schoolers too.

The manufacturers of Lifebuoy soap ran a series of advertisements with suggestions for those living through air raids with children:

Keep calm and cheerful . . . and the kiddies will share your mood. If they're very young, try not to wake them. Wrap them in warm blankets and carry them gently to the shelter. In case they should wake, have a hot sweet drink ready. Glucose sweets are good, too. Barley sugar, especially, combats the effect of shock. It is also a good plan to keep large sweets handy for the kiddies – these will keep their mouths open and the effect of this is to contract the ear drum which helps minimise the noise and effect of shock. See that there are plenty of toys and games in the shelter. And remember that it's worth a little trouble to have sufficient light. It's best to get an ARP lantern if you can. With ordinary candles, there's always some risk of their falling over or blowing out.

Housewife was on-message too:

Air raids will only mean a great noise to younger children and provided Daddy and Mummy won't mind they won't.

But it is no good pretending to older children that raids are of no importance. Far better to reassure them by admitting the danger, but stressing the very long odds against them being hit.

Explain that there are over 42,000,000 people in Great Britain, and even if the Germans were better shots than they are, they could only manage to kill a few out of that number, and the chances of your home being hit are therefore extremely small.

Also explain that the slightly shaky, sick feeling which they experience during raids is not really being afraid but is the result of the interference with the normal vibrations in the atmosphere due to the explosion.

That will help to take away that feeling of guilt that schoolboys and even schoolgirls are apt to experience when they fear they are not being as brave as they would like to be.

This sound advice ended on a rather wistful note. 'Those who have charge of children during raids are very much to be envied, for by concentrating all their wits and energies on saving the young things from mental and physical harm, they find they have no time or inclination to give in to their own fears.'

Mass-Observation reported on a family sheltering during a raid with three young children:

> Mummy told Jessica (6½) who was inclined to whimper and be jittery not to because that was what would please Hitler, and she shut up . . . The children got cotton wool put in their ears . . . we gave each child some of the bromide prescribed by the doctor, and a piece of chocolate afterwards, but it didn't seem to have the slightest effect. Patsy said hardly anything but sat on my knee shivering a little . . . Jessica worried 'Will a bomb fall on my Daddy in London?' 'Will Mummy and Sally be all right in Oxford?' 'Will a bomb fall on us here?' 'If a bomb falls on the house and all our things are spoilt, what shall we do?' Crispin appeared to be enjoying himself. Torrents of conversation poured from him . . . 'I do hope we'll hear something soon don't you? I do think this is exciting, where do you think they're bombing? I do hope we can have some bombs, it'll make it more exciting . . . can I have some more chocolate? Can I go and look outside?' (NO!) 'Hark, what was that? Maybe it's only a dud air raid and the All Clear will go in half and hour and it'll all be a sell.'

Most psychologists and psychoanalysts shared the common-sense perception that children took their cues from their parents. 'Children stand up to bombing remarkably well,' concluded Dr Crichton-Miller of the Tavistock Clinic. 'What they do not resist is the contagion of panic and hysteria on the part of their elders.' 'Small children are not afraid of raids – unless the adults are – because they do not fully realise the danger,' reported Melitta Schmideberg.

Mass-Observation investigated the effects of raids in the East End. In the months before the blitz, an investigator had watched a group of nine-year-olds playing 'air raids' in Bethnal Green. The girls' voices

> rose in a long low wail . . . rose, fell, and rose again in unison, imitating (most realistically) the sound of the air-raid siren. At last the wail died away, one of the little girls stepped forward in the role of 'Teacher'. 'No panic, girls, no panic please,' She commanded in perfect mimicry of a harassed teacher. ''As anyone forgot their gas mask . . .? Then go 'ome and get it . . .' At intervals a 'whistle' blew, and they all came out [of a cupboard which was standing in for an air-raid shelter] again, always under the heavy instructions from 'Teacher' . . . Meanwhile, boys at the same play centre were also playing air

raids ... In contrast to the relatively ordered make believe evolved by the girls, the nine-year-old boys interpreted the theme by racing wildly up and down, knocking furniture over, bashing into one another, and screaming 'Help!' at the top of their voices. The game became so wild that it had to be forbidden, and the boys agreed to play 'Gangsters and Cops' instead. 'To the onlooker,' Inv[estigator]. records dispassionately, 'this game appeared exactly the same as "Air Raids".'

Air-raid games of one sort or another were rife all over London during the early months of the war, and were indulged in by children of all ages. But even the most exciting game isn't the real thing: how would these enthusiastic players react to that? The answer came all too soon: they 'still seemed to keep their cool ... Observers all over London throughout the Blitz, tended to confirm the initial impression of all-round toughness and resilience in the face of bombing. In the shelters, in the streets, in their homes, they continued to play. ("Rescue Parties" was a favourite game, played with a clothesline with which children were no longer tied up and "captured" as they had once been, but were now "rescued" by the same method.) Children played in the bomb sites that had once been their "village", a little boy proudly showed an ARP man where his home had been – the top floor of a block of flats that had received a direct hit, while in Stepney, an excited seven-year-old emerged from the basement of his shattered home: "I had me socks and shoes on *in bed*!" he announced excitedly': this to him had been the big drama of the occasion. In a Bermondsey rest centre for the bombed-out, a woman helper, asking a six-year-old where her mother was, received the answer: 'Dad's been and gone and got blowed up, and Mum has got to look for 'is bits!'

Anna Freud, whose father Sigmund had died from cancer three weeks after the outbreak of war, had set up a temporary shelter for bombed-out families in a house in Hampstead in October 1940, but quickly realised that what was needed most urgently was somewhere for children to live, either if they could not be evacuated with their mothers, or if problems had developed with the families with which they had been billeted. At first Freud and her close friend and colleague Dorothy Burlingham were only able to accommodate ten or twelve children, some of whom came with their mothers, mainly from the East End. But early in 1941 the American Foster Parents' Plan offered financial support to the Hampstead War Nursery, and that summer a Babies' Rest Centre was opened in a nearby street, and a country house, New Barn in Essex, was made available for older children: in total 120 babies and children from six months old were gathered in for care, providing a unique – or as the *Lancet* called it, a 'glorious' – opportunity to study the effects of air raids on the young.

Anna Freud made a point of not separating siblings, and encouraged parents to visit as often as possible. When it became obvious that this was not always sufficient for the children, she organised them into 'families' of four or five, each with a 'mother', the role of 'father' being played whenever possible by local ARP workers and firemen if there were not enough resident staff to fulfil the paternal role.

Her work led Freud too to believe that children did not suffer particularly from the fear of air raids. For example, they did not associate a plane overhead with bombs falling, and when the staff took 'our big girls, 6 and 9 years old . . . for a walk and pass damaged houses [they] make expert casual remarks: "Incendiary bomb" (this is where the roof is burned out); "high-explosive" (where walls are badly shaken)'. When Stephen Spender came to talk about his work in the AFS, the children were less awed by the dangerous work he was doing than taken by the fact that 'Spender' sounded very like 'suspender'.

The children remained stable provided they were not separated from their mothers – and certainly not separated abruptly. The Hampstead War Nursery charges all had long experience of attacks from the air. The fathers of ten of them had been killed in raids, the houses of fifteen had been destroyed or badly damaged. Two children had been bombed three times and buried under debris once, while nearly all had experience of shelter life – either the tube, public or Anderson shelters, or under the stairs. In sum: 'all the children have seen their family lives dissolved by separation from, or death of the father. All of them are separated from their mothers and have entered community life at an age which is not normally considered ripe for it.'

Anna Freud's conclusions were much the same as those of *Housewife* and the Lifebuoy soap advertisement: 'So long as bombing incidents occur when small children are in the care of their mothers or a familiar mother-substitute, they do not seem particularly affected by them. Their experience remains an "accident".'

Things were very different if a child had become separated from or lost a parent during a raid. Then raids assumed a completely different dimension, and each would be a replay of the devastating one. 'For these children, every bomb that falls is like the one that killed their father and is feared as such.'

Parental anxiety communicated itself to the children. One five-year-old whose agoraphobic mother insisted that he should not go to bed during a raid but should stand, fully dressed, with her as she trembled in the doorway, became extremely anxious and started wetting the bed. Most young children would be afraid of fantasies such as lions or tigers or ghosts, of being left alone in the dark: in the blitz these fears would be translated into fear of Hitler, bombs and being attacked by planes at night. As far as Anna Freud was concerned, these worries were external, and her task (and that of parents) was to reassure and persuade children that there was really nothing to be anxious about.

But that was not how all psychoanalysts in Britain saw matters. Melanie Klein, who regarded herself as Sigmund Freud's intellectual heir, believed that anxiety, far from being externally generated, was internal, and had to be stimulated in order to be dealt with. In the psychologist Charles Berg's words, 'The war crisis is merely a screen memory for or a precipitating factor in bringing to the surface unresolved infantile conflicts.' So, while Anna Freud passed her war years running nurseries, Klein spent an entire year in Pitlochry in Scotland analysing just one child, the unfortunately named 'Little Dick', a precociously gifted ten-year-old evacuee, surfacing his repressed infantile anxieties. One result was 'the longest case history' ever published, in 1961. Another was a profound and bitter split in the British psychoanalytical movement.

The conclusions that Freud, Edward Glover, Melitta Schmideberg, John Bowlby, Donald Winnicott and other psychoanalysts drew from the blitz, that it was separation that was damaging for a child, not the fact of the air raids, was an indictment of the policy of evacuation, which invariably meant a sudden, often unexplained, rupture. One three-and-a-half-year-old boy in Freud's nursery compulsively put his coat on and off as if to go out, and sat mourning for his absent mother, refusing to play with other children until she was able to visit him. A four-year-old girl 'sat for several days on the exact spot where her mother had left her, would not eat, speak or play and had to be moved around like an automaton'. Observations of behaviour like this were to have a profound impact on the post-war work of child guidance, most notably perhaps in John Bowlby's influential, and sometimes inhibiting, theories of maternal deprivation.

As Edward Glover wrote: 'Long-drawn-out states of homesickness, upset and despair were observed [as a result of wartime separation], compared with which the mental conditions of children sleeping on the underground was a state of bliss to which, during their homesickness, all children desired to return.' All the advantages in safety, health or comfort to be gained under good evacuation conditions 'may dwindle down to nothing when weighed against the fact that the child has to lose his family in order to gain them'.

10

The 1940 Provincial Tour

Whoosh go the goblins, coming back at nightfall,
Whoosh go the witches reaching their hands for me.
Whoosh goes the big, bad wolf and bang go his teeth.
Are we sure we will be the lucky ones, the princess, the youngest son,
The third pig evading the jaws? Can we afford to laugh?
They have come back, we always knew they would, after the story ended,
After the grown-ups shut the book and said goodnight.

Naomi Mitchison, 'Siren Night' (1940)

The erratic pattern of the German blitzes . . . seems in retrospect to be nearly senseless. The sequences show no logic, no discernable theory of what such attacks – more or less indiscriminate bombing of all structures within a few limited areas nightly – were supposed to achieve; nor any reason why one place was left alone, while another was given serial assault, though still never with any consistency. This uncertainty was, of course, one explanation of the lack of pattern. No one in Britain could know or predict where the next bombs might fall . . . The repetitive but erratic aspect is crucial to any understanding of what it was like to live through the provincial blitzes, raising fundamental questions of human adjustment which did not arise in the same way in London, a huge target, with almost continuous bombing experience; or Coventry at the other end of the scale, with virtually no continuity . . . Southampton was the first town to experience this type of cycle, which was later to hit Plymouth even more savagely.

Tom Harrisson, *Living Through the Blitz*

On 6 December 1940, Anthony Heap, who wrote a regular diary each night in the shelter where he and his mother were pleased to go every evening not just for safety, but also because it meant they were 'saving no end of money in lighting and heating', noted, 'It seems a long time since we had a regular all night raid. People are deserting the shelters and staying in at night. In fact the shelter habit is on the wane.' But two days later London had another heavy raid. On 8 December 'wave after wave of planes flew over to the accompaniment of a gun barrage', dropping 380 tons of high-explosive bombs and 115,000 fire bombs. In some respects it was almost a reprise of the first night of the blitz, with the docks a target. Offices of the Port of London authority were badly damaged, as were factories, offices and housing in the area. However, this time the Luftwaffe fanned out wide over the city, and bombs fell in an arc that stretched from Wanstead in east London, Marylebone in the centre and out to Dagenham, Croydon and Slough. Two hundred and fifty people were killed and six hundred seriously wounded, but on the whole December 1940 was quiet in the capital. But not in the provinces. 'Southampton seems to have come in for most of the aerial attacks lately. It's been taking some very fierce onslaughts,' noted Heap, and then on 23 December, 'Manchester was the main target of last night's raids. London is being let off lightly for the time being while the provincial tour is in progress.'

The 'provincial tour' was a comprehensive one. By the end of 1940 the Luftwaffe had dropped bombs from Aberdeen to Cornwall, all along the coast from Swansea, Avonmouth, Plymouth, Portsmouth, Southampton, Hastings, Ramsgate, Folkestone and up to Hull. In the Midlands, Birmingham had endured thirty-six raids and Coventry twenty-one. While London held the unwelcome palm with 126 attacks, Merseyside – including Liverpool, Bootle, Wallasey and Birkenhead – was 'Hitler's number one target' outside the capital, and had suffered sixty raids. It was a natural objective. The Mersey was lined with granaries, power stations, dry docks and gasworks; its port was Britain's lifeline, with ocean liners bringing food and war matériel across the Atlantic, and though the 'second city of Empire' had suffered during the Depression of the 1930s, by the time war broke out the tonnage of shipping coming in exceeded that before the First World War. By November Liverpool had been attacked on average every other night – though this was never made clear in the press: Merseyside continued to be referred to under the general heading of 'the north west', to the chagrin of its people. During raids Walton prison had been hit, killing a number of prisoners, the central station badly damaged, warehouses and docks set alight.

But the attack of 28–29 November outweighed anything that had gone before. More than 350 tons of high-explosive bombs, thirty large land mines (eight of which failed to explode) and 3,000 incendiaries carpeted the area, killing almost three hundred people. The most distressing incident of a dreadful night happened at the Ernest Brown Junior Technical College in Durning Road, the basement of which had been converted into a large public shelter. When the alert sounded, two trams stopped outside and the passengers streamed into the already crowded space. At 1.55 a.m. the school was hit by a land mine. The three-storey building collapsed into the basement shelter, killing some people outright, and burying others alive. Gas and boiling water from the fractured central heating system poured in, and wooden beams ignited. An ARP warden, Mrs Taft, who happened to be sheltering there with her three-year-old grandchild, took charge. One survivor remembered her as 'magnificent in her courage and her commonsense. Even as we heard groans from the dying, some of them children, she never cracked up. None of us thought we would ever get out alive, but Mrs. Taft kept cheering everyone up. When people said "We'll never get through," she just replied, "They will get us out all right." ' As the water rose to the knees of the mass of people crammed so tightly that it was difficult to move, and acrid smoke from the fires threatened to engulf them, Mrs Taft was frantically searching for a way out, since all the exits were blocked with masonry and rubble. She suddenly shouted, 'I can see a light!': she had found a small window that was not blocked, and called for volunteers to dig a way through. Someone produced a torch, and shone it through the window. The beam was seen, and rescue parties were summoned to force a way into the building. One hundred and sixty-four men, women and children were killed in the shelter and ninety-six were seriously injured; only twenty got out unscathed.

The Lucas family lived in nearby Chantry Street. They used the school shelter nightly, but on 28 November Mrs Lucas decided that as other shelterers had complained that six-year-old Joe's whooping cough kept them awake, she would keep him and his baby sister Brenda at home with her. She sent her other four children to the school in charge of seventeen-year-old Florence, the oldest. All four children died in the shelter: Florence, George aged four, Frances, nine, and Winifred, seven. 'The trauma of that night was so terrible that for six months my mother couldn't speak,' remembers Joe Lucas. 'She never spoke a word. Brenda was only a babe in arms, but for a long time mam wouldn't let us more than an arm's length away from her.'

Three weeks later, Merseyside experienced a series of severe raids. Short raids on 20–21 December started fires all along the Liverpool dockside, where an estimated £4 million-worth of timber went up in flames and the contents of Latex rubber storage tanks burned for days. The Cunard Shipping Line headquarters, the municipal offices and the central police station were hit, as was the Adelphi Hotel: the lights went out and the band played 'There'll Always be an England' to the diners; two hundred bedrooms, the ball room and grill room were badly damaged. Passengers waiting at Lime Street station fell to the ground as glass from the shattered roof cascaded down. A railway viaduct received a direct hit; the heavy concrete structure collapsed, killing forty-two people sheltering under its arches. Ships in the docks were holed and damaged by fire. In Bootle the docks and the timber yards were set alight, the food offices at County Hall were hit and thousands of ration books destroyed in the blaze. In Birkenhead there was severe damage to the Town Hall, and rows of working-class houses were demolished, while Wallasey suffered its heaviest raid of the war, with at least 130 killed over the three nights.

The following night, 21–22 December, the bombers were back, and the raids were even heavier. Again the docks and shipping were badly damaged – in Bootle fire burned through a hawser and a ship drifted off: it was several hours before it could be remoored and the crew – several of whom were injured – rescued. In Liverpool the historic St George's Hall was struck by a shower of incendiaries, but quick action by Civil Defence workers and the fire services saved the building, though the Law Library and the Sheriff's Court were burned out. A delayed-action bomb breached the bank of the Liverpool to Leeds canal, barges and tugs were sunk, the seven-man crew of a fire engine were all killed when it drove into a bomb crater, seventy-four people died when a shelter was hit in Anfield, and at Pier Head the church of Our Lady and St Nicholas was completely gutted, while in St John's Fish Market chickens, turkeys and geese, ready for Christmas, sizzled fiercely.

The next night, 22–23 December, the Luftwaffe raided Merseyside and Manchester simultaneously, and Wallasey suffered damage to residential properties and 119 fatalities. Seven hundred and two people lost their lives in the three night raids, and almost the same number were seriously injured. Bootle claimed the unenviable trophy of being 'probably the most bombed town – bomb for square yard – in the country': 8,000 of its 17,000 houses had been destroyed or damaged.

Southampton, another important port, was attacked on the night of 23 November; much of the city centre was destroyed and seventy-seven people were killed. On the night of 30 November–1 December there was another raid, described in the city fire brigade's report as being 'of the most serious proportion', and by an observer as 'a blazing furnace in which every living thing seemed doomed to perish'. It lasted for six hours. The water mains were knocked out of action, and worse, the AFS was almost two hundred men under strength, depleted through sickness and exhaustion. Crews were sent from as far away as Nottingham, Peterborough, Ipswich and Tunbridge Wells to find fires raging throughout the centre of the city and the docks. Eight hundred high-explosive bombs had been dropped, killing 137 people and seriously injuring 242. The main shopping area running through the Bargate was razed and the business district had been seriously damaged, as had cinemas, churches and halls. The docks had been 'severely hit and a large part of the dock wharves and sheds are in a state of tangled chaos'. The toll on residential property was very heavy too, particularly in the 'densely crowded small shopkeeper and working class area east of the town [where] several acres of it virtually consist of debris . . . The Pirelli Cable Works is in a real mess . . . and one of the striking sights of the town is the huge Ranks Flour Mill – one side of the gigantic storage tower has been sheared away.'

Mass-Observation despatched several investigators to Southampton straight away. They found the town 'stunned and quiet, but not on the whole deeply depressed'. At first people talked about the raid being as bad as that on Coventry nine nights previously, but by Tuesday, 3 December they had begun to revise their opinion, and decided it was 'worse than Coventry'. One man was heard to opine that it was 'worse than Pompeii' (but whether he meant the ancient city or nearby Portsmouth, known as 'Pompey', is not clear). Little interest was reported in casualties: few clustered around the list posted up outside the Town Hall, though no one seemed to believe the official estimated death toll of 370. '3,700 is the more likely figure,' one man asserted. There was a general feeling that Southampton was 'done for', though at least it was believed that it would not be raided again, 'because there is nothing left to hit'. Gas, water and electricity were off in most districts, and it was announced on 2 December that water (which was being brought in in army water carts) was not fit to drink unless it had first been boiled; but without gas or electricity, that posed a problem. There were no communal kitchens, and there was a general complaint about the lack of hot food. A girl was seen making tea with the water from a hot-water bottle.

Part of Southampton's problem was that most of the municipal offices, including the library and the Registrar's office, had been housed in the large Civic Centre, completed just before the war started at a cost of £750,000 and described by Sir Nikolaus Pevsner as 'perhaps the most ambitious civic building created in the provinces in the inter-war years', and that had been largely destroyed. It was not just the civil buildings that were incapacitated: so were the civic leaders. The Municipal Health Clinic bore a scrawled notice: 'NO ENTRY. DANGEROUS'. The Pensions Office was deserted. 'A group of RAF officers virtually took control of Central Hall, the main evacuation depot. They did good work and produced considerable order out of chaos,' to show solidarity with the people of Southampton, and were 'absolutely disgusted with the official handling of the evacuation'. They were 'scathing about the leadership of the city as a whole. They considered that some of the top civil and civic servants had either panicked or failed by default to meet the needs of the crisis. Some, they said, refused even to see it as a crisis; these had quit intellectually, some of them actually, physically too.'

In addition, the offices of the local daily newspaper had been hit, so it was not on the streets until the following Thursday (5 December). Hence information was desperately scarce. M-O's investigator saw no notice displayed outside the Civic Centre other than 'a small typewritten announcement about identifying the dead'. Many people did not seem to know where the rest centres were located, and though a considerable number of Civil Defence workers, demolition squads and police had been drafted in from as far afield as Oxford, Northampton, Hove, Cromer, Guildford and London, it was rumoured that most of them didn't know the area, and were not much help when asked for guidance, so much frustrating misinformation was passed on.

Unsurprisingly in this situation, there was a rush of people heading out of Southampton. By 4.40 each afternoon it was a 'dead town. No cars, hardly any people. Buses full, men and women walking with their baggage. Some going to relations in outlying areas. Some to shelters, preceded by wives who had reserved sleeping spaces, some to sleep in the open, anything rather than spend another night there. Many trying to hitchhike, calling out to every car that passed: few stopped. Caused considerable annoyance – empty coaches went past. Trains full of women and children – little baggage – as if coming back the next day . . . In some neighbourhoods, whole streets evacuated – note on door giving new address. One read "Home all day: away at night".' Rumours were also rife: Sotonians were gloomily prepared to believe Lord Haw Haw's gleeful prediction that 'When Southampton is finished, Winchester will be next,' and that AA guns were being moved out of the city to defend Birmingham.

Dr Cyril Garbett, the Bishop of Winchester (translated to the Archbishopric of York two years later), was driven to Southampton on 2 December. He found his flock 'broken in spirit . . . with everyone who can do so leaving the town . . . For the time, morale has collapsed. I went from parish to parish and everywhere there was fear,' he concluded sombrely.

Alarmed – and infuriated – by such reports, Herbert Morrison sent Wing Commander E.J. Hodsoll, Inspector General of Air Raid Precautions (IGARP), to investigate. Hodsoll's report, which was not made public until 1973, was damning: 'There was no outstanding personality in Southampton's local government at all.' The Town Clerk and ARP Controller, Ronald Meggeson, was 'entirely unsuited' to cope with the situation, while the Mayor, William Lewis, was 'a poor creature'. The Regional Commissioner, Harold Butler, who could have 'jockeyed along' the Mayor and his Town Clerk 'with the right handling', had not been prepared to use his power to override local authority, and had failed to go, or send his deputy, to Southampton immediately to help sort out the situation. Only the Medical Officer of Health, Dr Maurice Williams, and the Water Engineer, Joseph Hawksley, 'clearly had the situation well in hand'.

'The civic organisation of the town was confined to the dug-out evacuated by the ARP control, where the Town Clerk in a mackintosh wandered about from group to group in gloomy inactivity without any concrete suggestions . . . throughout the time I was in Southampton. The Mayor's sole concern was to be out of town as soon as possible in the afternoon. If he missed his 3 o'clock train, he informed me, he would not be able to leave until 7 p.m.' The rather elderly Chief Constable of Police, who did not strike Hodsoll as 'particularly efficient', went sick on the second night of the blitz on Southampton after being knocked down by a car, while none of the councillors the IGARP met struck him as 'of such calibre as could be put in charge'. And the 'whole place was apparently riddled with intrigue'.

On 4 December a notice finally went up on the Civic Centre noticeboard, signed by the Regional Commissioner, Southern Region, and the Mayor. It informed the people of Southampton that 'some public services such as water and gas are interrupted, but will be in operation again in a few days' time'. Apart from telling 'everybody . . . to get in touch with his employer or the nearest Labour Exchange in order to resume work' it offered no practical information or suggestions, and concluded: 'THE BATTLE OF BRITAIN

MUST GO ON. ALL SOUTHAMPTON MUST CONTINUE TO PLAY ITS VITAL PART.'

On 5 December George VI arrived to boost morale in the stricken city. Even this was not well managed. His visit was not announced in advance, for reasons of security. Outside the ruins of the Civic Centre, the King inspected what an early historian of Southampton's blitz described as 'a proud cross section of the local civilian army which had defied the worst that Hitler could do' – that is, a parade of Civil Defence workers and representatives of the utility services. Then the royal party drove through 'the wintry streets', but since not a single loudspeaker announced the visit, very few people were lining them, and those who heard about it later were rather grudging, intimating that what they needed was not a royal walkabout but some hot food and new furniture.

An M-O report on 9 December made gloomy reading.

> Morale has deteriorated . . . public utilities are still seriously affected. Thousands of homes have broken windows and leaking roofs which make them extremely unpleasant, if not uninhabitable . . . The topic [of the raid] remains an obsession, and among many people is becoming dangerously near neurosis . . . The only gaiety to be found in Southampton was a pub which had a pianist and a singer. This pub was congested and did a roaring trade and had a higher degree of conversation than any other pub – most of the others were practically empty . . . The alleged dis-organization of the authorities and the failure of local authorities has now become a subject of comment in the surrounding countryside . . . The strong feeling in Southampton today is that the city is finished. Many will not say this openly, but it is a deep-seated feeling that has grown in the last fortnight. Yet many householders continue to come in every day, and quite a number of women spend the day in their homes and the nights in outlying billets . . . This 'instinct' for home and local associations remains, and the feeling of despair about Southampton could surely be much reduced by local leadership, propaganda and some brighter touches.

When M-O observers returned to the city in March 1941, they found that, 'Although Southampton life has returned to near-normal so far as most public utilities are concerned . . . many still are nightly evacuees, having moved out permanently or spending the night somewhere in the surrounding country.'

The night after the attack on Coventry, nearby Birmingham was bombed. Birmingham, Britain's second largest city, was another entirely predictable target. It was a crucial site of war production, with factories such as Austin, Rover and GEC, turned over to the production of Spitfires, Hurricanes, Lancasters, ringing the city, and four 'shadow' factories managed by Birmingham motor companies nearby, including a huge 345-acre site at Castle Bromwich. Metropolitan-Cammell Carriage and Wagon Company Ltd had produced the first tanks for use in the First World War, but had turned to producing railway rolling stock in peacetime. Now tanks were once again coming off the production lines in their factories at Washwood Heath and Wednesbury – almost 4,000 during the course of the war – while their works at Saltley became the leading manufacturer of radar vehicles, as well as producing spare parts for tanks. Dunlop's factory continued to make tyres (but now for aircraft rather than land-based vehicles), and had started a special training school to teach ground staff how to fit and maintain tyres for fighter and bomber planes. Other small factories and workshops turned from producing parts for motor vehicles to making ammunition cases, bomb cases, hand grenades, stirrup pumps and jerry cans. In peacetime Birmingham had been the centre of jewellery manufacture: in wartime these workshops and small factories threaded through the city used their tools and their workers' precision skills to contribute radar equipment, rifles and aeroplane parts to the war effort. Later in the war it was estimated that over a third of the city's population would be working in various branches of war production by the beginning of 1944.

Birmingham had been bombed before – the city centre was badly damaged in a raid on 25 August, before the main blitz started. And the raids continued throughout September and October, scarring the city, destroying factories, shops, places of entertainment, the City Art Gallery and many homes. On 19–20 November bombs fell on the BSA factory in Small Heath, which until 1936 had been making bicycles and motorbikes, but by 1940 was producing 50 per cent of all the precision tools in Britain, most notably Browning aircraft machine guns, Sten guns, Lee Enfield rifles and cannons, as well as bicycles and motorbikes for despatch riders and the folding bicycles British airborne forces would one day carry when they were parachuted into occupied countries. Many workers were trapped, and a desperate race to get them out of the burning building ensued: a member of the Home Guard and one of the company's electricians were awarded the George Medal for their bravery and fortitude through that long night, when fifty-three workers were killed.

After another heavy raid on 21–22 November, when over six hundred fires were started, Birmingham's water supply was in a critical state – only about one-fifth of the usual quantity would be available if there was another raid that night. Sixty pumps arrived from London, 250 firemen were drafted into the city, and water carriers positioned; but the situation was still critical, partly because of the state of affairs that recurred throughout the country: one fire brigade's hoses would not fit on the hydrants of another's. 'Birmingham will burn down if the Luftwaffe comes again tonight,' the Regional Commissioner, Lord Dudley, predicted. Fortunately there was no raid on 23 November, but during the previous two nights at least 682 people had been killed and 1,037 injured, and approaching 2,000 houses were uninhabitable and many more damaged. Communal feeding centres were set up: such was the demand in districts where there were no cooking facilities that forty pounds of potatoes, twenty pounds of meat and fifteen pounds of carrots were used to make a filling dish known as 'Exeter stew' – all of which was consumed in a single day. Birmingham was bombed again on 3–4 December and again 11–12 December, the latter being one of the longest raids of the blitz: thirteen hours. It was to be the final raid until Easter 1941, by which time Birmingham had become Britain's third most-bombed city after London and Liverpool, with 2,241 people killed, and 12,391 houses and 302 factories destroyed.

Ronald Cartland, the brother of the romantic novelist Barbara Cartland, had been the Conservative MP for the King's Norton constituency in Birmingham. Major Cartland was killed in the retreat from Dunkirk on 30 May 1940, aged thirty-three, but news of his death was not confirmed until January 1941. General elections had been suspended for the duration of the war, and an electoral truce agreed by the major parties meant that they would not oppose each other in any seats that became vacant, which would be filled by the party already in possession. However, this was not binding on minor, single-interest parties, so some by-elections were contested. King's Norton was one. In March 1941 a 'Reprisals Candidate' stood in the by-then badly blitzed constituency. He lost his deposit, as did his pacifist opponent: the Conservative candidate, an ex-army captain, romped home. However bad the bombing, calls for vengeance or for the cessation of hostilities never rallied public opinion to any appreciable extent.

Bristol was another obvious target. There was a large docks complex at

Avonmouth and the ancient city was ringed with aircraft manufacturing plants, the largest of which was the Bristol Aeroplane Company at Filton, which were badly hit in raids in late August and September 1940. It is probable that Bletchley Park had decoded German 'Enigma' messages revealing that Bristol was to be raided on the night of 25 November, and an advance call had gone out for extra ARP units, firefighters and engines to supplement the city's below-strength resources. Enemy planes were spotted and the alert given at 6.22 p.m. – not that Bristolians took much notice: this was the 338th alert the city had had, and people were blasé on that cold, foggy November evening. But this time it was for real. A force of 134 Heinkels, Junkers and Dorniers were making for Bristol, intent on eliminating as much of it as possible.

At first it was hard to see the city from the air, obscured as it was by swirling fog and broken cloud, but soon the incendiaries had fulfilled their task, acting like a flare path for the bombers. A gasholder, hit by a bomb, exploded in a sheet of flame. Within an hour forty-five large fires were burning. They could be seen from over sixty miles away. By 11 p.m., having dropped 1,540 tons of high-explosives, 4.7 tons of oil bombs and 12,500 incendiaries, the German bombers turned back to France, catching a last glimpse of the conflagration as they started across the Channel. They left behind a razed city with 175 UXBs littering the streets or embedded in buildings, 207 dead (including nineteen men, three women and a messenger from the Civil Defence services), 187 seriously injured and 703 slightly hurt.

The narrow old shopping streets of the High Street, Wine Street and Castle Street, built on the site of Bristol's Norman castle, had been consumed by flames, and much of the city's architectural heritage had been destroyed or badly damaged. The timbered Dutch House, which was supposed to have been built in Holland, it was thought in 1676, and later dismantled and re-erected in Bristol, was now little more than a skeleton, and with so much for the authorities to attend to, two days later the army was sent in to demolish the structure, rather than attempt to preserve it. The medieval St Peter's Hospital, once a Royal Mint but in 1940 the place the poor went for public assistance payments, was nothing but a shell. Park Street, leading down from Clifton to College Green, was a mass of rubble and debris; the art gallery, incongruously modelled on the Doge's Palace in Venice, was ablaze; and the University Great Hall had been burned out too.

Despite the presence of extra Civil Defence equipment and personnel, Bristol had not been able to mount much of a defence: the Ack-Ack guns achieved little, nor did the barrage balloons. Damage to water mains meant that supplies ran out by 11 p.m., and water had to be obtained from a floating harbour on the river Frome. In a grim presentiment of the 'second great fire of London' at the end of December, since it was a Sunday night many offices were not occupied, so fires could get a grip unchecked. Reinforcements of men and machines were not able to reach the city through cratered and blocked roads in time.

There was a large decoy site, part of Britain's war of deception, intended to lure bombers away from their intended targets to drop their bomb loads relatively harmlessly in the countryside, in the Mendip hills, with smaller ones dotted around the Somerset and Gloucestershire countryside. These sites (code-named 'starfish', for 'SF' – Special Fires) were supplied with large tanks of oil, and tinfoil, lighting and apparatus to mimic the sparks produced by trams, and glow boxes that looked like poorly blacked-out windows, while the actual likely target would be in darkness. As the enemy planes approached the mock city, creosote fires would be lit to simulate buildings ablaze after incendiaries had been dropped. However, those intended to protect Bristol had not been fired that night (and in fact there is little firm evidence of the success of starfish sites in general in the early days of the blitz).

Mass-Observation reported on Bristol a fortnight after the raid. The 'Investigators' reported hearing remarks such as, 'I can't see how we're going to win this war.' 'Why don't we call an armistice?' 'Of course we're losing, we're only one little country.' Bristolians were heard gazing at their ruined city and mourning, 'It'll never be the same again.'

Notwithstanding the facts that Bristol had suffered less damage than Coventry or Southampton, and that telephones were working and hot meals were being provided for the homeless – partly because the offices of the Regional Commissioner General Sir Hugh Elles were in the city, and post-raid problems 'seem to have been tackled with particular energy' – M-O concluded that:

There is more depression in Bristol than in any other area studied in recent months. There is quite open defeatism, especially among the young workers, though the Lord Mayor and others appear to have a somewhat exaggerated idea of its potentialities. There is also much more wishful thinking about the war being over than in other areas, in itself probably an indication of depression . . . The main grumble is about shelters. There is a violent minority dissatisfaction with Bristol shelters and this is often spontaneous, non-political, and actually justified. Moreover, among the very large poorer communities in the Knowle area, which has been badly hit, there are Andersons which are most frequently flooded. It is also commonly stated in the town that there are seven underground tunnels available for deep shelters, and that two are being used for museum and art treasures . . . one . . . is now being used by people and there is violent feeling about attempts which the BBC are said to be making to buy this tunnel for their own use. [The BBC had moved its main studios to Bristol, which had been designated a 'safe area' suitable for evacuees.] About half the tunnel is flooded now, while the other half has bunks. Conditions here are similar to those in the East End at the worst period. About a thousand people are crowded under the worst possible conditions; but this shelter is crowded to capacity well before blackout every night . . . Police, health authorities etc. have apparently tried to cut down the numbers without success. There are no canteen or other facilities; two closets with sackcloth doors.

Investigators with a wide comparison of experience with town shelter facilities consider those in Bristol to be strikingly inferior and inadequate in many parts of the town.

However, there was 'a low degree of private evacuation or desertion. The working-classes, in particular, have overwhelmingly "stayed put" – unlike Southampton or Coventry,' though some people were reported to be sleeping in their cars. This was because the upper and middle classes had largely absorbed the limited accommodation in the surrounding countryside, compounded by the 'extraordinary' situation that since Bristol was regarded as a place to be evacuated *to*, there were neither grants nor billeting allowances for those who wanted to be evacuated *from* the city.

M-O concluded that 'morale is being left to drift far too much, and there is a dangerous lack of imaginative leadership in the area. It would seem quite possible that depressive and defeatist feelings, which at present exist only in embryo, might heavily and quite rapidly increase in Bristol unless something is done to give the people positive feelings, feelings of pride and purpose.'

The Ministry of Information's report was more upbeat, mentioning 'co-operation and practical good neighbourliness' and concluding that 'the fact remains that the people of the West Country are stout hearted and without thoughts of surrender'. Though even Home Intelligence (reports gathered from police, ARP controllers and others in the locality, who were inclined to paint a rosy picture since the reverse might reflect badly on their handling of the situation) admitted that despite citizens taking the blows suffered by the city almost light-heartedly at first, 'by November 28, when people were becoming tired from their exertions, when the lack of water here of gas there and transport difficulties, nearly everywhere became increasingly irksome, this mood became more serious'.

It was not only weariness and lack of utilities that were depressing Bristol's spirit: it was what seemed to be the neglect of their suffering. Bristol was not identified by name in the national press for several days; the morning after the raid, the *Bristol Evening Post* spoke of 'comparatively few casualties', and of course it was not permitted to print the numbers of those killed or injured, nor to identify streets or buildings by name, which was frustrating for a city anxious to know the extent of its devastation. Most galling was the fact that newsreels shown in Bristol cinemas in the days following the raid showed film of the Coventry blitz, with a sententious commentary on the plight and pluck of the Coventarians, but no mention of what had happened in Bristol only ten days later. Although Bristol did not suffer so many deaths as Coventry, in the macabre taxonomy of war the city ranked sixth, with 1,159 deaths, fewer than London, Liverpool and Merseyside, Birmingham, Clydeside and Coventry, but more than Manchester, Swansea, Belfast and other major cities – yet for several days Bristol was identified only as 'a town in the west country'.

For much of the first two weeks of December, weather conditions were such that the Luftwaffe did not set off on any major bombing raids; but on the 12th and 15th Sheffield had its 'Coventration', 'Operation Crucible'. The city had been expecting a raid since the attack on other industrial centres had started, since it had been one of the world's major centres of armaments manufacture since Henry Bessemer had invented the process that revolutionised steelmaking in the 1850s. The British Steel Corporation factory on the river Don in Sheffield was the only one in the country with the capacity to manufacture the crankshafts for the Rolls-Royce Merlin engines that powered Spitfires and Hurricanes. The loss of this facility would have been a body blow to Britain's fighting capability.

Sheffield was to experience the 'doppelgänger' attacks that were becoming a pattern: two raids in short proximity, the second coming when a city was still reeling from the chaos of the first. On 12 December the city was attacked by a total of three hundred German bombers. The Marples Hotel, on the corner of the High Street, had a direct hit at 11.14 p.m. The seven floors of offices, concert rooms and bars, the orchestra dais and furniture, came crashing into the basement, where seventy people were sheltering. 'Sheffield's most famous pub had become a tomb.' Just seven got out alive, and though the search for survivors went on for twelve days, only fourteen bodies could be identified. Many bombs presumably intended for Sheffield fell wide of the mark, so Leeds, Barnsley and Batley shared the suffering.

Three nights later the bombers were back, showering Sheffield with incendiaries and bombs. Fires coursed through the city, and four hundred UXBs blocked roads and the Sheffield to York railway line. It was not until the following morning that Geoffrey Hill, a fifteen-year-old Sheffield boy, 'realised how bad it was. On street corners there were stretchers with bodies on them covered in tarpaulins waiting to be moved . . . about 500 yards from where we lived was a crater in the middle of the main road with a tram 20 feet from it . . . for weeks water wagons had to supply people [and there were] no toilets or electricity.' The casualties of the two raids were tragically high: 750 civilians were dead or missing, and around five hundred were seriously injured. Nearly 3,000 homes and shops were demolished, and the same number again would need major repairs. The steelworks escaped serious damage, but the city centre was devastated, and many smaller factories and business premises were put out of action, with the result that Sheffield added unemployment to the other miseries of war.

As Christmas approached, there were two more heavy raids. Merseyside was bombed again on 20 December, and Manchester, another large city in the front line of war matériel production, suffered what was becoming a pattern: raids on successive nights, 22–23 and 23–24 December. Two hundred and seventy-two tons of high-explosive bombs were dropped that first night, with over a thousand canisters of incendiary bombs, designed to ignite as many fires as possible. Fires were still burning in Liverpool from two nights previously, which helped illuminate the bombers' path, and unfortunately many of Manchester's 3,500 full- and part-time firefighters and other Civil Defence workers had been called to help quell the Liverpool conflagration, leaving their own city depleted and vulnerable. Soon more than four hundred fires had taken hold in Salford alone. The next night another 195 tons of high-explosives and nearly nine hundred incendiaries were dropped. The historic Manchester Free Trade Hall was destroyed, as was Cheetham's Hospital, the Corn Exchange, Smithfield Market, the Gaiety Theatre and St

Anne's church. The main roads, Deansgate and Oxford Road, were cratered and blocked by UXBs and piles of debris.

'Bombing is a messy business,' concluded the journalist Cyril Dunn.

> There were big fires everywhere, the air stank of smoke and the streets were full of black ash as if there'd been a volcanic eruption . . . The destruction was enormous & spectacular, but it's ceased to make any impression on me. Even to see the whole of the Royal Exchange gutted & burning, whacking great buildings blasted into ruin, water spurting into the road from burst mains, the cathedral; shattered glass everywhere like dirty drifts of pack ice – this scarcely interested me.
>
> I went around nervously collecting the same old stories. 'All I want to do,' said one publican who'd been blasted out of his cellar, 'is to get out of here and stop out. I've had enough.' And a woman, 'If only I could feel it was worth it, was helping to win the war. But this (the ruins of her pub) is every-thing we've worked for . . .'. I wrote the usual story about the cheerful courage & determined endurance of the Manchester folk.

By morning, one side of Piccadilly recalled that powerful image of total devastation from the First World War that so often resonated in the blitzed cities of the Second: that of the ruins of Ypres. More than 8,000 homes were destroyed or rendered uninhabitable, many in Salford. An estimated 684 people died – 215 in Salford alone – while 2,364 were wounded.

Since it was Christmas and newspapers, just like other workplaces, gave as many of their staff as possible the holiday off, stories were prepared in advance. Mancunians were amazed to read in the *Manchester Guardian* that on Christmas Day turkey was served to those in the city's rest centres. In fact most were overcrowded and struggling to find any hot food at all for their occupants. It was a bleak Christmas in the blitzed towns and cities of Britain.

11

Peace on Earth?

This evening I went to a children's party and carol singing. 'Peace on Earth and Mercy mild', shrilled the childish voices as the guns thudded overhead . . . The young voices were so soft that we could hear an enemy plane buzz buzzing across the night sky. It was all strange and poignant, but our emotions are all a bit dried up now, and scarcely respond to such obvious appeals . . . it is odd to think of 'Good King Wenceslaus', 'The First Nowell', 'Adeste Fideles' and 'While Shepherds Watched' rising from lips in every corner of the warring globe.   Phyllis Warner, diary for 18 December 1940

O give us back the old Noëls
The chimes and celebrations:
We dare not ring the Christmas Bells,
We'd break the regulations!
O where has gone the Christmas tree,
The toys and coloured wax?
Sir Kingsley Wood [Chancellor of the Exchequer] go ask, not me,
He framed the Purchase Tax!

O where is Santa Claus today?
Our children are concerned;
Has Herbert [Morrison] taken him away
And had the man interned?
The Angels will not sing tonight –
What now can cheer the land?
Their old Conductor wouldn't fight –
Their broadcast has been banned . . .
                              Matthew Bird, 'Christmas Carols', *Daily Worker*, 24 December 1940

'A raid-less Christmas Eve. Does this imply a tacit understanding on both sides to hold a truce over Christmas as happened on the Western Front in 1914?' wondered Anthony Heap as he wrote his diary on 24 December 1940. 'The general consensus of opinion is that it doesn't, mistrust of the "jerries" being the dominant fixture in the English mind. Yet, I wonder . . .'

'No indication of impending action,' reported No. 80 Wing's 'headache patrol' at 5.01 p.m. on Christmas Eve from its HQ at Garston in Hertfordshire. 'Headache' was the RAF's code name for *Knickebein* (crooked leg), the German navigational aid, and jammers were appropriately known as 'aspirins'. No. 80 Wing's job was to monitor signals and undertake radio counter-measures, and even though they felt sanguine about their intelligence, they sent up three defensive patrols of Beaufighters just in case. Four tracks of enemy aircraft were plotted by Fighter Command that night, but it was presumed that these were weather reconnaissance planes. No bombs fell anywhere in Britain or Northern Ireland on the nights of Christmas Eve, Christmas Day or Boxing Day 1940.

There had been no formal truce, nor, given the nature of warfare in 1940, any informal Christmas laying-down of arms between German and British troops such as the football match that had been played in no man's land on the Western Front in 1914. But the British government had heard, via Washington, that attacks on Britain would be suspended over Christmas, provided that the RAF refrained from carrying out raids over Germany.

The war was not going well. There had been no victories yet, just defeats and retreats. Six months earlier the British army had been driven out of Europe. It seemed as if the Western Desert might become another Western Front – a war of stasis with small gains, followed by losses and reverses. The Tripartite Axis of Rome–Berlin–Tokyo, the result of a pact signed on 27 September 1940, would later stretch hostilities across the globe. Those at sea – in both the Royal and the Merchant Navy – were leading perilous existences, under constant threat from U-boats as they ploughed across the Atlantic carrying war supplies and food, while nearer shore, fishermen faced constant risks from mines as they trawled to supplement the nation's rations.

Families were divided: men conscripted into the armed forces, women volunteering for the ATS, the WAAF, the WRNS, the Women's Land Army. Some overseas, most training or endlessly waiting in camps in Britain. Leave was occasional, short and never guaranteed. Airmen, already battle-hardened and depleted by war, were flying a punishing number of sorties in fighter or bomber planes. Young men and women were working away from home in munitions factories, living in digs or hostels. Children were evacuated, sometimes with friends or relatives, often billeted on strangers. Some were happy, revelling in the country life, but many were unsettled, anxious, worried about their parents back in the cities in the blitz. Some were overseas, sent to safety – it was fervently hoped – in America, Canada, South Africa, Australia.

Then there were the refugees: many Jews from Germany and Austria, who had managed to escape the Nazi regime of terror and persecution, others from German-occupied Europe – 10,500 had arrived from Gibraltar alone in 1940. Deracinated, separated from their families, often without news for months on end, unsure what they would find when they returned home, whenever – if ever – that might be.

To those in the 'blitz towns', still devastated by the effects of the raids, often without water, gas or electricity, their houses patched up, dark, cold, uncomfortable, with nowhere to cook, nowhere to live in many cases, Christmas must have seemed a bleak prospect.

Everywhere people were tired: working long hours in war production, in hospitals or social work, dealing with the casualties and the dead of war. Soldiering on in peacetime jobs, with reduced staff, doing jobs that were essential to keep the population fed, clothed and transported. Men and women fitting in AFS, ARP, WVS, bomb-disposal work or Home Guard duties, most after an ordinary day's work. Transport was disrupted, journeys discouraged. Women queued endlessly, having to be ingenious with rations, worrying about shortages, doing without small pleasures, longing for letters from men serving abroad or in PoW camps, or news of those missing in action. Men waiting to be called up; women wondering when conscription and direction might be extended to them. Young people having to grow up too fast, facing the realities of war and uncertainty about the future. Lives disrupted by raids, fear, anxiety.

As the journalist Guy Fletcher put it: 'This will be a brave Christmas with many a church that would have echoed to the singing of "Christians awake!" now lying in ruins, or a mere shell silhouetted against the sky; with some of us sleeping under tables, and others not sleeping at all; with children hanging up their stockings in Anderson shelters, and carols being sung in the London tubes; with this family separated, and that family spending Christmas up the road because their home was "pancaked"; with most of us serving in the Services, in munitions factories, or in some form of civil defence.' And, he went on with a certain edge, 'as Douglas Young [an entertainer] would say, it makes you think, doesn't it? Christmas is essentially such a German feast with its Santa Claus and Christmas trees. And yet that great nation gave itself up to a leader who had no time for a legendary Father Christmas bringing through the sky peace and goodwill and presents for everyone in a legendary reindeer-sledge. No – the presents he prefers to bring through the sky are incendiary and high-explosive bombs.'

On 20 December Phyllis Warner travelled home for Christmas in 'a crowded and rather sober train which left London punctually and arrived in a Midland city [unspecified because of the censor] dead on time. Then the sirens went and all the lights in the train and station were switched out. I don't care for a train in an air raid, first because you know you're a target, second because you stumble into a pitch dark coach and have to feel to see if seats are occupied or not, third because you can't see to read or even look at your watch, and fourth because you are so liable to lose some of your baggage. Once the lights were out we drew up the blinds and crawled along at fifteen miles an hour watching the gun flashes light the sky. A new way of coming home for Christmas.'

Such rail travel was discouraged. 'Is Your Journey Really Necessary?' read an admonitory poster pasted in railway and coach stations. Troops and essential supplies needed to be moved, fuel saved. The newspapers took up the theme: 'Now let's get this clear: there will be no extra trains this Christmas and no Christmas excursions,' emphasised the *Daily Express*. 'Vital war supplies will have first call. The Government asks everybody to stay at home. But already Christmas holiday-makers are jamming the booking offices. Mothers travelling down country to bring their children back to the cities for Christmas are among the worst offenders. There are plenty of others too. A high official of the Great Western Railway gave [the reporter] this message for them yesterday: "Do you want to spend Christmas Eve and Christmas Day in the waiting room? Because that's what will happen unless you come to your senses quickly." '

In fact a Sunday train service would run on Christmas Day, and on Christmas Eve and Boxing Day there would be a normal weekday timetable in operation (an improvement for travellers on what is on offer seventy years later). But the pressure was relentless: 'Those who are thinking of going by coach should think twice. Only one third of the normal long-distance motor coaches will leave London on Christmas Day . . . The Army has put London out of bounds for troops at Christmas – except those living within ten miles of Charing Cross. Men crossing London must have a special permit, though this does not apply to Dominion or Colonial troops. If you want to spend Christmas in comfort – Stay at Home. You will also be helping Britain win the war.'

It was clear that not everyone was toeing the line. Apart from people like Phyllis Warner, or Vere Hodgson, who worked in a welfare organisation in Notting Hill and was also going home to see her family in Birmingham, the *Daily Express* reported that 'hotel keepers in Devon and Cornwall and along the South Coast are preparing for a bumper harvest. Demand for accommodation is the heaviest for years and prices are going up like AA shells – high and fast.' Presumably, anyone who could do so was desperate to leave London for a few nights' quiet, a chance to catch up on uninterrupted sleep.

But leaving the capital could make people aware how badly other parts of the country were faring. Vere Hodgson 'reached Brum an hour late. Dr Hillier waiting for me and amazed I was so early . . . As I came out of Snow Hill station I saw the Arcade opposite black with fire and closed. Broad St. had some hits, but not Hagley Rd; and so far no bomb on Francis Rd. Cath and I went down to the Market Place. Not much to buy. Apples were ¼d a pound and oranges difficult to obtain . . . Saw New Street Marshall and Snelgrove's is like John Lewis'* – only the damage is on a smaller scale. Smallbrook St. and John Bright St. are a mess. However, New Street has not gone on both sides.'

Most people, however, had little option but to stay put. Doris Melling, a twenty-two-year-old typist in a hospital library in Liverpool, was 'afraid we won't get to Frodsham [to see her mother]. Everyone saying: Where will it all end? Poor old Liverpool . . . What a miserable Xmas, haven't even got a pudding!'

Even so, people made a great effort to make Christmas a special day that blitz year, though it took ingenuity: scouring the shops, saving up ingredients for the usual Christmas fare, scaling down expectations. The *Daily Worker* printed a recipe for a Christmas cake, 'even if it is a travesty of its former self', supplied by a reader from Potters Bar. It substituted three-quarters of a wineglass of vinegar for scarce eggs, and the other ingredients included flour, lard and whatever dried fruit a housewife could manage to procure.

---

* The Oxford Street department store had been completely burned out, and looked like a 'charred skeleton with its blackened walls and gaping windows and rust-orange soot and wax models lying like corpses in the street' after a raid on 17 September during which D.H. Evans and Bourne & Hollingsworth were also badly damaged.

In south London, Sidney Chave found 'Christmas shopping a bit dismal this year. Meat is rather scarce. There is a good deal to be had, but not much choice. Fruit is very dear, lemons almost unobtainable, nuts scarce and dear. Figs and dates are absent. Marmalade and cheese are rather scarce. Turkeys again are few, chickens dear.' Frank Edwards, a thirty-two-year-old buyer for a London war factory, member of the Home Guard and keen neighbourhood fire-watcher, 'spent the best part of [16 December] in and around the big stores in Kensington. There were plenty of shoppers amongst which many men were in evidence. Things are much more expensive than this time last year, but everyone seems to be purchasing practical gifts; things to wear and use was the order of the day. Most of the stores have a toy fair for the children, but I saw few children in the three stores I visited, which is doubtless accounted for by evacuation. There were not so many decorations about but there was plenty of colour about and all the departments looked bright and cheerful.'

Mass-Observation noticed that the Christmas shoppers in Oxford Street were rather short-tempered, that there was a shortage of Christmas bazaars and Father Christmases in the shops, and fewer decorations than usual. Even so, one investigator was buttonholed by a woman in north London complaining, 'Have you seen the Christmas decorations some shops have got – the butchers in particular? They've got masses of them there. I think it's downright scandalous. They keep telling us about salvage and waste paper in particular, and then you get people doing things like that.'

Christmas cards were a different matter: it was as if keeping in touch in this ritualistic way was a sort of reassuring affirmation in such uncertain times. Gwladys Cox, a West Hampstead housewife, found the cards she received 'rather dingy as if in an effort to damp down Christmas high spirits. One plain card without the relief of a robin, or any holly wished me "A Merry Xmas" in plain black letters!' She nevertheless noted that she received quite a number of cards. A man told a Mass-Observation investigator that he had received more cards in 1940 than ever before: 'Lots of people who didn't send presents sent cards and some people I haven't heard from for years sent them. It's a funny thing, but for no reason at all I sent cards to some people I haven't seen or heard of for five years or more.' It was the same for the *Daily Express* gossip columnist 'William Hickey' (Tom Driberg): 'Like many other people, I thought, "No cards this year . . . no presents . . . at least, hardly any . . ." Then the cards came trickling in . . . The trickle grew to a stream . . . Now my desk is flooded out with them. Thanks to all who have sent them, particularly readers serving in the Forces. In reply I can only wish you as peaceful a Christmas as possible – inwardly if not outwardly peaceful – and a New Year considerably brighter than this has been.'

Sidney Chave and his wife managed well in Upper Norwood. On Christmas Eve, 'Lee [his wife Eileen] had the house looking Christmassy' by the time her parents and younger sister arrived for the festivities, and that evening the family sat around the fire opening their presents. Sidney gave Lee 'some gloves and a record of "Fingal's Cave" while I had some slippers, having recently had a coloured photograph of Lee and Jillian [the Chaves' seventeen-month-old daughter]'. That evening the grown-ups sat by the fire listening (or 'listening-in', as was the parlance of the time) to the wireless, though they had missed the Festival of Nine Lessons and Carols announced in the *Radio Times* as being broadcast from 'a college chapel' – in fact King's College, Cambridge: the censor again – at 2.45 p.m. The Kentucky Minstrels had 'a splendid programme. They sang "Bless This House" and "Star of Bethlehem".' Then it was time to fill Jillian's stocking: 'Actually we used a pillow-case as she had so many presents.'

On Christmas Day Sidney and Eileen Chave went to Matins at their local church, St Oswald's. 'It was a wartime service, the choir consisted of two boys, five men and a number of girls. The congregation included many uniforms. However we sang old carols with great vigour – and enjoyed them too. The Vicar preached a short sermon – and a good one. He emphasised our prayer for peace, but said that there could never be peace until there was goodwill between men.' Back at home, 'We sat down to roast veal (which Mummy [Eileen's mother] was lucky to get), roast potatoes and a few new boiled potatoes – a gift from Jock Tweed's allotment* – cabbage from the garden, and our runner beans stored [in salt] from the summer. Then we followed on with Christmas pudding and mince-pies. We drank a toast in sherry to absent friends and relatives in the forces.'

Alan Don, chaplain to the Archbishop of Canterbury, assisted at Holy Communion in the Lambeth Palace chapel on Christmas morning, 'where a good number of parishioners assembled despite the blackout. To [Westminster] Abbey at 10.30 perhaps for the last time as an ordinary worshipper [he had accepted the post of Canon of St Margaret's, Westminster, which was bombed out and closed]. Attended a children's tea in the crypt

---

* The 'Dig for Victory' campaign encouraged people to be as self-sufficient as possible in food production.

at 5pm with Christmas tree and all. The crypt has never witnessed such a scene before I imagine.'

In the shipbuilding town of Barrow-in-Furness, Nella Last managed very well too. 'Everything was perfect – chicken stuffed with slightly flavoured "Sage and Onion" [onions were notoriously scarce during the war; this was probably Paxo stuffing] with added sausage meat and browned sausages cooked with potatoes in a tin. I steamed sprouts and cooked creamed celery and there was a good "light" Xmas pudding with rum sauce. Celery, coffee and biscuits and cheese. The table was gay with my embroidered cloth and lovely chrysanthemums I had bought and there was port and nuts to end with.'

The journalist Cyril Dunn, who had just come back from reporting on the Manchester blitz, 'had Christmas at home [in Leeds] . . . It was very much a normal Christmas. Neither on Christmas Eve nor last night [Christmas Day] did the Germans bomb this country, nor did we bomb them. It almost seems as if bombers have a conscience about bombing, consider it something unsuitable for Christmas; or perhaps they want some moral propaganda; or else it's just *reculer pour mieux sauter* . . . We got the kids a goodish show of toys. It featured soldiers for the boys and I tried to teach them how to play war. Nothing like giving them the Right Idea early. But they were not really amused, preferred their own play with the soldiers, which was mostly non-military. They fixed up a long route march, drummers and khaki buglers out ahead. I zoomed overhead with a model bomber and hard balls of brown paper. "*Don't* bomb them!" said John. "*Don't*".'

Robert Baltrop was determined to have a good time.

It was the first Christmas when the war was really on, and there was a sense of Christmas taking place in the thick of it . . . People made the best of it . . . I used to do ARP work . . . and we had a marvellous party in the ARP HQ . . . underground. Everybody who could be raked in was, standing round the piano singing and party games, all kinds of games. We had a wonderful time. Creeping outside into the office . . . to toast teacakes over an electric fire and all of that. It was just one night, very much disapproved of by the high ups . . . They said afterwards there was never to be anything like that again. Beer flowing and people behaving like that. Well, of course there wasn't because a few nights later the bombers came back . . . It was the same at home – the feeling of let's have a good time while we can . . . my father brought friends home, a chap who could play the piano, so we had a sing song . . . I think it was the only wartime Christmas that was intense like that. After that, well the austerity was biting a bit too hard. But that blitz Christmas was a very jolly one. We made damn sure of that.

It wasn't a particularly jolly Christmas for Stan Wilkinson, a Private in the Manchester Regiment who was one of a group of soldiers detailed to help clear up the blitzed city. He had hoped to be issued with a leave pass for Christmas Day. 'No such luck. We were issued with picks and shovels yet again . . . We were taken down the Oldham Road where a large power station had been bombed. The rubble was about seven feet high. We were given two hours off for lunch as a special treat for Christmas and then got back to the barracks at about 7.30 p.m. Eventually we were served our Christmas dinner – stone cold. We were so mad, Christmas Day, we could not go home, we had worked like navvies and been given a cold dinner. We banged our mugs on the table but there were no officers or NCOs about to take notice, they had probably gone home! Eventually the Sergeant cook appeared so we relieved our feelings by telling him what to do with his rotten Christmas pudding!'

Clara Milburn's Christmas was particularly poignant that year. She had gone to church in Balsall Heath, near Coventry, in the dark on Christmas morning: 'Though there was little decoration, a lovely variegated holly cross hung on the pulpit and the white altar flowers shone in the light of the candles,' and had then come home to prepare lunch for her family and friends. 'Before long we were eating a very good turkey and accompanying sausages (instead of the usual ham) and filling in corners with celery and home-grown potatoes, bread sauce and gravy . . . we all paid proper attention to everything – even the dessert [two plum puddings, mince pies and "some little glasses of trifley peaches"] – and it is marvellous to think of such a feast in these war days.' The Milburns' son Alan had been reported missing on 31 May 1940 during the retreat from Dunkirk, and it was not until 16 July that she had heard from the War Office that he had been taken prisoner. The 'great joy' on Christmas Day was 'the telegram which came with the day's post. It came via the British Legion and said that Alan was well and had not heard from us since 13th May. We wired to the British Legion Geneva: "Please inform Lieut. A.J. Milburn, Oflag 1XA, No. 3604, glad to hear that he is well, all well at home . . ." Evidently Alan soon began to think about getting in touch with us when he got to a prison camp, and that makes us feel he has really recovered and that his spirits are good. We do thank God this is so. A happy Christmas Day indeed!'

Doris Pierce had no need to be anxious about Christmas that year: 'Food rationing was tight – although there was worse to come. So far Mum had managed fairly well with the rations, we had never had an excess of food because money was short, so she had learnt to be economical with what-ever provisions were available and was an excellent cook. Now with Christmas upon us, she had conjured up enough rations to make a fruit cake, and acquired a Christmas pudding and a small chicken.' 'Food and drink was in abundance,' at her Uncle Ted's house, where the family went on Boxing Day, 'and Christmas 1940 was no exception.' The children were regaled with tales of how it had been much worse in the 'hungry thirties' of the Depression, when Doris's mother's family were often 'half starved' and relied on food Ted had 'scrounged or pinched from somewhere'.

The afternoon was another chance to 'listen-in' in the Chave household.

There was a programme called 'Christmas Under Fire', with interviews at Coventry, with the chiming of the bells of the ruined Cathedral there,* troops being interviewed in Iceland, Bethlehem, Egypt, merchant sailors, airmen on patrol duty, and civilian evacuees in this country, followed by an interview in a large London shelter where a grand party was being held. Then greet-ings from the King – and a speech from His Majesty. He spoke fairly well, somewhat haltingly as usual [George VI had a pronounced stammer, which he practised hard to overcome]. Then the National Anthems of our Allies – Free France, Norway, Poland, Belgium, Holland, Greece, Czechoslovakia and the British Commonwealth.

Naturally, the King tried in his message to encourage his subjects and raise their morale: 'Remember this: if war brings separation, it brings new unity also, a unity which comes from common perils and common sufferings, willingly shared. To be comrades and good neighbours in trouble is one of the finest opportunities of the civilian population, and by facing hardship and discomfort cheerfully and resolutely, not only do they do their own duty, but they play their part in helping the Fighting Services to win the war . . . The future will be hard, but our feet are planted on the path of victory and with the help of God, we will make our way to justice and peace.' But this was measured encouragement, as was the rest of the BBC output that

---

* Presumably this was a recording, since a feature of wartime England was the much-regretted absence of church bells, which were only to be rung to warn of an invasion.

day: there was to be no over-the-top 'blitz spirit', no 'thrilling or fearful entertainment'. The BBC had learned the lesson that people suffering the dangers and hardships of continual bombardment did not wish to have a false picture of cheerfulness painted for them. That Christmas producers had been warned that there must be 'no jollity stories from shelters anywhere in BBC programmes', and a planned broadcast from a Manchester shelter party was dropped.

Had Jillian Chave been a little older that Christmas of 1940, she might have listened in to *Children's Hour* at 5.15 p.m., which that day offered a dramatisation of Charles Dickens's *A Christmas Carol*, with the ubiquitous Norman Shelley (who later claimed to have stood in for Winston Churchill, reading his speeches on the radio) playing the Ghost of Christmas Present. At 7.15 p.m. Jillian's parents (and thousands of others) tuned in for *Christmas Star Variety* with Arthur Askey, Richard Murdoch, Jack Warner and, topping the bill, his real-life sisters Elsie and Doris Waters, whose resourceful chars Gert and Daisy were stalwarts of the 'Kitchen Front', with their ration-book cooking tips and recipes every morning after the eight o'clock news. The Forces Programme joined the Home Service for *Christmas Star Variety* as it had for *Christmas Under Fire*, but eschewed the Home Service's Christmas Community Singing from South Wales in favour of *Stars in the Shelter*, an entertainment put on by ENSA.

On Christmas Eve Anthony Heap and his mother had spent the night as usual in the basement shelter near Euston station. 'Despite the small attendance – some 15 or so, something of what is termed the "Christmas spirit" – i.e. refraining from jumping down each other's throats in order to do so with all the more vigour after Christmas for the rest of the year – prevailed in the shelter. Hatchets were buried for the nonce. After lights out, some seven or eight of us lay in the dark listening to the other seven or eight singing carols out in the passage and in the morning small paper stockings containing five sweets and a nick nack (mine was a collar stud, mother's a bath cube!) were found pinned to our bunks. Charming!'

Heap's lunch on Christmas Day consisted of 'rump steak, chips, beans, mince pie and a glass of port. I could wish for none better.' In the afternoon he 'sat by the fire reading a book. Then after tea, round to the shelter for the Christmas Party. This was held in conjunction with the Quakers (who have a shelter of their own) . . . a jumble of concert, games and dances with nothing but soft drinks and sandwiches and such like as "refreshments". It was all very tame.'

Concerned at the number of returning evacuees, Herbert Morrison and his colleagues had decided at a meeting on 19 December 1940 that 'it was undesirable to give excessive publicity regarding Christmas festivities and general amenities provided in shelters. The Press should mention improvements in sanitation and medical precautions but not create the impression that public shelters were to be regarded as nightclubs. The general impression should be that shelters were clean but not gay.'

Others saw things differently. The *Subway*, one of the several news-sheets for tube shelterers distributed across the network, which had adopted the American designation since 'underground might mean anything from coal miners to foxes', reported that 'Xmas 1940 was spent by many thousands of people underground in the London tubes. Parties were organised for the kiddies after which they were given presents. A doll for a girl and a car or box of soldiers for the boys. Toys were sent from America's Air Raid Relief Fund and were presented by the LPTB [London Passenger Transport Board] to the children. It was wonderful to see kids – some of them homeless and some of them orphans, enjoying themselves.' Christmas trees were erected in ticket halls, and decorated with stashes of pre-war ornaments – tinsel, baubles, paper lanterns, balloons, miniature crackers, sometimes fairy lights, and invariably a celluloid fairy/doll/angel with a white crepe paper dress at the top. Paper chains were strung along the platforms and some 11,000 toys were distributed to 'underground children'. The *Swiss Cottager* announced that £4.10s. had been collected from among the shelterers for a Christmas party for the children sleeping in the station.

Flo Rollinson travelled by tube from the East End to Paddington, from where she took a train to spend Christmas in Taunton, Somerset. 'All the stations had parties going on. I've never seen so many Christmas trees in one night. Each platform had one at each end; there were accordions, banjos, trumpets, anything on which to play a tune, singing, dancing and even a Santa Claus. It was lovely to see Londoners really knew how to make the most of a rough situation. Of course throughout the Blitz many families made these platforms their home.'

The *Evening Standard* diarist described a public shelter beneath a Piccadilly store (probably Simpson's or Swan & Edgar) 'decorated with holly, mistletoe and paper chains. Plenty of beer . . . A full dinner was served. A butcher had given two turkeys. They were cooked by a woman who has lost all her home except her kitchen. Taximen were there dancing. Some had their wives . . . In the West End 25 to 75 per cent of the people changed for dinner and a few officers wore mess kit.' However, he 'did not see a white tie, a woman in uniform or a brightly coloured evening gown. Most women dressed plainly in black, grey and white, but all the restaurants were all the gayer for that. It gave the balloons and paper caps a chance to be seen. A chef told me he had collected the ingredients for the pudding by saving them up over a period of months.'

One person who did not allow himself much celebration that Christmas was the Home Secretary and Minister for Home Security, Herbert Morrison, who 'took no Christmas holiday. He has spent the whole week in the Home Office getting on with desk work,' reported the *Evening Standard* on 26 December.

> But he did have one Christmas party. On Christmas Eve he sat down among his staff in the office canteen. Paper chains and sprigs of holly hung above the Minister's head; he wore no paper hat. The turkey and plum pudding were excellent, I am told. And the Christmas spirit of the staff was in no way reduced by the presence of their chief who has a pleasantly informal manner . . . Afterwards he returned to his desk and later to his office camp bed. Christmas Day he spent at work, and the only time he left the Home Office was for lunch. His Christmas dinner was sent to his room. Again he slept at the office, and he began Boxing Day at his desk at the normal hour.

The Minister was not alone in his dedication to duty. Raids or no raids, Civil Defence workers, firemen, medical staff, were all on duty. 'I don't think we had a Christmas,' recalled Leonard Jeacocke, whose job was to defuse unexploded bombs. 'We were working seven days a week. There was no Christmas for us.'

'A working Boxing Day,' reported Anthony Heap on 26 December. 'At least it was supposed to be, and for us the Town Hall actually opened for "business as usual". But like the last two Bank Holidays which were likewise cancelled [in the interests of war production], it was a half and half sort of day. Practically every shop was shut as well as many business houses, and for the majority of Londoners it undoubtedly was Boxing Day. No morning papers were published, but the evening papers made a somewhat emaciated appearance.' That evening Heap went to another shelter party – this one held in the basement of the British Medical Association building. 'Collins, our fellow inmate at F[riends] H[ouse] gave a turn . . . an exasperating clown off stage, but a most entertaining one on with a decidedly professional touch

. . . I enjoyed it more than any part of yesterday evening – a much more robust affair.'

Two days later Heap had lunch at a Lyon's Corner House:

home to change, then to the Coliseum for the 4 o'clock performance of 'Aladdin', the West End's one and only pantomime this year. In fact almost the only show of any sort. But of all the awkward times – 12 noon and 4pm [because of people's reluctance to be out in the evening, with the blackout and fear of raids]. And this year when Christmas means so little and the evacuation of practically the entire infantile population leaves so little real demand for pantomime, surely the money lavished on it would have been better employed in providing a good, colourful spectacular musical show. It's not even an exceptionally good pantomime . . . and the break with tradition in the form of a female dame is no improvement. A good deal more robust knockabout comedy such as the old Lyceum panto used to flourish on, would have done it the world of good. Good house. Stalls about a third full; Circles packed.

'There was no raid after all,' Heap wrote on the night of Boxing Day. 'So they could trust each other. And if not for Christmas, why not for good?'

12

Long Shall Men Mourn the Burning of the City

Gone are the churches, tall watchmen of the city,
Gone are the landmarks that London used to know.
Great halls and ancient walls, fallen, warped and charred now,
Gone are the chiming steeples, cracked and jarred now,
Gone are the bookmen of Pater Noster Row . . .

Red roared the fire through the heart of London's city
Hurled from the clouds by a brute and savage foe . . .

Long shall men mourn the burning of the city,
As long as London shall stand, or London's river flow,
Mourn the long-treasured links with gentler ages . . .

'Sagittarius' (Olga Katzin), *New Statesman and Nation*, 25 January 1941

'After three blissful nights without even the sound of a plane, we wildly hoped that both sides might feel too ashamed of themselves to start this bombing horror again,' wrote Phyllis Warner. Or, as Sidney Chave put it, 'It may be that Germany dislikes these night bombing raids more than we do and only started operations again when we did.' 'But alas,' wrote Warner on 30 December 1940, 'the brief sanity of the truce was over and last night was grimmer than ever.'

On 27–28 December, forty-eight German aircraft attacked London, and one diverted to Brighton. Bus garages were damaged from Chelsea to Dalston, a tram garage in New Cross was bombed, railway lines were destroyed. Parachute mines dropped over a wide area of the capital caused many fires, and 141 people were killed, including fifty in a public shelter in Southwark which received a direct hit, and 455 seriously injured.

There was a full 'bomber's moon' on the night of Sunday, 29 December. The square mile of the City of London was largely deserted, offices, warehouses and churches padlocked. Soon after 6 p.m. the siren went, its mournful wail rising and falling, rising and falling in the clear night air. As the last notes died away, the bombs started to drop – over three hundred incendiaries a minute in the area around St Paul's Cathedral: 'like apples falling from a tree', thought a watching journalist. Within half an hour Luftwaffe pilots peering down on the scene below claimed they could count fifty-four major fires. In just three hours, 120 tons of high-explosives and 22,000 incendiaries were dropped on the City.

'With its warehouses filled with textiles, paint, paper and wood, its tightly-packed Victorian offices separated by alleys so narrow you could lean out of the window and ask the typist opposite to marry you . . . the whole City had been labelled a "Fire Zone"', wrote a historian of London before the blitz. And that night it fulfilled its destiny. The five fire stations – Cannon Street, Redcross Street, Bishopsgate, Whitefriars (by the Strand) and Carmelite Street – and the thirty substations, set up after the Munich crisis in 1938 in warehouses, garages and disused Corporation buildings to augment the main stations, were powerless to contain the voracious flames.

On 29 December the Thames was at an abnormally low ebb as the raid began. Though fireboats pulled as near as they could to the shore, the firemen found it impossible to get their suction pipes through the mud and into the water mid-stream. Falling bombs fractured water mains, and soon the hydrants were running dry. With the static water tanks empty, the firemen struggled desperately to fight the terrible conflagration with little more than a dribble of water issuing from their hoses. Embers and incandescent particles swirled in the air, pricking the faces of the firefighters and igniting more fires. Buildings crashed to the ground, blocking the narrow City streets and making it impossible for the fire and Civil Defence services to get through. To add to the odds stacked against those fighting the inferno, a strong westerly wind blew through the streets, whipping the flames to a greater frenzy.

It seemed as if the City was doomed. Like a tragic replay of the Great Fire of London of 1666, its greatest buildings were destroyed, hundreds of years of history and tradition reduced to rubble and charred wood. 'On Sunday night, as I was reading about the Great Fire, in a very accurate detailed book,' Virginia Woolf wrote in her diary on the first day of 1941, 'London was burning. 8 of my city churches destroyed, & the Guildhall.'

The numerous fires soon joined together to form two mighty conflagrations, the worst of which ravaged half a square mile between Moorgate, Aldersgate, Cannon Street and Old Street. Fire Brigade control centres had twice to be abandoned – on one occasion staff clutching vital papers fled to safety through a network of underground tunnels. In the Operations Room at Redcross Street Fire Station in the middle of the Barbican, the heat was so intense that Aylmer Firebrace, Chief Fire Officer for the Greater London Region, noticed the paint blistering on the walls while the telephonists tried to work by candlelight (though the light from the fires outside made that superfluous) as one by one their phones went dead. Suddenly a Civil Defence warden rushed in, shouting, 'Your bloody roof's alight!'

All the fire stations in central London were 'down to bare poles', meaning that all the engines, men and equipment were out, leaving the station empty except for the poles the firemen slid down when answering a call. Emily Eary's job at Redcross Street station was to log requests and send out appliances, pumps, turntable ladders and hoses. 'That night, all the tallies had gone on the board, all the vehicles had gone out. There was nothing anybody could do about it . . . Messages kept coming in "send more appliances, send more ladders", but there was nothing at all to send . . . the tide had gone out in the Thames, so there was no water, and the City just burned . . . We were the only building that was left standing in that whole area . . . it was very, very terrifying.'

There was nothing to do but evacuate the entire area from Gresham Street in the south to Golden Lane in the north, Aldersgate in the west to Moorgate in the east. Little groups of shelterers, wardens, policemen, heavy rescue men and firemen ran through streets which were alight from end to end. 'The high wind which accompanies conflagrations is now stronger than ever and the air is filled with fierce driving rain of red-hot sparks and burning brands,' Aylmer Firebrace recalled later. 'The clouds overhead are rose-pink from the reflected glow of the fires, and fortunately it was light enough to pick our way eastwards towards Fore Street. Here fires were blazing on both sides of the road; burnt out and completely abandoned fire appliances lie smouldering in the roadway, their rubber tyres completely melted. The rubble from collapsed buildings lying three and four feet deep, makes progress difficult in the extreme. Scrambling and jumping, we use the biggest bits of fallen masonry as stepping stones, and eventually reach the outskirts of the stricken area.'

That night eighty horses were killed when a bomb hit a brewery in Chiswell Street, and 'the tubes were as full as at any time since the blitz started. Large numbers of people without shelter tickets stood in rows beside the passage-ways while the raid went on,' reported the *Daily Express* the next morning.

Watching from the roof of the Bank of England, B.J. Rogers, a senior clerk at the Bank, was horrified. 'The whole of London seemed alight! We were hemmed in by a wall of flame in every direction. It wasn't just big fires here and there, but a continuous sheet of flame all around us ... it looked absolutely out of control.' Over on the Guildhall roof, R.C.M. Fitzhugh, a fire-watcher, was equally shocked. 'The block bounded by Brassishaw Hall, Fore Street, Aldermanbury, and Bassinghall Street appeared to be one solid mass of flame. St Stephen's, Coleman Street, was soon enveloped in flames, and we couldn't see the steeple and weathercock fall ... Fires were everywhere in the City area. From time to time, heavy high-explosive bombs or land mines were dropped ... There would be the sound of something rushing in the air – then a brilliant flash would light up the entire sky and horizon to be followed within two or three seconds by the most resounding explosion.'

The City had nebulous boundaries – archaeologists and historians would have considered it bounded by the Roman walls, but to the police and local politicians and officials it was more amorphous, stretching as far west as the legal quarter around Chancery Lane and Middle Temple, north to take in Holborn Circus and Fleet Street, bulging east to encompass Smithfield Market and Liverpool Street station, and meandering as far as Petticoat Lane and Aldgate, ending up at Tower Bridge. The City was the centre of Britain's financial life – 'the capital of capital', some called it – but it was not then the district of soaring steel and glass it has since become. In 1940 it was still full of warehouses and small workshops, jostling with banks, financial and other institutions, most constructed of flammable ancient bricks and dry timber. It was no longer a significant residential area. Although in 1800, 128,000 people lived in the City, by the time of the blitz the resident popu-lation had fallen to around 5,000 – most of them caretakers, policemen and nurses. So many buildings were empty and unattended that Sunday night that the fires spread like lightning.

To anyone standing on Bankside, looking across the Thames, the City looked like a seamless wall of flame. A warehouse storing Brasso polish burned like a blast furnace; a paint warehouse was ablaze; fires burned out of control in the wharves that ran between Queen Victoria Street and Upper Victoria Street. A bomb fell near the Monument, the 202-foot-high column close to the northern end of London Bridge built by Wren to mark where the 1666 fire started. The historic halls of such powerful City companies as the Brewers, Coachmakers, Coopers, Haberdashers, Stationers and Wax Chandlers, all clustered around the Guildhall, were afire, as were the small and dingy premises of haberdashers, furriers, tobacconists, brewers and barbers and other providers of the daily essentials of the City's life. St Lawrence Jewry, the church of the Aldermen of the City of London, and one of the costliest that Wren ever built, filled from floor to ceiling with wood carvings by Grinling Gibbons, was blazing too. Soon the church was 'desolate. The four walls stood fast and the masonry of Wren's square-built tower had withstood the fire; but the roof had collapsed and the whole church was knee deep in smoking, smouldering ash and wreckage.' The churchwarden, Douglas Clarke, arrived to find beams still burning. Alarmed for the church's ancient records and priceless plate stashed in the strong-room, he persuaded the firemen to turn their hoses on the walls to cool them. When, days later, a safe-cutter managed to open the door, the treasure was found to be safe.

But sparks in the scorching air ignited the roof of the Guildhall. The four-hundred-year-old building, the ceremonial and administrative centre of the City of London and its corporations, repaired after the Great Fire by Wren, and given a new façade by George Dance in 1789, was soon a mass of flames. Although in the opinion of the *Architectural Review* its architectural merit 'has often been overvalued', inside the Guildhall was a treasure house, with its marble hall paid for by Richard (Dick) Whittington, Lord Mayor of London and its Alderman's Court Room designed by Wren. Roman antiquities from the amphitheatre that formerly stood on the site, too large to display, were housed in the basement. Its annexes housed a magistrates' court, library and museum, and an art gallery containing paintings by Constable, Reynolds, Rossetti, Holman Hunt, Millais, Tissot and Brangwyn. Joseph Knight's life-sized portraits of the twenty-two judges of the Fire Court who had resolved disputes and supervised the rebuilding of the City after the Great Fire hung there, while 160,000 books, 20,000 manuscripts and 14,000 prints were stored under the hammerbeam roof of the library. At 10 p.m. the fire had taken hold and the building was evacuated, fire-watchers and telephonists taking whatever they could carry of the most valuable of the Guildhall's priceless treasures. Much was saved, but much was lost, including the figures of Gog and Magog, the wooden pagan giants that traditionally defended the City. The original carvings had been destroyed in the Great Fire; now their early-eighteenth-century replacements proved equally unable to protect the City, and the Guildhall building itself was badly damaged.

Paternoster Row, close to St Paul's, where medieval clerics had walked, reciting the Lord's Prayer (*paternoster* – 'our father'), was one of a labyrinth of passages formerly with a religious purpose: Ave Maria Lane, Creed Lane (where the *Credo* had been sung), Sermon Lane, Amen Corner. From the sixteenth century onwards it been home to the book trade, with offices and warehouses jumbled together, though more recently some publishers had begun to migrate west to the elegant squares of Bloomsbury, to be replaced by second-hand book dealers. But there were enough remaining for seventeen publishing houses to be destroyed and an estimated twenty million books destroyed – a grievous loss at a time when paper was rationed and book production severely curtailed. The offices of such household names as William Collins, Ward Lock, Hodder & Stoughton, Eyre & Spottiswoode, Hutchinson and Nelson were reduced to rubble. Longman, which had been trading in the Row since 1724, was demolished, as was its warehouse across the river in Bermondsey; that night the firm lost over three million books as well as the woodcuts, blocks, drawings and plates for such perennial sellers as *Gray's Anatomy*. However, Longman's losses were not entirely bad news, since the fires disposed of a lot of dead stock, and the firm no longer had to pay War Risks Insurance on thousands of backlist titles that weren't selling.

The most devastating blow was that suffered by Simpkin Marshall, the largest book distributor in Britain, which lost six million books in the fires of 29 December. The firm never recovered, and after the war it went bankrupt. The offices of the *Boy's Own Paper*, the Catholic paper the *Tablet* and the trade magazine the *Bookseller* were damaged too. One of the *Bookseller*'s staff wandered among the debris-filled, deserted wasteland the following day. 'As I picked my way gingerly from brick to brick, hot gouts of sulphurous fumes from buried fires seeped up between my feet; desultory flames played in the remains of a rafter here or a floor joist there, and on either side the smoking causeway fell sharply away into cavernous, glowing holes, once a basement full of stock, now the crematories of the City's book world.'

Eight Wren churches, all built after the last Great Fire, were destroyed that night (no Wren church escaped damage during the blitz), including much of St Lawrence Jewry and the 'wedding cake' church of St Bride's, 'the cathedral of Fleet Street', where the young Nicholas Hawksmoor had been one of Wren's assistants. All that was left of it was four walls and the steeple, described by a historian of the City as a 'madrigal in stone'.

With his camera strapped around his neck, Herbert Mason, a press photographer, walked from Fleet Street up Ludgate Hill. It was 'carpeted in hose pipes, a scampering rat here and there a reeling bird in the flames. The heat became intense as I approached St Paul's Churchyard. Firemen were fighting a losing battle. Pathetically little water was coming from their hoses. Suddenly a fresh supply would come in and a hose running riot would lash out and knock firemen off their feet. The heat was so intense that embers were falling like rain and clattering on your helmet.' Mason went back down the hill and clambered up onto the roof of the *Daily Mail* building in Tudor Street, between Fleet Street and the Embankment. He could 'see that this night I was going to obtain the picture that would for ever record the Battle of Britain. After waiting a few hours, the smoke parted like a curtain at the theatre and there before me was this wonderful vista.' It was the dome of St Paul's Cathedral, wreathed in heavy smoke, but seeming to rise – almost to float – above it, like a celestial guardian. This was the photograph that appeared in the next morning's *Daily Mail*, and would become the iconic, universally recognised image of the London blitz, indeed of the war, with the cathedral as a symbol of faith, steadfastness, resistance and survival. Stan Hook, a despatch rider who had been stopped by Civil Defence wardens in Queen Victoria Street, and forbidden to take his bike any further, saw the dome 'silhouetted against a blood red sky, and it showed up black, and the cross on the top, the orb was reflecting all the flames around, and it gave you hope'.

Herbert Mason was fortunate with his bird's-eye vantage point: the majesty of St Paul's was not easily discernible from the ground, hemmed in as the cathedral was by other buildings, its façade all but obscured by an undistinguished Victorian office block. Indeed, many visitors had difficulty in deciding which *was* the cathedral, often mistaking it for the Old Bailey law courts nearby, and vice versa. St Paul's had been threatened by bombs before, and for all its architectural glory, it was not well built. Constructed partly on sand, partly on clay, its foundations were so insecure that a special Act of Parliament had been passed forbidding tunnelling and excavating under the precincts. In the 1920s an appeal had been launched to strengthen and rejuvenate Wren's masterpiece, and on the tercentenary of the architect's birth, 20 October 1932, a service to give thanks for the newly glorious cathedral had been broadcast.

On 12 September 1940 a 2,200-pound bomb had fallen close by, and lay embedded in the ground perilously near the front of the cathedral. Its removal was a highly dangerous task for the bomb disposal squad, and took several days. Finally the eight-foot-long missile was extracted, and driven gingerly on a lorry to the 'bomb cemetery' on Hackney Marshes in east London, to be exploded in controlled conditions, the streets on its route cleared in case it went off prematurely.

Aware of the historic importance of his cathedral, and of its structural fragility, the Dean, Walter Matthews, and the Cathedral Surveyors had had rising mains and supplementary water tanks installed before the outbreak of war, and several members of the cathedral staff were trained in fire-fighting. The tomb of the Duke of Wellington in the crypt, a fourteen-ton construction of Cornish porphyry on a granite base, far too heavy to move, was coated in Vaseline and bricked up for the duration, while the statue of the metaphysical poet John Donne, himself Dean of St Paul's from 1621 until his death ten years later, which had survived the 1666 fire, was laid in the basement. But more was required: it was recognised that the cathedral would be a nightmare for firemen, and was desperately vulnerable with its inner and outer dome of lead, its flat roofs of timber covered with lead, its ancient bricks and timber rafters, its 'pocket roofs' above the transept and other high-up hidden places in which an incendiary bomb could lodge and burn away undetected until it was too late.

Advised by the Surveyor to the Fabric (the cathedral architect), the Dean and Chapter put an advertisement in the Royal Institute of British Architects' *Journal* asking for volunteers to join the St Paul's Night Watch. Dean Matthews realised that architects would be his best bet because they would be able to read plans, and he called for 'men from forty to sixty who can walk up stairs and not fear heights'. James Richards, editor of the modernist *Architectural Review*, who occasionally used an office at the *Review*'s printers, Eyre & Spottiswoode in Paternoster Row (the business and production staff having decamped to the relative safety of Cheam), was one who volunteered, though he was younger than the specified age range. Matthews had specified men above forty because, according to Richards, 'he wanted to make sure he hadn't trained people who were then going to be called up'. John Betjeman, not an architect but a contributor to the *Archie Rev* (as he called it) and greatly interested in buildings, was another, as was Richard Titmuss, who would later write the most humane of the official histories of the Second World War. The Watch soon totalled about forty.

Each volunteer was required to spend one night a week in the cathedral, from 9.30 until six in the morning, but when the blitz started most came in on two nights or more, so usually there were about a dozen on duty each night, dressed in blue overalls and wearing a steel helmet and webbed belt with a torch attached and a steel tool for turning on hydrants. What now seemed like the blessedly long months of the phoney war had given them the opportunity to learn the intricacies of the cathedral. Ralph Tubbs, an architect and architectural writer who would come to national attention with his 'Dome of Discovery' for the Festival of Britain in 1951, was a team leader allocated to the roof level, and every evening he would train with his men. 'The Cathedral is really complex. There are over 20 staircases and . . . it was very, very dark. We used to ask each member of the particular team at that level to take someone to a remote point in the Cathedral, and then they'd have to find their way back on their own without any light, so they got to know it really well.' 'After the first weeks, the exercises were made more difficult,' recalls James Richards.

> We were told to assume that particular passages or stairs had been made impassable by fire or debris, so we quickly had to think out alternative routes to whatever corner of the building a hypothetical bomb had been reported from. We were not always successful, especially at first, telephoning with shame that we could not find it, or returning after such a long interval that our commander felt obliged to discover by cross examination what extraordinary route we had taken. It was like being back at school . . . We tried our hardest, and at the end of a few months most of us did know the cathedral intimately. We also had to learn as we went about the building, the location of fire hydrants and extinguishers, water tanks, stop cocks and telephones. If there was no raid the members of the watch would repair to the crypt to drink tea, read, play chess and sleep on a camp bed – alongside the Dean and his wife, since the Deanery did not have an air raid shelter.

On 29 December 1940, twenty-eight bombs fell on St Paul's. The Dean's wife thought it sounded like a coal scuttle being emptied. Some penetrated the roofs and landed on the upper side of the brick vaulting; some lodged in roof timbers; one stuck in the lead covering of the dome and, blazing away, gave the impression that the whole dome was on fire. Indeed the CBS correspondent Ed Murrow, watching the red glow, broadcast the cathedral's obituary to listeners in America: 'The church that means most to London is gone. St Paul's Cathedral, built by Sir Christopher Wren, her great dome towering above the capital of the Empire, is burning to the ground as I talk to you now.' But it was a premature death knell. 'I build for eternity,' Wren had said – though that was not to be the destiny of his other City churches. As burning lead dripped from the roof and it looked as if the Grinling Gibbons carved choir stalls and organ screen might catch fire at any minute, two teams of the Watch crawled cautiously along the wooden beams with stirrup pumps to try to extinguish the incendiary device. It was perilous work, high above the nave, balancing on a slender beam. The members of the 'dome patrol' were selected from amongst those 'with a head for heights and with a leaning towards acrobatics', according to the Dean, and since 'the dome was not a healthy place to be at the height of the blitz', the patrol was changed at half-hourly intervals. Suddenly, having burnt its way through the beam, the bomb crashed onto the floor below and 'was easily put out'.

At 11.40 p.m. an incendiary fell on an upholstery workshop in Creed Lane. It was the last bomb of the raid. By midnight the German planes had all gone from the skies over the burning inferno. Louise Savage, who lived only ten minutes from the City, was stunned.

The All Clear went . . . at 12 o'clock and we couldn't believe it, because up to then, the raids had gone on all night, from six o'clock in the evening until six or seven the next morning. So we grabbed the dogs and torches and rushed to the door . . . but you didn't need a torch, the whole place was red . . . there wasn't a sound, There was nobody about. The fires made it so bright that you could read a newspaper. We couldn't believe it. We kept looking over our shoulders . . . our ears alert, waiting for the siren to go off again . . . we were so sure it'd go off. They'd never leave a fire like this . . . we were so sure that they were going to come back that night and literally blow us to pieces . . . we felt sure there would be another huge bombing raid that would obliterate us all . . . but it never came – at least not that night.

The fires burned for two days. Robert Baltrop had been due to start a new job the day after the raid.

You could pick and choose jobs then if you were a young man, not yet called up, because there was a great shortage of able-bodied young men, and I had written to a firm in the City saying have you got a job for a fellow like me, and they'd said, start on Monday. So I got a train to Liverpool Street and I was going to walk through the City. But when I got there, there was no job, and there was no walk through the City. I turned the corner into Moorgate, and the City was in ruins. It was the most astonishing sight. Buildings demolished, smoke everywhere, firemen and hoses . . . so I went home, and the next day I rang up and the firm said, we'll get in touch with you . . . but they never did . . . You hear about raids on the wireless but you have to see something like this to realise what it was really like.

Down the hill in Fleet Street and beyond there were façades with nothing but smoking ruins behind them. Farringdon Road was little but piles of rubble between Ludgate Circus and Holborn Viaduct. A paperworks burned for nine days. Back up the hill to the Old Bailey it was the same. The Library of the Middle Temple had been gutted, and the attic in which Dr Johnson had compiled his dictionary was a wreck. St Andrew's by the Wardrobe, one of Wren's later churches, was a smoking ruin. In St Paul's a small service was being held to give thanks for deliverance: the cathedral reeked of charred timber, an acrid odour that would haunt the City for weeks.

'A most horrible and malicious flame' like the one Pepys had recorded in 1666 had revealed parts of the Roman London Wall for the first time in two hundred years. Cannon Street station was a bare iron skeleton, like some monstrous, crouching dinosaur, and the White Tower of the Tower of London had been damaged. The Barbican, which lay outside the City walls, was so devastated that the Home Guard used its ruins to train in street-fighting techniques, and gradually the site reverted to what it had been for thousands of years: a heath, seeded with willow herbs and fennel, buddleia, ragwort and nettles, alive with displaced feral cats, rabbits, mice, rats – and children who suddenly had rubble-strewn playgrounds where there had been no place to play before. But St Paul's still stood, more visible than it had ever been, even to Sir Christopher Wren, so many buildings had been razed around it. James Richards was not sure that was actually an advantage: 'St Paul's was meant to have buildings all around it. When Wren designed it, it was surrounded by buildings and that is why he designed it in two storeys, so you could always see what looked like a complete building over the roofs of the houses all round it . . . it looked rather absurd without any buildings, with an empty foreground, because it was never meant to be seen that way.'

Leo Townsend, an off-duty ARP warden, emerged on the morning after the raid

from a splintered Bank station into smoke-laden air, heavy with disaster. Traffic had ceased. Cheapside was sealed off; Lombard Street and Queen Victoria Street were impassable. A tangled skein of entrails, fire hoses twisting, interweaving among dust and debris, snaked up King William Street, coiled along Princes Street, as though a monster had been disembowelled . . . Some streets were cordoned off, but otherwise the steel Civil Defence helmets provided a passport to undisturbed wandering . . . Scarcely a door was on its hinges, not a pane of glass intact. No shops were open; those who would normally have been buying and selling found it all they could do to reach the site of the premises they had worked in. Many had decided it was useless to attend that day, others had arrived to find there was nothing left to attend to. Occasionally small groups of people stood talking in low voices.

The air grew heavier with soot, our feet stumbled among the undergrowth of charred wood, the steaming mass of warehouse goods, the sprawling tubes issuing from pump and hydrant. Piles across the roadway gave off a smell of burning rubber and smouldering cloth. Fires leaped within the gaping skins of buildings, smoke bloomed from shattered window sockets . . . Known buildings were rendered indistinguishable except when a spurt of fire licked a church tower into sudden prominence.

James Pope-Hennessy was writing a book, *History Under Fire*, for which Cecil Beaton was taking the photographs. On 30 December the pair visited the City, 'which was still in flames. It was an emotionally disturbing experience to clamber among the still smouldering ashes of this frightful wasteland . . . In the biting cold with icy winds beating round corners [the two aesthetes] ran about the glowing, smouldering mounds of rubble . . . We have trundled under perilous walls, over uncertain ground which, at any moment might have given way to the red-hot vaults below . . . We could not deny a certain ghoulish excitement stimulated us, and our angers and sorrows were mixed with a strange thrill at seeing such a lively destruction – for this desolation is full of vitality. The heavy walls crumble and fall in the most romantic Piranesi forms. It is only when the rubble is cleared up, and the mess put in order that the effect becomes dead,' wrote Beaton.

Pope-Hennessy found that the ten burned churches 'had suffered a disgusting change, a metamorphosis at first stupefying. How could these dear interiors, panelled, symmetrical, murky, personal, redolent of the eighteenth century . . . have been turned into dead bonfires, enclosed by windowless and roofless lengths of walls, with pillars like rotten teeth thrusting up from the heaps of ash? This was one's immediate reaction.' But soon Pope-Hennessy realised he had become 'an amateur in Wren ruins as I had never been an amateur in Wren'. And while to 'tabulate the damage to every Wren church would be redundant. It would also be dull,' he incanted a litany of names, a mournful roll call of dead churches. 'St Andrew by the Wardrobe; St Mary-le-Bow; St Augustine-with-St Faith; St Lawrence Jewry; Christ Church Newgate; St Alban, Wood Street; St Mary, Aldermanbury ["the night's worst loss", thought John Betjeman, also on the prowl around the ruins, with its "painted dome by Sir James Thornill, the father-in-law of Hogarth, a grand staircase and festooned pulpit, altarpiece and organ case"]; St Stephen, Coleman Street ["of little architectural loss" in Betjeman's opinion]; St Anne and St Agnes; St Vedast alias Foster [where only a "few baroque memorial tablets with sorrowing cupids and skulls remain", according to Beaton, while to Betjeman, its undamaged "Wren steeple of triangular shape [is] the most lovely of all in the City"].' 'Among these the destruction of St Lawrence Jewry is a crushing blow,' thought Pope-Hennessy, and Betjeman agreed: 'It was Wren's finest interior.' Pope-Hennessy and Beaton went to St Paul's, 'to offer our prayers for its miraculous preservation', while Betjeman worried about All Hallowes, Barking, 'another medieval church . . . full of treasures, the best of which was the font cover, three cherubs struggling round some fruit, probably the best work of Grinling Gibbons. I should like to know if that has been saved.'

Half a million commuters flooded into the City every day. As they arrived on the bleak, cold morning of Monday, 30 December, tramping over Blackfriars or London Bridge, broken glass crunching underfoot, the sight that met them was almost incomprehensible. It was a scene of utter desolation, with a smattering of snow falling on buildings that were still burning. Workers wandered through streets they thought they knew, took routes they could have sworn they would have been able to follow blindfold, they had taken them so many times before, but found themselves disorientated and lost, the cityscape cruelly disfigured and confusing. Firemen, exhausted beyond tiredness, grimy, smoke-blackened, their eyes red rimmed, were beginning to roll up their hoses, leaving a few fires, like the one still consuming a factory in Old Street with no other buildings nearby to ignite, to burn themselves out. As Dorothy Barton, a City worker, came over London Bridge, she saw such a group of firemen. 'Quite spontaneously, the office workers burst into a cheer, and several shook hands with the firemen as they passed. I was in tears as I walked along, it was such an emotional moment. I don't think anyone should ever forget the firemen were heroes during the entire war, but especially during the blitz.'

Fourteen firemen died in London that night, and more than 250 were seriously injured. Twenty-five-year-old Leonard Rosoman was 'fighting a fire in Shoe Lane just off Fleet Street. It was a narrow street and we didn't seem to be doing much good, so the man who was in charge said to me . . . "we're going into that building . . . we're going up onto the roof and haul the hosepipe – the branch as it's known – up onto the roof . . . we think that'll have a better effect" . . . so I did this and we handed this chap the hose, and walked back along this narrow lane. It must have been five, perhaps ten seconds, when there was the most really tremendous crunching sound, and the building opposite had fallen and crushed these two firemen, who were standing there, and I had missed it by seconds . . . it was a very chilling, traumatic experience, and I have to admit that I lost a fair amount of sleep over it.' But as well as being an auxiliary fireman (attached to the same Hampstead fire station as Stephen Spender), Rosoman was also an artist – he would later be appointed an official War Artist – and 'painted it out of my system . . . as a sort of therapy I suppose'. *A House Collapsing on Two Firemen, Shoe Lane, London EC4*, purchased for the nation in August 1941, became another iconic image of the blitz. Rosoman himself came to dislike it as 'sentimental and superficial' – though it is rather hard to see why.

At Moorfields Hospital on the City Road, five firemen died when another wall collapsed; two more died in an ambulance taking them to St Bartholomew's Hospital. Frank Hurd, an auxiliary fireman who wrote down his experiences of the blitz, and whose photograph had appeared in the press drinking tea with one of the old ladies whose life he had saved, died of injuries sustained fighting a fire at Smithfield Market. He was twenty-four years old.

Throughout Greater London as a whole a total of 160 people died and five hundred were injured, most of them in adjacent boroughs such as Westminster, Holborn, Stepney and Shoreditch, or across the river in

Bermondsey, Southwark, Lambeth, Deptford, Greenwich and Lewisham, others further away in Tottenham, Battersea, Camberwell and Fulham. Some were ARP wardens, Shelter Marshals, members of a demolition squad as well as firemen. Most were ordinary civilians, killed in their homes or shelters. Some were in their seventies, while one was only a few months old. In addition two people were killed in Bristol, fourteen in a raid on Crewe in Cheshire, one in Chelmsford in Essex, and one in Malling in Kent. Those of other nationalities, such as four Polish soldiers killed in an incident in Southwark, were not included in the official total.

On the morning of 30 December the BBC eight o'clock news reported in its usual uninformative way: 'Enemy aircraft attacked towns in the south of England during the night causing some damage. Fires were started and casualties have been reported.' However, the lunchtime news carried some cheerful tidings that had already found their way into the morning papers. The previous evening President Roosevelt had broadcast one of his 'fireside chats'. It was delivered at 9.30 p.m. in Washington DC, which was 3.30 a.m. in London, after the raid on London had ended but while the fires were still raging. Roosevelt denied that this was

> a fireside chat on war. It is a talk on national security, because the nub of the whole purpose of your President is to keep you now, and your children later, and your grandchildren much later, out of a last-ditch war for the preservation of American independence and all of the things that American independence means to you and to me and to ours . . . The British people and their allies today are conducting an active war against this unholy alliance [of the Axis powers]. Our own future security is greatly dependent on the outcome of that fight . . . The people of Europe who are defending themselves do not ask us to do their fighting. They ask us for the implements of war, the planes, the tanks, the guns and the freighters which will enable them to fight for their liberty and for our security. Emphatically, we must get these weapons to them, get them to them in sufficient volume and quickly enough so that we and our children will be saved the agony and suffering of war which others have had to endure . . . We must be the great arsenal of democracy . . .

In this broadcast, Roosevelt, while emphatic that the USA would not be sending 'fighting men' to Europe, had inched the country further along the path towards the resolve that Winston Churchill had expressed on 4 June 1940, at the darkest moment of the war, when Britain truly 'stood alone' (with her empire and dominion forces) during the battle for France: 'We will carry on the struggle until in God's good time the New World with all its power and might, sets forth to the liberation and rescue of the Old.'

'Everybody is enormously cheered by President Roosevelt's cheering speech,' reported Phyllis Warner, who wrote for the American press, including the *Washington Post*, and who probably took more notice than most people of the subtle nuances of US manoeuvrings. 'Respect for his righteousness is being added to admiration for his brilliance,' she added enthusiastically.

The next evening Warner celebrated the New Year. She found that although there were 'no wild bells to ring out the bad and ring in the good because this year bells can only ring for an invasion . . . and every theatre and cinema [is] shut, Piccadilly Circus blacked out and St Paul's surrounded by smouldering ruins . . . But never can every restaurant and club have been more completely packed, never can crowds have been more spontaneously gay.' The Meurice, 'London's newest resort . . . was packed as always for the Meurice dance band would fill an attic in Coventry . . . Favourite tune was "Oh Johnny, how you can love". Most of the women had blossomed into long skirts and backless dresses again. Fast waltzes, rhumbas and congas were the order of the day . . . As midnight struck we sang "Auld Lang Syne" and joined hands and waved our paper hats and danced a highland reel on two inches of space.' Warner was convinced that people's spirits were higher than they had been the previous year, when 'we were sober because the threat of the future was a threat still, and we knew the year was bringing us dread ordeals and hazards. 1941 will bring them too, but we have gazed right into the furnace, and recaptured our belief in ourselves, so we can look to the coming year with confidence and gaiety.' 'Looking forward with confidence and gaiety' was probably not how most people saw in the New Year in 1940, but Warner had a product that she hoped to be able to sell to her American readers: the dauntless British spirit and resolve.

Anthony Heap had celebrated the New Year too, but in his case at 'an informal party' in the Quakers' shelter in the Euston Road rather than a chic West End restaurant. 'At midnight we stood in a ring and sang "Auld Lang Syne" and it was all over. And so to bunk . . . Thus passed out 1940. Never was I so glad to see the last of a year than this unhappy one' (though, to be fair, Heap had affairs-of-the-heart issues that added to his blitz gloom).

Harold Nicolson was in pretty low spirits too. He felt that 'poor old London is beginning to look very drab. Paris is so young and gay that she could stand a little battering. But London is a charwoman among capitals, and when her teeth begin to fall out she looks ill indeed.' Nicolson, who was travelling around the country as the 'lightning conductor' for the Minister of Information, Duff Cooper – 'one just walks about in a fur coat and gets things done' – lunched on 30 December 1940 with General (later Field Marshal) Alexander, who had supervised the final stages of the evacuation from Dunkirk and was by then Commander-in-Chief of Southern Command: 'He thinks the Battle of England has already begun – Coventry, Southampton, Bristol, the City. They will burn and destroy them one by one,' Nicolson wrote to his wife, Vita Sackville-West, at home at Sissinghurst in Kent, from a train travelling from Bristol to Cardiff. 'I do think we are going through a hellish time.'

13

Standing Firm

Everyone has strong views about what to do in an alert. Miss Bousie: 'If I were in a munitions factory I would work during an alert. What good would I do here [in the Glasgow coal shipping firm where she worked]? I might be killed by a bomb. There is something glorious about being killed in battle, but not by a bomb.'   Mass-Observation diarist Edith Oakham, 10 January 1941

God is our refuge, be not afraid,
He will take care of you through the raid.
When bombs are dropping and danger is near,
He will be with you, until the all clear.

Verse of a wartime Sunday school hymn chalked on the walls of many air-raid shelters during the blitz

Vere Hodgson was distressed to hear about the destruction on the night of 29 December, particularly as the City offices of the accountant that kept the books for the charitable association for which she worked in Notting Hill had been bombed, and 'all the ledgers probably perished in the fire. It took [our accountant] seven years to make that Ledger, and the Balance Sheet was finished some time ago. Had the books been returned to us, it would not have happened. Everything of reference to the Association could be turned up in seconds in that book – and it has gone.' She was also somewhat censorious. 'We had further news of the damage to the City,' she wrote on 31 December, 'and all through neglect! Always the same – no one wants to take responsibility . . . let others do it. Common sense should tell us that it is madness to leave buildings to one caretaker, or to no one at times like these . . . It serves a lot of them right – but it has caused harm to many beautiful churches . . . Mr Herbert Morrison says it will now be compulsory for every building to be guarded. I should think so indeed! . . . Fancy leaving the City of London unprotected in days like these!'

It had been clear ever since the blitz started that firemen would not be able to deal with the thousands of incendiaries that might fall during a raid, and equally that a single undetected incendiary could wreak tremendous havoc. But although fire-watching had been encouraged, it had been a voluntary activity. The City raid had finally shown that voluntarism was not working, and that compulsion was needed in this as in so many other areas of the home front. In a broadcast on New Year's Eve Herbert Morrison had explained that no fire brigade could be expected to deal with mass incendiary raids without the assistance of the community. 'Some of you lately, in more cities than one, have failed your country,' he chided. 'This must never happen again . . . every group of houses and business premises must have its fire party. Fall in Fire Bomb Fighters!' he urged, likening fire-watchers to the Home Guard, as 'a Civil Defence Guard to back up the work of the ARP and the fire services'. It wasn't just damage to property that unchecked incendiaries could cause: the fires acted like a beacon for the enemy 'at which he will aim his high-explosive bombs'.

Charles Graves, a dedicatedly social journalist (and brother of the more famous Robert, the poet) who sat out the blitz in some of the smartest hotels and bars in London, heard Morrison's broadcast. Since Graves's wife, Peggy, thought it a waste of money 'to spend two or three pounds a head [not much less than the weekly wage of a working man or a private soldier] to have your champagne glass filled with streamers and the usual pellets which are thrown around on New Year's Eve', the couple dined at home that evening, and turned on the wireless to 'listen to Herbert Morrison making an appeal for fire-watchers before announcing that they were going to be compulsory anyway. It was a dull speech, poorly delivered. It didn't sound as though he had his heart in it. And yet, as a Cockney of Cockneys, he should have been quite passionate on the subject.' Then the Graveses set off in a taxi for the cocktail bar at the Dorchester, remembering to take a watch 'as there is scarcely a public clock in London which can still tell the time'.

Anthony Heap was predictably scornful too: 'The papers are full of the government's new scheme for a compulsory fire fighting service . . . unpaid of course. Surely a more ingenious scheme for mounting up air raid casualties couldn't have been devised. The government seems more concerned about the loss of property than the loss of life.'

In January 1941 Morrison returned to his theme and the microphone again, chiding his listeners that he would never have resorted to compulsion were 'all the people patriotic and courageous enough'. Eight million leaflets were sent out advising people how to organise themselves into fire-watching rotas with their neighbours, and telling them to contact their local warden's post about getting stirrup pumps and being trained how to use them. Until sufficient pumps were available, they were told, the best thing was to attack the incendiary with a rake and some sand. Local authorities were urged to make piles of sand widely available – Hackney provided three sand dumps at every warden's post for the neighbourhood, while Kensington Borough Council produced 5,000 sandbags and put a couple at the foot of every lamp post in the borough.

While fire-watching was important in residential areas, it was even more so at factories and other places of work. Morrison stated that in the workplace 'compulsion will apply to everyone of every grade – managers, office workers as well as manual workers. Factories and businesses of all kinds will be subject to severe penalties for any neglect of their obligations,' he warned. 'But don't wait for that. There isn't the time and there ought not to be the need.'

Although most newspapers welcomed the introduction of compulsory fire-watching as a necessary, if belated, measure, *The Times* was not the only one to point out the possible difficulties. Many workers were already working in Civil Defence as wardens, members of rescue parties or demolition squads, or carrying out other voluntary tasks, on top of a full working day, and had little spare time or capacity to give to fire-watching. The trade unions weren't very keen either, and complained that there had been no consultation. And while it was one thing to turn out on patrol in your own street, it was a bit rich to be expected to protect your employer's premises without remuneration, which could be seen as unpaid, compulsory overtime. The discontent rumbled on throughout the spring and summer of 1941. All over the country large numbers of employees refused to obey the order: it was estimated that nationwide around 60 per cent of those required to undertake fire-watching duties claimed exemption. There was a huge furore about the imposition when the TUC met in Edinburgh in September 1941. However, by that time Morrison had made some concessions, promising that there would be some limited financial compensation, and that employers were to be obliged to provide sanitary facilities and sleeping accommodation for their fire-watchers. But by then there wasn't anything like the same need for fire-watching as previously, since the blitz was over.

Later raids in 1944 would be of a rather different order, with V-1 flying bombs and V-2 rockets, rather than incendiaries that could be dealt with with sand or a stirrup pump.

Mass-Observation found that most people were in favour of compulsory fire-watching (though some, like Charles Graves, had been unimpressed by Morrison's speech), and many thought it should have been introduced 'months ago'. However, some could see no reason why fire-watching parties needed to be organised in residential streets: instead, every householder should be responsible for his or her own property. Nine out of ten men and six out of ten women polled said they 'vaguely' knew how to deal with an incendiary bomb (cover it with sand or earth), although a few thought water should be thrown over it, which was in fact dangerous and certainly ineffective. This was an improvement on the situation at the outbreak of war, when only about a third of those quizzed had any notion at all of how to deal with incendiary devices. Of those who thought that the best thing to do was to pick them up and throw them out of the house, many failed to remark that a long-handled shovel should be used for the purpose. Women admitted to being less likely to know how to deal with incendiaries, and were inclined to leave the matter to their husbands – a dangerous policy if the bomb fell during the day when the man was at work. M-O thought that women needed reassuring that it was relatively simple to cope with an incendiary, and that they should learn how to use a stirrup pump, while it was essential to get the message across to everyone that people should wait two minutes before approaching a device in case it was an explosive one, programmed to ignite spontaneously a little while after landing.

There were other personnel as well as fire-watchers on the roofs of factories and other places of work during air raids: aircraft spotters. Sometimes the roles were combined, though this was not recommended, as it was not possible to look up (for approaching enemy aircraft) and down (for smouldering incendiaries) at the same time.

Downing tools and stopping work to go to the shelter when an alert was sounded had become an increasingly contentious issue as raids grew more frequent. Official advice since Munich had insisted that in an air raid, civilians must take cover. But if they did this each time an alert was sounded, many hours in a shift could be lost; this would obviously have a disastrous effect on production, with serious implications for Britain's war effort. Winston Churchill suggested that the alert should be treated as just that, a warning to be on the alert, not necessarily a signal to take cover. Or as Ellen

Wilkinson rather more emotively put it, 'any needlessly stopping work is an act of surrender'. Employers developed various strategies to minimise the effect of interruptions: Bethnal Green Council, for example, allowed its staff to retreat to the basement when the siren wailed, but insisted that they must take the work they had been doing with them. This was hardly practical in munitions and aircraft factories, where instead workers volunteered (or were nominated) to stand on the roof and look out for approaching enemy aircraft, so that production could continue after the alert had sounded until these 'Jim Crows', as they were called – Churchill's name for them, since he was a naval man – signalled that raiders were actually overhead.

A group of seven North Country factories was reported to have perfected a system by September 1940. A pair of observers was posted on top of each factory building with a large compass so they could plot the direction from which German planes were approaching. They were linked by telephone to a central control room; if the phones were put out of action, messengers were used. When a call was received that the raiders were heading for the factories, an alarm was sounded from this control room, and the workers took to the shelters. The control room could also direct fire, first aid or decontamination services if bombs did drop. It was an ARP exercise *in parvo*.

Florence Rollinson's father was a fire-watcher at Bryant & May's match factory in the East End of London.

> The men in these fire-watch parties would go up on the roof in small groups and securing themselves with rope would watch out for fire bombs before they could take hold by kicking them off. The building was some hundred feet high and these tactics saved the factory. (The firm's Liverpool works had been burned down by incendiaries.) The men would change shifts quite often and come down for a breather with dad giving us a commentary of what was happening. As I was part of the First Aid party we had formed in the works, we would take care of any casualties, even those brought in off the street, and also keep the firewatchers supplied with tea and coffee. During those bitter cold nights in the blitz, we'd lace their drink with rum to keep out the cold! This was supplied by the directors of the firm, some of whom were also in the fire-watch party so everybody did their bit . . . These tactics did save the factory, and after the war the Chief Engineer in charge of the fire-watching was decorated with a medal.

Particularly concerned about the rate of aircraft production, Lord Beaverbrook, the Minister in charge, appointed Jennie Lee, a journalist, a past and future MP and the wife of Aneurin Bevan, to visit aircraft factories and impress on the workers the need to keep working after the siren had sounded. Lee, who believed that given her solid Labour background she would not be regarded as a government stooge, travelled the country speaking to shop stewards and addressing factory meetings, persuading workers to put in long hours and to work out a system of aircraft spotters so they would be away from their benches for the minimum time possible. On one occasion she was called to a Reading aerodrome where planes were tested as well as manufactured, because there was unrest among the workers at being expected to stay on the roof during an air raid. During her visit Lee found that while there were 'magnificent underground shelters' at the aerodrome, there were none for the houses where the workers' families lived nearby. So when the alert sounded, the men were apt to leg it across the fields to check on their homes. With Lee's persuasion, and Beaverbrook's famed disdain for red tape, cement was allocated and shelters built – although there was no publicity for this 'enjoyable act of piracy'.

A report on the Hawker aircraft factory in Kingston on Thames and 180 nearby businesses, published after the war, showed the efficacy of the roof-spotter scheme. At Hawker, spotters worked part-time during the day, ascending to the roof when they received notice from the Factory Defence Service that enemy planes were forty miles away; at night they were up there all the time. A chequered barrel would be hoisted on the factory roof, and similar ones on nearby large buildings such as the Guildhall, Bentall's department store and the local library, so that smaller premises could keep a lookout for this 'take cover' signal and instruct their workers. Between 1940 and 1945 the alert sounded for 1,250 hours fifty-nine minutes, but the actual 'take cover warnings' signalled by roof spotters and a network of alarms contingent on them lasted only 207 hours forty-one minutes – over a thousand hours of work time saved.

Aircraft spotting was skilled work. Although the favourite wartime reading matter of many British boys was the Penguin Special paperback *Aircraft Recognition*, by R.A. Saville-Sneath, and most people were confident that they could tell 'one of ours' from 'one of theirs', in fact they often couldn't. Initially, the RAF undertook to provide aircraft-recognition courses, and those thus trained disseminated their expertise to others. Soon aircraft-spotting courses were available all over the country, attracting employees not only from factories, but also department stores, newspaper offices, town halls, libraries and post offices, all of which had an interest in keeping their staff at work with as little interruption as possible, and adopted the rousing slogan of the *Daily Express* (owned by Beaverbrook) 'Look Out and Work On!' Though, if a popular ditty in the *Daily Herald* is to be believed, civil servants had to be named and shamed (as they were by Churchill) before they adopted the practices they recommended to others:

> 'Keep up your morale,' says Whitehall –
> While underground it delves,
> 'Work on,' they cry, to one and all,
> Then run to earth themselves.

It was cold, boring work standing on a roof hour after hour wearing a steel helmet (if you were lucky) with 'RS' painted on it, clutching a pair of binoculars and a map of the area. Torches were forbidden because of blackout regulations, though some organisations provided their spotters with silhouettes and photographs of German, Italian and British planes and cloud formations. It was not well-paid – £3 a week was about average – and there were dangers, both from enemy aircraft and from spotters falling from their vertiginous perches (or nests) in the dark.

Fire-watching carried similar – or greater – dangers. Although in January 1941 up to forty-eight hours' fire-watching a month was made compulsory for men aged between sixteen and sixty who worked fewer than sixty hours a week, women from twenty to forty-five who worked fewer than fifty-five hours a week (unless they were pregnant or had children under fourteen at home to care for) were not obliged to register for fire-watching duties until September 1942 – the same year that conscription and direction was extended to certain broad categories of women. In fact the available pool of fire-watchers was much smaller than these categories suggest, since the population of London and most large cities was only about three-quarters what it had been before the war, and many of those who were not in the forces were already engaged in voluntary Civil Defence or other war work. So although women were not compelled to fire-watch after the City blitz, they were certainly encouraged. Admitting that it could be dangerous work – 'though not as dangerous as the work wardens and firemen do each night the raiders come' – Herbert Morrison nevertheless felt that 'The time has long gone when women could be kept away from dangerous work in the defence of their country. The women of this country have shown that they have just as high courage and just as steady nerves as men. It may be that the idea of defending their homes, or the business where they work, as a front line fighter, will make a special appeal to them.' There were few women roof spotters (though the Bank of England used both sexes), and when it came to fire-watching, most women – certainly married women with children – preferred to carry it out at home rather than at their workplace.

On 1 February 1941 Sidney Chave went to a neighbour's house where were 'assembled most of the males of Glenhurst Rise [Upper Norwood]. We finally fixed up our arrangements for fire-watching. So that is settled at last. Most roads in London have their watching parties all fixed up ["the scheme is being supported throughout the whole country", Chave added the following week]. On Wednesday last, when incendiary bombs were dropped on Hampstead, there were about six men to each bomb, and not a single fire broke out.' A couple of Sundays later Chave and his wife were on duty from 11 p.m. to 2.30 a.m.: 'as bad luck would have it the sirens went at 10.45 just as I was in the bath, so Lee and I stayed up and "watched" until 2.30 by which time we were dog tired. Several planes came over and searchlights and guns sent into action but we heard no bombs.' It was not until 26 April that Chave was able to report that 'I was issued with a steel helmet for fire-watching at home today' – whether or not his wife also received one, he does not record.

The flat that Hope Cobb shared with two other young women in Tite Street, Chelsea, was rocked by a bomb and the ceiling collapsed while she was at work at the Admiralty on 16 April 1941. When her two flatmates 'had unravelled themselves, miraculously unhurt, they realised they were on fire-watching duty, so they bravely went out into the street. In the absence of tin hats' (presumably buried under debris), and pausing only to collect 'the tin containing the housekeeping money and her new suspender belt as well she might because we had no front door anymore and all the windows were broken', Dana put a saucepan on her head and Naidra lashed a frying pan to hers. So all that night they were addressed as, 'Saucepan, this way,' or 'Frying pan, over here, quick.'

There was one group of people who might well have been diligent fire-watchers before compulsion was introduced, but who refused to continue doing so when it was. In April 1939, in the face of Labour opposition and despite his own reluctance, Prime Minister Neville Chamberlain had introduced a Military Training Bill that allowed for conscription into the armed services – the first time such a measure had ever been taken in Britain in peacetime. The Act became law on 26 May. On the outbreak of war, the National Service (Armed Forces) Bill extended the categories of those required to register as liable to be called up for military service to men aged between eighteen and forty. As the war dragged on, the net trawled deeper into the pool of man – and later woman – power. There were exemptions for those in reserved occupations (often up to a certain age) and the medically unfit. And there was generous provision for those whose consciences – religious, ethical or political – meant they would not take up arms. Indeed, Chamberlain who had served on a conscientious objectors' tribunal in the First World War, was clear that it was 'both useless and an exasperating waste of time and effort to force such people to act in a manner which was contrary to their principles'.

Conscientious objectors (COs) were permitted to register not on the Military Training Register but on a special Register of Conscientious Objectors, on the grounds that they objected to undergoing military training or to performing combatant duties. Tribunals were set up specifically to hear the objections of such people and to decide whether they were sincere, consistent and deeply held, or opportunistic and cowardly. Obviously looking in men's (and later women's) souls in this way was never going to be easy: there were harsh, unfair or capricious judgements handed down by the bigoted or the confused on occasions, but on the whole the tribunals were more fair-minded than not, and wrestled long and hard to come to a decision – though those COs with a solid history of pacifism and religious objection to war, such as Quakers, tended to fare best. Those objecting to military service could be found all over Britain and from all classes, though there were fewer manual labourers and a preponderance of white-collar workers – plus creatives and intellectuals such as Ralph Partridge, Benjamin Britten, Peter Pears and Michael Tippett.

The tribunals could hand down one of three possible verdicts. They could reject an application altogether, in which case the applicant would then have to register for military service (and risk a fine or prison, or both, if he refused, though there were appeal procedures); they could require the applicant to do non-combatant service, where they would not be 'involved in the handling of military material of an aggressive nature'; or they could grant either an unconditional exemption or exemption from military service, on the condition that the applicant undertook some alternative form of war service under civilian control, such as ARP or other Civil Defence work, or working on the land or in the medical services. By the end of the war there were 59,192 COs, roughly 1.2 per cent of the five million 'called up'. Less than 5 per cent had been granted unconditional exemption; nearly 38 per cent were exempted on condition that they undertook a civilian alternative; almost 28 per cent were directed to non-combatant duties in the army; and nearly 30 per cent had their objections to military service dismissed altogether.

The blitz presented a particular challenge to COs – particularly the 'absolutists' who refused to undertake anything connected with war, or even to take a job that might release another person to fight (some even refused to appear before a tribunal). It was one thing to bear arms and actively engage in combat: it was rather another when combat came to you and your fellow civilians in the form of bombs and strafing.

The Royal Army Medical Corps (RAMC) was the usual choice of COs who had been directed, or were prepared, to work in a non-combatant role in the military, but by early 1940 it was said to be full and accepting no more recruits – there was some resentment about the number of 'lily-livered conchies' deployed in the Corps, and it was alleged that other applicants with specialist medical skills were being excluded because of them. So, in April 1940, a First World War innovation expressly for conscientious objectors, the Non-Combatant Corps (NCC, or as it was first called, the Non-Combatant Labour Corps –'Nancy-Elsie to genuine warriors') was revived. It consisted of fourteen companies totalling 6,766 men at its height, and was intended to be integral to all aspects of the war effort, apart from those that required the handling of weapons. Its members received their basic training at the Devon seaside resort of Ilfracombe, where they would drill without arms on the promenade and be trained in such skills as gas-detection, passive air defence, decontamination, cooking, cleaning and clerical duties. They could then be employed in administrative, construction or maintenance work, including the care of burial grounds, quarrying, forestry, filing in trenches and any other general duties. Occasionally there were problems when construction work involved such borderline tasks as building blockades and gun emplacements, or when an NCC company was detailed to fire-watch some warehouses in Liverpool which were found to contain shell cases – the court martial of the men accused was dismissed – or refused to build a road for an ammunition dump – no prosecution resulted.

During the blitz, NCC companies were stationed in Bristol, Coventry, Cardiff, Liverpool and other places that were frequent air-raid targets. Many of their members undertook voluntary rescue work in addition to their other tasks: two were awarded the George Medal for their services. In January 1941 two companies of the NCC were drafted to London to clear bomb sites and help with rescue work. The NCC also undertook some of the most dangerous work on the home front: disposing of unexploded bombs. The initiative came from the COs themselves, and when the War Office finally agreed, 465 NCC COs volunteered. Christopher Wren was one. He had been an 'absolutist' until Dunkirk, when he had been so horrified by the sight of civilians being shot at and bombed 'that we were prepared to go and help . . . do anything that was needed to save life. Germans as well.' When it came to dealing with UXBs, 'I thought that it would be very good to destroy armaments and at the same time protect people. Both aspects seemed to fit with why I had become a non-combatant. The training was minimal. We went to Chester and were under canvas on the racecourse . . . We were told we would be going to London because there was more to be done down there . . . A few weeks later we were sent to Chelsea Barracks for real training. We really enjoyed that. It was with the R[oyal] E[ngineers] and everything was enjoyable. No prejudice at all.'

The NCC (or 'Norwegian Camel Corps', as they were jokingly called, presumably to highlight their Dr Doolittle incongruity) volunteers worked alongside the regular soldiers and conscripts of the expert Royal Engineers. 'All you could do was be as useful as you possibly could be to the Royal Engineers. You couldn't take over from them. They were all very skilled men.' Wren was 'not a great handyman but I have got strength and the "sappers" liked that'. If the 'conchies' were ever taunted as cowards, there would usually be some old soldier who would 'say quietly "Don't forget [the conscientious objectors] did what they wanted. You waited for conscription." ' If a member of the public saw his NCC badge and asked Wren what it was, 'I would say "Non-Combatant Corps". You knew what they were thinking so I would say I was a coward straight away! Then sometimes they would see the bomb flash [the badge denoting his role in bomb disposal] and they wouldn't know what to make of it. I would just leave it.'

Tony White, a lifelong Methodist, was another CO who volunteered for bomb-disposal work.

It was doing something constructive in the sense that you were digging out bombs that were meant to harm, immunising them, and you could see it as a direct service for the community. But the major reason was my proving something to myself, that I wasn't 'dodging the column' . . . I didn't want to escape the risk and here was a chance to prove my sincerity, not in the front line but dangerous – I didn't know how dangerous at that time . . . There were several 1,000 pounders that we got, about 4 or 5 feet long, they were a pretty good size. They were heavy of course, and we got them out by winching them out, with a tripod type of rig to haul them out. We'd take them away and try to neutralise them. You'd screw in and make a hole in the casing, trying not to disturb the fuse . . . that job had to be done very carefully, and then we'd inject steam which would neutralise the powder or the explosive and then one could remove the fuse safely. And then the officer would retreat to what was theoretically a safe distance and then explode it with an electrical device. This was when the thing could explode before the officer had got far enough away, he was always the one at the greatest risk and we did suffer casualties.

You were never sure when you moved [the bomb] out of its hole . . . if you'd disturbed the mechanism and there was always the risk that the thing might explode. There were all sorts of things like sensible safe distances and safe times and so on to minimise the . . . danger, but it was always there.

The fact that they were volunteers was essential to COs who worked in bomb disposal; the introduction of compulsory fire-watching (or fire-prevention duties, as it was technically called) sharpened their wartime dilemma. By undertaking fire-watching duties they were, if they followed the logic of Morrison and other war leaders, making a contribution to the war effort and the defeat of Germany. If they did not, they might be allowing the homes of their fellow countrymen and women to go up in flames, perhaps incinerating the occupants.

There were further moral refinements. If you were prepared to defend your own property, why not that of other people, or your employer – or an aircraft-production or munitions factory? If, as a neighbourly or community-minded act, you were prepared to watch your neighbour's or other's property as well as your own, what happened when legal requirements were imposed on this moral duty? That would be complying with the *diktat* of a war-prosecuting state rather than acting from a wellspring of community responsibility and goodwill. Was the principle of individual liberty to be trampled upon, particularly as fire-watchers could be compelled by law to do their work in another district if the need were greater there?

The debate raged furiously – and illuminatingly – in the letters columns of the press, most particularly the pacifist press. A man writing from Wimbledon insisted that 'the grave question [of compulsion] with which we are faced . . . is the growing threat to individual liberty and judgement . . . It is not so much a matter of whether Friends [i.e. Quakers] and any of like persuasion can do fire-watching, civil defence, or other work, but whether they can give themselves to any of these things under State compulsion.' A woman with a historic Quaker surname, Elizabeth Howard, from Essex, however, reminded readers of the Quaker magazine *The Friend* that 'there is a conscientious *obligation* as well as a conscientious *objection*'. Another woman, with an equally illustrious Quaker name, Elizabeth Cadbury, writing from her manor house near Birmingham, agreed: 'One is getting a little tired of the efforts of some members to overweight our Peace testimony with self-made inhibitions; and we must hope that a more Christian attitude toward our fellow-countrymen and women and our country may be the basis for discussion.' A woman from Bridport could not understand why people objected to the compulsion clause: 'Friends are already agreeing to compulsion by complying with other war emergency laws e.g. paying extra income tax . . . complying with food rationing, blackout etc. Before the war Friends complied with compulsory education, lighting-up time and legislation to do with supporting a wife, and bankruptcy.' And an article by Carl Heath, a prominent Quaker leader since the First World War, urged:

> Do not let us be led into rejecting all compulsions alike because they arise out of the community's war-making. Where we can do so, let's turn them into creative acts . . . It is for us to transform all compulsions that can be discerned as having intentions of neighbourly act and concern. It is wrong to waste moral strength resisting these. Resistance is rather to be concentrated against those compulsions whose governing purpose is to destroy men. There is a world of difference in spiritual possibility between blacking-out and bombing . . .
>
> In submitting to, or resisting, the many infringements of civil liberty contingent on war conditions, we have to remember that there is little help for the cause of peace in attempting to resist war-in-progress on each detail. To do so is to get into an Ishmaelite position and to create nothing effective and much mere antagonism. There will be cases where the infringement involves a moral wrong to be withstood. But mostly we shall endure these ills, which the will of the community-at-war imposes, under protest, and seek

with determination their undoing in the peace. [As pacifists and Quakers] we are not outside the community of our nation. We are right inside. And because we are a minority our criticism and our opposition needs to be specially wise, constructive and discerning.

There was no 'conscience clause' in the compulsory fire-watching registration scheme. The penalty for failing to carry out duties under the legislation was up to three months' imprisonment or a £100 fine, or both, and employers who did not make suitable arrangements could be similarly penalised. Those in the armed forces, persons of unsound mind or registered blind, were not required to register, though ministers of religion were. Those already engaged in wartime duties such as the Home Guard or Civil Defence, or spending long hours doing vital war work, were required to register, but would not be enrolled for duty. A man not covered by any of these categories could apply for exemption 'on the ground that he is medically unfit to perform [fire-watching duties] or that it would be an exceptional hardship for him to be required to perform them'. This could provide a loophole for COs, who while they may have been perfectly prepared to put out fires, refused to register to do so. Probably through hasty drafting, local authorities had been given no powers to register those who refused to sign up.

Tribunals (distinct from the CO tribunals) known as 'Hardship Committees' were set up to consider exemptions from fire-watching on the grounds of ill-health or exceptional hardship. There was no appeal against their decision. Ill-health was usually fairly straightforward to assess; 'exceptional hardship' far less so. On 2 April 1941 a Mr Bell of Hook in Surrey applied to the City of London Hardship Committee for exemption from fire-watching duty at his place of work in the City. He gave as his reason that to be compelled to do something against one's conscience was a hardship. At first the Committee wrote to Bell's employers telling them that he had been granted 'indefinite exemption'; then, realising the moment of this decision, they withdrew it, saying that an error had been made. However, three subsequent applications – from a Bristol employer, a Bolton doctor and a ship-owner (though the Committee was divided in the case of the ship-owner) – were granted. These were the only successful applications for exemption until 1943, when the deputy editor of *Peace News* was granted indefinite exemption, since most Committees did not see that a sensitive conscience was equivalent to a broken arm or a dying mother.

In March 1941 the first prosecution for refusing to serve on a fire-watching rota at work was brought in Manchester: the miscreant was told to pay a fine of £5 or go to prison for twenty-five days: he chose the latter. Similar cases were brought in Nottingham (refusal to fire-watch for a bank), Glasgow and Exeter. On 30 May John Morley, a Newcastle upon Tyne employer who was chairman of the local War Resisters Group, was fined £50, with five guineas costs, for refusing to make fire-watching arrangements for his coach-making premises. Morley refused to pay, and was sent down for three months instead (though subsequently released after a few hours, only to be rearrested on the same charge).

Prosecutions for failure to enrol multiplied, including those of ten Christadelphians in Bristol who asserted that 'There comes a time when human laws conflict with the laws of God.' The Independent Labour Party MP Fenner Brockway had been a CO in the First World War, but had decided that Nazism was an evil that had to be met by force in the Second. Even so, though no longer one himself, he was very involved in the CO movement, and was also an active fire-watcher before the introduction of compulsion. He arranged a meeting with Ellen Wilkinson at the Home Office (ironically, her office overlooked the Cenotaph) to try to persuade her to insert a conscience clause into the fire-watching regulations. But Wilkinson refused to budge, arguing that 'In the serious condition of the present war, fire-watching was necessary to save life, and refusal to register for it was a serious offence, and the scheme could not be left to goodwill.'

The prosecutions continued; so did the odd acts of deception, with those liable employing others to do their duties for them; so did the 'funk expresses' taking people away from their fire-watching responsibilities to the safety of the countryside. And so did the shortage of fire-watchers. On 19 September 1942 the requirement to register for fire-watching duties was extended to women aged between twenty and forty-five (with certain exemptions). Within two months the prosecutions of women began, including those of the Misses Dungey, three sisters from Camberley in Surrey who each went to prison three times for refusing to register. The final prosecution for a fire-watching (or rather non-fire-watching) offence was brought on 26 February 1945. Compulsory fire-watching was abolished shortly afterwards, by which time a total of 555 prosecutions of COs had been brought, while several thousand more had fulfilled their obligations without noticeable demur.

Frequently people would take the often hard road of the conscientious objection for religious reasons. In addition to the Quaker Society of Friends, there was the Christian Fellowship of Reconciliation, which in 1939 had nearly

10,000 members, and there were small pacifist fellowships within most Churches, including the small but influential Roman Catholic PAX, the Anglican Fellowship (around 1,500 members) and the Methodist Peace Fellowship (around 3,500 members). There were COs who were Jews, Buddhists and Hindus, Seventh Day Adventists, Christian Scientists, Spiritualists and members of the Salvation Army. The Peace Pledge Union (PPU) was started in 1934 by Dick Sheppard, Canon of St Paul's Cathedral, who had invited men to send him postcards pledging never to support war: 113,000 responded. While it was not a religious organisation, the PPU appealed to many Christians. Its founder, the Reverend Dick Sheppard, had held the living of St Martin-in-the-Fields before becoming a canon of St Paul's, but most of its members could probably best be characterised as humanitarians.

Not all pacifists were Christians (or of any other religious persuasion). And not all Christians were pacifists: indeed, most were not. And many who had had pacifist inclinations in the interwar years, such as Fenner Brockway, the writer Storm Jameson and the philosopher and BBC Brains Trust member C.E.M. Joad, had come reluctantly to the conclusion that pacifism was not a viable option with the onslaught of fascism.

Bryan Richards, a Lieutenant in the Royal Engineers who was involved in bomb disposal, was also a Christian: 'I thought war was very stupid and wicked, but I think we have to live with people as they are and not as we think they ought to be . . . The only way of stopping [the Germans] was to fight them. That didn't seem to me in any way inconsistent with my religious beliefs.'

The Reverend John Markham, vicar of St Peter's, Walworth, in south London, was Chief ARP Warden for his district, in addition to his heavy parochial duties, and opened the crypt of his church as a public shelter. Other clergymen did the same, or joined the Home Guard. Father Groser was untiringly active on behalf of his Stepney parishioners, and those beyond his parish boundaries. The Reverend Ineson, a Nonconformist minister, opened the doors of his East End mission to anyone who had been bombed out, regardless of their faith. When the mission itself was bombed, a deaconess who worked there organised helpers to take boots and food, blankets and warm clothing to the shelters and arches where East Enders were sheltering. St Matthew's church, Bethnal Green, was bombed out, but the rector, the Reverend Ferraro, turned his rectory into a home for half a dozen bombees. Mr French, the Rural Dean of Stepney, noted that during the blitz the congregation of his bomb-damaged church, St Dunstan, had dwindled, and the collection plate on a Sunday now contained ten shillings rather than the usual £3. But he believed 'his real flock is out in the streets', and that is where he and hundreds of men of the cloth like him, vicars, priests and rabbis, worked tirelessly, searching for billets, helping fill in forms for compensation, organising evacuations, finding clothes, food and storage for furniture, giving practical help, succour and comfort. Most left their churches and went out into the community, holding services in shelters, praying with the bereaved, giving communion to the wounded and the dying, conducting the funerals of countless blitz victims, and, in the case of Groser, inviting high-profile people from film stars to visiting American dignitaries to come to see conditions in the East End for themselves so the publicity this engendered might galvanise the government into greater action. But in the end, the fact that 'we just carried on . . . was of the greatest importance . . . a reminder that life and hope endured in the midst of so much chaos and uncertainty', wrote Father Groser.

The churches were perceived as being on the front line – after all, many were bombed: one in every six Methodist chapels was destroyed or badly damaged, and both Coventry Cathedral and St Paul's became powerful national, and not just religious, symbols. Considering religion to be a potentially important force to encourage national unity and raise morale in wartime, the Ministry of Information created a Religions Division intended to impart 'a real conviction of the Christian contribution to our civilization and of the essentially anti-Christian character of Nazism'. However, the conviction that 'God is on our side' and that the war was a religious crusade against the dark forces of pagan Germany was inaccurate, and could prove counterproductive, particularly with thoughtful churchmen, most notably Bishop Bell of Chichester, who raised concerns about the British bombing of German cities as well as the internment of enemy aliens, many of whom had fled to Britain from Nazi persecution.

It was not intended that John Betjeman's poem 'In Westminster Abbey' should be a model:

> Gracious Lord, oh bomb the Germans.
> Spare their women for Thy Sake,
> And if that is not too easy
> We will pardon Thy Mistake.
> But, gracious Lord, whate'er shall be,
> Don't let anyone bomb me . . .

Think of what this nation stands for,
Books from Boots and country lanes.
Free speech, free passes, class distinction,
Democracy and proper drains.
Lord, put beneath Thy special care
One eighty-nine Cadogan Square . . .

Lord Macmillan, the first Minister of Information, had assured Church leaders: 'I realise that the Christian Church cannot be used as an organ of propaganda. It is in its essential nature ecumenical and supranational. But I trust that as individuals you will be ready and anxious to help us.' And Duff Cooper, Minister of Information during the blitz, encouraged the belief that 'You cannot spread Christianity by the sword, but you can defend a society in which Christian principles are allowed scope and in which there is freedom of thought and worship.' Church leaders were delicately circumspect. A joint declaration was published on 21 December 1940 and signed by the Archbishops of Canterbury and York (Anglican), the Archbishop of Westminster (Roman Catholic) and the Moderator of the Free Churches. This was careful not to mention bombing the enemy, or indeed the enemy at all. Rather it concentrated on the religious and ethical foundations of a future peace, and when that came, on a fairer distribution of the world's resources.

But what about ordinary people with no religious authority or vocation? Did the dangers and uncertainties of nightly air raids incline them to seek the comfort and certainty of a deity? Or did they turn away from religion, unable to comprehend how a supposedly all-loving and all-seeing God could allow such devastation, death and mutilation to be inflicted on the innocent?

Church membership had been in slow decline since the First World War: it was estimated that by 1939 only one in five English people went to church on Sundays, and fewer than that in London. On the whole, Catholicism had stood up better than Anglicanism, partly due to an influx of immigrants from Ireland, and partly because conversion was demanded of any person who married a Catholic. Wartime conditions – absence in the forces or working away from home in munitions factories, evacuation, the blackout, air raids, bombed churches – all conspired to reduce this number, so that in January 1941 Gallup found that only 9 per cent of people polled went to church more frequently than they had before the war, while 52 per cent went less often, and 32 per cent never went. In Hammersmith in west London, M-O found that by 1944, 61 per cent of the population never went to church other than for weddings or funerals, regarding church attendance as 'something of "a harmless hobby" '. In Paddington, a borough that had suffered badly during the blitz, though nothing like as badly as the East End, and had lost 42 per cent of its population due to damage to property, evacuation, etc., the average attendance at morning and evening services combined in the spring of 1941 comprised less than 4 per cent of the population.

After the raids on Southampton in December 1940, an Anglican church-warden told a Mass-Observer, 'The bombings put a stop to church going. They were never very religious round here before the raids, but any inclination people had to go and pray then has disappeared. I come in here [church] every day at lunchtime just for a few minutes' private devotion, but I haven't seen anyone else [lately].' The clergy hoped (or more often feared) that their congregations were getting all the religion they needed by tuning into the church services broadcast on the BBC, though this was not a new perception. National days of prayer, held regularly throughout the war, proved more successful in filling pews than regular Sunday services, though that may indicate patriotism rather than religious fervour.

When it came to religious belief rather than church-going, Mass-Observation found a remarkable continuity of faith in wartime, though it dipped from 1939 to 1942, when the progress of the war was at its grimmest, and the decline was halted as the hope of victory seemed more plausible. On the whole, those who were already believers found that war strengthened their faith, which gave them a rock to cling to, inclined them to seek the ritual and community of the church. Those who had been sceptical in peacetime turned further from religion, seeing the sight of man slaughtering man as confirmation that there was no benevolent God, and Churches had no more certainties than politicians. Few actually admitted to having lost their faith as a result of war, and some had it strengthened. In the experience of Ivor Leverton, a funeral director, the blitz 'did turn a lot of people away from religion. Or certainly established religions. On the other hand, there were a lot of people whose only comfort came from a belief in the future, a future life after death. So it worked both ways really.' People might pray during a raid, but that often seemed more an incantation of fear, a sort of insurance policy just in case there was a God, or an attempt to make a bargain – 'Save me this time and I'll . . .' – rather than evidence of consistently held belief.

Perhaps surprisingly, belief in spiritualism did not rise appreciably during the Second World War, as it had in the First. Gallup reported in March 1940 that only one in ten people believed that it was possible to get in touch with the dead. On the other hand, astrology, which was a ubiquitous feature in popular newspapers and women's magazines by the end of the 1930s, dipped slightly in popularity at the start of the war, but rose steadily throughout the blitz, so that by its end, two-thirds of the population admitted to looking at their 'stars' every day, hoping to find some cheerful prediction in an uncertain and bleak world.

14

Spring Offensive

Until the beginning of the re-grouping of forces for Barbarossa [the code name for the German invasion of Russia] efforts will be made to intensify the effect of air and sea war, not only to inflict the heaviest possible losses on England, but also to give the impression that an invasion of Britain is planned this year. Hitler's War Directive no. 23, 6 February 1941

Many of those here to-day have been all night at their posts and all have been under the fire of the enemy, under heavy and protracted bombardment. That you should gather in this way is a mark of fortitude and phlegm, of a courage and detachment from worldly affairs . . . I go about the country whenever I can escape for a few hours or for a day from my duty at headquarters, and I see the damage done by enemy attacks: but I also see side by side with the devastation and amid the ruins . . . a consciousness of being associated with a cause far higher and wider than any human or personal issue. I see the spirit of an unconquerable people . . .

Winston Churchill speaking at Bristol University on Easter Saturday, 12 April 1941

1941 was the grimmest year of the war for Britain. On land, Allied forces were defeated in every theatre of war in which they were fighting. Retreating in North Africa, in Greece and in Crete – a pattern that would soon be played out in the Far East too, with the loss of Hong Kong and Singapore. There were, however, straws in the wind indicating that the tide would slowly turn: Hitler's invasion of the Soviet Union in June opened an Eastern Front, while in December America abandoned its neutral stance when Japan bombed the US fleet in Pearl Harbor on 7 December and America, Britain, South American countries and the Dominions declared war on Japan, followed by a declaration of war on the USA by Germany and Italy. The circle of war was now clamped tight shut, although the British public would have been more optimistic had they known that on 9 January 1941 Hitler had given orders to cease preparations for Operation Sealion, the invasion of Britain.

At home it was a year of increasing compulsion: 1.5 million more people needed to be drawn into the war effort. There was a 'comb out' of industry to make sure that labour was being maximised for war production, the reserved occupations schedule was overhauled, study and apprenticeships were largely deferred for the duration, and in December Britain became the first nation in the modern world to conscript women. Food rations were lower in the first months of 1941 than at any other time during the war: shipping losses meant that imports had fallen to two-thirds of their pre-war level, and the Ministry of Food was continually having to revise targets downwards. Although farmers were managing to grow more food, this was at the expense of livestock production: the meat ration fell from 2s.2d in autumn 1940 to 1s.2d in January 1941, and hardly rose again for the rest of the war, while the cheese allowance plummeted to one ounce per person per week and jam went 'on the coupon'. In June clothes rationing was introduced. And the blitz continued, rising to a peak of attrition that spring.

The year opened with the country in the grip of freezing weather. Fierce north-east winds brought snow, the ground was rock solid, rivers froze, and venturing out was hazardous. Bomb-damaged houses that might have just about been fit for human habitation in more clement weather became almost unbearable as wind whistled under tarpaulins and through broken windows ineffectually patched with cardboard, while low gas pressure as a result of damage to mains and pipes, and shortages of coal and wood to burn, added to the misery of the biting cold.

On the home front, it was the firemen who were probably the worst affected. The turntables of fire engines were immobilised by ice, and firemen had to use blowlamps to get them moving again. If the water pressure fell – as it frequently did – hosepipes would freeze. Roads were treacherous for vehicles, and huge icicles hanging from buildings and even from their own ladders made their task hazardous for firemen whose wet clothes froze stiff on their bodies.

Although there were thirteen nights in January when weather conditions were too bad for the Luftwaffe to mount bombing raids, there was little let-up in the blitz once the so-called Christmas truce was definitively over. The German strategy had switched to attacking 'the most important English harbours for imports, particularly port installations, and ships lying in them

[and] to attack shipping especially when homeward bound'. Since Germany had not been able to overcome British air supremacy, and bombarding war-production factories was not yielding the hoped-for results, Britain's island status, her historic protection, now had to be violated, the country starved of food and war matériel, besieged into submission. Those at sea in the Royal and Merchant Navies, fighting a desperate battle against German U-boats in the Battle of the Atlantic, suffered yet more hardship in the appalling weather.

'Vital harbour installations' all around the coast of the United Kingdom (not just in 'England', which was how Hitler always referred to Britain) would be pulverised over the coming months as the blitz entered a new phase. Cardiff in south Wales was the first. On 2 January 1941 over a hundred Luftwaffe planes dropped high-explosive bombs and 14,000 incendiaries on the city. It was a cold, clear night with near-perfect visibility. The Luftwaffe's aiming point was the docks, though some bombers were diverted in the direction of a 'starfish' decoy site to the south-west of the city, and 102 high-explosive bombs fell there, which probably saved the vital ammunition dump at Barry. A sheet of flames more than 2,000 yards high could be seen from miles away and a rubber works, a paint factory and transport offices were hit, and railways put out of action.

But it wasn't Cardiff's docks and industries that suffered the most: it was houses and small shops, particularly in the west end of the city. More than sixty civilians were killed in the Riverside suburb within the first half hour of the raid that had started soon after sunset, at 5 p.m. Seven mourners in a funeral party which had decided not to take shelter were killed when a land mine hit a house, throwing a car a hundred yards. In a nearby street a rescue party dug for six hours to rescue a six-year-old child trapped under the staircase where he had been sheltering. Throughout the rescue operations the boy was reported to have sung 'God Save the King'. He had learned from his father, a coal miner, that when men were buried underground, they kept 'singing and singing', and he said that the national anthem was the only song to which he knew the words.

A land mine exploded at Cardiff Arms Park rugby stadium, and the city's white Portland stone Civic Centre reminded onlookers of a wedding cake as it stood proud amidst buildings on fire all around. Firemen and fire-watchers posted on the roof saved it by smothering the dozens of incendiary bombs that landed there, or shovelling them into Glamorgan canal that ran alongside it.

Llandaff Cathedral, built on one of the oldest Christian sites in Britain in 1107, at the instigation of Bishop Urban, the first bishop to be appointed by the Normans after the Conquest, had the roof of its nave shored off when a parachute mine exploded nearby, leaving a 'scene of utter desolation . . . stout oaken doors were split like matchwood and torn from their hinges . . . the floor was cluttered with fallen timber and broken slates, heavy pews had been thrown about and severely damaged'. The top of the spire toppled into the churchyard, making a huge crater, and the explosion hurled tombstones as far as half a mile. It was fortunate that twelve valuable stained-glass windows had been removed and put into storage at the outbreak of war. Dante Gabriel Rossetti's famous triptych *The Seed of David* had been packed into a wooden pallet and surrounded by sandbags, and that too was undamaged.

Cardiff had an unusually high percentage of volunteers in its Civil Defence services, and they were praised by politicians and the press for the courageous way they coped with the mayhem that night – a courage that *Front Line* suggested was 'not far in space or spirit from the mining valleys where the black dumps are always encroaching on the green hillsides and toilsome lives are lived in the shadow of daily risk of sudden catastrophe'. And like a mining disaster, the raid of 2 January 1941 was a catastrophe for the capital of Wales, its largest and most populous city. One hundred and sixty-five people died, and roughly the same number were injured. Many of the dead were given a mass funeral in Cathays cemetery the following week, with those who could not be identified sharing a common grave.

The writer Naomi Mitchison went to Cardiff three weeks after the raid to visit her oldest son Denny and his wife Ruth, who were both medical students, evacuated to the city to continue their training with University College Hospital. She had had to sit on her suitcase in the corridor most of the way from Paddington in a train crowded with troops, and when she did manage to find a seat it was in a compartment that was 'very crowded, all smoking'. She found the young couple 'very short of coal, although of course this is coal country. Also of meat, vegetables, fish and fruit. Other things patchy.' They were 'very fed-up because they are getting so few patients and so little teaching. Their hospital has been turned into a casualty clearing station, so most beds are empty . . . Talked a lot about the blitz, took me out to look at bomb craters; here, as in London, the thing strikes me as more untidy than dreadful, bits and pieces off everywhere, ornamental ridge tiles and so on. Often just looks like a place demolished on purpose. Sooner or later everyone in the South seems to talk about bombs.'

The next night, 3 January, Bristolians would also be talking about bombs – again. It would be the city's worst raid of the war. As 202 aircraft from Luftflotte 2 and then Luftflotte 3 moved along the coast, Bristol and Avonmouth were in their sights as they had been in November and December. Their mission was 'To complete the destruction of the harbour installations, large mills, warehouses and cold stores in Bristol in order to paralyse it as a large trading centre supplying southern England.' The raid lasted intermittently for twelve hours, with aircraft converging on the city from three directions. For the first time a 'Satan' bomb, measuring almost nine feet (with its tail) in length and weighing nearly 4,000 tons, was dropped on Bristol: fortunately it failed to explode. By midnight the flames of the burning city could be seen from a hundred miles away. At first the guns were silenced as wave after wave of Hurricanes were scrambled to intercept the enemy aircraft. They were not successful, and though the AA guns were reactivated and fired 1,317 rounds of shells, only one German plane was downed – and that was when it crash landed in Belgium on its return flight.

The temperature had plunged well below freezing on one of the coldest nights of the winter, and the roads were sheets of ice. As firemen struggled to contain the blaze, 'Two houses might be seen side by side, one in flames with the firemen at work on it, the other hung with long icicles where the streams of water had splashed and frozen.' WVS workers who valiantly struggled out with their mobile canteens to provide refreshments found that 'as the firemen put their cups down, the dregs froze and they froze. The tea froze. The hoses froze.' Sixty fire brigades, some from as far away as Surrey and Buckinghamshire, were ordered to Bristol to help contain the conflagrations. As the fire engines drove into the city along the treacherously icy roads, buses were being driven out to the safety of the countryside, so that Bristol's transport system would not be paralysed.

Several of the elegant Georgian houses in Berkeley Square in Clifton were hit that night. The YWCA hostel collapsed, and it was several days before the bodies of fifteen people buried in the wreckage could be recovered. Other residential areas such as Knowle, Bedminster, Easton, Hotwells, Cotham and St Paul's were also badly damaged. Temple Meads railway station was wrecked, as was Jones's department store in Broadmead. But the docks were not seriously damaged, and though one 'starfish' site at Chew Magna attracted six high-explosive bombs and about a thousand incendiaries, other similar sites were ignored. The historic centre of Bristol had been so badly damaged in earlier raids that there wasn't much left to destroy this time, but the Guildhall was gutted, as was St Augustine's church, one of the most historic in the city. Bristol General Hospital had a lucky escape, though the nurses' quarters on the top floor were destroyed by incendiary bombs, as were three wards, and high-explosives blew out most of the windows. Patients, none injured, were evacuated as water, debris and charred wood embers cascaded down stairs and lift ducts and ceilings collapsed. Throughout it all, the matron Annie Caroline Robins stayed put, calmly directing staff and comforting patients: she was awarded an OBE for her work that night and in previous raids.

One hundred and forty-nine people were killed, including eight local Bristol firemen, two fire-watchers, an ambulance driver and a police war reserve constable. The firefighters and the policeman all died in the High Street which had been so badly bombed in December. They were trying to put out a fire at the Posada restaurant when more bombs started to fall and some nearby buildings collapsed, burying them under tons of masonry; it would take hours to clear the debris to find their bodies. Three hundred and fifteen people were injured.

The next night, another bitterly cold one, the Avonmouth docks were the target. Although the sky was clear at first, thick cloud soon covered the port, making aiming harder, and the raid did not really develop – many bombs fell harmlessly in the Bristol Channel, and all the fires were extinguished by 10 p.m. However, Avonmouth's gain was Weston-super-Mare's loss, as the bombers followed the Bristol Channel, dropping high-explosives and incendiaries on Weston and the nearby resort of Clevedon, killing thirty-four people and wounding eighty-five.

London seemed to act like a powerful magnet throughout the spring of 1941. The Luftwaffe would fan out to attack the provinces – mainly the ports – then wheel back to bombard the capital again and again. George Orwell drew on his diary to capture those months in an article he wrote for *Partisan Review*: 'The aeroplanes come back and back, every few minutes. It is just like in an eastern country, when you keep thinking you have killed the last mosquito inside your net, and every time, as soon as you have turned the light out, another starts droning . . . The commotion made by the mere passage of a bomb through the air is astonishing. The whole house shakes, enough to rattle objects on the table. Why it is that the electric light dips when a bomb passes close by, nobody seems to know . . . Regular features

Bitter blitz. The water from firemen's hoses froze into long icicles on a fire engine's ladder during a raid on Bristol on 3 January 1941. The photograph was taken by Jim Facey, chief photographer on the *Bristol Evening Post* during the blitz.

The East End at war. Bert Hardy's photograph for *Picture Post* of an official taking statements from bombed-out local residents on the morning after a raid in September 1940.

A post-raid operation. A member of the War Reserve (WR) Police directs Civil Defence workers, including members of the light and heavy rescue squad and demolition workers clearing debris, in the search for victims trapped beneath a collapsed building.

A group of people gather outside an unnamed town hall to check the lists of air-raid casualties. This photograph was taken by Humphrey Spender, the photographer brother of the poet Stephen Spender, for *Picture Post*.

Swansea residents, their homes bombed,
queue up for tea and buns from a mobile
canteen in February 1941.

of the time: neatly swept-up piles of glass, litter and stone and splinters of flint, smell of escaping gas, knots of sightseers waiting at the cordons where there are unexploded bombs.'

The bombers were drawn back to London; Londoners were drawn back to the City to gaze in horror at its destruction. 'Everything is a shell . . . all burnt out inside. Smoke was still coming from one building,' wrote Vere Hodgson seven days after the Great Fire. 'It is no exaggeration to say that the bulk of the city is destroyed,' Anthony Heap had reported the previous day. 'Every street has its huge gaping voids, gutted buildings and debris-choked roadways. The odour of charred wood still lingers in the air. Never have I seen such widespread ruin and desolation. The damage in the West End is negligible compared with this harrowing sight' – though it appears that Heap never ventured to the East End to observe the even more 'harrowing sights' there.

Virginia Woolf came up to London from Sussex on 13 January. 'I went to London Bridge. I looked at the river, very misty; some tufts of smoke, perhaps from burning houses. There was another fire on Saturday . . . I wandered in the desolate ruins of my old squares [round the Temple]; gashed; dismantled; the old red bricks all white powder, like a builder's yard . . . all that completeness ravished & demolished.'

London suffered four major raids between 11 and 19 January. The smoke Woolf saw would have been from buildings still burning after the short, intense raid on the 11th, when a bomb hit Liverpool Street station, killing forty-three people including eighteen who were on passing buses, one of which was thrown across the road by the force of the blast and crashed into the wall of Bishopsgate Police Station. Two drivers, a conductor and twenty-two passengers were killed, and many more were injured.

Buses, trams and trolleybuses were particularly vulnerable during a raid, when they could be hit by bombs or shrapnel, or fall into craters in the road. By October 1940 so many had been damaged that buses were driven to London from as far north as Aberdeen and Inverness and as far west as Plymouth and Exeter to supplement the capital's diminished fleet, and the familiar red London buses were joined by others of a different hue, painted in the livery of dozens of provincial companies. Forty trolleybuses bound for South Africa were diverted for service in London, though they were six inches wider and considerably heavier than the usual vehicles, which could cause difficulties for drivers.

On the evening of 11 January underground stations were hit too – St

Paul's, Baker Street and Green Park. The most serious incident was the bomb that fell on Bank station just before 8 p.m. 'It is said,' Vere Hodgson reported, 'that the blast blew many people onto the live rails where they were electrocuted immediately.' One hundred and eleven people, fifty-three of whom had been sheltering in the station and four station staff, were killed, and a huge crater disrupted traffic and pedestrian passage until the army threw a temporary metal 'Bailey'-type bridge over it. The next night the Luftwaffe attacked the docks again, and again the Victoria and Albert Dock and Woolwich Arsenal burned. Buildings in Greenwich, and Lambeth Hospital across the river were hit. A week later the bombers reprised the first night of the blitz, hitting Beckton gasworks, and then on 19 January south London was the target. St Stephen's Hospital on the Fulham Road received a direct hit, killing nineteen people, and bombs fanned out across Wandsworth, Battersea, Chelsea and Richmond, as well as Hampstead in north London, Marylebone and St Pancras. That month 992 people across Britain were killed and 1,927 seriously injured.

Most people who died in air raids were killed either when masonry or beams fell on them, or were buried by falling debris and suffocated by rubble or brick dust ingested into their lungs. Those trapped under debris, or in basements or cellars or anywhere from where they could not escape, were at risk from fire, escaping gas or flooding. Others were killed by bomb fragments or shrapnel from AA shells penetrating their bodies. Splinters of glass could also kill, which is why people were urged to criss-cross the windows of their homes with paper sticky tape in order to hold any shattered glass together.

Another, though less frequent, cause of death was from bomb blast. An exploding bomb sends out shock waves which travel at very high velocity – with as much as six hundred times the force of a hurricane – and anyone close to the detonation, particularly if it happened in an enclosed space, would be affected by high-pressure suction impacting on the body's cavities: ears, lungs, the stomach and intestines. Such victims could appear untouched, and yet be dead within seconds.

J.D. (Desmond) Bernal, a monumental figure in physics in the 1930s, was attached to a newly formed Research and Experiments Department at the Ministry of Home Security, with headquarters at Princes Risborough, twenty miles from Oxford. One of his projects there was to investigate the risk of concussion from bomb waves to people in underground shelters. Bernal invited a colleague, the zoologist Solly Zuckerman, to help. The scientists 'devised the harness and fixings with which to restrain some monkeys against the wall of a concrete-lined shelter, and to detonate a bomb which was buried in the ground nearby'.

On 15 October 1939, a distinguished group of scientists (plus Mrs Zuckerman, 'along for the ride') gathered on Salisbury Plain to see the results. Although the concrete wall cracked, the monkeys appeared to be totally unaffected. So, to the consternation of the onlookers, Bernal and Zuckerman themselves sat in a trench as another bomb was detonated. The effect was so minimal that neither man realised the bomb had actually gone off until anxious faces 'peered in to see if we were safe. In those days no-one seemed to know anything about the precise effects of bombs,' Zuckerman reflected.

Zuckerman dismissed the idea of the 'powerful secretary' of the Medical Research Council, Sir Edward Mellanby, that 'from the public point of view, this is a case where ignorance is bliss'. He was also scornful of J.B.S. Haldane ('good scientist though he was'), who drew from his experiences in the Spanish Civil War the notion that 'when a big bomb explodes . . . the blast becomes translated at a distance into a wave of sound like that of the last trumpet . . . which literally flattens everything in front of it . . . It is the last sound which many people ever hear, even if they are not killed because their ear-drums are burst in and they are deafened for life. It occasionally kills people outright without any obvious wound.' Zuckerman was forced to draw 'the blunt conclusion that we knew practically nothing'. He believed that this was not a state of affairs that should persist.

He managed to persuade Sir Reginald Stradling, Chief Scientific Advisor to the Minister of Home Security, that more work needed to be done, and undertook investigations involving rabbits and guinea pigs and exploding gas balloons at the Road Research Laboratory near Slough. These echoed experiments he and Bernal had carried out with pigeons on the Maginot Line in France in the months before the Germans invaded. It was intense work, entailing detailed laboratory tests into the early hours, weeks studying tissue from deceased small creatures, killed by bomb (or rather gas balloon) blast, and sometimes chasing monkeys and goats that had made a bid for freedom across the fields. 'But it was a new experience and exciting – no-one minded.' And it paid off. Zuckerman was able to establish that bomb blast killed not by inhalation through the windpipe, as had previously been thought, but from external pressure to the body.

But there was more to do. How close to a bomb would someone need to be to be killed by the blast? And what should be done by way of protection? More experimentation. 'By this time food was being strictly rationed, with food coupons being the order of the day. Meat having become scarce, we used to distribute the rabbits which had been used in our experiments. Rabbit made a splendid dish. Goat was different . . .'

As well as experiments into the effects of bomb blast, Zuckerman and his colleagues were investigating death and injuries caused by shrapnel, sometimes using cadavers 'borrowed' from the local mortuary, lumps of meat (when meat was still available) or anaesthetised rabbits to test their theories. Again, the results were surprising. It was neither the size nor the shape of the fragment that caused the damage: it was the velocity at which it entered the body – and which organ it hit. Thus a quite large, jagged piece of shrapnel entering a thigh would do relatively little damage (unless it severed an artery on the way), whereas a pinhead-sized fragment of metal penetrating a kidney could be lethal.

Once the blitz started it was possible to test the conclusions of such experimental work against what actually happened in real life. Zuckerman and Bernal set up a Casualty Survey (which paralleled the Bomb Census) with a permanent team, many of them young women, based at Guy's Hospital in London, a central analytical group in Oxford and a 'flying squad' ready to investigate incidents elsewhere in the country.

It could be frustrating at first, as 'Des and Solly' rushed to an incident at St Pancras station only to discover that the damage had in fact been caused by an anti-aircraft shell. But when the pair visited a factory that had been blown up in Luton they found that 'a few men had been blown to bits, and some small pieces of human flesh [Zuckerman particularly remembered a piece of brain] had not been completely cleared from the fallen masonry'. He was 'deeply impressed by Bernal's objectivity as he tried to reconstruct exactly what had happened when the bomb burst. To me, destruction was still destruction.'

As well as his work with Zuckerman, Bernal was also heavily involved in experiments at Princes Risborough to defuse UXBs. He toured the country lecturing on their disposal and seeking them out where they had fallen, at such risk to himself that J.B.S. Haldane scribbled him a clerihew:

> Desmond Bernal
> Is not eternal
> He may not escape from
> The next bomb.

'An audaciously precise bombing attack' on Banbury in Oxfordshire was to prove the turning point in Zuckerman's work. The raid, on 3 October 1940, was a daytime one by a lone German bomber flying low along the railway tracks. The plane circled before dropping its bombs. The first few, aimed at gasometers near the station goods yard, caused considerable damage, but those aimed at the rail track and signal box destroyed a single-storey brick building on the end of the platform with eight men in it. One man outside the small building and two inside were killed instantly, and three more died subsequently: all had been injured by pieces of bomb casing or falling debris. The blast pressure in the building had been so high that everyone inside's lungs had been affected and eardrums ruptured. 'What seemed incredible at the time was that all eight had not been killed.'

By the end of 1940, with night raids intensifying, Zuckerman's Casualty Survey team had studied 111 incidents, mostly in London and Birmingham, carrying out post-mortems and interviewing as many people as possible who had been in the vicinity, whether they had been injured or not. In November 1941, helped by medical statistics experts, Zuckerman felt that 'between us, Bernal and I had learnt as much about the effects of bombs as could be known at the time, short of becoming victims ourselves', and sufficient data had been collected from more than 10,000 people (of whom about a thousand had been casualties) for them to be able to publish a report on the effects of bombing raids (though of course this was not declassified until several years after the war). Some of the findings were obvious: during daylight raids more people were likely to be caught outside or in factories or offices, while in night raids five times more people were in shelters than in the day. Equally, it was not surprising that the casualty rate varied according to the size of the bomb. However, what was unexpected was that, ton for ton, smaller bombs of 50 kg produced significantly more casualties than did larger bombs of 250 kg or even 1,000 kg. This was because a plane could carry more 50 kg bombs than heavier ones, which meant more strikes. More damage was caused by many bombs with small radii of what was called 'effective action' than by one large one, which would be likely to have thick walls within its area of 'effective action' that might protect some people who would otherwise be at risk. Furthermore, more people would be likely to be killed or injured by fragments from several small bombs than from one large one. In this macabre equation, 'biggest is not always best' when it comes to killing people.

Moreover, it turned out that in general most air-raid victims were not killed by the primary effects of bombs – blast or splinters or fire from the bomb itself – but by falling debris (including being buried by it) and flying glass. This was because during a raid most people were in their homes, which usually offered less protection than shelters. The conclusions to be drawn from Zuckerman, Bernal and their team's work was that during raids people should take shelter in places where they were least likely to be hit by flying debris, where thick walls protected them as much as possible from bomb shells, and where there were no windows to break. One might have thought that this was a conclusive argument for countrywide deep shelters, but by the time they reported their findings the scientists had become involved in their implications for the formulation of British bombing policy, rather than the protection of British citizens from enemy attack.

Intercepts of German messages suggested that Manchester was the target for the night of 10–11 January, but low cloud and heavy rain was probably the reason the raid was switched at almost the last moment to Portsmouth, a naval base with extensive docks, just along the south coast from the by-now much-battered Southampton. Portsmouth would be raided with sickening regularity – roughly every four weeks throughout the spring of 1941. On this night the 150-odd German bombers were guided by two VHF beams that intersected over Southsea Common, and dropped a total of 140 tons of high-explosive bombs and over 40,000 incendiaries on the city. Within two hours more than 2,000 fires were burning so fiercely that they could be seen clearly by the crews of the retreating German planes as they crossed the coast of France.

Portsmouth's Guildhall, built half a century before, was deluged by incendiaries: firemen and council workers valiantly succeeded in sweeping them off the roof, but then one fell down a ventilation shaft and proved impossible to extinguish. The Guildhall's two-hundred-foot tower became an incandescent beacon, with flames leaping into the night sky: it continued to burn all the following day. The roof fell in, the panelled interior was gutted, all the civic treasures except the mace were lost, and the heat was so intense that it was impossible for fire crews to get inside for several days: the city council was obliged to requisition the Royal Beach Hotel on nearby Southsea seafront to serve as its offices. Bombs fell on HMS Vernon, the shore station headquarters of the Royal Navy's mine counter-warfare establishment, but only part of it was damaged, and the wardroom was saved from destruction by a newly built blast wall. Sixty-eight people were reported dead in the raid, and 161 seriously injured.

The wet, cloudy and foggy weather in February gave some protection from aerial assault, and for the first time in five months night after night passed without any major raids. There were, unfortunately, exceptions. The important Welsh port of Swansea, which Dylan Thomas, who had a cottage on the Gower peninsula just along the coast, called an 'ugly lovely town', had been bombed before (and would be forty-four times in all). From 19 to 21 February 1941 it suffered a 'three-night blitz', a sustained bombardment that lasted for seventy-two hours and did more damage and brought more loss of life than to anywhere else in Wales. The docks weren't badly damaged, and though the ICI works on the edge of the city were hit, it was the centre and the residential areas that took the brunt of the attack. Over forty acres was left as little more than a desert of ruins and rubble, including 575 business premises and the department store David Evans. More than 2,000 people were homeless, and fourteen rest centres were opened to accommodate them. An estimated 2,000 to 3,000 other people trekked out of the city hoping to find accommodation at Mumbles and on the Gower peninsula. Many of the homes of those who remained in Swansea were without water and gas, and people scooped snow off the pavements to boil in a saucepan over a paraffin stove to make tea. The final night, 21–22 February, brought the highest toll of casualties (ninety-eight dead and seventy-eight seriously injured); 219 had been killed and 260 seriously injured over the three nights.

The welcome respite in the blitz thanks to the grim weather of February 1941 was definitely over by early March, though bad weather did prove something of an inhibition to the bombers towards the end of the month. This was to be the final phase of the blitz, and few large towns, cities or ports escaped as the ferocity of the German attack intensified before Hitler turned his attention east with the attack on Russia, Operation Barbarossa, in June.

In March, twelve raids could be classified as major. Again the main targets were ports, particularly along the west coast, but London was frequently and heavily attacked too. The Commander-in-Chief of Anti-Aircraft Command, General Sir Frederick Pile, agreed that Ack-Ack guns could be moved from the industrial centres and relocated in ports, while 'starfish' sites, which had not been spectacularly successful until then, began to prove their worth. By this time there were 108, and that number had increased to 164 by the end of the year. There was even one in London. Sited in Richmond Park during the blitz, it was moved to Hampstead Heath in May 1942, but given the proximity of so much residential property, it was only rarely fired. However, the sites near Cardiff and Bristol were particularly successful: on 18 April 90 per cent of the bombs intended for Portsmouth fell instead on the starfish at Hayling Island. On average the sites attracted sixteen high-explosive bombs and 130 to 140 incendiaries each time they were lit.

The pattern that had been set in Swansea, of pounding the same target for several consecutive nights, continued relentlessly, with places that had already suffered several raids being revisited in the spring. Other targets as scattered as Crewe, Ipswich, Brighton, Great Yarmouth (where twenty people were killed) and Bawdsey Manor radar station near Aldeburgh, which had escaped the blitz so far, were now drawn into the firing line.

The gazetteer of destruction included several more raids on Cardiff and Southampton. Portsmouth suffered its thirty-seventh raid on 11 March: again the docks, shipyards and factories were the targets, but the 193 high-explosive bombs that were dropped were heavier than previously – several a massive 5,500 pounds. Fuel-storage depots went up in flames and the naval barracks were hit before the bombers crossed the Solent to raid the Isle of Wight before turning back along the coast to attack Hamble, Selsey and Littlehampton. They came back on 17 April, and again the docks were set on fire. Ten days later Portsmouth was targeted yet again. The docks burned, parachute mines fell on the central railway station and twenty-eight people were killed when Madden's Hotel in the city centre was hit. Patients had been evacuated from the Royal Portsmouth Hospital, as it had already been hit twice in previous raids: it was bombed again on 17 April, and this time several staff were killed.

On the night of Good Friday, 11 April 1941, the raiders returned to Coventry, which had been bombed on 8 April, and several aircraft factories were hit. 'The effect on war production will be felt for some time to come,' warned Lord Beaverbrook. Winston Churchill, preoccupied with the stream of bad news from North Africa and Greece, and considering that 'Easter is a very good time for invasion,' was well aware that there was uneasiness in the country 'as a result of the gravity of the war situation'. He embarked on a fact-finding and morale-boosting tour of the West Country with his wife Clementine, daughter Mary, 'Pug' Ismay and a clutch of officials. He also took along John Winant, the newly appointed US Ambassador to Britain – 'a welcome contrast to his defeatist predecessor, Joseph P. Kennedy', and soon a personal friend of the Churchill family. Winant's remark on his arrival on 1 March 1941, 'I'm very glad to be here. There is no place I'd rather be at this time than in England,' had made headlines in the press and naturally endeared him to the British people, particularly coming on the heels of the visit of Wendell Willkie in January.

Willkie had been the Republican candidate who fought Roosevelt for the presidency the previous November. He had lost, but had polled an unprecedented number of votes for a defeated candidate, and Roosevelt had told his son James, 'I'm happy I've won, but I'm sorry Wendell lost.' The German Chargé d'Affaires in Washington, Dr Hans Thomsen, had recognised that Willkie's nomination was 'unfortunate' for Germany. Unlike most in his party, 'He is not an isolationist, and his attitude in the past permits no doubt that he belongs to those Republicans who see America's best defence in supporting England by all means short of war.' Less than a month after Roosevelt's 'arsenal of democracy' speech, Willkie had come to London, 'representing no one' but determined to see for himself the condition of Britain, and to carry reports home. He toured the blitz-devastated cities – London, Coventry, Liverpool and Manchester – then went to Dublin to meet the Taoiseach, Éamon de Valera, and tried unsuccessfully to persuade him to allow the British Navy to use Irish ports. Everywhere Willkie went, wearing his white-painted tin hat, 'he took the country by storm with hundreds turning out to cheer "Tell them we can take it!" and "Send us anything you can!" ', reported Lady Diana Cooper, wife of the Minister of Information, who had entertained Willkie to dinner.

Willkie was impressed by the resilience and fortitude of the people he met on his blitz tour, and when he got back to America in February he did what Lady Diana had 'prayed God he would . . . give a good account of us and our country, our needs and our hopes, when he comes to testify to the Senate'. On 8 March 1941, the day that the Lend Lease Bill was passed – the Republicans voting seventeen to ten against – Roosevelt told Harry Hopkins, his right-hand man who had also been in Britain assessing the country's Lend Lease requirements: 'We might not have had Lend Lease if it hadn't been for Wendell Willkie.'

The Prime Minister, the Ambassador and the rest of the party slept on the train to avoid putting pressure on accommodation in the blitzed cities they intended to visit, and woke up in Swansea on Good Friday. 'Spent morning among battered ruins and inspecting detachments of Civil Defence workers,' wrote John Colville, Churchill's private secretary. 'The centre of the town has not a house standing. I was amazed by the eagerness and cheerfulness of the population. W[inston] had a great reception.' Then it was off to Cardigan Bay, where they saw 'a noisy but interesting display of rockets', then back to the train, which stopped in a siding for the night.

Early on Easter Saturday Churchill and his entourage arrived in Bristol, and after breakfast 'led by the Lord Mayor we walked and motored through devastation such as I had never thought possible. Swansea is mild in comparison. There had been a bad raid during the night and many of the ruins were still smoking. The people looked bewildered but, as at Swansea, were brave and were thrilled by the sight of Winston who drove about sitting on the hood of an open car and waving his hat. At the University the PM, as Chancellor, conferred honorary degrees on Winant and Menzies [Robert Menzies, Prime Minister of Australia] and made an excellent impromptu speech in which he likened the fortitude of Bristol to that which we are accustomed "to associate with Ancient Rome and modern Greece" [which was at the time being overrun by German forces]. The gowns and pageantry were a strange contrast to the smoking ruins outside.'

'It was quite extraordinary,' remembers Churchill's daughter Mary (later Soames). 'People kept on arriving late with grime on their faces half washed off. They had their ceremonial robes on over their fire fighting clothes which were still wet.' Among those on the platform was the Regional Commissioner, Sir Hugh Elles, who had earned a reputation for himself in the blitz as one of the most active of controllers. The previous night he had been on hand to help the firemen, taking his turn training a hose on burning buildings, as he had on other occasions.

Churchill referred to being 'in battered Bristol, with scars of new attacks on it': as well as the scars inflicted in November and January, fresh wounds had opened up in another heavy raid on 16 March. That night the Luftwaffe had followed the railway line from Temple Meads, attacking Avonmouth, Clifton, St George and the centre of the city. Many residential areas had also been hit, particularly the working-class suburb of Easton. Two nurses from the Bristol Maternity Hospital who had volunteered to go to the aid of a heavily pregnant woman trapped in a partially collapsed house in Kingsdown, and had stayed all night with her in extremely dangerous conditions, were awarded George Medals. Scarcely a parish church escaped intact throughout the city, and 6,000 houses were damaged in addition to those destroyed. The Regional Commissioner announced that the city would require 2,000 men for repair and clearance work 'for an indefinite time'. The casualties were heavy: 257 dead, including forty people involved in Civil Defence work as fire-watchers, ARP wardens, shelter marshals, police reservists, members of a decontamination party and a casualty service auxiliary nurse, and 391 people were injured. More raids followed on Bristol and Avonmouth, but the 'Good Friday Raid' was the largest on the battered city that spring, targeting industrial installations in Bristol, Avonmouth and nearby Portishead. Two hundred high-explosive bombs and 35,000 incendiaries were dropped in a wide arc over the city, damaging houses, offices, factories, Colston Girls' School and Cheltenham public library. Taylor's department store was destroyed, as was St Paul's church in Bedminster. St Phillip's bridge, known locally as the 'Half Penny Bridge', which had replaced a ferry in 1841 and charged a halfpenny toll for the next forty years, was gone, and the cable supply severed, with the unfortunate result that after forty-six years' service trams would never run along Bristol's streets again.

When the All Clear sounded at 3.52 a.m., a hundred UXBs blocked the streets, 180 people had been killed and 382 were injured. Yet again Civil Defence workers, desperately vulnerable because of the requirements of their jobs, had been scythed down, thirty losing their lives. This was to be almost the end of Bristol's blitz ordeal, though there were minor raids in May, often it seemed by pilots returning off-course from raids in the Midlands, and anxious to shed the last of their bombs.

It was not only ports that were attacked. The Midlands were raided consistently that spring. Birmingham was bombed on 11 March, and again on 9 and 10 April. On the first night the Bull Ring and the High Street burned, hit by some of the 280 tons of high-explosives and 40,000 incendiaries dropped on the city, and fires were still alight the following night when 245 bombers droned over, but this time it was residential areas such as Small Heath (which had suffered so badly in the November raids), Kings Heath, Aston and Nechells that sustained the most serious damage. On 16 May it looked as if Birmingham would be raided again, and indeed the Wolseley car factory and the ICI works were bombed, as were several streets on the outskirts of the city. However, it seems that nearby Nuneaton took many of the bombs intended for Birmingham, with the result that more than eighty civilians were killed in the town.

Bombs had fallen along the South Shields coast between St Abbs and Flamborough Head in February, and the raiders came back on 9 April. Bombs fell across Tyneside, crashing onto railway lines, sending passenger coaches and goods trucks flying about like a toy railway, falling on South Shields (where the Queen's Theatre was set on fire), Jarrow, Gateshead, Sunderland (where the Town Hall was gutted), Tynemouth (where the docks burned furiously, as did warehouses and blocks of commercial premises and housing), Whitley Bay and Newcastle, most of them places of considerable military importance. It would almost be simpler to catalogue where bombs *didn't* fall on those April and early May nights in 1941, so widespread was the destruction that also took in Eastbourne, Bournemouth, Chichester, Rugby, Cromer, Bridlington, Thameshaven, Slough, Falmouth, Gloucester, Grantham, Lowestoft, Sheffield, Doncaster, Weymouth, Barrow-in-Furness, Cambridge, Hull, Leeds, Harwich, Holyhead, Ramsgate . . .

Winston Churchill claimed that British air intelligence successfully interfered with the German navigational beams on 8 May, when raiders were deflected from their target, the Rolls-Royce factory and other important industrial plants in Derby. If this was true (and no German source has authenticated it), the loser was Nottingham, where the historic Moot Hall and Lace Market were devastated by bombs, as was the red-brick University College, the cricket ground at Trent Bridge and Notts County's football pitch. It was a major raid: 90 per cent of the bombs that fell on Nottingham throughout the entire war fell on that night. Nearly a hundred fires were started in the city centre, 350 houses were destroyed or damaged beyond repair and 430 people perished in Nottingham and the surrounding area. A bomb hit two shelters beneath the Co-op bakery, entered at an angle and skidded across the floor, killing forty-nine night-shift workers. St Christopher's church nearby was also hit. The vicar, the Reverend Frederick Ralph, was anxious to help those wounded in the devastated shelter, but was dissuaded from doing so by Civil Defence workers, since 'there was nothing I could do . . . the wreckage was all mixed up with marmalade and jam and flour and bodies. It was terrible.'

On 21 February 1941 the Ministry of Home Security had issued a list of the damage sustained by domestic property up to 15 February (excluding Scotland): 33,575 houses had been destroyed or damaged beyond repair in London, and 60,290 elsewhere. In London 123,395 houses were seriously damaged but repairable; the figure elsewhere in the country was 175,520. In London 379,140 houses had been damaged; elsewhere in the country the number was 715,050. The Ministry estimated that it cost £750 (almost £30,000 in today's prices) to rebuild a house that had been destroyed, £100 to repair a seriously damaged one, and £30 to sort out minor damage. The total bill had already reached £113,115,390 – and although of course no one knew it then, there were still three more months of heavy bombing to come in 1941; followed by the 'Baedeker raids' in spring 1942, retaliation visited on England's most historic cities, those given three stars in the German guidebooks; 'tip 'n run' raids, mainly on ports; the 'little blitz' on southern England from January to April 1944; and finally, from June 1944, the V-1 and V-2 attacks would further raze great swathes of property, since on average each V-1 damaged four hundred houses in the London area, and each V-2 between six hundred and 750.

The human toll of the blitz was mounting inexorably too. Six thousand and sixty-five people were killed in April 1941. So far 29,856 British civilians had been killed since the start of the war as a result of aerial bombardment. Many people in places it had somewhat complacently been assumed that the German bombers could not reach, or had no interest in reaching, would be tragically disabused.

15

The Far Reach

Hitler is 52 today. Napoleon died at 52.

Diary entry of Sidney Chave, 20 April 1941

Things have been very quiet here of late and we have had quite a number of nights free from alarms . . . But when we have a quiet night I always fear that we are enjoying our peace and quiet at the expense of some other folk equally anxious to be left in peace and that the unfortunate folk may be our ain folk in Glasgow which heaven forbid.

Letter from Nellie Larson in Baldock, Hertfordshire, to her cousin Colin Ferguson in Glasgow, 25 March 1941

During the past financial year, national expenditure was £3,867,000,000 – or about £10,500,000 a day . . . £3,220,000,000 of it being war expenditure . . . Budget Day. Income Tax is to be increased to 10s in the £, and the highest scale of surtax to 19/6d. Tax will be payable on all incomes over £110 per annum, and allowances will be reduced; but the amount paid on account of the latter measure will be credited to the taxpayer as 'savings' repayable after the war. There are no increases in direct taxation.

Diary entries of Wren Audrey Hawkins, Plymouth, for 1 and 7 April 1941

In October 1935 David Kirkwood, who was seeking re-election as Labour MP for Clydebank and Dumbarton, received tumultuous applause when he declared, 'I am all out for peace in the real sense and would not send a Clydebank boy to war upon any consideration.' Clydeside had a long history of political militancy: in the post-First World War election Labour had won twenty-one out of the twenty-eight seats in the area, and in nearby Glasgow it had been ten out of fifteen seats. A huge crowd had gathered at St Enoch's station in Glasgow to cheer the 'Clydeside Brigade' (which included the striking figure of the ex-schoolteacher, now MP, James Maxton, and the brilliant, intransigent John Wheatley) on their way to Westminster. One worker had sported a badge that read 'High explosive, handle carefully', and as Kirkwood boarded the train, he turned to address the crowd. 'When we come back, this station, this railway, will belong to the people,' he promised.

Clydesiders had much to be militant about. Shipbuilding, the main industry on the Clyde, had been pole-axed in the thirties, leaving the area with one of the highest unemployment rates in the country, and widespread poverty and hopelessness. Indeed, engineering apprentices were on strike for better pay and conditions when the blitz struck Clydeside. Although strikes were illegal under wartime regulations, poor industrial relations in several industries, including mining and shipbuilding, made them all but inevitable. The apprentices voted to suspend the strike and to help clear up the bomb damage.

The Clydesiders' deep distrust of the National Government (made up of members from all three major parties, but predominantly Conservative), coupled with currents of pacifism that coursed through – and deeply divided – the Labour Party and the labour movement, had led them to oppose any preparations for war. When advice had come from the Scottish Office in September 1935 for local authorities to make preparations against possible enemy air raids, Clydebank's Labour council rejected it, and voted not to cooperate with other local authorities. In their view the answer to the threat of war was not appeasement, but collective security among like-minded nations, including Russia; to start making preparations for war would be to endorse the government's foreign policy. They were not alone in this stance: several councils throughout Britain, including Poplar and Stepney in London's East End, took the same line, while many more complained that it was all very well to advise such action, but where was the cash to pay for its implementation by hard-pressed local authorities still struggling with the effects of long-term unemployment?

But Clydebank was more intransigent than most – or was intransigent for longer. Two days after Hitler had reoccupied the Rhineland in March 1936, Clydebank council voted by thirteen votes to five not to send delegates to a conference on air-raid precautions, and by January 1937 Clydebank was one of only three Scottish boroughs still refusing to cooperate. On 1 January 1938 the Air Raid Precautions Act became law. It was no longer simply advised that local authorities should prepare for war: it was a statutory duty. Clydebank fell into line and started to plan for defending its citizens in the event of war. It could be argued that in fact the delay was to Clydebank's benefit: much of the earlier preparations had been unfocused and ill-considered. Clydebank could benefit from lessons learned in other boroughs (or burghs, as they are known in Scotland).

Although Hitler's key objectives since the start of 1941 had been ports and naval installations as well as war-production industries, Clydebank had so far escaped all but minor raids, and a degree of complacency had seeped into the minds of many of its citizens that maybe Glasgow and its environs were too far for the German bombers to come, and that they would escape the raids that were ravaging the rest of the country. 'It's England they're more for than Scotland'; 'If they'd wanted to bomb Scotland, they'd be here by now,' were some of the remarks made to Mass-Observation investigators when they came to report on morale in Glasgow on 7 March 1941, exactly one week before the Clydeside blitz.

On the warm spring evening of Thursday, 13 March, the alert sounded at a few minutes past 9 p.m. There was a near full moon – perfect bombing weather – and the first wave of German bombers, first Heinkel HE IIIs, followed by Junkers 88s, crossed the coast between the rivers Tees and Tweed from their bases in Holland and northern Germany (later waves would sweep up from northern France and down from airfields in Norway and Denmark), guided by the treacherous silver ribbon of the Clyde. There were no devices in Scotland to jam Luftwaffe navigational signals or 'bend' directional beams, as there were in most of the large English cities, so the planes had an unimpeded run towards the Scottish port. There was a follow-up raid to the previous night's massive attack on Liverpool and Birkenhead, and bombs were also dropped on Hull that night. But the main targets were Glasgow and Clydebank, which were about seven miles apart.

At 9.30 p.m. the bombs started to fall: the visibility was so perfect that the bomb aimers switched from automatic release to manual. The raid took the pattern that had become usual: smallish 50-kg bombs dropped first to drive everyone, including firefighters, to take shelter, followed by a hail of incendiaries which started fires that would act as markers to the target. In peacetime the Singer Manufacturing Company had produced sewing machines: in war the company's Clydebank factory had largely switched production to armaments, including machine guns. Next to the factory was stored an inestimable amount of timber – £500,000-worth belonging to the Singer company, plus huge government reserves. Soon it was all blazing furiously. Also highly flammable were the great vats of whisky at the Yoker Distillery in Glasgow, which were soon on fire, as were three of the Admiralty oil tanks at Dalnottar and Old Kilpatrick. The choking, sickly smell of burning rubber enveloped the streets near John Brown's shipyard in Rothesay Dock, though in fact the yard escaped relatively lightly, and a Polish destroyer in for repairs was able to put up a formidable barrage of Ack-Ack fire throughout the night – though as the Brigadier in command admitted, it was about 'as effective as shooting a bluebottle in the dark with an air pistol'. The Royal Ordnance Factory at Dalmuir was seriously damaged by fire, as was Turner's toxic asbestos factory. Within a couple of hours of the raid starting, RAF planes taking off from Dyce airport near Aberdeen could already see the flames.

That night about twelve of Clydebank's schools were destroyed or badly damaged: schools were particularly vulnerable to fire, with their assembly halls that provided a strong through-draught to fan the flames of incendiaries trapped in the roof, and pitch-pine floors that, once ignited, crackled like a giant bonfire. Churches too burned, and there was reputedly not a single pub left standing. But it was the homes of Clydebank that suffered the greatest devastation. The rows of tenement buildings, workers' dwellings that characterised Scotland's cities, had no room for Anderson shelters. More than 40 per cent were overcrowded: Clydebank was the third most overcrowded area in Scotland. People's protection came from communal arrangements: either brick-and-concrete public surface shelters similar to those found all over Britain, or, distinctive to Scotland, closes strutted with steel scaffolding. To minimise the effect of bomb blast, brick baffle walls had been erected on the edges of pavements and at the entrances to the closes – creating a painful hazard in the blackout.

The population of Clydebank in 1941 was around 50,000, with perhaps an additional 10,000 war workers billeted there temporarily; by the second night of their blitz, 35,000 were homeless. Hardly a single street in the whole borough escaped without at least one person dead or seriously injured. Some were simply destroyed, the 'faces pulled off the houses', and those inside killed. Many of the tenements were multi-occupied, some in effect lodging houses. There were eighty deaths in Second Avenue alone, with ten members of one family killed and eight of another, while the deaths in nearby streets were nearly all in double figures. In Pattison Street a high-explosive bomb fell on a shelter, killing fourteen neighbours who had been persuaded that they would be safer there than in their own flats. The cumulative effect was like that among the 'Pals' Battalions' of the First World War – friends and neighbours dying together, the effect on the local community hard to imagine.

The All Clear sounded at 6.25 a.m. 'Bankies' emerged from their homes or shelters to scenes of unimaginable horror: the city was still burning fiercely; bodies covered in blankets lay in the streets; the water mains had been hit; tram lines reared, grotesquely twisted, into the air. Thousands, traumatised, gathered what they could carry – or what they had left – and took to the hills. The next night the bombers came back. At 8.40 p.m. the siren sounded, and many who had not fled the city boundaries already did so then. Two hundred and three German bombers flew over Clydebank, dropping 227 tons of high-explosive bombs and 781 incendiaries (the previous night it had been 268 tons and 1,630 incendiaries), most of which fell on the same area that had been devastated the night before. Ten more tanks at Dalnottar, containing twelve million gallons of oil, were set alight. The damage throughout Clydebank, though terrible, was less than on the previous night: only one-tenth as many people were killed.

The Clydebank blitz was, in the almost unnecessary summation of the Scottish Regional Commissioner, Lord Rosebery, 'a major disaster'. The announcement from the Ministry of Home Security on 18 March that 'about 500' people had been killed in the raids was met with 'frank incredulity' and resentment by locals. ('Which street?' one man asked.) On 3 April the Regional Commissioner's office confirmed (but not to the public) that 1,083 people had been killed over the two nights in Glasgow, Dunbartonshire and the surrounding area, and 1,620 seriously wounded. In fact more people had been killed outside Clydebank than in: it was the concentration of the destruction in the area that had such a powerful effect. In Glasgow, though the toll was higher, the bombs were scattered across the city. The Lord Provost had been confident that 'Glasgow houses are more solidly built than those that collapsed from concussion in London.' His confidence proved misplaced when bombs carpeted the residential areas of Drumchapel, Maryhill, Partick and Govan. A parachute mine landed on three tenement buildings in Maryhill, killing ninety-two people, and at Yarrow shipyard eighty workers died after their shelter sustained a direct hit. Glasgow University was badly damaged, as were the shipyards at Scotstoun and the Rolls-Royce factory at Hillington, which in wartime was making aero engines.

Clydebank's greyhound stadium had been requisitioned as a mortuary, but it was destroyed in the first night of the raid, so emergency ones were established. By Monday, 17 March many relatives had arranged private burials for their dead, but there were still some 160 bodies unclaimed or unidentified. These were buried in Dalnottar cemetery in a communal grave dug with the assistance of gravediggers from Glasgow and Edinburgh. The burials were conducted at great pressure and with inadequate resources. Sir Steven Bilsland, the highly respected Civil Defence Regional Commissioner for Glasgow, complained bitterly that it was 'indecorous' that the corpses had been trussed in white sheets, tied with string at the waist and neck. He retracted his criticism, however, when it was pointed out that requests from Clydebank's Sanitary Inspector to the Department of Health at the Scottish Office for authorisation to purchase papier mâché or waxed cardboard coffins had repeatedly been turned down.

Only eight of Clydebank's 12,000 houses were reported to be undamaged. Four thousand three hundred were totally destroyed or damaged beyond repair. An inspector from the Scottish Office reported, 'There is a part, locally known as "The Holy City", situated on a hill and overlooking the riverside and this impressed me as being in a most distressing condition. The roofs of many of these houses had been of tarred felt with the result that they blazed with the greatest fury, and it was decided to let them burn themselves out. I understand that whatever preparations had been made for such a vicious assault, it would have been impossible to keep the fires under control.' Terrified dogs and near-feral cats roamed the gutted streets, displaced, disorientated. Dogs started to form howling, scavenging packs, as in a post-apocalypse movie. In a couple of days the Scottish Society for the Protection of Animals opened a sanctuary. Soon five hundred strays had been put down; by the end of the year it was almost 1,800.

Why had Clydebank burned so out of control? Had the high toll of casualties been avoidable? How were the 'Bankies' being cared for after the raid? Were there lessons that needed to be learned?

The answer to the last question would seem to be yes. Essentially, the local fire services were overwhelmed on the night of 13 March, though the circumstances make this hardly surprising: 'No fire master could possibly have coped with the number of buildings on fire . . . literally one got the impression that there was a fire in every tenement.' Three AFS stations were put out of action, telegraph lines were brought down, disrupting communication with the control centre for several hours, and the largest water main was put out of action, though the Forth and Clyde Canal was a useful resource. Fire engines and appliances sent from other districts encountered the same problems as in almost every raid throughout the blitz: no uniformity of equipment meant that hoses of different sizes could not be screwed together or be fitted onto hydrants, while firemen were trained in different procedures, and even used different terminology. Craters and debris prevented fire engines from getting near enough to the fires; while the fire trailers used by the AFS were more manoeuvrable, the throw of their hoses was shorter, and they were often damaged as they were manhandled across broken paving stones and heaps of shattered glass.

At eight o'clock on the morning of Friday, 14 March, Lord Rosebery arrived to assess the situation. Deciding that operations lacked direction, he in effect sacked the Firemaster, Robert Buchanan (making him a scapegoat, a local historian of the blitz, Dr MacPhail, himself a bomb disposal expert, thought), and replaced him with the Second Officer from Paisley. Much the same happened to Clydebank's Superintendent of Police, William McCulloch. When the Anderson shelter in which he and his family were sheltering was badly damaged by a bomb, he decided to get out, taking his family into the hills above the town. For this perceived dereliction of duty McCulloch was removed from his post and transferred elsewhere.

As well as problems with the fire services, Clydebank's voluntary fire-watching organisation was little more than embryonic. The Town Council had expressed dissatisfaction about the state of affairs at their March meeting. A demonstration of how to put out an incendiary bomb was 'poorly attended', and anyway there was an acute shortage of stirrup pumps for such purposes. It wasn't clear whether people were failing to volunteer for fire-watching duties, or the organisation was so poor that volunteers were not being registered. The ARP services were not in much better shape: there were anxieties that one of the beneficial effects of the war for the region, the increased employment in shipyards and in armaments manufacture, meant that men were working such long hours that they had little time for voluntary Civil Defence work. In addition, while hundreds of circulars had been issued from the Glasgow office of the Ministry of Home Security, dealing with every conceivable contingency in the event of a blitz, getting funding to implement these recommendations was a slow and tortuous process – and just before Clydebank's night of hell, a request to purchase additional fire hoses had not been approved. Moreover, the Ministry had insisted that the ARP control centre should be situated in the basement of the public library, despite objections that this was near John Brown's shipyard, an obvious target. The centre received a direct hit on the first night of the raid, and was subsequently out of action.

Thursday night was the weekly practice night for Clydebank Casualty Services, so when the raid started on 13 March, most of the first aid posts were fully staffed and the first aid parties, ambulances and other forms of transport were ready for action. Two ambulance drivers, Hugh Campbell and Mary Haldane, were awarded OBEs for their heroic work that night, driving through the blitz as bombs crashed down all around them to take the wounded to medical services, and tending to others themselves. At one point a first aid post was burned to the ground, and those injured who were able to walk made for a nearby one. There many people were tended by medical students from Glasgow Royal Infirmary whose final examinations were still nine days away. Summoned by a young nurse who had seen how bad conditions were, they had packed medical supplies – excluding morphia, which the Medical Superintendent refused to give them – and gone by ambulance straight into the inferno. They worked all through the night, returning bloodstained and exhausted to the hospital. Their actions won the concession that in future final-year medical students *would* be allowed to administer morphia.

Clydebank's rescue parties had harrowing experiences, several of them working for seventy-two hours without a break. Again, when it was all over rewards for bravery were handed out to them: two George Medals and two OBEs. A rescue party of miners, brought in from West Lothian, pioneered a recently-devised rescue technique, burrowing into the rubble from the bottom, rather than uncovering it from the top. This method soon found its way into the manual of instruction for rescue parties working to release those trapped after an explosion.

Some 3,500 people were evacuated by buses on Friday, 14 March, most to the Vale of Leven, others to Helensburgh and Kirkintilloch, while many more took themselves off to stay with friends or relatives. Others remained in rest centres in Clydebank. Of the original nine of these, three had been obliterated in the raids; 'the remainder had to accommodate from three to four times the number of persons expected in them' by lunchtime, though most had been cleared by the time the second raid started that night. However, some shelterers were marooned for two nights in an Episcopalian church when, in what threatened to be a dreadful reprise of the South Hallsville School incident in the first days of the blitz, the promised buses failed to materialise.

On Saturday afternoon, after a second night of raids, a further 12,000 people fled Clydebank, many in a shuttle service of around two hundred buses. That day 7,000 arrived in the Vale of Leven, in addition to those who had turned up the previous day. The Vale had not been designated as a reception area for evacuees, and no preparations had been made. Schools and village halls were requisitioned, but although they could just about serve for a night or two, the homeless of Clydebank would need accommodating for several weeks. Each rest centre had been issued with a hundred cups, but that was all – no cutlery, food, bedding or cooking equipment. The local Co-ops tried to help with supplies of rolls and milk, but when sacks of turnips and carrots were delivered, they could not be cooked.

Schoolchildren were sent round to houses in the neighbourhood to solicit the loan of cutlery and crockery, and sterling souls managed to set up kitchens in various places to provide meals and cups of tea, with teachers taking kitchen-maid duties, heating babies' bottles over bunsen burners, obtaining the necessary nappies and sanitary towels, and assisting at the birth of a baby in the headmaster's study at one school-now-rest-centre. The WVS in Edinburgh was contacted, and Lady Ruth Balfour arranged for four lorryloads of clothes to be sent to the rest centres.

By Thursday, 20 March there were 3,500 people in rest centres in the Vale of Leven. The total had fallen to 1,164 a fortnight later, but after that the departures slowed to a dispiriting trickle. In addition to those in rest centres, 4,049 evacuees had been billeted in private houses in the Vale. Some were fortunate enough to end up in hospitable homes, but others were made to feel an imposition. There were stories of families being put up in garden sheds, or sleeping for weeks on the floor, and generally being made to feel like war spongers rather than war victims. 'The success of [the billeting] depends on the spirit of co-operation among those who have been more fortunate, whose assistance will be necessary to complete it,' said Sir Steven Bilsland. But when the MP David Kirkwood urged that big houses should be taken over for homeless families, a young man yelled, 'What about your house?', to which Kirkwood replied that three families were already under his roof.

Those who remained in the shattered city hardly fared any better: gas and electricity supplies were restored by Saturday, but gas pressure was low, and many people had to rely on candles for light. Water was brought in in barrels from Glasgow, and hot meals were also sent. With no cooking facilities in most homes, people were dependent on mobile canteens and army field kitchens. A communal feeding centre was set up at the Town Hall, supplemented by mobile canteens, most run by the WVS. It was estimated that between 15,000 and 20,000 people were eating meals provided in various ways by the Ministry of Food and voluntary bodies. In those hectic days wrapped and sliced bread, a novel commodity in England at the time, but common in Glasgow, proved its worth, since as a WVS organiser reported, 'Nearly 5,000 meat sandwiches were made between breakfast time and 11.45, and sold for 4d each.'

'It was one of the worst, if not the worst example of enemy ruthlessness,' said Herbert Morrison when he visited Clydebank, days after the raids. Sir John Reith, ex-Director General of the BBC, ex-Minister of Information and himself a Scot, agreed that the damage was 'worse than anything he had seen in any part of the country'. J.P. Hutchinson, who had been Education Officer for Clydeside, was equally sombre. Clydebank had suffered 'a bad knock, probably severer than Coventry or any English town since the whole town "got it" and no single area or district escaped. It is difficult to discover another place of similar size in Britain that was virtually obliterated.'

'Our patch on the outer edge of Europe would have a pretty low rating in the German plans,' wrote civil servant Patrick Shea. And many in Belfast shared his complacent conviction. Like Clydeside, their city was at the far reach of the German bombers. Indeed, Northern Ireland had seemed to be having a rather different war from the rest of Britain. In March 1940 it was still possible for a resident to observe, 'We are unbombed and we have no conscription and life is relatively normal.' But the price of that normality would be high.

The government at Westminster had 'absolutely turned down' Stormont's request that the Province should be included in the legislation for Civil Defence – the provision of shelters in particular. Although this was partly due to cost, it was also because Major-General 'Pug' Ismay, Secretary of the Committee of Imperial Defence, shared the complacency that Northern Ireland was unlikely to be a military target. Belfast, he had argued as late as June 1939, was 'the most distant city of the United Kingdom from any possible enemy base. It is 535 miles from the nearest point in Germany. An attack on Northern Ireland would involve a flight of over 1,000 miles. For aeroplanes of the bombing type, loaded, this is a very big undertaking. To reach Northern Ireland the attacking planes would pass over targets which would appear to be more attractive than anything Northern Ireland has to offer.' For Ismay the relationship of Northern Ireland to mainland Britain could be compared to a Woolworth's store, the only entrance to which was through Carrington's, the biggest jewellery store in London. The Vice Chancellor of Queen's University, Belfast, might have been less than happy with this patronising colonial attitude, but he wondered 'if there isn't some force in the suggestion that the immunity of Northern Ireland from aerial attack may be connected with the absence of important munitions plants here. It is at least possible, and the corollary might well be that immunity would cease were ordnance factories to be set up.'

It was not only those in authority who were complacent: Moya Woodside, a Belfast housewife, persisted in her conviction that the ARP in the city was redundant, and that somehow the neutrality of the South would provide a protective shield for the North. She repeated the rumour that 'De Valera indicated to the German Legation that Ireland is to be *regarded as a whole*. As long as the English keep out of Eire, this [state?] of affairs will be respected.' Then there was the matter of logistics: 'We are another 240 miles and back from Liverpool and why should the Germans come all that distance when they have plenty of important targets to hand.' She refused to prepare for war: 'Soon [our house in a professional and middle-class suburb of the city] will be the only house to remain normal. I prefer to run the risk of bombs falling nearby rather than live for the duration in rooms which remind one of a dungeon or a meat safe! Besides it has never been proved, or if it has, I have never seen it stated, that all this sticky paper, muslin etc. are of the slightest use.'

As the war progressed and France and the Low Countries were occupied, bringing Northern Ireland within closer range, and the blitz started in earnest, the vulnerability of Belfast to attack, and the probability of that attack given the importance of its port, its shipbuilding and aircraft manufacturing industries, were more seriously considered. But the political will, under the ageing and near senile Prime Minister Lord Craigavon, remained seriously undergalvanised. There was an acute shortage of ARP workers, and no legal compulsion on local authorities in Northern Ireland to prepare air-defence schemes. Blackout regulations were only patchily observed, and it seemed rather illogical to be draconian about this when across the border the lights of neutral Southern Ireland burned bright every night. By the summer of 1940 there were only two hundred public shelters for the entire 425,000 population of Belfast, though around 4,000 low-income households near the vulnerable harbour area had each been provided with a domestic shelter.

The main reason for the delay in accelerating a shelter-building programme was the shortage of building materials, since so much was required for military purposes. By the spring of 1941, although almost all the 12,000 householders considered to be in a target area had been provided with shelters, public-shelter provision remained woefully inadequate. There were still only 750 shelters, capable of holding a total of around 37,500 people, ready. This meant that roughly three-quarters of Belfast's population had no shelter accommodation when the raids came. Added to which, there were only thirty-eight Ack-Ack guns (twenty-four heavy and fourteen light), one RAF Hurricane squadron, six radar stations, no efficient Observer Corps, two barrage balloons and a single bomb-disposal unit, while the AFS had not been trained how to use the recently acquired fire pumps and hoses. The Minister of Public Security, John MacDermott, in his post only since June 1940, had conceded that Belfast was 'less well-defended than any comparable city or port in the Kingdom', and even given his fast-track efforts to improve the situation, it still held true in April 1941.

On the night of 7–8 April, Belfast suffered its first raid, attacked by aircraft most of which were on their way to or from dropping bombs on the British mainland. The docks and the Harland & Wolff shipyard were the main targets. Incendiaries rained down 'like hailstones' on the poorly-built working-class housing around the docks. St Patrick's church was gutted, leaving only the altar and one wall standing. There were two tragedies half an hour before the All Clear sounded at 4 a.m. The Rank flour mill by the Pollock Basin was hit by a parachute mine, ripping the building apart: twenty men trapped inside the twisted steel and asbestos structure died. At about the same time, workers at Harland & Wolff's aeroplane fuselage factory, believing that the All Clear had gone, emerged from their shelter and rushed over to inspect what they thought was a German parachutist who had landed on the roof: it was in fact a parachute mine, and the explosion killed several men and injured others. Thirteen people died in the raid that night, and more than eighty were injured.

Easter Tuesday is a traditional Northern Irish Bank Holiday. On that day in 1941, 15 April, the Belfast siren sounded at 10.40 p.m. Within an hour 180 German aircraft were over the city, dropping flares to illuminate their targets. William McCready, a post office worker, looked out of his bedroom window in north Belfast and saw what looked like 'the powerful headlights of a car shining straight down from the sky . . . I had a sinking feeling . . . that on this occasion the Germans meant business.'

A black smokescreen, put up as a precautionary measure, obscured the docks, so that the back-to-back working-class houses in the north and east of the city, 'where the poor of Belfast lay unprotected', took most of the onslaught. More than two bombs fell every minute – 674 during the five hours the raid lasted. Many were specially adapted, their noses covered with a steel plate intended to prevent them from embedding deep in the ground, and thus causing the maximum damage over as wide an area as possible. But to William McCready the most terrible bombs were the 'screamers', which had tubes shaped like organ pipes welded to their tailfins so they emitted a terrifying, eerie sound as they plunged to earth.

There were few shelters in the narrow streets, and when two streets were flattened, whole families were wiped out, and those who survived ran in panic and terror from their homes, some crouching in ditches, others huddling under bridges. Others just kept running for their lives. The huge bulk of York Street flax-spinning mill was hit by a parachute mine, and the six-storey-high, sixty-foot-long brick rear wall collapsed into the street, pulverising houses and flattening shelters. Thirty-five people were killed, their bodies laid in a row along the pavement.

Forty-five people were killed in nearby Hogarth Street when bombs hit both ends simultaneously, and incendiaries 'rained down like confetti'. Those who did manage to find shelter were not necessarily any better off. Revellers, many still in party clothes, on their way home from a dance in the Floral Hall, alighted from a tram and dived into a shelter at the corner of Antrim Street. When a bomb fell nearby, many of them were killed, along with other shelterers. A single bomb could wreak untold havoc in the narrow streets with their shabby, poorly built houses: around the Crumlin Road, terraces simply concertinaed, and seventy people were killed; Ewart's weaving mill on the corner was still burning twenty-four hours later. The Shankill Road and the Falls Road were largely untouched, but a parachute mine fell near a public shelter at the corner of the Shankill Road and Percy Street: the walls were sucked out and the roof collapsed. A local doctor decided that the only way to save some of the survivors was to amputate their legs to release them from the tons of concrete that was trapping them. Thirty people died. Belfast's most exclusive undertakers, Wilton's, was hit, and dozens of the black Belgian horses that, wearing elegant feather plumes, were used to pull the carriages containing hearses, perished.

Nearly forty fires were burning in the docks, but a number of parachute mines fell harmlessly into the water and failed to explode. Four Stirling aircraft, almost ready for service, were destroyed, four fire-watchers were killed and high-explosive bombs brought cranes crashing down.

Although the city centre escaped relatively lightly, Trinity Church was hit by a parachute mine; no trace was ever found of the Hill family who lived next door. At an ARP warden's post in Unity Street twelve people were killed, including five ARP wardens. Other off-duty wardens, returning from a concert in Ulster Hall where, at the suggestion of the popular singer Delia Murphy, they had sung loudly to drown out the noise of the attack, were killed as they walked home.

The central telephone exchange was put out of action by a parachute mine which cut connections to mainland Britain and also meant that it was not possible to coordinate Civil Defence and anti-aircraft activities. The radar plotting lines were broken between Aldergrove airport and the filter station at Preston in Lancashire, which meant that the RAF had no idea how many aircraft were raiding Belfast, nor from which direction they were coming. At 2 a.m. British fighters withdrew to beyond a five-mile radius of Belfast, and the Luftwaffe 'had the sky to themselves'. By 1.45 a.m. it was clear that fires were burning out of control, and containing them was beyond the capacity of the fire services as pumps ran dry, and rubble and craters blocked roads. Flames leapt into the sky, turning it blood red.

Fortunately, just before the phone lines went down, John MacDermott, crouching under his desk in the study of his home near Stormont Castle, as the bombs crashed around it, shrapnel clattered on the roof and an explosion blew the windows out, managed to get a telegram through to Éamon de Valera, asking for assistance. De Valera, who would experience the blitz on his own doorstep when Dublin was bombed twice (most seriously on 30 May 1941 in error: the German government apologised), took 'what was possibly the fastest decision of his career', and agreed to send some of Eire's resources over the border to Ulster. 'They are all our people,' he said. Thirteen fire engines and their crews raced from Dublin, Dundalk, Drogheda and Dun Laoghaire to Belfast. Most did so because, like their Prime Minister, they believed that 'The people of Belfast are Irishmen too,' though one, Patrick Finlay from Dublin, had his suspicions that their Northern counterparts might concern themselves only with Protestant areas.

When Moya Woodside, who had spent much of the raid crouching with her husband under the stairs, shaking and trying to pull herself together by drinking neat whiskey, heard of this, she was very pleased, believing that 'An action like this does more for Irish unity than any words of politicians.

I hear that the brigades were wildly cheered in towns and villages in Ulster as they passed through.' But not by the British government, which rewarded the Republic's firemen, who had spent a miserable night with no water-proof clothing to protect them from the freezing water from their hoses, many of which they had in any case been unable to fit to Belfast's different-gauge hydrants, with five shillings to cover the cost of their meals. Moya Woodside also drew comfort from the fact that forty-two fire engines and four hundred crew arrived from mainland Britain, crossing the Irish Sea from Liverpool, Glasgow and Preston in a destroyer and several ferries. 'It makes us conscious of a comforting solidarity with Britain,' she thought.

The All Clear sounded at 4.55 a.m. Since electricity supplies had been ruptured in many areas, the police went around the streets ringing hand bells to advise people that it was safe to come out. What they found was 'a scene of utter desolation . . . men [were] digging out dead women and children who had been killed in their homes'. Glass lay inches deep on the pavements. 'Houses [were] roofless, windowless, burnt out or burning, familiar landscapes gone, and in their places vast craters and mounds of rubble.' People wandered about with 'tear stained, mourning faces' or looking 'wild-eyed and dazed'.

The next day it was announced that 173 people had been killed; but the figure kept rising. A week later the Ministry of Home Security stated that 'The dead at present is known to be 500 based on the number of bodies removed to date.' By 1944 the official toll was 745 dead and over 430 seriously injured. But the Northern Ireland Fire Authority insisted that 950 had been killed and six hundred seriously wounded.

The mortuaries were unable to cope. Belfast had lost about as many people in a single raid as Liverpool had, and was not far behind London's tragic record. The novelist-to-be Brian Moore was an ARP warden attached to the Mater Hospital, and he wrote of a 'stream of corpses . . . in the stink of excrement, the acrid smell of disinfectant, these dead were heaped, body on body, flung arm, twisted feet, open mouth, staring eyes, old men on top of young women, a child lying on a policeman's back, a soldier's hand resting on a woman's thigh, a carter still wearing his coal sacks on top of a pile of arms and legs, his own arm outstretched, finger pointing as though he warned of some unseen horror. Forbidding and clumsy, the dead cluttered the morgue room from floor to ceiling.'

Identifying bodies and body parts was always a deeply distressing task, but in Belfast the pain was compounded by sectarianism. In the Falls Road public baths the dead were segregated, as were the living, by their religious faith. If the victim was unknown, there was a meticulous search to find evidence of his or her religious denomination – perhaps a rosary, or a crucifix – so that no Protestant would be inadvertently buried among the Celtic crosses of Milltown, or a Catholic interred in the city cemetery at Roselawn, to lie for eternity denied the proper rituals of their own faith.

Some 20,000 people were made homeless; 3,500 houses had been demolished or were uninhabitable, and 10,000 more were in need of urgent repair. Rest centres and emergency feeding centres struggled to cope, and hundreds of 'ditchers', the Irish equivalent of trekkers, left the city each night to sleep wherever they could on Cave Hill or Divis Mountain, or chalked 'Gone to Ballymena' or similar on their doorposts. Others crammed into trains to travel further afield, many of them crossing the border into Eire.

Belfast had not been alone in Northern Ireland in its agony. On the same night the walled city of Londonderry, with its ports and shipyards, had been hit by parachute mines, one poignantly falling on a group of ex-servicemen's homes, killing fifteen and injuring another fifteen. The aerodrome at Newtownards was also hit, killing ten guards and injuring three civilians, and in Bangor, County Down, five civilians were killed and thirty-five injured. There was little possibility that the ditchers from Belfast would find much of a welcome in these afflicted places, where 'there is absolutely no provision for the reception or feeding of those vast numbers'.

Soon Moya Woodside noted that 'Public opinion is veering round to disapproval of those who bolted from undamaged houses particularly those who did not even have young children.' In an area where 'more than six weeks since the last raid . . . still everywhere one looks are roofless houses, or great piles of bricks and mortar where houses once stood', Woodside saw 'painted on a wall in two different places, "Be a man not a mouse/Come down from the hills and sleep in your house" '.

The story went round that Lord Haw Haw had informed the citizens of Belfast that Hitler would give them 'time to bury your dead before the next attack. Tuesday was only a sample.' The propagandist's chilling broadcast proved accurate. Belfast was bombed again on 4 May; the only precautions that had been taken against fresh attack had been to try to camouflage the Stormont building with black paint and a cinder path, and to hire a Royal Ulster Constabulary marksman to shoot six wolves, two raccoons, a puma, a hyena, five lions, two lionesses, a tiger, a black bear, two brown bears, two polar bears, a lynx, a vulture and a black rat at the city's Bellevue Zoo as the Head Keeper watched, 'tears streaming down his face as the executioner moved from cage to cage', in case Belfast was bombed again and they escaped.

This time the target was the harbour, shipyards and aircraft factory, and as it was a clear night some two hundred planes honed in on the area, dropping 235 tons of high-explosive bombs and 96,000 incendiaries. Harland & Wolff, among the largest shipbuilding yards in the world, employing 23,000 people, was hit by high-explosive bombs, parachute mines and incendiaries. Two-thirds of its entire premises were destroyed, including workshops, drawing offices, administrative buildings and repair sheds. The firefighting equipment proved inadequate – the hoses were too short to reach the water in the harbour as the tide ebbed. Given the layout of the city, which had taken shape long before the concept of industrial estates away from town and city centres was in planners' minds, residential streets around the yards suffered terrible damage too, regardless of the fact that they were not the main target. Again, the streets around St Patrick's church were devastated, and one, Chater Street, was entirely demolished. In the centre of Belfast, the historic City Hall banqueting chamber was badly damaged.

A parachute mine fell near a public shelter, pushing it along the pavement and killing twenty-five of the occupants. Seven young policemen who had just finished their training were killed when Glenraven Street Police Station received a direct hit. York Street mill, damaged in the April raid, was hit again, and this time was totally consumed by flames. The pavements of nearby streets were so hot that walking on them was like treading on burning coals. Women splashed their windows with cold water to try to stop the glass from cracking. At one point in the night two hundred separate fires were burning: it looked as if the entire city was ablaze.

In the comfortable house in Elmwood Avenue where he was a lodger, civil servant Patrick Shea and his fellow lodgers 'listened to the frightening drone of the raiding aircraft, the sounds of the city centre being torn apart, the detonations of the exploding bombs and the return fire of the anti-aircraft guns. On that night fear was in every heart in Belfast.' When the All Clear finally sounded, Shea made his way to the city centre, 'past burning buildings, through streets criss-crossed with fire hoses, around areas in which unexploded bombs had been found, to the Law Courts which had been designated as the meeting place for the emergency group [for which he was working]. From the roof of the building, as the dawn broke, I watched the city centre being consumed in flames and down below where I stood open vehicles were bringing dead bodies into St George's Market.'

Fires burned for more than forty-eight hours after the All Clear – again signalled by the ringing of hand bells, since the harbour power station had been blasted out of action. They may have been a beacon for the German planes, probably making for Clydeside, that dropped bombs on east Belfast again the next night. Two adjacent public shelters and some nearby houses were demolished by a parachute mine: fourteen people were killed, forty were seriously injured and three hundred were made homeless. The entire city of Belfast was without electricity for twenty-four hours, one area had no gas for a week, the main sewerage plant was unable to function, food was almost unobtainable in the shops, and many people were still having to get water from standpipes in the street ten days after the raid. One hundred and fifty UXBs blocked roads and added to the transport chaos.

It seemed almost unbelievable given the conflagration, but Harland & Wolff was not destroyed – though its compensation claim of £3 million for bomb damage to its yards and plant in Belfast and on the mainland was the highest amount claimed by any British company throughout the entire war. At first its workers, terrified of another blitz and aware of the minimal level of air-raid protection, refused to work night shifts, but by November production was pretty much back to where it had been before the blitz, and that was true of most of Belfast's other war industries too.

The 'Fire Raids' of early May claimed fewer casualties than the Easter raids: 191 dead, 189 seriously injured and three people unaccounted for. In total the air raids on Belfast left over a thousand people dead and 650 seriously injured. The toll on property was devastating. In a city that already had an acute housing shortage before the war, and a considerable slum problem, 56,600 houses were damaged, and of those 32,000 were completely demolished.

The 'blitz spirit' of unity and endurance had been strong during the raids as Protestants from the Shankill Road area crammed into the Clonard monastery with Catholics. Women and children sheltered together in the crypt, and at one point, when it looked as if the chapel would be hit, one of the priests, Father Tom Murphy, donned a tin hat and offered absolution to all present. Refugees from the blitz flooded into Dublin and other places in the South. An editorial in the *Irish Independent* on 18 April 1941 ventured that 'If anything further was needed to demonstrate the utter unreality of the artificial border that divides our country, the welcome that has been given to the refugees from Belfast provides it.' De Valera reiterated the point two days later: 'In the past, and probably in the present too, a number of them did not see eye to eye with us politically, but they are all our people – we are one and the same people – and their sorrows in the present instance are our sorrows.' Though when the government at Westminster had asked to be allowed to use Eire's 'Treaty Ports' to help the Navy in the Battle of the Atlantic against German U-boats, the request had been refused.

The spirit of unity didn't last. Unionist politicians from the North were soon emphasising that the raids proved that Northern Ireland was an integral part of Britain's war, from which the South's neutrality made it remote (though not entirely immune from attack). Belfast Protestants accused Catholics of suffering less in the raids: fewer Catholic churches were hit than Protestant, but more Catholic schools suffered damage than Protestant ones. In general, Protestant areas suffered more damage than Catholic ones, but this was likely to have been accounted for by the fact that Protestant homes were more likely to be in industrial areas than because 'the Pope was in the first aeroplane', or because Catholics were allegedly parading up and down the Falls Road with lighted matches in their hands to 'encourage' the German bombers flying at over 20,000 feet above Belfast.

'Bigotry is rampant in Belfast,' concluded Moya Woodside in August 1941, after she had seen that 'in Roman Catholic districts the police barrack buildings are almost completely bricked-up; and brick structures, apparently for machine guns, built out over the pavement. It looks as though riots were expected. On the walls in these same districts are painted up such slogans as "Join the IRA", "No Conscription Here", "ARP Stands for Arrests, Robbery, Police" etc. Some of these have been defaced, but some look quite recent.'

Of the three British ports united by their attraction to the German bombers in the spring of 1941, and by their optimism that they would escape bombardment, Plymouth was the westernmost. With a population of around 200,000, Plymouth is located in Devon, near the border with Cornwall. Behind the city stretches the huge, often bleak expanse of Dartmoor; to the fore, it juts out into the open sea. Plymouth, from which the Pilgrim Fathers set sail for America on the *Mayflower*, and which gave thanks for the defeat of the Armada, is a historic seafaring town, dominated by its naval connections. In 1941 the Royal Navy base HMS Drake spilled its many functions, and ever-changing personnel, into the city, with fine Georgian houses for Admirals and other high-ranking officers, barracks in Devonport named for great seafarers – Drake, Hawkins, Grenville and Raleigh – and the vast King William victualling yard. Dockyards provided much work for the civilian population, repairing and refitting ships while other vessels laid at anchor in the harbour: ocean liners and trawlers in peace-time, battleships and destroyers in war.

Its prominent position on the south-west coast, and its key role in the defence of Britain, meant that Plymouth has been attacked many times over the centuries – probably the first time was during an unsuccessful invasion attempt by Bretons in August 1403. More than five hundred years later it had to be recognised that while the seaport remained vulnerable to attack from the sea, it could also be at risk from the air, although for some time there was uncertainty about the reach of German bombers, and a certain amount of confidence that Plymouth would either be spared aerial bombard-ment or, for some reason, would receive 'more warning of impending attack than any naval base in Britain'.

By the summer of 1940, the war had definitively come to Plymouth. It had been designated one of the reception ports for thousands of British, French and Belgian soldiers evacuated from Dunkirk as France was overrun by German troops, and on 18 June it received 110 survivors from SS *Lancastria*, sunk by German air fire as she left Saint-Nazaire loaded with Allied soldiers. Plymouth Sound was awash with boats of all sizes, many from the French fleet; Devonport dockyard was fully occupied in repairing ships like HMS *Exeter* and HMS *Belfast* that were scarred from battle. The Home Guard was on alert, conscious that detachments of a seaborne German invasion from occupied France might attempt to land at Plymouth and secure the port as a supply base.

Throughout the autumn and winter of 1940–41 Plymouth was subjected to intermittent air raids, many on RAF Mount Batten on the peninsula, where a squadron of Sunderland Flying Boats was stationed to attack German U-boats. These culminated in a severe raid on 14 January 1941, with consid-erable damage to property and some loss of life, after which the Mayor gave a speech in which he suggested that Plymouth's Civil Defence arrangements had been tested and found to be adequate. He gave the impression that the city could now tick that off, and would not be tested again. It was.

On 12 March Plymouth suffered its thirty-first air raid of the war. Buildings were damaged, shop windows broken, and the city received one of the marks of recognition as a war zone when it was honoured with a royal visit on 20 March, the eve of the vernal equinox, one of the two days in the year on which the earth is in equilibrium. The King and Queen arrived in the royal train at 10.30 a.m. They were met by Lady Astor, Plymouth's Conservative MP (and strong advocate of appeasing Germany before the war), who combined her parliamentary duties with the *de facto* role of Lord Mayor, since her husband Waldorf, whose job it really was, was frequently indisposed, as he was on this occasion. The morale-boosting visit included a tour of the dockyards and naval barracks, the inspection of Civil Defence workers lined up in front of the Guildhall, a call on a rest centre, tea with the Astors in their constituency home (they also owned the stately Cliveden in Buckinghamshire), and finally a quick look-in at the YMCA before the royal couple returned to their train, which pulled out of the station at 5.45 p.m.

Less than three hours later, the alert sounded: within minutes Heinkel 111s, the undersides of their wings painted black to make them less visible against the night sky, started dropping their bomb loads. They were followed by a pathfinder force which, once it had located the target area, dropped iridescent blue, green, red and crimson flares to guide the bombers that were following. Soon the centre of the city was ablaze, the flames fanned by a strong wind. With an acute shortage of fire tenders, water (despite the fact that Plymouth is surrounded by sea) and firemen (only 263 part-time firemen out of a force of 537 reported for duty that night), the fires soon coalesced into seamless sheets of leaping, out-of-control flames. The Navy rushed in pumps to help. A connection was made from Sutton harbour to the water tank by the Guildhall, and urgent calls went out to neighbouring brigades for vehicles and water carriers, since so many of Plymouth's mains had been damaged, and much of the water supply to the city cut off.

Within an hour the police HQ was out of commission, all but five police telephone boxes had been hit, and the only way messages could be relayed was by motorcycle despatch riders loaned by the Navy. The Palace Theatre, where Billy Cotton was playing, was hit, and the lights went out. A factory adjacent to the theatre was on fire, but the safety curtain saved the Palace. The Alhambra Music Hall nearby was packed with servicemen watching the striptease artiste Phyllis Dixey go through her routine. Because of the mayhem outside, the manager persuaded his patrons to spend the night on the premises.

By midnight when the All Clear sounded Plymouth was 'a ball of fire'. Since many fires could not be brought under control, they were left to burn all night; some were still smouldering seven days later. The following morning BBC news bulletins referred to 'enemy action being on a small scale'. The Home Intelligence Unit was unable to correct this, as its phone lines were down. A German reconnaissance plane that flew over the city to photograph the damage received a more accurate impression. When Audrey Hawkins, a Wren (Women's Royal Naval Service), waited for a train at North Road station on the morning of 21 March, at the start of a week's leave, she found it 'a bit of a mess. One platform had been hit and a train burned out. There was a dead man on the [station] roof . . . there was a time bomb on the line . . . we had to wait for two hours in frost and fog, getting very cold.'

The next night, the first of spring, the bombers came back – more of them this time, and with heavier loads. The pathfinder force circled over the city for more than twenty minutes before releasing an explosion of flares. This was immediately followed by a hailstorm of 7,000 incendiaries and sixty-four high-explosive bombs. Again a strong westerly wind fanned the flames, and again there was a desperate shortage of firefighting equipment, water and manpower. The tide was out, fire crews were 174 men under strength, and communications broke down. The situation was worse than on the previous night, because while once again the only way to transmit information was by messengers, their motorbikes and bicycles had all been destroyed. Locked buildings burned since no one could get in to extinguish the incendiaries. When a call went out to Exeter for more ambulances to convey the wounded to hospital, the request was refused by the controller. Fortunately the Navy again came to the rescue, allowing civilians to be transported in naval ambulances. Others were carried through the burning streets on stretchers, only for their rescuers to find that the Prince of Wales Hospital was almost out of blood plasma, and could not contact any neighbouring hospitals to obtain more. The telephone supervisor at Devonport finally managed to get through to Barnstaple Hospital, and additional stocks were sent by plane.

Union Street, which linked the shopping areas of Plymouth and Devonport, was burning all along its eastern end, and the mainline railway station had also been hit. The General Post Office was a burned-out shell. The Guildhall had been hit, and the ARP control centre in the basement had to be evacuated to Devonport. A tar distillery was blazing, and the fifteenth-century St Andrew's, Plymouth's mother church, had almost nothing but its walls left standing. The children's ward and recently opened maternity ward of Plymouth General Hospital were hit, killing twenty-five children and six nurses. Naval barracks and the victualling yard were hit. When the wind rose, it whipped the flames so fiercely that there was talk of dynamiting buildings to form a fire break; throughout great swathes of the city, with eighty water mains destroyed, there was no water to be had to fight the fires.

There was almost a mutiny in Devonport that night when sailors aboard HMS *Jackal* refused to return to their stations unless they were promised shore leave to see how their families were faring. Lord Louis Mountbatten, Captain of the 5th Flotilla, finally acquiesced to the men's request. There was no subsequent court martial after it became apparent that when the men did go ashore many found they had lost homes, relatives and friends in the raids.

The sight next morning was one of utter desolation. A hundred Royal Engineers were drafted in to clear the eighty-five UXBs that blocked the roads and made buildings unsafe. Hoses wielded by blackened and exhausted firemen played on still-burning buildings. Steamrollers were flattening the piles of rubble. Fourteen of Plymouth's forty-six rest centres had been damaged and had to be closed. Urgent calls went out for billets for the homeless, and though Devon, which had been designated an evacuation area, seemed to have no spare capacity, representatives from Exeter, Totnes and Dartmouth arrived to see if they could help. There were virtually no food shops open in the centre of Plymouth until emergency vans arrived. Staff from Spooner's department store, which had been gutted, opened for business in a car showroom. One member of staff was despatched to Devonport 'to buy as much calico as he could find, which was then tacked onto the showroom's window frames, and sized over to keep out the rain'. Staff went as far as Exeter, Bristol and Totnes to buy supplies of food, and the 'shop' stayed open until 9 p.m., using tables borrowed from a local dance hall as counters and lit by candles, providing customers with parcels of tea, sugar, bacon, butter and sausages, without requesting coupons. In order to notify the public of the improvised store's existence, since the local newspaper, which had to be printed in Exeter, had no space for advertisements, John Bedford, the manager, 'took most of the large hoardings that were available in Plymouth, and when considering what to put on them, remembered the words from St Paul's "Letter to the Corinthians", "We are pressed on every side yet not straitened, perplexed, yet not in disrepair, smitten down, yet not destroyed." ' Bedford 'therefore headed all our advertisements with "SMITTEN DOWN YET NOT DESTROYED".'

The German report noted that Plymouth's defences had been 'very weak', and there were also undoubtedly some shortcomings in the response to the raids. Although the army and navy provided cooking facilities outside the rest centres that were still open, and managed to produce hot meals, they could not cope with the demand. The Emergency Meals Service, detailed to feed the population, closed its doors on 23 March, observing the Sabbath in a way that was hardly humane. Herbert Morrison resolutely refused to name Plymouth as the city that had been so brutally attacked, despite complaints from Lady Astor, who dubbed the Ministry of Information 'the Ministry of Inflammation', so profoundly angry were so many who had suffered so grievously and, as they saw it, with so little recognition. 'No-one in Whitehall cared about us or our safety,' wrote the Town Clerk, Colin Campbell. 'We were left alone to get on with it, to bury our dead and clear up the mess. No-one had warned us what to expect.'

The Ministry of Home Security expressed disquiet at the firefighting capabilities of the city, and demanded improvements. Plymouth's Emergency Committee rejected most of the charges, but agreed to erect more stand-pipes and to standardise hydrant fittings throughout the city.

Two hundred and ninety-two people had died in the raids. A military funeral was held to bury the forces' personnel, while the civilian dead were accorded a mass funeral and buried in a communal grave, wedged side by side in wooden coffins covered by Union Jacks.

There was worse to come. At 8.39 p.m. on Monday, 21 April, 120 planes of Luftflotte 3 started to mass over Plymouth. Within a quarter of an hour 10,000 incendiary bombs had landed on the city; in the course of the six-hour attack 35,000 incendiaries and seven hundred high-explosive bombs were dropped. A large underground shelter in the centre of the city received a direct hit. Seventy-four people were sheltering there: only two survived. One child lost her father, mother, sister and grandfather in the incident. Another terrible shelter tragedy took place at HMS Drake naval base when one of the towers, Boscawen block, housing petty officers, was hit. Those sheltering in the basement were killed when the bomb crashed through the floor, and others were trapped when the floors above collapsed. The next day seventy-eight bodies were recovered, and it was thought that another eighteen burned corpses were still somewhere in the debris. But the next day a sentry, thinking he heard a cry for help, alerted the watch. The boarding that had been nailed over the site was removed, digging recommenced, and several sailors were brought out alive.

It was clear that Plymouth's public shelters were inadequate, built without proper mortar, as many London ones had been in the early days of the blitz. In many cases the roofs had no reinforcement – 'Morrison sandwiches' waiting to happen. The fire service was obviously deficient in a number of ways, and in the eyes of the South-West Regional Commissioner, Sir Hugh Elles, who arrived in the city from Bristol the next day, the Civil Defence services were lacking leadership, organisation and motivation in a city in which 105 bodies had been found so far, 60,000 homes had been damaged, and water and gas cut off.

There was no respite: the bombers came back on 22 April, when Devonport dockyard was the main target. A destroyer, HMS *Lewes*, was hit, the railway goods yard was badly damaged, the telephone exchange was knocked out of action, and the casualty department of the Prince of Wales Hospital was demolished by a bomb as the wounded continued to be brought in; emergency operations were carried out in a basement filled with brick dust and without adequate supplies of water, or gas to boil water to sterilise surgical equipment. The terms 'front line' and 'battle zone', sometimes hyperbolically used, were entirely appropriate to Plymouth that night. Again, fires burned out of control. The London Fire Service sent men by train to help.

On 23 April Plymouth was bombed again, for the third night in succession. Devonport was again attacked: 8,700 tons of petrol and 3,000 tons of diesel were ignited; the fires burned for four nights. Hundreds of houses in the area were badly damaged. The situation had become so acute that Sir Aylmer Firebrace, the Chief Superintendent of the Fire Service, was ordered to fly to Plymouth from the north-east of England, where he had been on a tour of inspection. His opinion confirmed that of Elles: there was a total lack of authoritative leadership in the city. Again, exhausted firemen had been summoned from London and elsewhere, their gallant efforts often frustrated by lack of water. Devonport seemed little more than ruins and debris, with many dead and wounded, and most of the equipment and medical stores at the naval base destroyed.

Plymouth's terrible ordeal was still not over. On Monday, 28 April, 124 bombers headed to the city. The pattern was sickeningly familiar: widespread showers of incendiaries followed by high-explosive bombs. Yet again water mains were damaged, docks alight, telecommunications out of commission, bomb craters hindered the movement of fire-fighting equipment. This time Saltash was bombed; it was impossible to reach the area because of UXBs and roads made impassable by craters and rubble. Forty-three sailors were killed when two adjacent shelters at HMS Raleigh were hit, and many more were injured.

On Tuesday, 29 April the bombers returned again. This time the fleet of

162 planes initially had difficulty locating their target, and some bombs fell in the countryside outside the city, but soon they were falling on Plymouth, Devonport, Saltash, Milehouse and Keynsham. A gasometer was set on fire at Milehouse, and forty houses were destroyed in Saltash. Nearly 8,000 tons of fuel oil were lost when an oil depot at Torpoint was torched, a railway station was demolished and a steam train fell into a bomb crater at Keynsham. Plymouth's Central Library burned to the ground with the loss of 100,000 books, and though the Swindon Fire Brigade had arrived in the city, there was no water for their hoses, and they could do little but stand and watch the inferno. The only good news was that the art gallery and museum, which housed the valuable Cottonian collection, including paintings by Sir Joshua Reynolds, were saved – though their treasures were sensibly packed up and evacuated the following week.

The official death toll for those three nights was 591. The actual total was almost certainly more, as many bodies were never recovered. Students from Bristol University's Medical School were asked to help with piecing bodies together for burial. In what Churchill, following naval tradition, called the 'butcher's bill', the cost to Plymouth of all the raids in the spring of 1941 was 928 civilians dead. They included nineteen Civil Defence workers, the youngest of whom was a fifteen-year-old messenger (though the official minimum age for enrolment was sixteen), twenty-six firemen and one firewoman, sixty-six Fireguards, ten policemen and seven nurses. Add service deaths to this and the total is 1,172, although since so many witnesses were killed, and so many records destroyed, it may well be higher. The youngest person to die was just seven days old: Harold Santilla was killed with his twenty-four-year-old mother, to whom he was attached by a cord, when the Maternity Wing of the City Hospital received a direct hit. The oldest killed was ninety-two. Three thousand two hundred and sixty-nine people were injured. An overall total of 5,748 civilians and service personnel were killed or injured.

The two main shopping centres of Plymouth and Devonport were razed, and for many months people had to shop at stalls set up by stores like Woolworth's in the covered market, in rows of Nissen huts with hastily installed shopfronts, or even in private houses. The number of houses demolished totalled 3,745, and another 18,398 were seriously damaged. Forty churches were wrecked, nearly every civic building had gone, and so had twenty schools. Plymouth was like a city of the dead, its buildings scrawny, misshapen skeletons.

It has been estimated that as many as 30,000 people left the city every night after the raids had begun. They would pour out into the countryside by train (vouchers were issued), car or by lorry if they could manage to hitch a lift, by bicycle, or trudging on foot. An endless column, clutching all they could carry, most of them with no specific destination, no idea who might put them up, just determined to get away. They were sometimes dubbed the 'yellow convoy' or the 'funk express' by a judgemental press. While it is hard to think of a more rational response to the raids, their absence cast a heavy burden on those who 'stayed put' as they were instructed to do. On them fell increased fire-watching duties and other Civil Defence functions, and it is no wonder that resentment smouldered against those who left.

Soon nearby towns and villages were full to capacity with the refugees. Bere Alston and Bere Ferris, a few miles from Devonport, were overwhelmed with trekkers. Places which have since been absorbed into Plymouth's urban sprawl were outlying villages in 1941. Two thousand trekkers flooded into Plympton, where the grammar school had been turned into a rest centre. Others went to Roborough, where the asbestos village hall was set up to accommodate as many people as possible, though that meant that only blankets were available, not mattresses or palliasses. A rest centre had also been arranged at Bickleigh, and others ventured to Yelverton, Horrabridge or Tavistock. A few fortunate people found billets with sympathetic families. Many were put up in far too overcrowded village halls and schools. Others slept in huts, tents, ditches or hedgerows. Some went as far as Dartmoor, prepared to sleep 'wrapped in blankets on the drizzling moors', so profound was their fear of the seemingly magnetic pull of Plymouth for the Luftwaffe.

Most trekked back to the city during the day if they could: men to work, women to wander the streets trying to find food, to rummage through their bombed houses for their lost possessions, shattered furniture, trying to piece their lives together again, queuing endlessly at Public Assistance offices for money for food and clothes, forms to fill in for compensation, for new ration books, identity cards.

Plymouth claimed to be the 'worst-bombed city in Britain'. That was not true, but it came unenviably near the top. Of those places that suffered major attacks (classified as raids in which a hundred tons or more of bombs were dropped), Plymouth had eight (the same as Merseyside and Birmingham, but fewer than London, with fourteen). In terms of the number of high-explosive bombs dropped, Plymouth came fifth in a table on which no city would wish to feature. With 1,228 bombs it was behind Glasgow/Clydeside as well as Merseyside, Birmingham and London, but above Coventry (often seen as the benchmark), Bristol and other ports such as Portsmouth, Southampton, Cardiff and Hull. And Plymouth was a much smaller city than London (with a wartime population of around eight million) or the Merseyside/Clydeside conurbations. Apart from London, more high-explosive bombs per acre fell only on Liverpool/Merseyside than on Plymóuth. And the tonnage of bombs did not necessarily equate to the amount of damage done: 449 bombers hit Coventry in a single night, killing 555 people and seriously injuring 865. Moreover, if a place had already been heavily raided, subsequent bombs might simply fall on the ruins, doing minimal additional damage.

By early May 1941 Mass-Observation had built up a thick dossier of reports on how 'blitztowns' coped with raids. Plymouth was a particularly well-studied example. M-O teams spent a considerable amount of time in the city after each raid, making contacts, including 'an unskilled observer with special qualifications for obtaining information' about sailors' problems. The report it produced on the 30 April raid was its third on the city.

'The civil and domestic devastation in Plymouth exceeds anything we have seen elsewhere, both as regards concentration through the heart of the town, and as regards the random shattering of homes all over the town. The dislocation of everyday. life also exceeds anything we have seen elsewhere, and an enormous burden is being placed on the determined spirits of the people,' M-O investigators reported. While they recognised that these were 'exceptionally difficult circumstances', and singled out some individuals, like the Public Assistance officers and those running mobile canteens, for praise, they were in general deeply unimpressed by what they observed of the organisation in the city, and particularly the post-raid evacuation, which they described as 'disastrous chaos', 'disgusting, degrading and tantamount to sabotaging the war effort. Who can let things get in such a mess and get away with it?'

This was a rerun of the 'Lesson of London' – it seemed as if everything had to be relearned every time there was a heavy raid: 'Each part of the post-blitz problem is treated as ad hoc, uncoordinated, locally, and only *after* the worst has happened.' M-O found the same shortcomings in almost every city that it had first highlighted in its report on Coventry, six months previously. There was no 'morale *policy*', no clear guidelines or arrangements in place to ensure that information about what to do, where to go for help, was readily available, that the plight of the homeless was recognised and prepared for, that evacuation was not left to individual enterprise, but was firmly and clearly regulated – otherwise it would be the survival of the fittest, winner takes all. M-O was particularly concerned about the elderly, who were bewildered and with few resources, and cited the heartbreaking case of 'eight old women, all over 70, and all dressed in Victorian bonnets and lace, sitting in a large, bare underground room in one of Plymouth's rest centres. They had been sitting on the hard seats (there were no others) in this uncomfortable room for several days, the Home from which they came having received a direct hit, killing and injuring many. The people in charge were doing their best to look after them, but with inadequate facilities and perhaps not much imagination. No billeting officer had been, and no arrangements were said to be underway for their movement, these might take some days yet.'

The people of Plymouth, with their 'strong local pride and tradition of toughness associated with the sea', were determined to show that they could 'take it', but anyone would have to be of '*superhuman* character to come through [the] raids unaffected and unshaken'. The report was critical of the official definition of good morale as 'cheerfulness', as expressed in facile displays such as 'cheers for the Prime Minister, thumbs up to the camera man', rather than consisting of 'citizen co-operation, work and the determination to work on and on, long term endurance, and confidence in victory and leadership'. Although the people of Plymouth talked of little else than their city being 'as flat as a pancake', and admitted to being 'scared stiff', and to thinking that 'people have had just about enough', the M-O observers did not think they were being 'defeat*ist*, far from it. But they are defeated. Their town has suffered a major military defeat, and they, the untrained and undisciplined soldiers of the Home Front, can (at present) do nothing much about it.'

The Prime Minister came to visit these home front 'soldiers' on 2 May. Churchill went first to Royal Naval Barracks, 'where bombs had killed a number of sailors. There was a gruesome sight in the gymnasium: beds in which some forty injured sailors lay, separated only by a low curtain from some coffins which were being nailed down. The hammering must have been horrible to the injured men but such was the damage that there was nowhere else it could be done.'

The Ministry of Home Security was incandescent when M-O's first report on morale in Plymouth was widely circulated among government ministers by the Admiralty, regarding it as less a report on low morale than a contributory factor. The Conservative MP Victor Warrender, a Junior Minister at the Admiralty, sent the report to Sir John Anderson, the Lord President of the Council: 'I think it is most dangerous to give these reports any kind of circulation at all . . . they give what I believe to be, in many cases, an entirely false impression. I presume they were written by what are known as the "intelligentsia" and I think they would be very much better employed doing something useful for the community.' 'I don't think I've heard of Mass-Observation,' ventured Anderson.

The M-O 'intelligentsia' were also inclined to be dubious about the Prime Ministerial visit. It was four o'clock in the afternoon by the time Churchill arrived in the devastated city centre (presumably because he had been delayed in the naval barracks), and by that time the nightly exodus had begun, so 'only a small proportion of Plymouth people saw him . . . we suggest about 500 people saw him closely enough to feel in personal contact . . . another 1,500 saw him clearly passing . . . and another 2,000 glimpsed him as he passed, often not taking in who it was until after he had passed . . . the car travelled too quickly'. Rather than going on a walkabout Churchill sat in a Daimler with Lady Astor (who had done her bit for morale, initiating dances on the Hoe and, rather improbably, 'doing cartwheels to cheer people up in some of the shelters'). However, for those who managed to see 'this great man, fierce faced, firmly balanced on the back of the car, with great tears of angry sorrow in his eyes . . . a man overflowing with human sympathy, an epic figure riding through an epic of destruction', and who were 'close enough to hear his few remarks, "God bless you all," "Well done Plymouth," ' it was a moving moment, beautifully summed up by a man standing outside the Guildhall: 'He's like a *lighthouse*.'

16

Attrition

Let's be gay. It's Easter Day –
And Spring, at last, is on its way.
It's Hitler's habit in the Spring
To do some dark disgusting thing,
But you and I may still decline
To sign on Hitler's dotty line . . .

A.P. Herbert's 'Postscript', broadcast on 12 April 1941

The street was as flat as this 'ere wharfside – there was just my 'ouse like –
well, part of my 'ouse. My missus was just making me a cup of tea when I
come 'ome. She were in the passage between the kitchen and the wash 'ouse
where it blowed 'er. She were burnt right up to her waist, 'er legs were just
two cinders. And 'er face – the only thing I could recognise 'er by was one
of 'er boots – I'd 'ave lost fifteen 'omes if I could 'ave kept my missus. We
used to read together. I can't read mesen. She used to read to me like. We'd
have our armchairs on either side o' the fire, and she read me bits out o' the
paper. We'd a paper every evening. Every evening.

ARP warden, Hull, reported by Mass-Observation

There was a little woman from Dovehouse Street sitting on a bench . . .
Dovehouse Street had had a parachute mine on it and the Chelsea Hospital
for Women had dealt with many casualties. Suddenly her control gave way
and she began screaming in a frenzy of grief . . . 'He's gone . . . He's gone and
I'm all alone and no home, nothing. No one wants me . . . Why didn't I go
with him, it's cruel, it's cruel, cruel. Why? Why?' Her anguish was terrible.

In the appalled silence with which officialdom treats such outbursts –
almost as if she had said or done something obscene – a sleek, well-dressed
clergyman . . . told her sternly to desist – that what had happened was God's

316

will and that she must accept it and thank Him for her own deliverance from death. She looked at him in dazed misery as if he spoke a foreign language and began screaming even more wildly. 'God! There's no God! There's only Hitler and the Devil' . . . I looked at his well-kept hands, and his beautifully tended nails, and I thought of the Reverend Arrowsmith and his curate digging frantically with their bare hands in the rubble, of the Reverend Newsom sitting night after night on a hard bench with his parishioners sharing the perils of the Blitz, and then of the vicar of Old Church, fighting incendiaries and looking after his fire parties so wonderfully, and now his church was gone. I thought of how Kathleen and Anne were dead [that night] . . . and I said nothing. It did not seem to me that there was anything to say.

Red Cross nurse Frances Faviell, writing about the morning after 'The Wednesday' raid on London on 16–17 April 1941

April and May were the cruellest months. The vital east-coast port of Hull was a natural target, standing at the confluence of two rivers and highly visible to any plane flying overhead. In early March the *Yorkshire Post* journalist Cyril Dunn, who was living in Leeds, reported, 'We've only had one or two air raid alarms lately, but nothing dropped. They've been slamming Hull again, tho' it's not up to Blitz standard, and have taken one more crack at Bridlington.' But there were two heavy raids in March: the first on the 13th–14th, which targeted industrial sites along the river, destroyed two hundred homes and killed thirty-nine people; in the second, on the 18th, three hundred tons of high-explosive bombs and 77,000 incendiaries were dropped, but in the fog that night most missed their target, the port, and caused widespread devastation in residential and commercial districts. Dunn found these raids 'a curiously ordinary experience', though 'some very substantial fires got going'. He was sent to the Bellevue Road area,

and got some good stories from a man who had been digging people out of the ruins [of some bombed houses], a woman with dirt in her disordered hair who was half daft with shock and who spoke to me with exaggerated refinement. The All Clear went while we were there and an ambulance arrived and they carried quiet bundles out of the houses on stretchers and policemen made notes by car light and everybody came out laughing, and boasting and hugging each other . . . We drove round a bit looking for damage and policemen at strings of red lights headed us off & said there were 'sleepers' [presumably UXBs] lying over there. We had a puncture driving over snow-drifts of broken glass & while the driver mended it we walked on to where a great army of rescuers worked in the moonlight to dig some trapped people out of a very quiet ruin in Institution Street.

Thereafter I saw the Town Hall roof on fire & I was rebuffed when I tried to interview the Police Chief – and after a lot more comings and goings and writings of stories, I went home about 6.30am. The smoke from some great fire smirched the cold virginity of the dawn & there was white dew all over our lawn and a bird sang very lustily in our tree & made me feel ashamed of being human.

There were 42 killed, 79 seriously injured, 116 injured, and 12,000 made homeless. The Germans call it 'a sharp attack'.

Hull was the unwilling beneficiary of bad weather over Merseyside when on 31 March bombers on course for Liverpool were diverted to the east at the last moment. The missiles this time were mainly parachute mines. The ARP HQ was hit, and Dr David Diamond, Hull's Deputy Medical Officer of Health, who had recently introduced a comprehensive blood transfusion service to the town, was killed as he talked in the basement to the newly appointed Medical Officer for the Civil Defence service. The policeman guarding the door, PC Robert Garton, was never seen again: all that was ever found were torn scraps of his uniform. Fire-watchers on the roof were killed instantly too.

Easter Sunday fell on 13 April, and Cyril Dunn paid a visit to nearby Bridlington, which he found 'very grim'. In anticipation of a possible inva-sion, 'whole blocks of private hotels and apartment houses have bleak and curtainless windows. The seafront is festooned with rusted barbed wire and there's not a footprint on the empty sands. The place is stiff with troops living in the deserted houses. I walked down Richmond Street – & it was just like going down the lines of a military camp, soldiers going around in their khaki vests, carrying enamel mugs and plates.'

On 16 April a parachute mine fell on a crowded public shelter in Hull, and between forty and fifty of those inside were killed. Twice again in April parachute mines fell on the city. On 8 May high-explosive bombs, para-chute mines and incendiaries fell on Hull, and the bombers returned the following night. 'The night before the RAF bombed Hamburg, so last night the Luftwaffe bombed Hull. And so on, I suppose, to infinity,' wrote Dunn. 'This is the worst blitz damage I've seen so far – although I always say that

... I can't possibly detail it all.' Even so, the list of places destroyed or badly damaged ran to five pages of Dunn's exercise book. They included

streets not bombed, but bombarded . . . Hammond's great store, the most majestic ruin I ever saw, its huge floors laid open and sagging under debris . . . the huge ghastly pile of the Prudential building down, all except the high corner tower, with 14 W.R.N.S. buried under tons of rubble with sweating soldiers patiently carrying it off brick by brick . . . Feren's Gallery had its white front splattered with red brick dust, just like blood, from the exploding Prudential. The lovely Dock Offices just had windows broken. The City Hall had missed the worst. West Street was still blocked with the ruins of the Metropole. Like ancient tribesmen, the people have made a new West Street – a track across the Metropole's foundations . . . The old Alexandra Theatre was a heap of muck, its tower pinnacle set on top like a fool's cap . . . Then up to Dantom Lane, to the back streets of poverty. I got some good stories & saw a ragged child digging for her toys . . . I heard tell of much more damage, along the Docks, for instance, but this is the kind of damage that doesn't happen officially.

I heard the usual wild rumours, shelters hit, the Bus Station fired by a crashing Nazi, German pilots baling out. One is said to have fallen in the docks and been drowned by keelmen. Another was almost certainly arrested on Holderness Road, and a fireman whose home had been destroyed, went up and kicked him hard in the balls. The police threatened to arrest him & he said 'I don't care if you do; I've had my satisfaction.'

I told this story later in the 'Mail' office [in Hull, where Dunn used to work] and Giles said even if this one wasn't true, it was a fact that a Nazi plane crashed in Bridlington Bay & some fishermen went out to rescue the pilot, believing the plane to have been British. When they found it wasn't, they threw the pilot back in the sea & kept him under with a boat hook. The RAF launches later got the body &, said Giles in confirmation of his story, the pilot had a great boathook stab in his bottom.

'They must have got close to the appalling limit in Hull,' Dunn wrote on 10 May, the day that would come to be seen as the finale of the blitz.

There was a second blitz raid in the early hours of yesterday morning. It will take years to rebuild the city. I spent five hours there yesterday and I only saw a small part of the disaster. Today I've temporarily resigned from the

Y[orkshire] P[ost] pretending illness to get over the numbing dejection of my experience. The biggest achievements of the Nazis yesterday were – complete destruction of whole stretches along the Old Harbour, Rank's huge flour mill, for example, is an epic ruin; they set fire to the whole of King George Dock, a policeman told me, 'on fire from end to end', with all the ships in it, including two destroyers. But I can't convey the fantastic thoroughness of it all. I stood, for instance, in Clarence Street. Everything I could see was wrecked, the vast Gehenna of Rank's mill filling the skyline. I walked round into Church Street. All the houses were shattered. St Peter's Church was just a dead shell. But the whole thing has lost meaning. It is too fantastic, too stupid for the ordinary human mind. And what relief can there be in hoping that the same kind of havoc exists in Germany? . . .

The City Hall is damaged by fire. The Cecil cinema is gutted, a lump has been carved out of the Guildhall, there have been two direct hits on the charming Trinity House almshouses, the Constitutional Club is rubble – curious to remember that it was here I heard those aged Tories eagerly prophesying war years ago. The geography of Hull's city centre has been abolished. In 10 years people will only talk of it as an antiquity . . .

People were really afraid, too. One of our machines flew over the city – why do the fools after a blitz? – & I saw several women run into the shelter of the shops.

And at teatime Ferensway was crowded with people with suitcases, waiting for buses to take them to hell out of it for the night. The same sort of thing happened at Coventry & Plymouth; people just went out into the fields.

Commercial areas were the worst-hit during the first night of Hull's May raids; the docks were devastated on the second, and it was said that the fires raging along the quays could be seen from the coast of Denmark. Riverside Quay was gutted as embers ignited the timber stacks. The contents of the huge grain warehouses lining the docks were on fire, and would smoulder for days. As Dunn noted, Rank's flour mill was razed, and horses stabled nearby had to have sacks put over their heads so they could be led to safety. The Central Fire Station was destroyed, as was the Corporation garage and a telephone exchange, a tannery and the Eagle oil mill, among other industrial buildings. The railway network was damaged, and the main bus garage burned out of control, leaving just the iron skeletons of buses standing when the flames were finally doused. So many gas mains were either fractured or flooded that Hull was without gas, and the Corporation offered to rent out electric kettles and hotplates to people without the facilities to boil water or cook. More than four hundred civilians were killed over the two nights, and 550 injured, many seriously. Forty thousand people were homeless, and in the weeks following the raids nearly half a million hot meals were served to people who no longer had the means to provide their own.

Although the *Yorkshire Post* 'was able to come out with a lovely front page splash [about the raid] and the *Mail* nobly rushed out a first leader about it, other papers were less fortunate'. In the national press reports Hull was referred to for reasons of security simply as a 'north-east town' or a 'northern coastal town', so it was not for some time that many people were aware of the city's plight. Out of a population of 320,000 when war broke out, 1,200 civilians were killed and 3,000 seriously injured; 86,715 buildings were damaged and 152,000 people made homeless. The emergency services and the thousand-odd-strong WVS were strained to breaking point. However, the port, amazingly, was never so devastated that it could not function.

If Hull had taken the bombs intended for Liverpool in March, Merseyside received its full complement during the devastating 'May Week' when it was raided for seven successive nights, by the end of which the city had 'a depressed and sordid atmosphere', according to a Home Intelligence Report. 'This is partly due to the blackness and the number of the very poor seen in the streets, and is enhanced by the Blitz debris.'

During those seven nights, 2,315 tons of high-explosive bombs and 112,000 incendiaries fell on Merseyside. On the night of 3–4 May alone, four hundred fires were burning. Again the docks were the target, since they were key to Britain's wartime survival: over 90 per cent of war matériel came through Merseyside's eleven miles of quays, which were Britain's main link to the United States.

On 3 May a burning barrage balloon tugged free of its moorings and came to rest on SS *Makaland*, moored in Huskisson Dock and packed to the gunwales with a thousand tons of bombs. Despite frantic efforts to extinguish the fire, many of the bombs exploded, destroying the quay completely and damaging others, while parts of the ship's plating were hurled over a mile by the force of the explosions. Mill Road Infirmary was hit by a heavyweight high-explosive bomb, completely destroying three buildings and damaging others. Ambulances and other vehicles parked on the forecourt were consumed by fire. Seventeen members of the medical staff were killed as were fifteen ambulance drivers and thirty patients, although one who was on the operating table in the basement at the time of the attack was buried by debris but was eventually dug out alive.

On 5 May an ammunition train parked in Clubmoor sidings near Anfield received a direct hit. Ten LMS railwaymen struggled valiantly to contain the fires, and with ammunition exploding all around them, managed to decouple some of the rear coaches and push them to safety. One of the men, George Roberts, was awarded a George Medal for his bravery. St Luke's church in the centre of Liverpool was gutted; only a few retaining walls remained: it was never rebuilt, and remains today a stark reminder of 'May Week'. Several other churches were also destroyed, as were Liverpool's Head Post Office, the Mersey Dock Office, other historic buildings connected with the work of the port, the Corn Exchange and the Public Library.

The casualties were numbing: 1,453 were killed in Liverpool, 257 in Bootle, twenty-eight in Birkenhead and three in Wallasey. One thousand and sixty-five were seriously injured in Liverpool, and the Civil Defence services lost many of their personnel: twenty-eight ARP wardens and WVS workers killed and fourteen seriously injured; eleven police killed and fifty-one injured; twenty-seven first aid workers, ambulance drivers and stretcher-bearers dead and six injured; while the heavy and light rescue services lost five men and the same number seriously injured. However, the government, anxious not to alert the Germans to how devastating their raids on Merseyside were being, was even more careful than usual not to let such figures escape the scrutiny of the censor.

Although the docks had been the target in Hitler's final attempt (as it turned out to be, though no one could be sure of this at the time) to disable Britain's capacity to wage war before preparing to veer east to attack Russia, as was usual streets of small terraced houses ran alongside the docks, the homes of those who laboured in the port. The devastation of these was appalling. Six thousand five hundred houses were destroyed in Liverpool, 16,400 were seriously damaged and 45,000 sustained slight damage. In Bootle only 15 per cent of the total housing stock was undamaged, and 25,000 people were made homeless; the number of those who lost their homes in the raids on Liverpool was 51,000.

The local authorities in the area were alleged to be 'too easily satisfied with the provisions made and are inclined to ignore public opinion . . . [and] be on the defensive and unwilling to discuss difficulties', concluded the Intelligence Report the Ministry of Home Security received. Cooperation between the ARP services and voluntary organisations broke down, food supplies were limited, conditions in public shelters were 'indescribable', and evacuation, particularly of the elderly, was chaotic.

Those who could fled into the surrounding countryside. On 8 May, when Bootle was attacked and 262 people were killed, all the main roads of the town were blocked, and a third of all shops were destroyed. Only one house in ten was undamaged, leaving one person in every four homeless. To add to the misery, eleven of the town's twelve rest centres had been destroyed or rendered unusable. That night almost half the population had trekked out of Bootle, and ten days later nearly a fifth were still going as far as twenty miles away to escape the bombs, though many returned each day to work.

On 10 May, the last night of the raids, 50,000 trekkers left Merseyside by any means they could: by special trains and buses laid on for the purpose, a few by lorry, car or bicycle, many just by trudging along the roads. This weary column of the fearful and the dispossessed, a familiar feature of wars in all places and at all times, imposed an intolerable burden on nearby towns and villages, most of which were totally unprepared for the mass of dispir-ited and disorientated humanity that settled like an exhausted swarm on their inadequate facilities. Maghull, a small town a few miles north of Merseyside, had made arrangements to take 1,750 refugees: in the event 6,000 arrived, almost the equal to the town's normal population of 8,000. They had to be put up in every school, church and village hall in the vicinity, and the wards of an empty hospital were opened to accommodate the over-spill. Dreadful though they were, the number of casualties in May Week would have been much higher if it had not been for the nightly exodus into the Wirral and as far away as North Wales.

London had enjoyed two virtually raid-free months, but on 8 March 1941 30,000 incendiaries fell on the capital: three railway termini were hit, and rolling stock damaged. Buckingham Palace was hit again: this time the North Lodge was almost destroyed. Bart's Hospital near Smithfield Market was hit too. In the West End two 110-pound bombs fell near Leicester Square, damaging the Rialto Cinema and crashing down into what was advertised as 'the safest and gayest restaurant in town, 20 feet below ground', the Café de Paris, where the phenomenally popular singer Ken 'Snakehips' Johnson had just started to croon the second chorus of the thirties revival 'Oh Johnny (How You Can Love)'. One bomb failed to explode but split open, spilling its contents on the floor; the other exploded in front of the stage, killing Johnson, a member of his band and the Café's head waiter, Charles. The room was packed, with a smart crowd of officers on leave and elegant women in evening dress sipping cocktails and enjoying the music. Thirty of them were killed and many more injured, including Betty, the daughter of the pre-war Conservative Prime Minister Stanley Baldwin. A dustman who happened to be passing wept at the sight of 'young men in uniform carrying out their dead girlfriends'. Due to a communications mix-up, it took some ambulances over an hour to arrive at the incident while the dead and injured lay among the rubble, twisted girders, shattered mirrors and chandeliers and matchsticks of furniture, all that was left of a nightclub that was reputed to have been constructed on the site of a bear-baiting pit, and had the sinuous, elegant lines and chromium-plated décor of an ocean liner – indeed, its design was ominously similar to that of the ill-fated *Titanic*, which had been built around the same time.

Barbara Nixon described the Café de Paris raid as 'a gory incident', and recounted how 'the melodramatic nature of the incident caught the fancy of reporters and for three days the papers were full of the gallantries of expensive girls who had torn their expensive frocks into strips to make bandages . . . but the same week another dancehall a mile to the east of us [in Finsbury, where Nixon was an ARP warden] was hit and there were nearly two hundred casualties. This time there were only 10s 6d frocks, and a few lines in the paper followed by "It was feared there were several casualties." Local feeling was rather bitter.'

But there was one aspect of the 'melodramatic incident' at the Café de Paris that the papers did not report. As the dead and injured lay among the debris, looters picked their way among them, easing rings from dead fingers, or reputedly if that was not possible, cutting off the fingers with a penknife, denuding corpses of earrings and necklaces, shoving gold compacts and cigarette cases into their pockets. Looting was the largely unspoken, un-acknowledged underside of the 'blitz spirit', the fissure that crazed the pulling-together to face a common enemy – and it was widespread. 'I lost more through looting than by bomb damage,' a London trader told the *Daily Mirror* in February 1941.

Some looters were bomb-chasers: when a raid was on they would converge on a target area and smash shop windows as the bombs fell and official attention was distracted, the streets empty with most people having taken shelter. The thieves' network would pass on information about houses damaged by bombs where rich pickings might be had. The Reverend John Markham in Walworth, south London, had learned that 'nothing helps the recovery of [air-raid victims] more than the knowledge that their personal treasures were safe. The usual practice of those who took shelter was to put all their cash, Savings Certificates, items of jewellery, and personal papers such as birth and marriage certificates in their handbags, which they kept under the chair on which they were sitting, or by their side if they were in bed. As soon as it was daylight, I used to take two of my wardens and tunnel through the mountains of rubble to find these handbags. We dared not leave them, even for a few hours, or they would be gone.'

After a particularly heavy raid on 17 April the Reverend Markham borrowed a ladder belonging to one of his wardens who was a window cleaner to reach the top flat in a block round the corner from his rectory, since the staircase had been destroyed when a bomb fell on the building.

We let down on ropes all the furniture and other fittings we could find . . . I can picture to this day a tin bath which we loaded with a complete dinner service, slowly and jerkily descending three floors on two ropes . . . We stored all we saved from this flat in the crypt, from which Mr and Mrs Marsh were able to recover it when they came out of hospital . . . that made a lot of difference. If we had waited another day it would have been looted . . . a few days later a family of another of the blasted flats came to collect their furniture and found that a piano had been taken from an upstairs flat. Two other relatives came to ask me whether they could enter their old mother's flat in Merrow Street, which had been blasted and made unsafe, and I took them there, and found all her trinkets, including her son's First World War medals, were gone. In fact, the very morning of the raid, the Borough Treasurer's men came to empty the gas and electric meters in the blasted flats only to find that every one had been broken into and rifled. That was less than six hours after the bomb exploded . . .

A rather more macabre side to looting is illustrated by another precaution that I had to take when I recovered dead bodies. As soon as we found them, I had to put them in an empty room, under the guard of two wardens, until the stretcher party could remove them to the mortuary. Otherwise their clothes would be rifled, there in the midst of the darkness and dust and falling bombs. It was a good thing I was not armed with a pistol or a gun . . .

A more comic side of looting was shown the same night. I arrived at the scene of the explosion within a couple of minutes of hearing it. I quickly found the body of one of my fire-watchers, lying in the rubble. Then I found his wife, shouting and swearing her head off. 'Some bleeder,' she cried, 'has nicked a couple of pounds of bacon I had in my meat safe.' It transpired that the said meat safe was sitting on top of the rubble of the block in which she had occupied a top flat. I do not think that she knew that her husband's dead body lay a few yards away . . . Shock can play funny tricks with people.

Others without a conscientious warden like the Reverend Markham, alert to his parishioners' every need, might return home after a raid to find that all that remained was destruction, rubble, broken glass, smashed furniture, gas and electricity meters broken open, everything of value cleaned out. The mansion block in West Hampstead where Gwladys Cox and her husband Ralph lived was bombed in October 1940. When they went back the following morning, 'we wandered from room to room, our feet squelching in the saturated carpets . . . I found that my silver cigarette lighter had disappeared from its drawer. Under my bed, my trinket box was lying open, its contents scattered over the wet carpet. It had been taken out of my dressing table drawers which had been forced and everything of the least value taken. Ralph's room had been ransacked and most of his underclothing, as well as a gold watch, taken. All the work of looters.'

In September 1940 there were 539 cases of looting reported in London alone. The figure rose to 1,662 in October and 1,463 in November, and there was talk of appointing a 'Director of Anti-Looting'. The appalled Lord Mayor of London urged that notices should be posted warning that 'the Legislature has provided that those found guilty of looting from premises damaged or vacated by reasons of attacks by the enemy are, on conviction, liable to suffer death or penal servitude for life. Thus the law puts looters into the category of murderers, and the day may well be approaching when they will be treated as such.' They never were (though in Germany looters were routinely shot): the maximum penalty a magistrate could impose was three months' imprisonment, or remitting the case to a higher court where sentences could be exemplary.

After raids in Sheffield in December 1940, the Assize Court had to sit for a full two days to hear cases of looting. The presiding judge pronounced: 'When a great city is attacked by bombs on a heavy scale, numbers of houses and their contents are left exposed and deprived of their natural defences. Necessarily these are the homes of comparatively poor people, since they are by far the most numerous . . . The task of guarding shattered houses from prowling thieves, especially during the blackout, is obviously beyond the capacity of any police force.' While this was said in Sheffield, regrettably it could have applied anywhere: Liverpool, Glasgow, Birmingham, London – where on the night of the 10–11 May raid thieves stole the great bells of the bombed St Mary's church near Elephant and Castle, to the deep distress of its vicar, the Reverend Christopher Veazey, and his wife Joan.

That same night, the American journalist Larry Rue, in London for the isolationist paper the *Chicago Tribune*, filed a story that would appear under the headline 'Air Raid Blitzkrieg Breeds Crime, London Learns'. It reported the comments of the Metropolitan Police Commissioner, Sir Philip Game, that juvenile crime was on the increase, accounting for 48 per cent of all arrests, and that there had been 4,584 cases of looting since the start of the blitz. For Game, the most distressing feature was 'the number of cases in which various members of the public services abused what is in fact a position of trust'. When the figures of prosecutions for looting in England and Wales were finally released in 1947 it was revealed that in 1940 there had been 701 (including forty-six women), and in 1941 the total had been 2,763 (including 163 women). Clearly the police did not have the resources to investigate or prosecute anything like the number of cases reported.

The blitz, like the blackout, provided cover for all sorts of nefarious activities – in one case a murder was attempted to be passed off as death in an air raid: pickpocketing; protection rackets; racketeers charging fabulous sums for 'reserving' a place in a shelter or the tube, or to store bedding; 'inspectors' carrying notebooks who would strip out anything of value from normally locked shelters, including such things as ventilation pipes or escape hatches, the absence of which could render them lethal. People made false claims for the loss of ration books or ID cards, or said they had been bombed out when they hadn't: a Wandsworth man claimed to have been bombed out nineteen times in five months before the authorities realised his game and he was sent to prison for three years in February 1941.

The sheer overburdening of bureaucracy during the blitz meant that legitimate claimants for damage to property could wait for months for their claims for repairs to be processed; in the meantime many of them had to live in intolerable conditions, unable to afford to pay a builder to do the work. Loan sharks took advantage of this, offering to advance money to desperate householders at exorbitant rates of interest. Damaged, unprotected houses were often cannibalised for their fixtures and fittings, sometimes by local authorities which in seeking to repair one house, might strip another.

Many looters were petty criminals in peacetime, who found that the blitz provided them with unprecedented opportunities as previously inaccessible premises suddenly spilt forth bounty. Others were simply opportunistic, in the right place at the right time, pouncing when they saw watches, jewellery, silverware, radios, cartons of cigarettes spilling out from the windows of a blitzed shop onto the pavement. Previously honest citizens impetuously yielded to temptation in these times of stress and chaos, picking up what could seem like discarded goods. Many were children or young people, 'scrounging' in urban wastelands: New Scotland Yard reckoned that 50 per cent of looters were under twenty-one, and many were a good deal younger than that: one seven-year-old boy was described in the *Daily Mirror* as 'a looting ringleader' and 'a menace to the community'. Such young offenders were dealt with severely, often being sentenced to several strokes of the birch.

Glass shattering sounded the same whether caused by a bomb blast or a hurled brick. The noise of the AA guns blotted out sounds of illegal entry or demolition. Sometimes ARP wardens, firemen or members of demolition squads and rescue parties would succumb to the temptation to plunder. In 1941 thirty-three Royal Engineers, including NCOs, sent to clear up bomb sites, appeared at the Old Bailey wearing battle dress, charged with stealing over nine tons of lead. Four were acquitted, but the rest went to prison, including the sixty-three-year-old 'fence'. In May that year the Metropolitan Police claimed that out of a sample of 228 men prosecuted for looting, ninety-six held official positions. At one point a despairing magistrate expostulated, 'I'm beginning to wonder if there is an honest demolition worker in London' (though that was clearly not the case), and the Home Secretary admitted that no enquiries were made into the background of those employed to carry out such duties.

To ensure that there were no misunderstandings – one part-time ARP warden in central London claimed that the 130 pairs of ladies' gloves, 214 towels, seventeen bottles of hair lotion, two fur coats and a fur collar he had managed to accumulate were 'tips' – it was made clear to all involved that they were not allowed to accept gifts from grateful victims. These must be handed to the Incident Officer or a senior police officer at the scene.

In July 1941 Mass-Observation reported on a demolition squad where the childhood ethos 'finders keepers' seemed to be the norm, with the men taking anything they came across that was 'useful and portable'. The foreman, however, was outraged: 'They're not doin' anything to 'elp the country, they're a fuckin' 'indrance. I'm no angel meself, but I'm not 'avin that goin' on.' On finding a handbag with an empty purse in a bombed building, he exploded: 'It's the funniest bloody bomb I ever come across. I been all through the last war and I done several jobs like this, but I never come across a bomb like this. It's blown every bag open and knocked the money out of the gas meters, yet it didn't break a single light bulb in the basement.'

The big boys, the career criminals, usually eschewed such chancey pickings. They preferred to identify houses that had been closed up for the duration, the owners evacuating to a safer berth, and organise comprehensive raids, taking a pantechnicon and loading up the entire contents of a home, unchallenged since there were so many moves, so much coming and going, in wartime. When the owners returned all they would find would be curtains flapping in the wind, and maybe pools of water on the floor, since the lead had been stripped from the roof. Dover had been largely evacuated in the summer of 1940 when an invasion looked imminent: when the residents were allowed to return in 1942, most found their homes stripped bare of everything remotely portable. In Cardiff, the Regional Officer of the War Damage Commission reported that 'the evil is at its height immediately after a blitz but it continues until there is little left that is worth removing. Even fruit trees in gardens are uprooted and stolen. Baths, fireplaces, copper tanks, whole staircases, etc. are removed undamaged, which demands a certain amount of skill. It is evident that the looting (as distinct from wilful damage) is not the work of irresponsible youths. How the culprits succeed in carting the articles away without being detected is a mystery to me . . . in Ninian Park Road, Cardiff, the new work is disappearing as fast as it can be reinstated by the Corporation, who appear quite helpless in the matter, despite the vigilance of the police.'

It was the fear of looting as much as anything that made many people unwilling to leave their blitzed homes, and an urgent priority for local authorities was to provide secure storage for furniture and effects so their owners could decamp with confidence. This was another charge laid on their overstretched resources which many signally failed to fulfil.

Looting is a particularly invidious and mean-spirited crime, taking advantage of the adversity of others, making someone's recovery from a traumatic incident so much harder. Penalties were often harshly exemplary, particularly if a person employed to help abused his authority. Several Portsmouth policemen who had been posted to guard bombed premises in Southsea in the autumn of 1940 looted them instead, taking a fur coat and cape among other things. Each was sentenced to ten years behind bars. In October 1940 six London auxiliary firemen were accused of looting. In pronouncing sentence the judge chided, 'Each of you was sent to trade premises for the purpose of extinguishing or of dampening down such parts of the debris that were still smouldering. While so engaged all of you seized the opportunity of stealing such stock on the premises which you could conveniently carry in your water buckets or by hand, and of hiding the stolen property in the motor vehicle entrusted to you for carrying yourselves, your hoses and other fire gear . . . As a deterrent to others the sentences must be severe. You have disgraced the uniform you wear and have failed to carry on the great tradition of the London Fire Brigade, which has won the respect and admiration of all.' He sentenced each of the men to five years in prison.

If anything, the press was even harsher than the law. *Daily Mirror* headlines urged 'Hang a Looter and Stop This Filthy Crime' twice in November 1940, the *Sunday Dispatch* weighed in with 'Forward the Gallows' in the same month, and the *Observer* talked about 'the dregs of society'.

However, the definition of the crime could be cruelly rigid. There could be a thin line between looting and salvage, and many accused pleaded, with some justification, that the goods they pocketed were damaged, and would go to waste if left, which in times of chronic shortages seemed profligate. There are stories of ARP wardens prosecuted for filling their pockets with a few lumps of coal, a couple of battered tins of soup or an orange that no one would ever claim. A Bristol man was sentenced to four months' imprisonment with hard labour in May 1941 for stealing sugar from a bombed house; he claimed that it was being trampled underfoot. An auxiliary fireman was 'made an example of' by being sent to prison for five years for filling two buckets with food (though his sentence was quashed on appeal). A seaman whose ship had been torpedoed and who had spent twenty hours in an open boat, which was then machine-gunned, was prosecuted for stealing a bottle of cough mixture and a jar of hair cream. Leonard Watson, in charge of a Heavy Rescue Squad digging for victims or their remains after a pub was hit, found a quarter-bottle of gin among the debris and passed it round his fellow workers to strengthen their sinews for their laborious and gruesome task. He was jailed for this 'crime'.

As Liverpool would suffer its devastating 'May Week', earlier newspaper headlines had read 'The Big Blitz Back Again' in the capital. On 15 March it was the turn of south-east London. Thirty boroughs were carpeted with a hundred tons of high-explosive bombs and 16,000 incendiaries. The docks were damaged, as were three hospitals, shops, offices and houses. In Southgate on the northern edge of London forty-two civilians were killed in a single incident. A raid on 19 March devastated a large area, with five hundred planes dropping 470 tons of high-explosive bombs, 122,000 incendiaries plus a large number of parachute bombs, which caused widespread damage. ' "All Clear" didn't sound till 5.30 this morning. The longest alert this year so far,' noted Anthony Heap. The next day, on his route to pay ARP wardens' wages, Heap saw 'the damage caused by a land mine which fell in the centre of a block of buildings near the corner of York Way and Hungerford Road [in north London] . . . in order to pay some of the stretcher-men digging for bodies there, I was able to go right to the thick of it and see the whole works. Not a building in the entire block was left standing. It was just a gigantic pile of debris surrounded by jagged shells of shattered walls. Every window and shop front in many streets was blasted out. The total casualties were unknown, but likely to prove heavy. These land mines are the very devil.'

The mines razed whole streets in the East End too, in Poplar, Stepney and West Ham. Several of the bombs that fell that night were the massive SC 2500s, known as 'Maxes', weighing 5,500 pounds. The destruction was fearful: a public shelter in Poplar was hit, killing forty-four of the occupants, other public shelters were bombed as were nine hospitals, and bombs fell in an arc from Bromley in Kent to Leyton in east London. Two thousand fires burned; the utility services and transport systems were severely disrupted.

Then came a lull, or as Anthony Heap, who was chuckling wryly at the 'latest rationing joke – cheese to be 1 oz. [per person per week] from the beginning of May', put it: 'There is this to be said for the Germans' particular tactics. They do spread the blitz fairly over the country and give the provinces their due share instead of concentrating solely on London as they did at first. The effect is that we now have time to digest our weekly dose before being served up with another.'

When the next dose was administered, on the night of 16–17 April, it came with unprecedented ferocity. 'About the worst "blitz" we've yet experienced broke over London after 9pm last night and lasted a good seven hours. It took us right back to last September, though neither then nor since has there been anything to match the raid for non stop intensity,' wrote Heap

331

of a night that would become known in its awfulness simply as 'The Wednesday'.

On that evening Harold Nicolson dined with Sybil Colefax, the socialite interior decorator who during the blitz held 'ordinaries' (dinner parties at the Dorchester Hotel at which guests paid for themselves) and ran a canteen in Belgravia. Walking back to the Ministry of Information where he sometimes slept, since there was no transport, Nicolson noted, 'There is a hot blitz on. To the south, round about Westminster, there is a gale of fire, as red as an Egyptian dawn. To the north there is another fire which I subsequently see at close quarters. The stump of the spire of Langham Place church is outlined against pink smoke. I walk under the guns and flares and the droning of the 'planes. I fall over a brick and break my glasses. I limp into the Ministry to be told that we have sunk a large convoy between Sicily and Tripoli. This is the news we wanted.' (But five days later he would write, 'We are evacuating from Greece. The Americans will take this badly and there is a wave of defeatism sweeping the continent.')

Less than half a mile from Senate House, where the Ministry of Information was located, Anthony Heap found that the basement shelter of the Friends' Meeting House in Euston Road 'was packed by 9.30pm and though we turned in as usual the incessant drone of relays of planes flying overhead (they recurred at least one a minute), the continued gunfire, and the frequent explosion of bombs in the near vicinity all made sleep impossible. Finally, when somewhere around 3am a bomb hit the other end of the Friends House itself, penetrated two floors and shook the building from top to bottom, we all got up and dressed and kept on the qv until the all clear sounded around 4.45.'

Heap 'immediately went out to look round and in the course of an hour's walk witnessed the following fires still raging – the whole of Maples [furniture store] main building between Tottenham Court Road and Gower Street (by far the largest and most destructive of the lot). The Hotel Russell – Hebrand Street School – the Express Dairy head offices in Tavistock Place – the south wing of University College and a number of houses further along Gower Street – a factory and a block of flats in Chenies Street, one side of the Embassy cinema in Torrington Place – a block of buildings on the south side of Oxford Street – Flemings restaurant in Oxford Street and a road crater by Warings further up – and one or two minor fires off Charlotte Street. So numerous, in fact, were the fires that there couldn't have been sufficient firemen to cope with them and some were burning away and spreading unattended . . . Dawn had broken by the time I got back to the shelter for a final hour's courting of sleep. Courting was all it came to.'

June Spencer, a young ambulance driver who lodged in Cheyne Walk, Chelsea, had been out to dinner that night. After leaving the 'ARP-wine cellar' of a Spanish restaurant in Soho, she emerged

> to find Piccadilly blazing – to the 400 [a nightclub in Leicester Square] to dance for 2 hours – bad news of Chelsea.
>
> Impossible to find a taxi-driver so we walked (I was wearing a long pink and black tulle dress!) Fires were raging all around – very heavy bombing. We threw ourselves to the pavement a few times. Got a lift from Cadogan Square. Incendiary bombs all down the King's Road.
>
> Got to the ambulance station (opposite the Old Church). It was quite flat, and most of Cheyne Walk too. Glass in windows puffed out as you looked at them . . . One huge sheet of glass from the garage roof moved in the moonlight. Sydney pulled it and from underneath rose a very tall policeman with a long beard [the painter Stanley Grimm, a special constable]. Very drunk. He said he had no legs. To reassure him he was standing on them, I pulled up his trousers. In his relief he danced down the street holding Sydney's hand.
>
> Back to 97. Windows out and many holes – but all was well . . . Changed – out again – amazing sight – brilliant moon – blazing wreckage – glass, glass everywhere – ambulances and cars with flat tyres – had to carry dog home.

Nine Chelsea pensioners, one of them 101 years old, were killed when a bomb hit the Royal Hospital. And at Lambeth Palace, 'four HE bombs exploded . . . the fourth exposed a grave dating from over 100 years ago and hurled bits of corpse, still not fully decomposed, all over the place – the head landed on the roof of the church and the stench was terrible – the coffin with an inner lead casing must have been airtight – a horrible thought. The sooner cremation becomes universal the better,' wrote the Reverend Alan Don.

Theodora Fitzgibbon, an artists' model and aspiring actress, was living with the painter Peter Rose Pulham in Kings Mansions, Lawrence Street, in Chelsea. The couple were in bed when

> there was a thud as if a gigantic sack of coal had been dropped, making the room shudder, almost immediately another thud, and a tremendous explosion.

333

The window blew in and a dense cloud of greenish dust moved slowly through a gaping hole, forming the shape of a weird monster. Peter flung himself on top of me on the bed, his eyes wide and dark with fear. His face and lips, pressed onto mine, tasted gritty.

'Dear Pussy, dear Pussy.'

There was a noise like exceptionally heavy rain, and his weight became almost unbearable. The bedside light was still on: the clock said twenty-five past one. All the furniture had moved, not far, it had just moved round about a foot, except for the chair with my clothes on which was under the window. There was no sign of that. I could move only my head, for the bed was covered with lumps of plaster, broken glass, wood and what looked like small stones . . . 'I'm all right, darling, I think. But what happened? There were all those thuds, it didn't sound like a bomb.'

'Well if it wasn't a bomb, I don't know what has brought the ceiling and walls down. You're right though, it wasn't the usual long shriek' . . . Through the open window came the sound of excited voices. I turned my head to look out and saw leaping flames quite nearby.

'I can see fires.' 'That's not unusual.' 'But it is. Normally I can see the church clock tower.' He framed his face in his hands and peered out through the fog-like dust. 'I can't see the church either. I think it's gone. There are fires everywhere. I must get you out, Pussy.'

The stone staircase was littered with debris.

'Some of the banisters have gone. Go slowly, sit down if necessary and come down that way.' We slid down, slithering on our bottoms like children.

In the streets were the occupants from the lower floors, wardens, ambulances, nurses, firemen and police, all lit by torchlight, the wardens with their log sheets hanging round their necks. Someone tried to herd me into an ambulance, but I pulled away and Peter and I went into the Crossed Keys which was wide open, the door and one wall blown into the bar. The elderly couple who ran it, never known for their generosity, were sitting down sipping brandy, covered in white plaster looking dazed and very, very old, amongst the people gathered there. A local resident was in charge and gave us all a drink.

'The old church has gone!' This was repeated frequently: that they were alive seemed incomprehensible.

We soon left, and went towards the remains of Chelsea Old Church ['that rare thing, a church which no restorer had ever spoilt', mourned the *Architectural Review*] to see if we could help. The nurses' home of the Cheyne Hospital for Children had the top floor blown off: a neat nurse's bedroom, the ceiling light still shining, looked like a stage set. A warden perilously climbed up the staircase and switched it off, although there was a flaming gas main burning round the corner which floodlit the entire area. The church was nothing but an immense heap of timber and stone, flames licking through it; a large vaulted tomb with a stone urn on top rose up undamaged at the front. The New Café Lombard and all the large and small houses at the end of Old Church Street had been flung together into a giant mountain of shale-like destruction, all lit by fires and the gas main. Under that fantastic mountain were people, some still alive. Heavy stones were flung aside like pebbles: the local grocer of the street, Mr Cremonesi, put his hand down through the space and felt warm flesh. A naked unhurt woman was pulled up. An old lady appeared, staggering, from the far side of the mountain, having been flung at least thirty yards and then covered with glass, wood and bricks from which she had extricated herself. She seemed unhurt. A curious rattling sound like a time bomb made us cautious: a battered tin was moving on a stick. Below, a young woman had forced it through the bricks to attract attention. She was rescued by a war reserve policeman. A sixteen-year-old girl, pinned, only her head showing, talked to a rescue worker: she was freed but died several hours later.

Young and old brought buckets of water to supply stirrup pumps to douse fires. The dust was like a great fog. Charred papers and smouldering wood choked the helpers. Still the raid continued with whining bombs, cracking, thudding guns, droning aeroplanes, both German and our own night-fighters. Huge chandeliers of flares hanging in the sky like Roman candles illuminated the bombers' targets. Our hands were cut and bleeding . . . Several wardens, police and onlookers were talking together [on the Embankment]. Two land mines had been parachuted down on the church which is why the usual whining sound was absent. All the firewatchers at my post had been killed except Arthur Mallet.

The next day, in borrowed clothes, Fitzgibbon struggled into work half an hour late. 'No one was interested in my bomb story, they had become like fisherman's tales. I was "the one who got away".' When she went home that night Pulham greeted her with the words, 'Not a flat any longer, Pussy, a bed-sitting room . . . There's nobody else in the whole block but ourselves.'

The artist Frances Faviell, who was working in a First Aid Post in Chelsea, found 'it was now almost impossible to sketch anywhere – and absolutely forbidden to make drawings of bomb-damaged buildings without a Ministry of Works permit. Every drawing had to be passed by them and was stamped on the back as having been permitted, but not for reproduction. After Rex Whistler had told me to apply for such a permit I did do some drawings of blitzed houses in Chelsea.' Faviell was scornful of suggestions that April's heavy raids were in retaliation for the concentrated British bombing of Germany. In her view they were retribution for Roosevelt's announcement of the Lend Lease scheme for Britain, which would come into effect in June.

On 18 April Faviell's own house was hit: '*One in a million!* And the feeling I was conscious of was furious anger . . . It was our worst night yet and when news came that the Old Church [where Faviell had attended "the Day of National Prayer ordered by the King on 23 March 1941"] had gone it seemed the climax to the mounting horrors . . . "It's a pile of dust," one of the stretcher bearers said. "The whole of that bit – all Petyt Place seems to have disappeared and the firewatchers with it" [including a seventeen-year-old boy, home for the school holidays].'

Yvonne Green, a thirty-year-old Canadian woman, newly married to a Canadian army officer, lived in Old Church Street, Chelsea, and was a part-time Auxiliary Fire Service driver. On 15 April she and her husband 'dug for victory in the garden', as she wrote to her mother. 'I have carrots, beets, *onions* [which were in very short supply, since before the war most had been imported from the Netherlands, Brittany or the Channel Islands]. Lettuce and tomatoes perhaps.' The next day, although she was not on duty, Mrs Green went along to the wardens' post in Petyt Place to see if she could help. She was one of the six killed in 'The Wednesday's' raid. Her clothing 'was torn to shreds, the following remains only', recorded her death certificate: '1 AFS tunic and slacks, 1 man's blue sock, 1 portion white vest, 1 tank corps brooch, pink brassiere, part of red belt, 1 lipstick, 1 lighter, 1 wallet, 1 Identity Card, Driving Licence, AFS card, 6 stamps @ 2½d.' The cause of death was given as 'bomb blast', and Yvonne Marie Green was 'deemed to have been buried by Council'.

Across the river from Chelsea the Battersea house in which Doris Pierce lived with her parents, sister and brother was also hit. Her brother Jim had been badly hurt, and was taken to hospital. The rest of the family had been dug out from the rubble, and though cut, bruised and shaken, were not badly injured. But taking stock of the situation we all came to the conclusion that we had lost everything apart from a few items in the front room. We had no clothes, beds, kitchenware, furnishings or personal belongings, it was as if we had never been. Dad looked white and haggard and didn't seem to be able to say anything coherent but 'b[loody] hell' again and again, but it was Mum who was most affected . . . she stood with tears in her eyes looking at the shattered remnants of twenty years of marriage. All her hard work and sacrifices over the years had ended in a flash . . . For the first time in our lives we had to comfort her instead of the other way round. We had to be optimistic, Daphne and I, and assure her that we could get another home together, this wasn't the end, we would fight back. There were all the usual words said to bolster ourselves, but they were really empty words without substance. We had reached rock bottom and were frightened, we had been bombed by day and night and in spite of everything had managed our daily lives and achieved a sort of routine, we had come through a number of hazards and believed ourselves invincible, but we weren't, the worst had happened. Could we really pick ourselves up? Had we still enough energy to cope with what was to come? I had always been optimistic . . . but the events of that night had drained the optimism all away. I could only dwell on the fact that what had happened once could easily happen again.

Our reveries were interrupted by a neighbour's daughter . . . on hearing that Daphne and I hadn't a coat between us, Jessie offered to find us something from her own clothes. We assured her it would only be a temporary loan, by the next day we would have an allocation of money from the council to buy essential clothing. Jessie was a lot thinner than us, so inevitably things didn't fit very well, but she did her best. There was an oatmeal-coloured cardigan for Daphne and a full length lilac-coloured coat for me. It was too small to do up but it went perfectly with my mauve footwear [a pair of bedroom slippers with Cuban heels and matching silk bows that she had been issued with from the emergency supply at her local rest centre].

Doris worked at the Army and Navy Stores in Victoria Street, and the next morning she and her sister set off to inform the shop that Doris would need a few days off to sort her life out.

We caught the train to Victoria and on the way there was plenty of evidence of the ferocity of the night's air raid, but there were no diversions, and we alighted at our stop. Walking along classy Victoria Street, I suddenly felt conscious of our appearance. Daphne in her grubby plimsolls [also a rest-centre issue] and too-small cardigan, me in my fancy slippers, too-small coat and both of us with grey dusty hair . . . because we hadn't been able to have a bath and hair wash yet as the water and gas was still dodgy. Strangely, we didn't get many odd looks, I suppose in wartime London, the unusual wasn't unusual any more. In the normal course of events, I would never draw attention to myself, but I think I felt a certain pride that we had 'risen from the ashes' so to speak and had survived our baptism of fire. Seeing the well-heeled shoppers of Victoria and feeling the warmth of the spring sun I found my natural optimism beginning to surface; things could only get better now.

For several days after the raid Anthony Heap roamed around London looking at the devastation: the 'high explosive wreckage around the BMA [British Medical Association] building in Woburn Place . . . St Pancras Square, where a land mine demolished the entire block of flats and shattered all the surrounding houses with heavy casualties [this was one of the worst incidents the borough had, with seventy-seven killed and fifty-two wounded out of a total of two hundred shelterers]. The First Aid Post at the back of St Pancras Hospital . . . some schools at the foot of Haverstock Hill – a land mine between Grays Inn Road and Kings X . . . The West End . . . is in a sorry state. Among the buildings completely written off – the Shaftesbury Theatre and the block of tenements opposite . . . Stone's Chop House in Panton Street. Buzzards in Oxford Street. Slightly damaged were Selfridges and Peter Robinsons (this is the fourth time PR's windows mid frontage have been blown in). Big slabs of Oxford Street were damaged beyond repair on both sides . . . Any number of thoroughfares blocked with debris and the air was thick with dust and smoke and the smell of smouldering ruins.'

By Friday, 18 April 'the ruins of the Bourne Estate and Gray's Inn [which] were laid waste were *still* smouldering . . . the City Temple and St Andrew's [a Wren church] behind it were completely burnt out. So were several shops and buildings in Leather Lane, High Holborn, Gray's Inn Road and Red Lion Street . . . such was but a fraction of the total havoc wrought on London during this "one night of the blitz" which the press and radio both here and in Germany agree to have been the worst we've had so far.'

In the eight and a half hours that the raid lasted, German bombers had made a total of 685 sorties, some planes making the return shuttle to France three times that night. Eight hundred and ninety tons of bombs were dropped, including 151,230 incendiaries. Bombs fell indiscriminately from

Maidstone to Grimsby, Yarmouth and Bury St Edmunds, to Exeter, Margate and Warlingham in Surrey, where seven people died. But it was London that suffered the worst. Most of the capital was affected: from the docks, along the Thames, Holborn, where Heap peregrinated, the West End and out to the suburbs. Bomb damage was recorded in sixty-six of the 101 boroughs covered by the London Civil Defence Region, and over 2,250 fires burned, of which fifty were classified as 'major'. The South Metropolitan Gas Works at Rotherhithe exploded, the granaries opposite the Tower of London were on fire, and air-raid shelters in Holborn, Camberwell, Ealing, Lambeth and Leicester Square were hit with heavy casualties. The Houses of Parliament were damaged, as were the Admiralty and the Law Courts. St Paul's Cathedral received a direct hit, but once more the symbol of London's fortitude survived.

The jazz singer and crooner Al Bowlly, who had had such success in the 1930s with Lew Stone's Band at the Monseigneur restaurant with hits like 'Blue Moon' and 'My Melancholy Baby', had been trying to revive his career in Britain after his return from America by playing out-of-town engagements. On 16 April he had been singing at High Wycombe, but declining an invitation to stay the night, returned to his flat off Duke Street near Selfridges, and was reading in bed when a bomb hit the block. The force of the explosion threw Bowlly's bedroom door across the room, hitting him on the head and killing him. The last song he had recorded was 'When that Man is Dead and Gone'.

Two fire-watchers on the Reverend John Markham's patrol were killed when a large bomb fell on a block of flats at Elephant and Castle and damaged another nearby. The next morning Markham consulted his list of occupants and reckoned that two people were still unaccounted for. Most of the rescue parties had withdrawn, convinced that they had done their job. But the vicar persisted. 'We called and listened by a heap of bricks and mortar. Then we heard what sounded like the faint mewing of a cat. I told the [one remaining] Rescue Squad to dig, and very soon we found two girls, one dead, under the remains of a kitchen table where she had sheltered, the other still alive, sitting in the remains of an armchair nearby. She was the source of the faint sound, which was all she could make when she regained consciousness six hours later. Her throat and lungs were choked with white mortar dust, which still remains in my memory as one of the most vivid sensations of all the bombing. It had an acrid, damp sort of smell. She was rushed to hospital where she recovered quite quickly from a broken arm and severe bruising. I do not think that she ever knew how close we had been to leaving the site that April morning before we heard that faint mewing sound.'

'London looks bleary-eyed and disfigured,' wrote John Colville the next morning. 'There is a great gash in the Admiralty, St Peter's, Eaton Square has been hit [the popular vicar Austin Thompson, who had gone out onto the steps to urge people to shelter in his solid-brick church, was killed there by a bomb], Chelsea Old Church [famous from Whistler's painting] is demolished, Jermyn Street is wrecked, Mayfair has suffered badly.'

James Lees-Milne had been caught out in the raid, and had spent the night sheltering in the Piccadilly Hotel, which was hit by a bomb. When he emerged into the street as dawn broke,

Piccadilly resembled a giant skeleton asleep upon an ice floe. The eye sockets of the houses looked reproachfully at the dawn. Like lids, torn blinds and curtains fluttered from every window. The brows of the windows and portals were wrenched and plucked. On pavements and street a film of broken glass crunched under the feet like the jagged crystals of lush icicles. One had to take care they did not clamber over the edge of one's shoes. The contents of shop windows were strewn over the pavements among the broken glass. Silk shirts and brocaded dressing gowns fluttered upon area railings. The show cases of a jeweller's window had sprinkled tray loads of gold watches and bracelets as far as the kerb of the street. I stooped to pick up a handful of diamonds and emeralds – and chuck them back into the shop before they got trodden on, or looted.

The sky had the gunmetal solidity of sky before a snowstorm. Cinders showered upon our hair, faces and clothes. On all sides columns of smoke sprang from raging fires, the glint of whose flames could be seen above the rooftops, trembling upon chimney stacks and burnishing the dull surface of the sky . . . I wished to see all the damage there might be, to be saddened and maddened thereby. We could not walk up Piccadilly because a stick of bombs having fallen from the Fifty Shilling Tailor's to St. James's Church had pene-trated a gas main. Tongues of flame were belching from craters in the road. We could not walk down Jermyn Street which was blocked by rubble from collapsed houses. Here I noticed a stripped, torn trunk of a man on the pave-ment. Further on I picked up what looked like the mottled, spread leaf of a plane tree. It was a detached hand with a signet ring on the little finger.

For the *flâneur* Charles Graves,

London is definitely an unedifying spectacle. The annoying part is that we claim to have destroyed only five bombers out of the hundreds that came over last night . . . Fortnum and Mason's have been blitzed . . . Jermyn Street is a shambles . . . walked along Piccadilly with further bomb craters en route into Leicester Square, where the whole of the north-east corner has disappeared including the Café Anglais and Jack Bloomfield's pub. I hope Jack was not there . . . The cockney has a marvellously morbid sense of humour. Thousands of people were taking a Roman holiday [looking at the devastation]. We walked on to the Strand; traffic even pedestrians were diverted . . . Farringdon Street and Clerkenwell Road were blitzed. It might have been unnecessary to destroy the one remaining tower of the Crystal Palace [the rest had been destroyed by fire in 1936, but there was fear that the radio tower might be a landmark for the bombers], which happened yesterday because the Germans would probably have done it last night. The Germans have reported that it was in revenge for our bombing the centre of Berlin last Wednesday . . . They claim that it was the largest force of bombers ever sent over London. I am glad to think so. I should hate to imagine that it had been done by a small force of bombers . . . Injured people were taken into the Ministry of Information where three of them died. So the MoI has been really useful in a direct way . . .

Wherever one goes from pubs to clubs and back again to clubs, pubs and offices, there is further news of the raid last night. Streatham, Brixton, the Old Kent Road have all caught it badly. Old grey London sprawls so much that she can conceal her wounds very adequately. Walked home by a different route this morning. There are shocking sights in Holborn and Bloomsbury. They are still dampening down the burning ruins of Gerrard Street which is cordoned off. In Portland Place whole blocks of flats have been shattered. Marylebone [where Graves lived] (touch wood and don't look round) is largely undamaged. Went on a Home Guard parade but only six people turned up for street fighting. So we paraded at the Stag's Head and had a drink.

On 'The Wednesday' 1,180 people were killed, including many ARP workers, and 2,230 were seriously injured.

'The Saturday' three days later was the heaviest attack of the war on Britain so far. Again it was London that was the primary target, though there were widespread attacks throughout the Home Counties. There was no deadly 'bombers' moon' that night, but low cloud, mist and intermittent rain, though this proved little deterrent. More than a thousand tons of high-explosives were dropped between 9.15 p.m. and 4.15 a.m. on the night of 19–20 April, the most ever in a single night's raid, plus 153,096 incendiaries.

This time areas along the Thames, from Tower Bridge downstream to the docks in the east, took the brunt. The Royal Victoria Docks were once again consumed by fire, as were the East and West India Docks, the granaries at Millwall Docks and the streets around Greenwich Power Station. The Royal Naval College was hit, and so were St Peter's Hospital, Stepney, and innumerable houses and tenements. East Ham was heavily bombed, with whole terraces of houses being razed. In Nutall Street, Shoreditch, three blocks of LCC flats and an underground shelter were destroyed: forty-six people were listed as killed, and another forty-six were missing.

The toll mounted: across the country a total of 6,065 civilians were killed in April 1941. The sense of material loss was palpable too. Cityscapes were reconfigured, familiar landmarks erased. People felt disorientated as they wandered through streets that had been familiar to them all their lives, unsure what a jagged wall, a heap of bricks represented. The sound of glass being swept up, of crashing masonry as unsafe buildings were dynamited, became the sombre symphony of those late spring days as dust hung like an ochre pall in the air. Piles of rubble lay everywhere, despite the Herculean efforts of the energetic mandarin Sir Warren Fisher, formerly head of the Civil Service but since September 1940 the Special Commissioner for the London region in charge of the restoration of bomb-damaged roads and public utilities, the demolition of unsafe buildings, and the salvage of valuable materials such as timber, metals, bricks and hardcore. Fisher, an impatient man with a tendency to fall out with everyone, was determined to organise the clearing up of blitz rubble as soon as possible, since he thought there was 'nothing worse for morale than to have this debris untouched for everyone to see'. Five thousand Pioneer Corps soldiers had been drafted in to help with clearance work in mid-October 1940. They were joined by a large workforce of the unemployed, and by early December this force had been swelled by a further 8,000 troops, many skilled engineers. A number of Indians from the Punjab, specialists in railway construction, arrived to assist in getting vital transport links operational again as soon as possible.

Transport was frequently disrupted, with diversions to avoid UXBs and bomb craters. In any case, as Anthony Heap wrote, 'Travelling by bus these days isn't what it used to be. For on most of them the windows have been rendered opaque by green gauze material spread thereon to prevent flying glass and dim the lights at night.' Heap had 'never realised what an innocent pleasure one used to derive (and still can on some) from looking out of bus windows. Just another case of not appreciating anything until deprived of it.'

Bricks and rubble were carted away to be used in the building of runways, some sent to the United States in ships that had carried food and supplies across the Atlantic as part of the Lend Lease arrangements. Whatever might be useful in rebuilding – timber, bricks, girders – was stored; everything else was burned. Since it was spring, nature, abhorring a vacuum, crept into the crevices of destruction. Soon willow herb, buddleia, conch grass, brambles and weeds pushed through cracks, reclaiming the bomb sites, often for years, sometimes for decades.

May 1941 was bitterly cold, and the 4th saw what Anthony Heap thought was 'a splendid idea really', the introduction of Double Summer Time: 'The clocks were advanced a further hour overnight in addition to the already existing hour which has been maintained throughout the winter. So that it doesn't get dark now till after 10pm and we need only go down to the shelter to sleep and not waste half the evening there.' The primary purpose of the extended daylight hours was to enable those working on the land to extend their productive hours, though according to Heap, 'the farmers with their usual pig headedness opposed the measure, but fortunately it made no difference. It's to last till August 10th, and will of course mean regular evenings' entertainment again.' The Metropolitan Police agreed that cinema performances could finish an hour later than previously, at 10 p.m.

On Saturday, 10 May a crowd of 93,500 spectators crammed into Wembley stadium, its roof camouflaged with black paint, where Preston North End were playing Arsenal in the FA Cup final. One man was censorious. The Labour MP Emanuel Shinwell, while proclaiming himself to be 'no killjoy. I want to see the people of this country getting a fair measure of recreation,' nevertheless wondered 'whether we are crazy. Think of the petrol consumed, the transport used and the services used for this so-called recreation and ask yourselves whether we are really organizing our resources for war.' The young Tom Finney, playing on the right wing that day, was Preston's greatest hope; for the 'Gunners' it was Denis Compton, both a cricket and a football international, and the full-back and England captain Eddie Hapgood. But when the final whistle blew at 5 p.m. there was no victor. The game was drawn 1–1, with Compton scoring Arsenal's goal. Preston would win the replay 2–1.

There was still plenty of evening ahead: since it was Double Summer Time the blackout began at 10.21 p.m. Less than an hour later, the alert sounded. Since the London boroughs received a signal from Scotland Yard, near the Houses of Parliament, to activate their 'air raid imminent' signals, there was usually a slight discrepancy between the 'awful warbling-like sound of a howling wolf' ululating across one borough and another. That evening was no exception. In Westminster the alert sounded at 11 p.m.: in Croydon in south London it had been seven minutes earlier, and in Kennington two minutes later.

In South Norwood, Sidney Chave prepared to start his shift as a fire-watcher, sitting in his box room peering out at the sky – 'It was a perfect moonlit night, almost as clear as day' – while his wife took their daughter Jillian to the shelter. At 11.15 p.m. the first bombs fell. Five hundred and seven aircraft converged on London, wheeled, turned back, reloaded and returned. By the time the All Clear sounded at 5.24 a.m., 711 tons of high-explosive bombs and 86,173 incendiaries had fallen on the capital.

Again the docks were the main target, and soon both sides of the Thames were alight from Victoria Docks to Waterloo Bridge. Fires joined up to form conflagrations from Stepney and Bow to the City, with smoke rising as high as 10,000 feet in the loop of the Thames. Other fierce fires fanned north to Hackney Marshes. With 2,154 fires burning across sixty-one of the London Defence Region's boroughs, the fire services were stretched to breaking point. That night the Thames was low, and many mains were fractured, reducing water pressure to little more than a dribble as firemen struggled with the flames. Soon every route across the city was impassable.

The buildings hit that night read like a tourist's guide to London: the Royal Naval College at Greenwich (again), the War Office, the Law Courts in The Strand, the Public Record Office in Chancery Lane, Fleet Street, the British Museum, the Palace of St James, the Houses of Parliament. In the City the destruction included the Mansion House, the official residence of the Lord Mayor of London, Sweeting's famous oyster bar in Queen Victoria Street, another Wren church, St Nicholas Cole Abbey, and a number of guild halls such as the Butchers', Cordwainers', Mercers' and Salters'. St Mary-le-Bow and St Stephen's Walbrook were hit – St Stephen's, a Wren church, had been damaged in the 29 December raid; now it was destroyed.

The nine-storey, white-concrete Faraday House, the largest telephone

exchange in the world, with its frontage on Queen Victoria Street, strad-
dled ten acres. It was built like a citadel, and inside sheltered the former
Home Secretary Sir John Anderson and the Minister of Labour Ernest Bevin.
Also at stake were Britain's links with the rest of the world: if Faraday House
were to be destroyed, the island really would stand isolated and alone. A
fleet of lorries carried thousand-gallon loads of water through the cratered
and burning streets, then tipped them into a 5,000-gallon steel dam to feed
the fire hoses. So essential was the exchange's survival that if that didn't
work, orders were given to dynamite nearby buildings to create a firebreak.
But that might threaten the foundations of St Paul's Cathedral just up the
hill, the symbol of London's survival.

From the offices of the *Daily Mirror* in Fetter Lane, the newspaper's
chairman, Cecil King, gazed on a desolate scene. 'The smoke was such that
you could not see that it was a full moon with no clouds, the air was full
of flying sparks; every now and then there was the roar of a collapsing
building . . . The Temple Church, one of the great monuments of English
history, was on fire . . . St Clement Dane [of the famed nursery rhyme
"Oranges and Lemons", where Dr Johnson had worshipped] had been gutted,
and only the spire was alight half way up the top and sending out showers
and sparks – an odd and rather beautiful spectacle.'

Alan Don, now a canon, had been appointed rector of St Margaret's
church, Westminster, in January 1941, and with his wife Muriel had moved
from their apartment in Lambeth Palace into 20 Dean's Yard, from where
Don had a perfect view of the nine-hundred-year-old Westminster Abbey's
damage that night. Many of the windows had been blown out in earlier
raids, but 60,000 sandbags were stacked around the tombs of the monarchs
buried there, including Edward the Confessor, behind the high altar and
Henry V under his Chantry Chapel, while the Coronation Chair on which
George VI had sat during his coronation four years earlier had been removed
to Gloucester Cathedral for safekeeping. The Stone of Scone had been
'removed and hidden privily', the choristers evacuated to Christ's Hospital
in Sussex, and an 'internal ARP' team of forty or so Abbey staff and volunteers were always on duty. St Margaret's, the fifteenth-century parish church
of the House of Commons, always a fashionable venue for weddings –
Samuel Pepys had married there in 1614, as had Winston Churchill and
Clementine Hozier in 1908 – had also been damaged in earlier raids.
Westminster School had evacuated to Herefordshire, and the firemen and
women stationed in Little Dean's Yard made use of its premises for offices

and sleeping quarters now the boys had gone. Alan Don would lend them the key to the gate of the Abbey gardens so they could enjoy the sunshine while they waited for a summons.

Soon after midnight a shower of incendiaries dropped on the Abbey roof: with its 'crevices, ledges, little variegated knobs of stone abound[ing] every-where . . . each one of these myriad ornaments became a possible fire-trap'. The fire-watchers were able to deal with most of them, though one fired the lantern roof, causing it to crash down onto the pavement 130 feet below and burn out.

The Victoria Tower, part of the House of Lords just across the road, was surrounded by scaffolding, since the limestone was being cleaned and repaired. This meant that an incendiary could smoulder there unseen. Police Sergeant Alec Forbes caught a glimpse of a small fire that threatened to take hold, and climbed three hundred feet up the scaffolding carrying a heavy sandbag to extinguish it. Nearby, two auxiliary policemen had already plum-meted to their deaths when a high-explosive bomb struck the octagonal turret of the Royal Gallery in Victoria Tower, used on ceremonial occasions, and brought down a shower of debris, and the policemen with it. The rubble had to be cleared, because if there was not a clear passage through the maze of the Palace of Westminster's miles of corridors, the risk of a fire being impossible to reach would be high.

At the Abbey, the deanery was blazing out of control, and a bomb had lodged in the roof, burning directly over the tomb of the unknown warrior from the previous world war. Over the road, the hammerbeam roof of Westminster Hall, the finest in the country, was on fire. A message was sent to Downing Street by the desperate Dean. It was relayed to Churchill, who was watching a film at Ditchley Park near Oxford, the home of Conservative MP Ronald Tree, who had offered it as a weekend sanctuary because Chequers was vulnerably near to London. 'The Abbey must be saved at all cost,' the Prime Minister replied imperiously. However, at 1 a.m. 'the water supply gave out and there was no water in the hoses', reported Don.

While firemen were concentrating on controlling the fires in the House of Lords, the Commons, at the other end of the Palace, was also alight, and there was an unexploded bomb beneath the ARP control room. The fires, fed by draughts from the labyrinthine heating ducts below the floors, were soon burning out of control: by morning the walls of the chamber of the House of Commons had bowed outwards in the heat, the roof had collapsed, the speaker's chair was no more, and the green leather Members' benches, embossed with gold portcullises, were charred and saturated by water. It took two days to extinguish the last of the fires.

At about 5 a.m. Canon Alan Don 'looked across the river and saw that Lambeth Palace was on fire'. As he raced across the Thames he passed the much-stricken St Thomas's Hospital, which, a Casualty Sister wrote, was experiencing 'quite the noisiest and most nerve-racking raid we had so far experienced. It was a night of fire, when incendiary bombs fairly whistled and rained down on us without ceasing . . . falling on the old theatres and the wards and the piles of wood and debris from former raids. There were not enough people to cope with so many fires, and firemen and engines were in demand everywhere . . . Many firemen and girls from mobile units came in, not only bringing patients, but as patients themselves. Besides injuries many had sore eyes from dust and smoke. The noise was so terrific that we in Casualty were advised to descend to the basement and receive patients there.' Burning debris intermittently crashed down the lift shaft to the basement, and 'to make matters worse, a large pipe burst and there was a flood and there was a loss of precious water. This was squeeged [sic] and swept away from the patients in the corridor for about two hours by an army of willing workers, some of whom were the First Aid staff already on the spot in the basement.' Fortunately no patients or staff died that night, though two firemen lost their lives in a bomb explosion in the hospital's garage yard.

When Alan Don arrived at Lambeth Palace he found the Archbishop, Cosmo Lang, safe: he had retired to bed at three in the morning, after having been knocked off his feet by bomb blast, though the mass of humanity sheltering in the Palace's corridors, added to the cacophony of the raid, kept the prelate from sleep. Lollard's Tower, with its iron rings to which heretics, followers of John Wycliffe in the fourteenth century, had been tethered, was gutted by fire, as was the chapel.

In St Paul's Cathedral, the architect Ralph Tubbs was on duty that night as a fire-watcher. 'We had an unbelievable view of the fires round St Paul's . . . everything within a hundred yards of the Cathedral was burnt to the ground. And we had this extraordinary view – mind you, we didn't have much time to look at it because we had our own job to do. But it was remarkable . . . I remember coming down at four in the morning into the main body of the Cathedral. The glass had been blown out at high level all round the dome, and these great sparks were blowing – the sparks from burning buildings all around were being blown in through the windows and circling down, and it was really, one shouldn't say it I suppose, but it was almost poetic seeing these great sparks circling round and round the dome.'

The Tower of London had been deluged by incendiaries early in the raid, setting fire to the Constable Tower. Near Lincoln's Inn the Royal College of Surgeons, founded in the reign of Henry VIII as the Barber-Surgeon Company, was hit, and over half the 6,000 anatomical and pathological specimens and surgical instruments collected over four centuries were lost, though stretcher-bearers salvaged as many pickled specimens as they could. Fortunately, two of the key exhibits, the skeleton of the thief and thief-taker Jonathan Wild, immortalised in Daniel Defoe's novel and by John Gay in his *Beggar's Opera*, hanged in 1725, and that of the seven-foot-ten-inch Irish giant Charles Byrne, had been evacuated to the country.

Gray's Inn burned too, despite the valiant efforts of its fire-watchers. The Great Hall, where Shakespeare's *Comedy of Errors* had first been performed, was razed to the ground, the library of over 30,000 books reduced to little but ashes. At the other two of England's four Inns of Court, Middle and Inner Temple, resident barristers acting as fire-watchers joined firemen in a night-long battle to save the buildings despite scant water and a stiff breeze that ignited dormant flames and scattered smouldering wood. When it was clear that the fires were unquenchable, the benchers darted into the 750-year-old Temple church, rescuing what they could of the valuables within, and managed to wrest some oil paintings of their famous forebears from the walls of Inner Temple Hall. But the 90,000 books in the library went up in flames, and Lamb Building burned like matchwood. 'There were moments,' reflected one of the Inner Temple barristers, 'when it seemed there was no limit to the havoc being wrought.'

At the Queen's Hall, home since 1895 of the 'Proms' founded by the impresario Robert Newman and the conductor Sir Henry Wood, an audience of over 2,000 had listened that evening to Malcolm Sargent conducting the Royal Choral Society and the London Philharmonic Orchestra in a performance of Elgar's *The Dream of Gerontius*. In the early hours of Sunday morning an incendiary fell through the roof and blazed as brightly as an acetylene welding lamp. The hall's fire system was found to have run dry, and though the fire brigade promised to come, they were delayed and the building was devoured by fire.

A 'bread basket' of incendiaries fell through the roof of the British Museum, where the domed Reading Room had been damaged by an oil bomb in the autumn, and a high-explosive had destroyed over 250 valuable old books in the King's Library. Many of the galleries had been closed, and at weekends visitors were restricted to three hundred a day, but gradually more galleries had been reopening. But now, on 10 May, the fires took such a hold that the museum's fire-watchers were powerless. It took forty-five minutes for the fire brigade to arrive, by which time the roof of the Roman Britain Gallery was burning furiously, and the library and other galleries full of priceless antiquities were threatened.

London's transport system was seriously disrupted: a 1,000-kg bomb fell on the concourse of King's Cross station and ripped through to the Circle Line below. Paddington was damaged too, as were many underground stations, starting with Rotherhithe, where incendiaries started a fire at 11.33 p.m. A bomb exploded in the tunnel between St James's Park and Victoria; forty-five minutes later a bomb blasted a milk train off the rails between East Acton and Wood Lane, and throughout the night bombs fell on stations and mainline rail lines across the capital, including Paddington, Tufnell Park, Hammersmith, Great Portland Street, Drayton Park, Moorgate, Clapham South, Victoria, Stepney Green, Surrey Docks and High Street Kensington. Baker Street station was deluged with incendiaries, and a train waiting at Platform 4 burst into flames.

General Raymond E. Lee, the US Military Attaché in London, looked out from his room in Mayfair, where he was entertaining the American writer and journalist Vincent Sheean and his wife. 'The whole night sky was lit up by a huge yellowish disc of a full moon, while the horizon was illuminated by a great number of fires which extended around us in a huge ring. As a rule, the fires before had appeared like rose red illuminations, but tonight a large number of them had huge forked flames leaping up towards the heavens, which indicated to me that they were buildings which had been ignited on top by incendiary bombs. I could count no less than fifteen of them all around us, and it really looked as if Claridge's hotel was the exact hub and center of the whole design.' Not far away in Eaton Square a trench shelter situated between the 'Dig for Victory' allotments took two direct hits; among the dead was Westminster's Mayor, sixty-seven-year-old Councillor Leonard Eaton-Smith, who was on his usual nightly tour of the shelters. Only that afternoon Canon Don had been trying to persuade Eaton-Smith to accept the post of 'People's Warden' at St Margaret's. An hour or so earlier, another Mayor, Albert Henley of Bermondsey, was also killed as he stood near the borough's fire-control centre.

Soho had a bad night. Two high-explosive bombs, and an oil bomb that did not explode, fell on the corner of Dean Street and Old Compton Street. Fortunately there were no casualties, but the Patisserie Valerie, a Soho institution, was destroyed. The Central London Electricity Company in St Martin's Lane was hit by a 1,000-kg 'Hermann'. The caretaker and his wife were killed in their basement flat, and firemen had to deal with a nightmare cauldron of boiling oil and sulphuric acid.

At least twenty flats were destroyed by another 1,000-kg bomb which fell on the Millbank Estate, a pioneer of the LCC's municipal housing provision, built on the site of the old Millbank Prison at the turn of the century, but rescuers were able to reach most of those trapped in an underground shelter. A building in Stratton Street, Mayfair, was hit, and its top floors demolished, but its steel-framed construction proved more able to withstand bomb damage than traditionally-built brick-and-mortar buildings. Carr's Hotel, off Piccadilly, also received a direct hit, as did the Alexandra Hotel in Knightsbridge, where twenty-four people perished when a bomb brought five floors crashing down; three small private hotels on Vauxhall Bridge Road in Pimlico were razed too. Since these hotels were the workplaces of a number of prostitutes, the proprietors were unable to provide a definitive list of who might be buried in the ruins, which made the search for survivors even more problematic than usual. Nearby, the Palmolive soap factory was destroyed, and also in Pimlico, Dolphin Square, a purpose-built complex of flats much favoured as London *pieds à terre* by MPs and top civil servants, was hit, with numerous casualties. In Belgravia and Chelsea, three churches were hit: St Michael's, Ebury Street; Holy Trinity, Sloane Square; and St Columba's, Pont Street. St John's, Smith Square, across the river from Lambeth Palace, known as 'Queen Anne's footstool' because of the monarch's petulant response to its design, was gutted; its services decamped to Canon Don's St Margaret's until it could be restored as one of London's finest classical music venues. The vicar of St Silas church in Nunhead, south London, was killed by a bomb, as were the six ARP wardens he was in conversation with outside his church.

At Elephant and Castle, 'an area of about five acres used as shops, dwellings, cinemas, churches, railway arches, warehouses etc, [was] severely damaged by explosion and fire'. Of the six roads that radiated from the Elephant, only one, London Road, was clear for the fire services to get to the conflagration. Water mains had been blasted apart, and water was haemorrhaging uselessly into the ground, while the Emergency Water Supply tanks in the area, in basements and swimming pools, were getting dangerously low. Nearby, along the New Kent Road, a block of tenement flats had collapsed, killing twenty-four people, including a couple and their five children. By 2 a.m. there were nearly three hundred firemen fighting the inferno at Elephant and Castle: as they managed to douse one fire, another flared up. Seventeen were killed when a bomb fell through the roof of the Surrey Music Hall where they were fighting a fire: the force of the blast hurled one of the engines across St George's Circus and into the Salvation Army hostel where George Orwell had once lived as a 'down and out'. Water supplies ran low, and the rubble that fell continually on the hoses flattened, blocked and tore them open, rendering them useless.

Government regulations, framed in a gentler age, forbade using anything but fresh water from the mains on fires in food warehouses or shops, for fear of pollution. That night, fighting fires in the docks, around Waterloo station, all over London, firemen were desperate for water, any water, including 'contaminated water' from the Thames and canals.

Kenneth Sinclair-Loutit had experienced bombing during the Spanish Civil War, when he had led a British Medical Aid Unit in support of the International Brigade. He had returned to London to finish his medical studies at Bart's Hospital, and was elected a Labour Councillor for Holborn. In 1939 Admiral Sir Edward Evans, the Senior Commissioner for London Civil Defence Region, offered Sinclair-Loutit a job as Finsbury's Medical Officer for Civil Defence. 'So at the age of 27, I found myself in charge of an autonomous municipal department employing several hundred men and women spread out in First Aid Posts (situated in the empty schools), a Mobile Unit, a Depot for Stretcher Parties with their transport as well as a mortuary. This service worked in cooperation with the Municipal Engineers Light and Heavy Rescue Parties, together with a central staff of instructors and supervisors plus local doctors who had volunteered to help.' After the blitz started, Sinclair-Loutit 'was out every night of that weird period, the Finsbury group worked with courage in conditions that were certainly intimidating. The noise of descending bombs with the shake of the ground under your belly while tunnelling underground to dig out people already imprisoned by an earlier bomb, leaves you with nothing to imagine. You are face to face with a form of Russian roulette in which the trigger is pulled by someone else.'

His wife at the time, Thora, had been born in Abertillery in South Wales, the daughter of a miner: 'Once, when I was tunnelling to get at casualties through a mountain of debris that had once been a block of flats, I realised I was faced with the same problems as those of rescue after a fall in a mine. I got invaluable lessons from Abertillery and a miner's pick which I always had with me during air raid duty. It probably saved my life on more than one occasion when a cave-in was stopped by switching it to the vertical with the blades acting as a short roof beam.'

On the night of 10–11 May, Sinclair-Loutit 'was picking my way up City Road when I scented the most wonderful aroma of good coffee. Lipton's warehouse was blazing: it was a major incident and the Control Officer had been calling for reinforcements.' Nearby there were a number of crowded air-raid shelters, and he feared that a major fire would serve as a marker for the next wave of bombers. The water mains had been hit, and supplies for the fire engines were insufficient. 'The coffee aroma was real, torrents of good freshly infused coffee were rolling out of the carcass of the warehouse as the stocks burnt and the water percolated back into the sewers . . . as the fire gained the water supply diminished. I suggested the unthinkable: we opened a sewer manhole and pumped the torrent of newly infused coffee back onto the fire. The [fire]man [from Chalfont in Buckinghamshire, part of the "ultimate reserve force"] who was to direct the hose went up and up that narrow ladder until it was swung over towards the blazing warehouse. He was frightened when he went up the ladder. He was a brave man, on top of it, fighting an apocalypse. This must be the only example of firefighting with . . . café espresso.'*

'London was in flames,' typed the American journalist Quentin Reynolds in his room in the Savoy as Fleet Street, Ludgate Circus, Shoe Lane, Fetter Lane, Holborn and Blackfriars were consumed by flames. 'Across the river a solid sheet of maddened fire banked the river for nearly half a mile.' In Hackney at least twenty people died when a tenement block was hit; nine were killed in a similar incident in Islington; twenty-five in Peckham; five people were blown to pieces when a bomb exploded in the tram tunnel in Lancaster Place where they were sheltering. When a shelter at Peek Frean's biscuit factory in Bermondsey was hit, the bodies of those killed or fatally injured lay in the yard while ambulances ferried those with any hope of

---

* Sinclair-Loutit was awarded an MBE for his service during the blitz. He went to Buckingham Palace with his wife and mother to receive it. 'The King, George VI . . . had the gift of making the brief phrase, "It gives me much pleasure to decorate you" sound extremely personal. When he went on to say "Please tell them in Finsbury how proud I was of London during those times," I also felt very proud myself.'

survival through the craters and falling bombs to Guy's Hospital. An entire family died in Barking in the East End when a stray 1,000-kg bomb was dropped, presumably in error, on a residential street.

It was the worst night of the blitz. The carnage and destruction went on all night, leaving whole areas of London in ruins. Not until eight minutes to six did the flat, steady sound of the All Clear finally sound. 'The day seemed unable to dawn,' wrote Canon Don, gazing a few minutes later from Westminster Bridge at 'the thick pall of smoke that hung across London' and the flames still leaping from St John's, Smith Square. Westminster Abbey stood roofless, and when John Colville arrived there for communion at 8 a.m., 'burnt paper, from some demolished paper mill was falling like leaves on a windy autumn day . . . there were fire-engines, and the policeman at the door said to me "There will not be any services in the Abbey today, Sir," exactly as if it were closed for spring cleaning. I turned towards Westminster Hall, on the roof of which I could see flames still leaping. Smoke rose from some invisible point in the pile of Parliament buildings beyond. I talked to a fireman. He showed me Big Ben, the face of which was pocked and scarred, and told me a bomb had gone right through the Tower. The one thing that had given him great pleasure during the night was that Big Ben had struck two o'clock a few minutes after giving the proper time.'

Colville, who only three weeks before the raid had 'look[ed] at London's landmarks more carefully now, with a feeling that it may be the last time I shall see them' as he walked through the streets, now 'stood on Westminster Bridge . . . St Thomas's Hospital was ablaze, the livid colour of the sky extended from Lambeth to St Paul's, flames were visible all along the Embankment, there was smoke rising thickly as far as the eye could see. After no previous raid has London looked so wounded next day. After breakfast I rang the P.M. at Ditchley and described what I had seen. He was very grieved that William Rufus's roof at Westminster Hall had gone. He told me that we had shot down forty-five [German planes] . . . which is a good result.' (In fact Fighter Command had exaggerated: the correct number was thirty-three.)

But Churchill was rather distracted that Sunday morning. The previous day Rudolf Hess, Hitler's deputy, had parachuted into Scotland, apparently intent on speaking with the Duke of Hamilton, whom he had met at the Berlin Olympics in 1936. The motives of Hess, who first gave his name as 'Horn', were bound to be suspect, though his intention seemed to be to broker some sort of compromise peace. Churchill sent the deluded and confused German to the Tower of London while he decided how best to deal with him. 'There has never been such a fantastic occurrence . . . the rumours and theories are diverse and amusing,' commented Colville. Cyril Dunn noted that 'the evening papers had, of course, the unhappy duty of deciding *why* Hess was in Britain. Untrammeled by responsibility, the general public are talking about nothing else, and with wild originality . . . It is assumed that the Germans have announced his madness in order to discredit anything he may say. To this the British officials have replied by painting him as the least offensive of the Nazis, a young man [Hess was in fact forty-seven] of real if somewhat reckless political ideals who has been misled by the Nazi villains, in a word, one who up to last week was a brutal sexual pervert & drug fiend, is now almost a gentleman. "I should think that tomorrow *The Times* will call him "Mr. Hess," ' said one of Dunn's colleagues. 'We must not make a hero of him,' Churchill warned Harold Nicolson when he tried to probe the Prime Minister about Hess's arrival.

Most Londoners had neither gas nor water, and that would remain the case for more than forty-eight hours for many. The transport system was in chaos. For twenty-four hours Marylebone station was the only one with trains still running: King's Cross, Euston, Paddington and Liverpool Street were open by Monday, but Waterloo and Victoria remained closed for a week. Thirty miles of underground track had been destroyed, and stations closed. It was nearly the end of July before the Circle Line between King's Cross and Baker Street reopened. Nearly a thousand roads were closed, made impassable by UXBs – there were 162 – bomb craters or fallen masonry. There were few trams or trolleybuses, and no buses at all in the City or crossing the river until Blackfriars Bridge was reopened on Tuesday. Higher wages than those that could be earned in war production were offered to workers to get the craters cleared of debris so vital services could be reconnected. There were few takers.

The battle to save Faraday House was still being waged at mid-morning on Sunday, 11 May. All fire officers' leave was cancelled, and a thousand reinforcements had been drafted in from outside the capital. Many firemen, coughing continuously from the effects of smoke and dust, their uniforms sodden, soaked through to the skin, cold and uncomfortable, had been on duty for twelve hours. They were exhausted, their faces blackened by soot and smoke, their eyes red-rimmed. It was not until six o'clock on Sunday evening that it was officially declared that Faraday House was out of danger and that St Paul's, again threatened by fire, had once again survived. But hundreds of the 2,154 fires started by the raid continued to burn.

The *Daily Herald* journalist Mea Allan, who intended to survey the damage 'from the East End to Chelsea . . . left Golders Green station in the morning in brilliant sunshine; stepped out at Leicester Square station into a grey overcast day, leaden clouds above and visibility bad – like a November fog threatening to come down and envelop the city. The sun did not break through the smoke pall till 12.30 . . . all morning we had a black snowstorm – burnt out paper, etc., drifting down. It was incredible – every street littered with it. I have never seen such widespread damage.'

Every Londoner was affected by the loss of or serious damage to landmarks that were long familiar to them, even if their own homes had escaped. Many felt an urgent compulsion to see the damage for themselves. Charles Graves was contemptuous of such 'blitz tourists', or 'gawkers', but his scorn seems misplaced. The tragedy of the blitz was not a private affair; the sense of bereavement was not vicarious. If London called upon its citizens to defend it, to endure the endless assaults, to 'Keep Calm and Carry On' in the slogan of the times (appropriated today for mugs, tea towels and mouse mats), they had to be able to try to make sense of their city's wounds in whatever way they could.

Anthony Heap set off on his customary post-raid walk to check out the damage on Sunday morning. He noted

various shops burnt out in Tottenham Court Road, houses demolished in Fitzroy Square and Fitzroy St.; a good part of both Charlotte St. and Old Compton St. . . . completely destroyed by fire . . . But it wasn't until I hit Fleet St. that I came across the really big stuff. Huge areas on both sides of it had been burnt right out – not so much the 'street' itself as behind it. Ludgate Circus was a shambles and New Bridge St. one gigantic network of hose pipes leading up from the river at Blackfriars to fight the fires burning in Ludgate Hill, Old Bailey, and elsewhere. Ludgate Hill was in fact ruins and nothing was left of St Bride St., Shoe Lane, Charterhouse St., and the whole length of Farringdon St. north of Holborn Viaduct and very little of Smithfield and the south end of Farringdon Rd. These are plain, unexaggerated facts. This whole area has been virtually laid waste . . . but it didn't end there . . . what little had been left of Gray's Inn from the last show-down was finally disposed of. The north front of Lincoln's Inn too had taken a rap and more of High Holborn, including the stadium has been hit. The best part of Red Lion Street and Eagle Street were burnt out. Bedford Row had taken three direct hits and, as a piece de resistance, the whole of Theobald's Rd. (both sides) from Bedford Row right up to Southampton Row, together with the south end of Lamb's Conduit Street had been brought to the ground. The casualties must have been enormous and though the main brunt of the attack must obviously have been concentrated on this extensive area adjacent to the city, I should think the total damage sustained was as great as anything inflicted in any previous single raid. And this is the price we have to pay for so called 'democracy'. Is it worth it? I shall leave posterity to judge. The world is too insane for anyone to hope to make any sense out of it.

Charles Graves's world had been turned upside down by the raid too. 'Lunched at the Savoy. For the first time in the history of the Savoy we had our vegetables served *à la Lyons* [Corner House], already placed on a dish . . . Walked back by Paddington Street, but had to make detour. The "Pitt's Head", one of my favourite local pubs, had a direct hit. The rubble is only a yard or two above the level of the ground. The publican's wife was miraculously saved, but he was duly killed. Dined at the Moulin d'Or, which was also hit last night but is still carrying on by candlelight. We even had steak.'

Moyra Macleod, a FANY (First Aid Nursing Yeomanry, women volunteers who worked mainly with motor transport for the ATS and Special Operations Executive) who was in London on the Wednesday after the raid to attend a lunch at the English Speaking Union in Charles Street, Mayfair, found it difficult to walk through the streets: 'cascades of glass still tinkling down and almost impossible by car as there was a diversion on every corner and one landed up miles from one's objective . . . Hans Place [behind Harrods] was a complete shambles and chaos, and Victoria Street sliced up – a half block of tall buildings swept away laying bare the mews behind. The little streets behind the Cavalry Club are grievously punished and Sunderland House – where our "coming out" dance took place and we danced all that summer of Jubilee year [1935] – is gutted by fire. That grandiose, gutted ballroom with the burnished cherubs and the glowing ceiling is ravaged and open to the sky. We have seen the end of an era.'

General Raymond E. Lee's beat was around Mayfair. 'Park Lane is blocked, with a huge crater in the middle of it. Not far from Lord Londonderry's house. Part of Shepherd's Market is completely burned out, together with a large building across the street, and a number of mansions in Hill Street are simply brick shells, still smouldering. In Clarges Street there is a house down. As we passed this morning we saw the Salvage Corps digging furiously through a heap of rubbish to rescue some unfortunate who was buried beneath it. When I walked by there this afternoon, they were still digging, but rather more slowly and it is easy to see that the ambulance which was standing there awaiting the removal of bodies is now going to take only corpses.'

Virginia Woolf, who had been so often stricken with a terrible sense of loss as she wandered around blitzed London after a raid, was not there to see these final wounds. In the morning of Thursday, 28 March 1941 she had taken her own life by weighing her pockets down with heavy stones and slipping into the fast-flowing river Ouse near her home, Monk's House in Sussex. Her body was not found until three weeks later, on 18 April. Naomi Mitchison heard of her death in 'a very nice letter from Leonard Woolf, explaining that she had killed herself because she was afraid of going mad. I do sympathise with that: one so often feels like that.'

Upper Norwood had not been much affected on the night of 10–11 May, but when Sidney Chave set off for his laboratory at the School of Hygiene and Tropical Medicine in Bloomsbury on Monday morning, his bus 'ran into an enormous traffic block at Kennington. Eventually I, like thousands of others, got off and walked as far as Trafalgar Square. Four bridges being closed (Westminster, Waterloo, Blackfriars and London Bridge) was the cause of the traffic chaos. When I arrived at the School I found the place a terrible mess. The first of a stick of bombs had struck the east side and the whole building was blasted out. The damage is quite severe but the steel skeleton held well. I donned a boiler-suit and spent the morning working in the wreckage rescuing papers. The Prof's office on the ground floor was unrecognizable. Our labs have not suffered too badly but the building had lost virtually all its windows and the Public Health, Physiology and Chemistry departments and workshops are no more . . . I returned home by another bus route tonight. It was very roundabout and took about 1½ hours. The district around the Elephant and Castle has suffered terribly and street after street is wrecked. The fire brigade was still pouring water on huge wrecked smouldering ruins all around. It is the worst destruction I have ever seen.'

Harold Nicolson went along to his work too. 'I go to see the ruins of the old Chamber [of the House of Commons]. It is impossible to get through the Members' Lobby which is a mass of twisted girders. So I went up by the staircase to the Ladies' Gallery and then suddenly, when I turned the corridor, there was the open air and a sort of Tintern Abbey gaping towards me. The little Ministers' rooms to the right and left of the Speaker's Lobby were still intact, but from there onwards there was absolutely nothing. No sign of anything but *murs calciné* and twisted girders.' Winston Churchill had wept when he saw the destruction to the Chamber, but the independent-minded MP Josiah Wedgwood told the often lachrymose Prime Minister, 'Don't be distressed at the ruins. Such ruins are good assets all around the globe, and especially in America.'

On Sunday, Naomi Mitchison, in Scotland, was 'worrying about London' because she had not heard from her husband Dick, who had been there the previous night. 'And if anything had happened, I easily mightn't for a long time. The evening news: a pity if Westminster Hall was smashed badly and I'd hate Big Ben to come down, but not much affected by Westminster Abbey. The Brit. Mus. doesn't sound much. But will they come again tonight? Awful to think of these young men on both sides starting out, these lovely evenings, set for hell fire.'

Whether the bombers would return was the question everyone was asking. At an emergency meeting held at the Imperial War Museum on Sunday, Alderman Len Styles, Southwark's Defence Chief, had given Admiral Evans his opinion that 'two more nights of this and London will be at standstill'. The capital's losses were the most devastating in its nearly 2,000-year history: 1,436 people had been killed on the night of 10–11 May, and more would die later of their injuries; 1,800 were seriously injured; 11,000 houses had been damaged beyond repair, and 12,374 people were homeless – not that anyone knew that appalling toll as they waited for the alert to sound on Sunday evening.

It came at 9.30 p.m. 'We've had it,' one fireman would say to another. But thirty minutes later the All Clear sounded. On 12–13 May twenty people were killed in a raid on Falmouth in Cornwall, and bombs dropped on Plymouth, Lowestoft, Gorleston and London. Over the next few days more bombs fell on Veryan in Cornwall, Falmouth, Weymouth, Cardiff, Nottingham and Lincoln. On Friday, 16 May Birmingham was the target of a three-hour raid, but the bulk of the bombs fell on nearby Nuneaton instead, causing widespread damage to industrial and residential property, killing eighty-three people and requiring the services of Coventry Fire Brigades and Civil Defence. The ICI works at Birmingham were hit, as was the Dunlop Rubber Company, but the damage was relatively minor, though utilities were put out of action and thirty people were killed. Stray bombs were dropped over the Midlands, and as far south as Plymouth and as far north as Aberdeen. But the blitz was over – nearly.

However, Hull continued to suffer raids: on 2 June, the fiftieth raid on the city since the start of the blitz was a particular disaster. The All Clear was sounded prematurely and people making their way home from the shelters were hit, killing twenty-seven; the Deputy Chief Constable, also believing the raid to be over, was killed as he drove to inspect the damage. 'The Nazis have given Hull its chance to rebuild,' wrote Cyril Dunn after he wandered around the damaged city and docks, uncertain what had fallen in which raid, just aware of a near-deserted wilderness of ruins and rubble. 'Whatever the inhabitants decide to do about it, the Old Town of Hull – the part once enclosed by walls and then the docks – will have to be re-built. What a *chance* there is here! And how certainly it will be neglected.' There were more raids throughout July, most of them light. But all did damage, and brought death and injury. On 18 July the docks, the industrial area and the terraced houses of East Hull were devastated; fifty inhabitants of one street were killed, as were a further twenty when a shelter received a direct hit. This time, for the first time, the name Hull appeared in the national press.

Essentially, the blitz – or the 'big blitz' as it was sometimes called later, when other attacks gave a point of comparison – started with a devastating attack on London on 7 September 1940, and ended with an even more devastating one 243 nights later. 'We got hit in the beginning in West Ham . . . And we got hit in the end. The Germans never left us out of their favours . . . It seemed like we were their same target throughout the whole blitz,' recalled East End fireman Cyril Demarne. 'It took a long time to realise that raid on 10 May was the last one. We'd been so used to having a raid every night, or them stopping and then starting again . . . And then of course we got the answer. We found out what it was all about. Hitler had attacked Russia. What Churchill called the biggest blunder in history. He attacked Russia. And we realised that the Luftwaffe couldn't possibly come to us, so it was safe to go to bed at night and have a good night's rest, dry our clothes and get our breath back.'

During this time, much of the rest of the country had suffered grievously too – particularly the ports and industrial centres. More than 43,500 civilians were killed nationwide during those seemingly endless months of the blitz. Officially, 71,000 people were seriously injured and 88,136 slightly injured, while 98,500 were treated at First Aid Posts, a fifth of those being transferred to hospital. The true total is probably higher, since records were not always kept fully at times of crisis and chaos, criteria were different –

one report's 'serious' might be another's 'slight' – and not every injured person sought medical help. But what can be definitively said is that during the blitz Britain's civilians were on the front line of battle. It was not until the autumn of 1942 that the enemy had killed more British soldiers than civilians.

'Of course we knew the map of London, we knew it very well,' said Hajo Hermann, a Luftwaffe bomber squadron leader. 'And I only thought that it doesn't have an end. London is too big . . . what should we do to destroy London – that is quite impossible.' And for London, read Britain.

After

It was an extraordinary thing. All the best sellers in the bookshops were books on architecture, because there was tremendous hope. We were always being told we were working for a better Britain, and we really believed it. I really believed every word. So instead of saying how awful about the cities being blitzed, it was a wonderful opportunity to build the most beautiful city in the world. I met my husband [Michael Foot, who became MP for Plymouth Devonport in 1945] when I was making a film about the Plymouth plan, and one of the things that almost made me fall in love with him – although I found his eyes rather fetching, and his smile – was that he said 'We are going to build the most beautiful city in the world,' and that was the spirit of things then. But I suppose the architects and the local authorities didn't really live up to their promise . . .

Jill Craigie, film-maker

Writing of the blitz, the American magazine *Time* used the memorable phrase 'the past bombed out of our lives'. The article referred to the material destruction, the loss of historic buildings, of landscapes of memory. But the losses caused by the blitz were far more profound and far more widespread than that. They encompassed loss of life, of home, of workplace and of hopes for the future. Thousands of people's worlds were blown apart by the bombs.

Nothing can be listed in the credit column against such a crushing debit. Yet the inferno did reconfigure more than the nation's town and cityscapes. The past was in many senses 'bombed out of our lives' between September 1940 and May 1941, and though the future was bound to be less of a clean slate than that phrase suggests, the war did change Britain. As the conflict's most intense and concentrated expression for most British people, the blitz powerfully shaped that change.

One almost immediate effect of the 10 May raid was Herbert Morrison's announcement that the fire services were to be unified. During the blitz they had comprised a nucleus of fewer than 5,000 professional firefighters supplemented by a 'transient horde' of more than 50,000 auxiliaries or volunteers – London alone had 23,000 of these. Hours for firefighters were long – forty-eight hours on, often in exhausting conditions, twenty-four off – far more than most civil defenders worked. A very great deal was demanded of firemen, both regular and wartime auxiliaries, in the blitz, but many worked with the equivalent of one hand tied behind their backs when it came to conditions and equipment, and their rewards were hardly commensurate with their labours and the risks they took, despite the prediction made back in 1935 that 'In a national emergency, the man with the branch-pipe and hose is probably going to prove more valuable to the nation than his fellows with machine-guns, and other warlike material. On him, and other members of the passive defence force, the *morale* of the public will depend.'

The fire services required to cope with the German onslaught were a heterogeneous collection of 1,668 local brigades, few having more than twenty men before the war, and most being poorly equipped. This multiplicity of brigades had a hotchpotch of different standards for training, technique, equipment, even terminology; again and again this would undermine the usefulness of firemen from one place coming to the assistance of those in another during the blitz. Moreover, when help was required, brigades often sent relatively inexperienced AFS men rather than their best regulars, and there were endless wrangles about who would pay for their work: on occasion buildings burned down because this had not been agreed, so no men or engines had been sent.

In his autobiography Morrison would claim that he had decided on the amalgamation of the brigades after the attack on Coventry in November 1940. But his biographers point to his reluctance to do so. Having seen how difficult and sensitive a matter it had been to wrest authority from one seriously deficient ARP Controller in Stepney in October 1940, and how unsatisfactory the outcome of that spat had been, the Minister for Home Security was loath to pluck out what he referred to as 'the brightest jewel in the local authorities' regalia', and replace local fire services with a unified national one.

The raids on Plymouth at the end of April prompted the local MP, Nancy Astor, to write to *The Times* to complain about 'how totally inadequate local fire fighting organisations, even when expanded, are to deal with the effects of a real air attack when tens of thousands of incendiary bombs start widely scattered fires simultaneously'. Lady Astor's solution was nationalisation, and even though her husband was Lord Mayor of Plymouth at the time, she confessed that she found herself unable to understand the 'worship for local authorities'. The Plymouth blitz had also finally convinced Morrison that action would have to be taken without delay. On 8 May he secured the agreement of the War Cabinet, and embarked on a round of consultative exercises with local authorities, securing the reluctant agreement of most by promising that although 'fire fighting, in substance, has become a military operation', the fire services would be returned to local control at the end of the war. Some authorities, most notably Glasgow, objected bitterly, but the proposals were steamrollered through the Commons, and by 22 May 1941 the Fire Services (Emergency Provisions) Act was law.

Although the fire service was nominally national, it was in fact subject to regional control. The task of coordinating firefighting activities was vested in the twelve Regional Commissioners, and England and Wales were divided into thirty-three Fire Areas (including four for London), and Scotland into six, with the aim of bringing the whole of each important urban or industrial fire-risk area under single control, regardless of local authority boundaries. Sir Aylmer Firebrace, who had done such sterling work in London, was appointed Chief of Fire Staff, while each fire force was led by a Commander who reported to the Chief Regional Fire Officer in his area. Below the Commander came a pyramid of officers variously in charge of firemen and women, fire engines and pumps.

The Treasury made government funds available to equip this National Fire Service with standardised and updated equipment, and a new uniform training programme and promotion ladder were introduced so that firemen and women could rise throughout the service, and not just in their own brigades. Henceforth fire forces could move anywhere in their area, and if necessary across the country, confident that procedures and equipment would be standard, and that they could work as a team with the local force.

These reforms, which were largely achieved by July 1941, may have been necessary, but they were not universally popular. The premises for these new forces were often either inadequate or non-existent, and most had to be entirely re-equipped. The reorganisation made all existing fire service jobs obsolete, and positions in the new national service had to be applied for centrally. There had frequently been tensions between the regulars and the auxiliaries, with the former both fearing that the wartime imports might be after their jobs, and regarding many of them as 'soft' and not up to the physically demanding work of firefighting. The terms and conditions of employment of AFS members were worse than for regular firemen: they were paid less, often inadequately trained, poorly equipped and housed in distinctly substandard accommodation. If an AFS man was injured on the job he would receive thirteen weeks' full pay, and then if he was still not fit for duty he would be dismissed, and would have to rely on means-tested benefit if he had no other source of income. This divide was powerfully portrayed by Henry Green in his 1943 novel *Caught* (Green, the poet Stephen Spender and the novelist William Sansom were early recruits to the AFS, and were all stationed in Westminster).

While the reorganisation meant that pay and conditions were standardised, tensions could increase when men were demoted, relocated or pensioned off; and career firemen might find themselves commanded by a former auxiliary who, though probably better educated, did not have the experience in the job that the regulars had. All administrative staff lost their former civilian status, and were required to wear a uniform, given a rank and subjected to the same working conditions and regulations as firemen and women; the new professionalisation of the service came as a rude shock to some rural brigades for whom firefighting had been an occasional, voluntary calling.

The problem with the fire brigades was just one example of the relationship between central-government and local-authority control, many manifestations of which had been simmering since the First World War, but which presented themselves with painful clarity under the strains of the Second. Looked at one way, local-authority control could mean incompetence or even anarchy, pointlessly and time-consumingly reinventing the wheel with every challenge. From another perspective, the *diktat* of central government could ride roughshod over the people who had to make policies work, ignore the specificity of local conditions and enervate local initiatives. And over all such discussions hovered the question of money. It was all very well for central government to prescribe, but too often the prescription came with little or no funding attached, and local authorities were obliged to empty their own coffers to carry it out. This would mean either rate increases or cuts in other areas of expenditure, neither of which was likely to please the voters on whom councillors depended for their office.

While bombs showed no respect for local authority (or any other) boundaries, the old Poor Law mentality of not accepting responsibility for people from elsewhere (even if elsewhere was only the next borough, or even the next wardens' post) persisted, with disastrous consequences for the homeless in the early weeks of the blitz. Again, this was partly a matter of a lack of clarity about what government would pay for (or reimburse) and what it would not. In this, as in other areas such as health and industry, the notion of a national community, of the standardisation of services and equity of provision, while not a new concept, was given urgency by the crisis of the blitz.

Indeed, the whole notion of the reach and competence of the state in people's lives was brought into sharp focus at this time. It had become clear before war broke out that the military could not be brought up to the required strength by voluntary enlistment, and conscription was introduced for the first time in peacetime Britain in May 1939, and the first men were called up in July. Its sweep was extended throughout the war, as the blitz (and the Battle of Britain that preceded it) showed that neither the forces nor industry could recruit sufficient numbers by exhortation, cheering posters and patriotic rhetoric. It was the same with fire-watching and other defence requirements: appeals to altruism and civic duty were not always sufficient. Increasingly there had to be a degree of compulsion and direction, and as the war progressed Britain gradually became a command economy, in the broadest meaning of that phrase.

This was a response to exceptional times, of course, and the vast majority of people accepted it as such; but the blitz undoubtedly made that acceptance easier: the war came home in September 1940, and the need for extraordinary measures was pointed up daily. Britain was under direct attack, and normal responses, time scales and consultations – the traditional liberal niceties – were frequently disregarded and discarded in combating this.

This would have important post-war consequences. People would ask why, if the government could act so decisively and directly in wartime, it could not do so when peace returned. The state, so often seen in the thirties as passive in the face of unemployment, harsh economic circumstances and aggression abroad, had assumed powers of direction in the war that many believed should translate into an active role in building a more equitable society than the one that had existed in 1939. When Jennie Lee visited a Lancashire aircraft factory she heard the mechanics singing what she took to be 'There'll Always be an England', but on closer attention she realised that what they were singing was 'Will there always be an England with a job in it for me?'

The war would not have been won had the British people not on the whole showed unity and resolution of purpose in the blitz. A social contract, no matter how informal and unspoken, had been forged during those months of attack. People who 'took it' should be entitled to 'get it' – if 'it' meant better housing, a fairer education system, more job opportunities. It was partly for this reason that when the Beveridge Report was published in December 1942, a year and a half after the blitz ended, what was essentially a tidying-up operation of welfare provision assumed iconic status, appearing to offer a new beginning, a safety net from the cradle to the grave, an attack on the five 'giant evils' in society: squalor, ignorance, want, idleness and disease. Churchill's guarded response to Beveridge's recommendations, and his refusal to make any commitment to implement them after the war, would prove to be a political misjudgement.

If the blitz reconfigured Britain's cityscapes, how much did it reorder people's attitudes and expectations? To what extent did the acute threat posed by an external enemy weld the British people into a seamless unity? Did bombs break down the stark divisions and class barriers of the pre-war years? Did a more altruistic society emerge from the ruins? In short, how much was the blitz a laboratory, a forcing house for change? And was that change sustained? Did it light a candle that would flicker into the post-war years, lighting the years of austerity with resolution for reform?

As Richard Titmuss pointed out in his official history of social policy in the Second World War, one of the most striking things about the conflict, and particularly about the blitz, is how much depended on volunteers. On people taking on tasks because they were too old or too young to be conscripted or directed into the forces or munitions factories, or had other responsibilities that prevented them from doing so. And these tasks – firefighting, fire-watching, ARP duties, the Home Guard, the WVS and dozens more – were undertaken, usually without pay, in addition to people's normal daily work. Although the word 'volunteer' became increasingly elastic as regulation and compulsion eroded voluntarism, such people were essentially 'on duty' for the almost six years of the war, and during the 246 days the blitz lasted (and later during the V-1 and V-2 attacks) they were on constant alert, prepared but uncertain.*

One consequence of this was that people often found themselves in contact with situations and people they would never have encountered in the normal course of their lives. Young women who had led leisured lives within a charmed social circle might find themselves nightly driving ambulances through some of the poorest streets in Britain, ministering to people in places they would never have visited in peacetime. Cambridge-educated Barbara Nixon's account shows how socially mixed an ARP post could be, with wardens who might be lawyers or doctors, factory workers, strippers or dustmen. The multifarious functions the WVS undertook often (though not always) involved comfortably-off middle-class, middle-aged women who had never worked outside the home before – Nella Last is an obvious example of the latter category – coming into regular contact with the poor. The evacuation programme is often held up as an example of how many people in Britain saw for the first time how the other half lived, as children from inner-city slums were dispersed around the country. The blitz had the same effect. Walls sheared off in a raid poignantly revealed how mean so many homes were, how few possessions the poor might have, what a narrow margin there was between them and destitution.

Violent death or injury are the same tragedy for rich or poor, belted earl or unemployed labourer, but their ability to cope with attack from the air was not equal. Docks and industrial installations were the most frequent targets, and the streets around such areas were invariably made up of small, poorly built working-class houses. The families in them had few alterna-

---

* By October 1940 Herbert Morrison, recognising that there were severe shortages in the Civil Defence services, ordered that full-time (i.e. paid) ARP wardens over the age of thirty should be 'frozen' in post, since so many younger men were being called up into the forces or directed into war work. This meant that they could not leave their job without official permission, usually from the Regional Commissioner. By the end of the year full-time members of the ARP services were compulsorily enrolled as an alternative to joining the armed forces. This marked a decisive end to the voluntary principle in recruitment, but in March 1941 Morrison insisted in the House of Commons that voluntarism had not failed, and that the amazing achievements of Civil Defence on a voluntary basis had been 'one of the greatest successes in history'. In January 1941 the Ministry of Home Security was given powers to compel men and women to perform Civil Defence duties for a maximum of forty-eight hours a month. The final step in 'freezing' part-time Civil Defence workers was taken in January 1942, when all CD personnel were obliged to continue their duties until dispensed with by the authorities.

tives but to stay put: they did not have the resources to relocate, rarely had relations or friends in safe areas able to accommodate them if they were bombed out, and did not have savings to cushion them through a period of dislocation.

On the whole, the middle classes did not frequent rest centres: they had other options. When the Queen pronounced that she could 'look the East End in the face now' after the bombing of Buckingham Palace, not all East Enders saw the parallel. They did not have a home in the country (in fact several) to repair to; having a wing of your London base damaged was of a rather different order from losing the only home you have ever known, and all your possessions with it.

It was the same with sheltering. Those who could afford it were able to leave the most bombed areas. If they elected to stay, they had shelter options: their own Anderson, a reinforced basement, a sturdily built house. On the whole the middle (and upper) classes were not found clutching their meagre bedding waiting to go down the tube for the night, or crammed into an overcrowded and malodorous public shelter, unless they had been caught out on the way home.

These comparisons are not intended to diminish the impact of the blitz that many people, certainly those living in towns, suffered. The loss of a home, of a former life, is devastating, regardless of class or wealth. But the sense of a shared experience was unifying, examples of extreme bravery and resilience (as well as the reverse) were found across the country, and there was great sympathy for what those in the East End of London, on Merseyside, Clydebank and other badly bombed places suffered. Everyone had a bomb story. Everyone could lay claim to a blitz narrative.

If the commonality of experience did not stretch evenly across the classes, nor did it across other divides in society. Anti-Semitism, a regrettably prevalent feature of thirties Britain, was not diminished by the shared threat of the blitz, nor by reports of the Nazi persecution of the Jews. There had been accusations that the war was a 'Jewish conspiracy' but such views – sometimes expressed by graffiti scrawled on propaganda posters to alter their message, for example: 'Your courage; Your cheerfulness; Your resolution; Will bring Jews [rather than Us] victory' – were only held by those on the wilder shores of fascism. Nevertheless, grumblings about the Jews rumbled on. They were accused of being military-service dodgers or black market dealers, of fleeing danger areas. Jewish shopkeepers were blamed for overcharging for rationed goods. In the East End, Jews were accused of pushing

Tension erupts in Coventry, with people's possessions scattered in the street after a raid in February 1941.

The devastation that was Clydebank. A steady stream of dispossessed residents, some of the 35,000 made homeless, stumble past a tenement in which a large number of people had been killed, still burning after the raids of 13 and 14 March 1941.

A soldier stands guard in front of a bombed-out grocer's shop in Birkenhead in March 1941 to prevent salvaged stock from being looted.

'Blitz broth'. Members of the WVS working in the open air to prepare a large vat of soup for those affected by a raid on Liverpool in December 1940.

'I think I am the only Dean in history who has no bible and no prayer book,' mourned the Dean of Westminster Abbey, Dr Paul de Labillière, seen here inspecting the ruins of the abbey's cloisters on the morning after the last raid of the blitz, on 10 May 1940.

A garden city. Hollyhocks, buddleia and willow herb had colonised bombed-out buildings in the City of London's Gresham Street by July 1943, a little more than two years after the blitz ended. Wildernesses such as this would persist on many urban bombsites for decades.

others out of the way to get the best places in shelters, and refusing to move, and Jewish women were reported to be seen sporting expensive mink coats after a raid. All the old smears about Jews on the make, Jews and sharp practice, were given a bitter wartime topicality. A Mass-Observation investigator was told by a Birmingham woman that she considered Jews to be 'parasites who live on mugs like us', and that she hoped their local neighbourhood would be wiped out by Hitler's bombs.

Robert Baltrop considered that while there was little strong anti-German sentiment during the blitz, 'If there was any group of people who suffered from prejudice, certainly in the East End, it was the Jews. There were feelings that the Jews were financiers, they manipulated things behind the scenes, and if anybody was cowardly, it was likely to be them, because they weren't English and that kind of thing' – though many Jewish families living in the East End had settled there more than fifty years before the blitz started.

A civil servant sent to investigate the bombing of Coronation Mansions in Stoke Newington in October 1940, where a large number of Jews had been among those killed and injured, 'talked to several of the people waiting at the desk [to get help and advice]. Two Jewish women were very down on their luck and the elder of the two was in floods of tears because she said she had lost "everything". As a matter of fact her house was only damaged and her furniture was being removed to store, so she had on the whole very little to complain about. Two sisters, on the other hand, of 76 and 84, non Jewish, were joking about their shocks and losses.'

A letter to the *Hackney and Kingsland Gazette* in October 1940 claimed that 'from personal observations, I should say that 90 per cent of those who recline nightly on Tube platforms are of the Jewish persuasion . . . Besides men with black patriarchal beards, the observer cannot fail to detect a considerable number of robust and obviously well-nourished men.' When George Orwell went to check the rumours about air-raid shelters in Chancery Lane, Oxford Street and Baker Street underground stations, he found that the shelterers were '*not* all Jews, but I think a higher proportion of Jews than one would normally see in a crowd of this size. What is bad about Jews is that they are not only conspicuous, but go out of their way to make themselves so . . . Surprised to find that D. who is distinctly Left in his views, is inclined to share the current feelings against Jews.' And, Orwell reported, 'With reference to the advertisements in the Tube stations, "Be a Man etc." (asking able-bodied men not to shelter there but to leave space for women and children), D says the joke going round London is that it was a mistake to print these in English.'

The Jewish Board of Deputies was so concerned by the allegations about behaviour in air-raid shelters that it commissioned a non-Jew to investigate. He reported that 'In those districts where Jews lived in large numbers they behaved just as well as the British people as a whole.' Likewise, when the charge that a disproportionate number of Jews were black marketeers was looked into, it was found that the number of Jews and Gentiles prosecuted for such offences was in line with their proportions among traders as a whole.

The blitz added to paranoia about Jews, particularly in the East End of London. This was no doubt partly because of suspicion of the easily identifiable 'other' in wartime, whose loyalties might lie elsewhere. It was also because the blitz was a time of raw emotion, of fear and competition for scarce resources both of food (during the most acute period of rationing) and safety (in terms of shelter and protection). And there already existed a pool of anti-Semitism, 'not violent but pronounced enough to be disquieting', from which to draw. This did not mean, as Orwell wrote, that anyone 'wants actually to *do* anything about the Jews', other than grumble about them and use them as an easy scapegoat for wartime difficulties, anxieties and ambivalences.

If the blitz did not dissolve prejudice or definitively break down class barriers, it did forge a certain determination and a defiance that was noticeable and unifying. This might be local rather than national – a response to the feeling that London had become emblematic of the blitz, and received nearly all the publicity and an unfair share of resources, while the sufferings of the provinces tended to be overshadowed. But these localisms did coalesce into a national resolve.

Virginia Woolf, who felt the destruction of London's buildings deeply, wrote to Ethel Smyth after the Woolfs' house in Mecklenburgh Square had been hit by a bomb in September 1940: 'London looked merry and hopeful, wearing her wounds like stars; why do I dramatise London perpetually? When I see a great smash like a crushed match box where an old house stood I wave my hand to London. What I am finding odd and agreeable and unwonted is the admiration this war creates – for every sort of person: chars, shopkeepers, even more remarkably, for politicians – Winston at least, and tweed wearing sterling dull women here [in Sussex], with their grim good sense: organising First aid, putting out bombs for practice, and jumping out of windows to show us how. We burnt an incendiary bomb up on the down[s] last night. It was a lovely tender autumn evening, and the white splutter of the bomb was to me, who never listened to the instructions, rather lovely. I'd almost lost faith in human beings, partly owing to my immersion in the dirty water of artists envies and vanities while I worked at Roger [Fry, a study of whom Woolf was writing]. Now hope revives again.'

For Robert Baltrop, 'people were heroic in the blitz. Tremendously so sometimes. But the greatest quality of all was not the acts of bravery that took place – they did but there were acts of meanness and cowardice too – it's all part of human nature – but the sheer fortitude. The way people stuck it out.'

It was this defiance, the stalwart determination that that 'bloody 'itler' wasn't going to beat Britain whatever the odds, that best characterised the blitz . 'Business as usual was the survivor's reaction to air raids,' wrote Jean Crossley, an army wife who was working for the photographic section of the Ministry of Information. 'This was not something imposed on us by government decree. Each one of us, no matter to what class of society we belonged, instinctively rebelled against allowing Hitler – that silly little man with a toothbrush moustache – to rule our lives. It was a feeling that united the nation as never before or since.' This was a time, it should be remembered, when optimism might have been expected to be in very short supply. Britain's former allies had either been knocked out of the fight or had held up the white flag. America, though increasingly helpful, was maintaining its position of neutrality, and there had been no substantial victories abroad. Nor would there be until El Alamein in November 1942, which, Churchill cautiously allowed, was not the end, or even the beginning of the end, but was, perhaps, the end of the beginning.

Defiance did not on the whole mean a call for retribution. After a particularly bad raid, there would be a call to 'Let 'im have it' in letters to the press or reports to Home Intelligence, or in conversations overheard by Mass-Observers. But it appears that most people would echo Robert Baltrop: 'I didn't personally have any great animosity towards the Germans – they were just people like ourselves who had been hauled into war . . . the general feeling was that Germans were victims of war like we were. After all, they were bombing us, but we were bombing them too.' A total of 635,000 German civilians were killed as a result of Allied bombing raids (in which 55,000 British airmen died). At first both Allied and Axis planes targeted war-production factories, docks and military installations, though every raid resulted in cruel collateral damage to homes, hospitals and lives. However, as the Butt Report showed in 1941, only one bomber in four managed to drop its bombs within five miles of the target. Essentially, targeted bombing failed: area or carpet bombing was to be the new strategy. On 14 February 1942, Directive 22 was issued to Bomber Command by the Air Ministry in London: henceforth bombing was to be 'focused on the morale of the enemy civil population and in particular of the industrial workers'. The first Allied raid on Cologne had been on 12 May 1940: on 30–31 May 1942 over a thousand bombers converged on the city, and area bombing raids followed on other German cities, including Bremen, Leipzig, Berlin, Hamburg and finally Dresden in February 1945.

As Vera Brittain wrote, 'It is relevant . . . perhaps to inquire what we ourselves have destroyed in Cologne, in Hamburg, in Frankfurt and Munich. What Germany has to forgive us who centuries ago, by our Balance of Power policy, committed Europe to ceaseless national conflict. Policies as well as buildings are historic; we must not forget that.'

The blitz literally smashed down the old and made ruins of the past. Some of what was lost was regretted. But not all. Writing in the BBC magazine *London Calling* in 1941, the journalist Macdonald Hastings weighed the balance: 'If Wren's most beautiful churches and some of the City's most noble and historic buildings are damaged irreparably, they have taken with them in their passing some of the meanest stretches of Victorian office buildings in the whole of the City . . . The Hun has given us a priceless opportunity to reconceive the City on a more rational and liveable plan.'

It was an opportunity that was eagerly seized upon. In 1941 two very different periodicals published plans for the post-war world. In July the *Architectural Review*, having previously taken 'a disinterested attitude to the war' which, its editor admitted, might 'invite the charge of fiddling while Rome burns', plunged into the fray. 'We hear it said on every side that this is a peculiar war . . . that it is not a war at all, in the old-fashioned sense of a mere military campaign, so much as inevitable *change* passing through one of its most intense (and unpleasant) phases . . . In due course we shall presumably again be, in a sense, at peace, but we shall not be *back again* at peace. We shall be living in a world as different in its own way from the world before the war as our present war-time world is.' 'Translated into terms of architecture', this seemed to mean being able to admit that 'the old days have gone for good and to keep in touch with the new days . . . [so that] architecture remains an essential part of the machinery of civilisation'.

And this in turn meant not just providing obituaries for buildings lost, but accepting that bomb damage 'only wipes out some of the evidence of inadequate or unintelligent planning in the past. It does nothing to prevent the same mistakes being made in the future.' What was needed was 'an informed and active public opinion, aware of the real issues and sufficiently familiar with the principles on which reconstruction can be founded to be able to do more than take the proposals of the experts at . . . face value'.

On 4 January 1941 *Picture Post* published 'A Plan for Britain'. This, the magazine insisted, was 'not something outside the war, or something after the war. It is an essential part of our war aims. It is indeed our most positive war aim. The new Britain is the country we are fighting for . . . The war . . . has been a crisis for our country's whole economic and political life. We have been forced into a knowledge of our dependence on each other.'

The thrust of the *Picture Post* articles was 'never again'. Britain must not repeat the mistakes made after the First World War: the 'homes for heroes' that were never built, the rapid decline of manufacturing industries, intractable unemployment, disputatious industrial relations, continued inequalities in health and education. The answer was planning, a mantra of the left throughout the thirties. 'Given the will to plan, we could in a quarter of a century transform our worst towns . . . we could replan and reconstruct many of our outworn public services, to stop the drain of money to no purpose,' argued the architect and town planner Maxwell Fry.

J.B. Priestley was of the same mind, and took a dig at Churchill, among others. In Cyril Connolly's magazine *Horizon* in March 1941, Priestley wrote, 'I do not trust the man who promises to do everything for me after the war so long as nothing is changed or even discussed now. I suspect that once Hitler is out of the way and the danger to property is past, he will ask me not to speak nonsense about reconstruction but to go and mind my own business . . . There is no doubt that the general mood of this country favours progressive and fairly thorough reform, a remodelling of the whole political, economic and social structure, and is suspicious of the diehards. But it is frightening to find oneself in mid-air above a chaos. Something must be done at once. Better anything than nothing . . . if we are not careful, we shall find ourselves back in August 1939 with the same old voices talking the same old drivel, all as it was before, except that now the Government in power will have a good deal of unrepealed war-time legislation to help it quieten any real opposition . . . the blueprints [for change] must already exist.'

Sir John Reith, the towering, austere former Director General of the BBC, since October 1940 Minister of Works and Buildings, had from the start of the blitz (which almost coincided with his tenure in office) urged local authorities to 'plan boldly' in reconstructing their blitzed towns and cities. In January 1941 he set up an Expert Committee on Compensation and Betterment (the Uthwatt Committee) to look into the financial implications of the land acquisition that would be required to do this.

The fate of Reith's vision can serve as an allegory for the 'lessons of the blitz'. After the war, there were conflicting impetuses: that identified by Priestley as 'progressive', which looked for opportunities to build on what had been razed, to use the central controls of wartime planning to regulate the peace. To nationalise land, industries and services, standardise provision, centralise administration, codify practices. Much of this drive was realised by the Labour government's post-war reforms, most particularly the creation of the National Health Service in July 1948, and the nationalisation of coal, the railways, gas and electricity, iron and steel (the latter briefly), road haulage, the buses.

In the case of the health service, the blitz had brought the medicine of the battlefield to the home front, and with it came unprecedented opportunities to study the effects of serious injury and to advance methods of treatment, especially surgery. It had given prominence to the acceptance of universal entitlement for treatment and care, free (for a time) at the point of delivery. It had also demonstrated the value of what Richard Titmuss would later highlight as a key example of altruism – blood transfusions and the growth of blood banks, so essential in the conditions of air raids, when one person would make a gift literally of his or her lifeblood, without expectation of reward or thanks, to another unknown person.

The other thrust was a wish to turn away from the imperatives of war, not to harness them. To return to an individualistic society of home, work and family, as it had been enjoyed before the war. This natural impulse would cut across radical plans for reconstruction. Where town planners envisaged grid patterns and sweeping boulevards, zoned areas, commercial centres and traffic-free neighbourhoods, many citizens saw the priority as building new houses or quickly and thoroughly repairing old ones, having schools functioning again, shops back as and where they had been. They would fight against the compulsory purchase orders that were necessary to make the planners' dreams a reality, resist attempts to flatten more of Britain's cities than the bombs ever had.

The debate was not resolved then, nor has it been now. Principles were eroded, plans nibbled away at. The great cross-axis of Plymouth's Armada Way, with a never-before-seen sweeping view to the Hoe, and the phoenix of the modern rebuilt Coventry Cathedral, were radical exceptions. Most reconstructions, whatever the original intentions, were compromises, a balance between planners' schemes and local vested interests – and the ever-present problem of lack of money and materials in an impoverished, indebted post-war economy that would persist for decades after the end of the blitz, leaving hundreds whose houses had been destroyed then, or in the subsequent V-weapon attacks, living (often contentedly) in prefabs, some of which persisted into the next century – as did the willow herb, buddleia and rubble that held sway on bomb sites in city centres.

In 1941 the *Architectural Review* made a suggestion: 'The ruin, looked on as architecture in its own right, represents the apotheosis of the past: the intense experience of these active days [of the blitz] crystallised in architectural form. When it is all over, a few of the wrecked buildings might well be left as permanent ruins – not, one hastens to add, as object lessons to future war mongers, or for any other moral purpose, but for the sake of the intensely evocative atmosphere common to all ruins, which gives them a . . . vitality of their own: and frankly their beauty. To posterity they will as effectually represent the dissolution of our pre-war civilisation as Fountains Abbey does the dissolution of the monasteries.'

ACKNOWLEDGEMENTS

This book could not have been written without a lot of help. Starting with its genesis, my thanks go first to my agent Deborah Rogers and her assistant Mohsen Shah; at HarperPress Arabella Pike commissioned it and encouraged its writing, while Robert Lacey made it a far better book with his legendary editorial skills. My thanks too to John Bond, Helen Ellis, Minna Fry and Sophie Goulden at Harper Press for their enthusiasm. I am grateful to Christopher Phipps's skill as an indexer, and to Anne Rieley who read the proofs

Dr Robin Woolven, an absolute mine of information on blitz-related matters, has saved me from many cringe-making errors, pointed recondite material my way and answered endless queries. Terry Charman at the Imperial War Museum did likewise with equal encyclopaedic knowledge, patience and good humour. Both they and Professor Roger Morgan read the entire manuscript, and the corrections and comments of all three have been invaluable. My thanks too for their expert readings to Professor Paul Addison, Dr Robin Hiley and Professor Edgar Jones.

I am grateful both to the trustees of the Imperial War Museum and to the individual copyright-holders for allowing me access to the collections of papers held by the IWM and for permission to publish extracts from them. At the IWM Roderick Suddaby, Keeper of the Department of Documents, and his colleagues have been extremely helpful in making material available and coming up with a stream of useful suggestions. I am indebted to the IWM Department of Photographs for their help, and I am also most grateful to Caroline Theakstone at Getty Images for her deep knowledge of the collection, so generously shared.

Catherine Bradley, formerly of The National Archives, guided me through many of the complexities of the Archive. I would like to thank the Trustees of the Mass-Observation Archive at the University of Sussex for permission to quote from diaries, file reports and topic collections held in the M-O

Archive. Under the terms of deposition of diaries kept for Mass-Observation, the diarists are anonymous. Occasionally, a diary has been published or permission given to use the name of the diarist. My research was made easier with the help of Dorothy Sheridan and her colleagues at the M-O Archive, as it was by the staff of the British Library; the Bodleian Library, Oxford; Clydebank Local Studies Library; the Mitchell Library, Glasgow; the Friends Meeting House Archives and Library, London; the LSE library; and Liverpool Central Library. Those working in the London Library have, as usual and despite the inconveniences of long-term building work, been cheerfully accommodating and helpful. I am grateful to Elke Tullett for information about people interviewed for a Thames Television documentary on the blitz transmitted in September 1990; to Darren Treadwell of the Labour History Archive and Study Centre, Manchester, for his help with the notebooks of Alan Hutt and for permission to quote from them; and to the Trustees of Lambeth Palace Library for permission to quote from the papers of the Reverend Alan C. Don and Father John Grosser. My thanks to Peter Dunn for the loan of his father Cyril's wartime notebooks and for permission to quote from them, and to him and Lis Dunn for generous and repeated hospitality. I am grateful to Charles Strachey for permission to quote from his father John Strachey's book *Post D*. (While every effort has been made to track down the owners of copyright material, in some cases this has not proved possible. I will happily remedy any omissions in future editions of this book.)

Conversations with and material supplied by Terence Bendixson, Professor Joanna Bourke, Hazel Court, Dr Lara Feigel, Mark and Lucy Le Fanu, Professor Richard Overy, Dr Nicholas Stargardt and Gillian Tindall have been stimulating, and the interesting things a large number of people have told me about their own or their parents' blitz experience are much appreciated.

My children and their partners have been patient, supportive and interested through an overlong dereliction of grandmotherly (and thus parental) duties. I am very grateful to them, and to Henry Horwitz, who read and listened – rather a lot.

Juliet Gardiner
July 2010

NOTES

Preface

xiii 'These are the Facts': In Julian Symons (ed.), *An Anthology of War Poetry* (Penguin, 1942), pp.188–9

xiv On that day: George Orwell, 'London Letter to *Partisan Review*', 3 January 1941, *The Collected Essays, Journalism and Letters of George Orwell, Vol. II: My Country Right or Left, 1940–1943*, (eds) Sonia Orwell and Ian Angus (Secker & Warburg, 1968), pp.54–5

xv either we turn: George Orwell, *The Lion and the Unicorn: Socialism and English Genius* (Secker & Warburg, 1941), reprinted in *My Country Right or Left*, p.58

Before

1 I think it is well: *The Times*, 11 November 1932

2 quite suddenly: IWM 67/262/1, Thames Television interview with Robert Baltrop for a documentary on the blitz, September 1990

3 at something of a loss: Horst Boog, 'The Luftwaffe's Assault' in *The Burning Blue: A New History of the Battle of Britain*, (eds) Paul Addison and Jeremy Crang (Pimlico, 2000), p.40

4 The tide would be: Quoted in *Plague Year, March 1940–February 1941: Being the Diary of Anthony Weymouth* (George G. Harrap, 1942), p.164

5 it switched to trying: Boog, p.39

5 The collapse of England: Quoted in Richard Overy, 'How Significant Was the Battle?' in Addison and Crang, p.268

5 all but annihilated: In fact by late September 1940 the Luftwaffe had only 276 serviceable single-engined fighter planes as compared to the 665 in the RAF's Fighter Command. Ibid.

6 'cripple' Britain: Richard Overy, *The Battle* (Penguin, 2000), p.126

Chapter 1: Black Saturday, 7 September 1940

8 We lay on the grass: Virginia Cowles, *Looking for Trouble* (Hamish Hamilton, 1941), p.435

8 wave after wave: Harold Nicolson, *Diaries and Letters, 1939–1945*, (ed.) Nigel Nicolson (William Collins, 1967), p.111

8 We are growing: Weymouth, p.163

8 People are becoming: Nicolson, p.109

8 Whoohoo: Quoted in Tom Harrisson, *Living Through the Blitz* (William Collins, 1976), p.42

9 The purpose of: Quoted in *The Blitz: Then and Now, Vol. II*, (ed.) Winston G. Ramsey (Battle of Britain Prints International, 1988), p.49

9 We have had many: Weymouth, p.175

9 waited for an hour: Ibid., p.176

10 their warehouses and sheds: *The Blitz: Then and Now, Vol. II*, p.57

10 Keep the home fires: Neil Wallington, *Firemen at War: The Work of London's Fire-Fighters in the Second World War* (Newton Abbot: David & Charles, 1981), p.21

10 it was quite: IWM 67/262/1, Cyril Demarne, pp.16, 23. Demarne, an instructor with the AFS at West Ham, moved to Australia after the war to train staff in the outback in how to deal with air-crash fires. He died in February 2007, aged 101.

11 an endless queue: Peter Blackmore, 'Early Days' in *Fire and Water: An NFS Anthology* (Lindsay Drummond, 1942), pp.20–1, 24–5

12 the drone of approaching: Cyril Demarne, *The London Blitz: A Fireman's Tale* (After the Battle, 1991), pp.223–4

12 I was frightened: IWM, Demarne, p.18

12 That day stands out: Bernard Kops, *The World is a Wedding* (MacGibbon & Kee, 1963), p.63

12 It was very exciting: Len Jones quoted in Joanna Mack and Steve Humphries, *The Making of Modern London, 1939–1945: London at War* (Sidgwick & Jackson, 1985), p.40

14 an extraordinary spectacle: Quoted in Wallington, p.80

15 Chaos met our eyes: IWM 80/30/1, F.W. Hurd, 'Blitz over London. An impression of the first large-scale night raid on the capital 17/9/40', handwritten ms.

16 a patch of burning: Quoted in John Crossland, 'Black Saturday' in 'Blitz', *Sunday Times*, 2 September 1990

16 You'd go round: IWM 67/262/1, Stan Durling

17 They scream: IWM 67/262/1, Stan Hook

17 saw an astonishing: A.P. Herbert, *Independent Member* (Methuen, 1950), pp.169–71

18 others were evacuated: Demarne, p.52

19 absolutely amazed: Crossland, p.37

19 It was chaos: Quoted in Jane Waller and Michael Vaughan-Rees, *Blitz: The Civilian War 1940–45* (Macdonald Optima, 1990), pp.21–2

19 Come on girls: Gladys Strelitz in Les Miller and Howard Bloch, *Black Saturday: The First Day of the Blitz* (T.H.A.P., 1984), p.12

19 Not funny: Alan Hutt notebook, Labour History Archive and Study Centre, Manchester

20 I came out: IWM Department of Documents 99/66/1, Private Papers of Miss I. Naish

22 Then quite suddenly: Hurd, 'Blitz over London'

22 sounded a beautiful: Kops, p.64

23 She turned up: IWM, Baltrop, pp.9–10

Chapter 2: 'The Most Grim Test in its History . . .'

25 The Most Grim Test: Hannen Swaffer, 'The Cockney is Bloody but Unbowed', *Daily Herald*, 9 September 1940

25 With our enormous: House of Commons *Official Report*, 30 July 1934. *Parliamentary Debates* Fifth Series (HMSO, 1934), Vol. 292, Column 2368

25 Darling Kat: Lady Diana Cooper, *Trumpets from the Steep* (Rupert Hart-Davis, 1960), pp.58–9

25 War Damage Survey: The maps have now been collected and reissued with an introduction by Robin Woolven. Ann Saunders (ed.), *The London County Council Bomb Damage Maps, 1939–1945* (London Topographical Society, 2005)

26 In that month: Quoted in ibid., p.20

26 There is also a list: LCC/CE/War/2/66

27 lifted and moved: Jones in Mack and Humphries, p.43

27 ragged sleepless army: *Daily Express*, 9 September 1940

28 looked like one: John Colville, *The Fringes of Power: 10 Downing Street Diaries 1939–1955* (Hodder & Stoughton, 1985), p.752

28 a million to one: *Daily Herald*, 9 September 1940

29 the big crowd: *The Memoirs of General the Lord Ismay* (William Heinemann, 1960), pp.183–4

29 had a long job: Martin Gilbert, *Finest Hour: Winston S. Churchill, 1939–1941* (William Heinemann, 1983), p.775

30 third-class accommodation: Colville, p.242

30 The question of where: Richard Holmes, *Churchill's Bunker: The Secret Headquarters at the Heart of Britain's Victory* (Profile Books in association with the Imperial War Museum, 2009), pp.62–3

30 the whole bloody world's: Demarne (1991), p.28

30 he said it was: Hutt notebook

31 His pulpit still: Ritchie Calder, *The Lesson of London* (Secker & Warburg, 1941), pp.18–20, and *Daily Herald*, 11 September 1940

33 locals still believe: *The Blitz: Then and Now, Vol. II*, p.79

33 They call it crater: *Daily Herald*, 12 September 1940

33 backless houses: *Daily Herald*, 10 September 1940

34 Later that day: Sarah Bradford, *George VI* (Weidenfeld & Nicolson, 1989), pp.427–8

34 We had depended: IWM Department of Documents, Conservation Shelf, Violet Regan

34 Most Ack-Ack guns: Basil Collier, *The Defence of the United Kingdom* (HMSO, 1957), p.238

35 with the noise: Lambeth Palace Library, Mss. 2686, Alan C. Don diary, 14 September 1940

36 a curtain of exploding: *Daily Herald*, 12, 13 September 1940

36 some angry voices: General Sir Frederick Pile, *Ack-Ack: Britain's Defences Against Air Attack During the Second World War* (Harrap, 1949), pp.132–4

36 What a fantastic: IWM 95/14/1, Phyllis Warner, 'Journal Under the Terror', 14 September 1940

38 Acacia Avenue: *Daily Express*, 10 September 1940

38 Emergency Medical Services: *The War Diary of St Thomas's Hospital*, p.6

39 for most of the war: *The War Diary of St Thomas's Hospital*, (eds) Frank and Dorothy Cockett (Starling Press, 1991), pp.3, 4, 10–34; *Daily Herald* and *Daily Express*, 10 September 1940

39 My darling Mama: Quoted in William Shawcross, *Queen Elizabeth, the Queen Mother: The Official Biography* (Macmillan, 2009), pp.522–3, 524

40 There is much bitterness: Nicolson, 17 September 1940

40 helped people who have: Quoted in Shawcross, p.524

40 wearing in turn: Quoted in Piers Brendon and Philip Whitehead, *The Windsors: A Dynasty Revealed* (Hodder & Stoughton, 1994), p.114

41 might perhaps have been: Norman Hartnell, *Silver and Gold* (Evans Bros, 1955), pp.101–2

41 A sense of invasion: *The Diary of Virginia Woolf: Vol. V, 1936–41*, (ed.) Anne Olivier Bell (Chatto & Windus, 1984), p.320

41 It may be this weekend: *Daily Herald*, 12 September 1940

42 by the morning: Terence H. O'Brien, *Civil Defence* (HMSO, 1955), p.223

42 rumours rapidly spread: Ibid., p.224; *Daily Herald*, 9 September 1940

43 27,500 high-explosive bombs: Philip Ziegler, *London at War, 1939–1945* (Sinclair-Stevenson, 1995), p.118

43 This was the night: *Few Eggs and No Oranges: The Diaries of Vere Hodgson 1940–1945* (1971; Persephone Books, 1999), p.210

44 heard of all sorts: London Metropolitan Archive, Acc. 2243/14/1, The Diaries of Anthony Heap, 9, 10, 16, 22, 25 September, 12, 13, 15, 16, 26 October and 10 November 1940

45 Bomb entered roof: Don diary, 18 October 1940

46 the Bishop of London: Ibid., 10, 17 October 1940

46 I almost wish: Warner, part III, p.3

46 to see London: *Leave the Letters Till We're Dead: The Letters of Virginia Woolf, 1936–1941*, (ed.) Nigel Nicolson (The Hogarth Press, 1980), pp.431, 460

46 perhaps our strangest: *The Diary of Virginia Woolf: Vol. V*, pp.316–17

Chapter 3: Sheltering

49 John Strachey, *Post D* (Victor Gollancz, 1941), p.48

49 other options: Holmes, p.64

49 deep underground rooms: Colville, pp.240–1

49 Pray let six: Ibid., p.280

50 knock-out blow: O'Brien, p.172

51 Each stage of alert: Ibid., pp.224–6

52 Once the blitz started: Ibid., pp.363–4

52 government funding: Ibid., pp.107–9

52 probably the most: Quoted in ibid., p.150

52 a large amount: Government circular of 28 March 1938, pp.121–2

53 refuge room: *The Protection of Your Home Against Air Raids* (HMSO, 1938), pp.124–5, 148

53 stand the test: Quoted in O'Brien, p.153

54 still no public shelters: Ibid., 162

56 Defence Regulation 23B: Ibid., p.368

57 specified areas: Ibid., p.504

57 When the alert sounded: Patrick Shea, *Voices and the Sound of Drums: An Irish Autobiography* (Blackstaff Press, 1981), pp.148–9

58 We are lucky: Warner, 'Journal Under the Terror'

59 This going up: IWM 79/27/1, 'War Diary. A Chronicle of events, personal and political. Which took place during three years of War against Oppression which commenced in September 1939 recorded by Sidney Chave', 21 October 1940

60 It was so small: IWM 67/262/1, Margaret Turpin

62 which in those days: Barbara Nixon, *Raiders Overhead: A Diary of the London Blitz* (1943; Scolar/Gulliver, 1980), p.7. Finsbury is now part of the borough of Islington.

62 During September 1940: Ibid., pp.53, 54, 55

63 It is amazing: IWM PP/MCR/199, The Papers of Joan Veazey, 16 September 1940

64 potentially lethal public shelters: O'Brien, p.369

64 Of course you had: IWM 67/262/1, Margaret Turpin

Chapter 4: Underground

66 'In Civvy Street': IWM Department of Documents, 88/49/1

67 For days on end: Nixon, p.45

67 The Jewish dead: *The Blitz: Then and Now, Vol. II*, p.181

67 rising to the problem: TNA HO199/324, Winifred Holmes, 'Personal Visit to Stoke Newington – October 14th 1940'. I am most grateful to Robin Woolven for drawing my attention to this report.

69 a strong tendency: Quoted in O'Brien, p.507

69 The vicar of Haggerston: H.A. Wilson, *Death Over Haggerston* (A.W. Mowbray, 1941), pp.14–15

69 A small party: IWM 01/3/1, The Papers of Mrs M. Fenlon, pp.2–3, 5, 6

71 60,000 people: *Picture Post*, 5 October 1940, pp.16–18

71 as there was no: An eighteen-year-old Wren, Helen Sandys, quoted in Waller and Vaughan-Rees, p.257

71 a gypsy squatters' camp: TNA PRO 207/1101, Letter from E.J. Hodsoll to the Head of Home Office ARP Department, 4 February 1941

71 'Rock of Ages': M-OA, 'Living Through the Blitz', Box 233

71 a light touch: O'Brien, p.531

71 Runcorn: Ibid., p.199

72 cold and dark: Sylvia Cooke, quoted in Waller and Vaughan-Rees, p.256

72 men, women and children: John H. Smith, quoted in ibid., p.257

72 not only the most: Ritchie Calder, *Carry on London* (The English Universities Press Limited, 1941), p.39

72 an enormous place: IWM, Baltrop

72 On one side lay: Constantine FitzGibbon, *The Blitz* (Allan Wingate, 1957), pp.149–50

73 never forget the stampede: Calder, *Carry on London*, pp.40–1

73 confused mass of bodies: Hilde Marchant, *Women and Children Last: A Woman Reporter's Account of the Battle of Britain* (Victor Gollancz, 1941), pp.89–91

74 It does seem: Diary of Euan Wallace, Bodleian Library, Oxford, GB 161, Mss Eng. Hist. C.495–8, 9 October 1940

74 slept the night: Calder, *Carry on London*, pp.41–2

74 night out with: *Stepney Letters: Extracts from Letters Written by Rachel Reckitt from Stepney During the 'Blitz' of 1940–1941* (privately printed, Milthorpe, Cumbria, 1991), pp.26, 29–30

76 an extensive system: Letter to *The Times*, 17 February 1938, p.8

77 The concrete industry: J.B.S. Haldane, *ARP* (Victor Gollancz, 1938), pp.210–13

77 £12 for each person: Ronald Clark, *The Life and Work of J.B.S. Haldane* (Hodder & Stoughton, 1968), pp.122–3, 126–9; O'Brien, p.190 n.4

77 sandbagged basements: *Architect and Building News*, 21 October 1938, pp.57–8

77 danger volume: John Pinckheard, 'The ARP Exhibition at Finsbury Town Hall' in *Keystone* (Journal of Architects, Surveyors and Technical Assistants), March 1939 (Ove Arup Papers, Churchill College, Cambridge)

78 favourably impressed: John Allan, *Lubetkin: Architecture and the Tradition of Progress* (RIBA Publications, 1992), pp.353–61

78 It is quite certain: Quoted in Robin Woolven, ' "Playing Hitler's Game" from Fitzroy Road NW1. J.B.S. Haldane in controversy in WWII', *Camden History Review*, Vol. 23, 1999, p.25

78 These people are not: *The Listener*, 4 November 1940

79 By that time Haldane: Woolven, p.25

79 lying like sardines: IWM Department of Documents 91/5/1, The Papers of the Reverend J.G. Markham

80 sleep was, for most: Don diary, 7 September 1940

80 The most compelling: Joanne Buggins, 'An Appreciation of the Shelter Photographs Taken by Bill Brandt in November 1940', *Imperial War Museum Review*, 1989, pp.32–42

80 stretched on the rough floor: Calder, *Carry on London*, pp.36, 37, 38–9

81 We decided what was: Phil Piratin MP, *Our Flag Stays Red* (Thames Publications, 1948), p.73

81 No one snores: Cooper, p.60

82 electrically operated gates: John Gregg, *The Shelter of the Tubes: Tube Sheltering in Wartime London* (Capital Transport Publishing, 2001), p.14

82 The LPTB: *Daily Worker*, 13 September 1940, p.1

82 So during the day: IWM 67/262/1, Irene Moseley, pp.5–6

83 From the platforms: *South London Press*, 1 October 1940, p.2, quoted in Gregg, p.24

84 I had not realised: Veazey, 17 September 1940

84 It was frightening: IWM, Moseley, p.7

84 troglodyte communities: Barbara Castle, *Fighting All the Way* (Macmillan, 1993), p.91

85 shelter census: *Front Line, 1940–1941: The Official Story of Civil Defence in Britain* (HMSO, 1942), pp.67–8

86 the Blitz Team: *Herbert Morrison's Work in the War Government 1940–1945* (The Labour Party, 1945), p.4

86 son of a Lambeth policeman: Bernard Donoughue and G.W. Jones, *Herbert Morrison, Portrait of a Politician* (Weidenfeld & Nicolson, 1973), pp.284–7; *Oxford Dictionary of National Biography*, entry by David Howell

86 Dear Herbert Morrison: *Daily Herald*, 4 October 1940

86 Improving the shelters: Charles Graves, *London Transport Carried On: 1939–1945* (London Transport, 1947), p.45

87 The next day: Betty Vernon, *Ellen Wilkinson, 1891–1947* (Croom Helm, 1982), p.187

87 What does money matter?: *Daily Herald*, 7 October 1940

87 I met [Wilkinson]: Marchant, pp.94, 101

87 She said to me: Nicolson, 20 November 1940, p.128

88 bombed out of her flat: Vernon, pp.186–7

88 a straggling queue: Clearly not all followed Irene Moseley's mother's precaution that bedding should be carried in a suitcase, though the long queues must have made it obvious that these were 'squatters' or 'tunnellers', as the press called those who sheltered underground, rather than travellers.

88 by 6pm there seemed: *Sunday Dispatch*, 22

September 1940, quoted in Gregg, p.24

88 the good sense: Report in the *Daily Herald*, 19 September 1940

88 Trains must run: *The Times*, 30 September 1940

88 twenty unattached young men: *Daily Express*, 28 September 1940; Mass-Observation Archive (M-OA) FR 465, 'The Press and the Blitzkrieg'; TNA HO 45/18540, quoted in Gregg, p.25

88 I am 29: M-OA FR 425, 'Young Men in Tubes: Behaviour in the Underground'

89 whatever type of shelter: Mr W. Mabane, Ministry of Home Security Under Secretary, quoted in the *Daily Herald*, 24 September 1940

89 police supervision: *Daily Herald*, 27 September 1940

89 7,600 had been erected: Gregg, p.56

89 Holland Park station: M-OA FR 436, 'Shelter in London'

89 Old Street station: Gregg, p.42

90 We didn't have: IWM 67/262/1, Emily Eary, p.15

90 Lifebuoy Boys: Idle, p.81

90 at least 700 people: *Daily Herald*, 28 September 1940

90 It was better: IWM, Moseley, pp.9–10

90 to head a committee: Vernon, p.188

91 highly undesirable: Hansard, House of Commons debates, Vol. 365, 20 November 1940

91 Horder's recommendations: *Recommendations of Lord Horder's Committee regarding the Conditions in Air-Raid Shelters with special reference to health; and a brief statement of action taken by the Government thereon* Cmd. 6234 (HMSO, November 1940) and *Further Recommendations of Lord Horder's Committee regarding the Conditions in Air-Raid Shelters with special reference to health; and a brief statement of action taken by the Government thereon* Cmd. 6235 (HMSO, December 1940)

91 Hilde Marchant: *Daily Express*, 14 October 1940

91 PLEASE stop: Camden Local History Archive, H 355.23, *Swiss Cottager*, Bulletin 1

92 a simple snuff: IWM 79/27/1, Chave, p.200

92 two white lines: Nigel Pennick, *Bunkers Under London* (privately printed, 1985), p.12

92 terrible hindrance: IWM Conservation Shelf, Veronica Goddard, 'My Scrapbook, Part I (1939–1943, 1946)', 21 October 1940

92 Should women have: Graves (1947), p.45; *Picture Post*, 10 November 1940, pp.16–17

92 *Subway Companion*: Gregg, pp.67, 72–3

92 Greetings to our: *Swiss Cottager*, Bulletins 1–4

95 I should like: TNA HO 186/639

Chapter 5: Front Line

97 *Front Line*, p.143

97 There is no public record: Strachey, pp.2–21

97 an old Etonian: Michael Newman, *John Strachey* (Manchester University Press, 1989)

98 killed anything else: 'Reporting the War', *New Statesman and Nation*, 5 April 1941, p.371

98 At first he took: Strachey, pp.17, 18–19

99 I wanted an active: Nixon, p.8

99 Herbert Morrison himself: Donoughue and Jones, p.266

99 the ARP Act: O'Brien, pp.109–10; Mike Brown, *Put That Light Out: Britain's Civil Defence at War, 1939–1945* (Alan Sutton, 1999), p.4

100 This still fell short: O'Brien, p.214

101 must have been drunk: M-OA FR A24, 1 June 1939

101 very comfortable: IWM Department of Documents, 09/37/1, Frederick R. Bodley, 'ARPing On It', pp.1–2

101 railway workers: Nixon, p.78

102 had been to the: Ibid., pp.82–3, 85

102 smoke drills: Bodley, pp.2–5

102 training can never: O'Brien, p.122

102 the multitudinous things: Nixon, p.10

103 ticking off the names: Frances Faviell, *Chelsea Concerto* (Cassell, 1959), p.115

103 eyes and ears: *Front Line*, p.144

103 Where are you?: Graham Greene, *The Ministry of Fear* (William Heinemann, 1943), p.27

103 tennis racket: Strachey, p.46

103 just crashed: IWM Department of Documents, 95/8/1, The Papers of Miss M.E.A. Allan, 12 September 1940

104 great, torpid, iron pigs: Major A.B. Hartley, *Unexploded Bomb: A History of Bomb Disposal* (Cassell, 1958), p.60; M.J. Jappy, *Danger UXB: The Remarkable Story of the Disposal of Unexploded Bombs During the Second World War* (Channel Four Books, 2001), p.183; *The Blitz: Then and Now, Vol. II*, pp.84–9

105 delay mechanism fuses: My thanks to Dr Robin Hiley for this information, plus *The Blitz: Then and Now, Vol. I*, pp.147–77 and http://www.fortunecity.co.uk/melting pot/oxford/330/fs

105 he with a balaclava: Bodley, p.13

105 I go into a house: Quoted in Juliet Gardiner, *Wartime: Britain 1939–1945* (Headline, 2004), p.386

106 left to the local authorities: Robin Woolven, 'First in the Country: Dr Richard Tee and Air Raid Precautions', *Hackney History*, Vol. 6 (2000), pp.50–8

107 Some of the mortuaries: Frank R. Lewey, *Cockney Campaign* (Stanley Paul, n.d.; probably 1941–42), p.83

107 It was a terrible: Faviell, p.115
109 No amount of training: Nixon, pp.31, 10, 32
109 unmistakable, indescribable: Strachey, pp.78, 93
110 They had evidently: Ibid., pp.32–40
112 A huge bomb: *Southwark at War*, compiled and edited by Rib Davies and Pamela Schweitzer (Southwark Council Local Studies Library, 1996), p.12
112 A motley crew: Stanley Rothwell, *Lambeth at War* (SE1 People's History Project, Morley College, 1981), pp.8, 17, 23

Chapter 6: The Test of War
116 wandered about for: Kingsley Martin, 'Report on East London', *New Statesman and Nation*, 5 October 1940, pp.324–5
118 grudgingly permitted to spend: Richard M. Titmuss, *History of the Second World War: Problems of Social Policy* (HMSO, 1950), pp.45, 47, 52–3
118 the ebb and flow of people: Ibid., pp.203–35, 413
119 unforgettable picture: Ibid., p.261
119 rarely translated: M-OA FR 431, 'Survey of Voluntary and Official Bodies During the Bombing of the East End', p.59
120 When they come out: Ibid., pp.v–vi
121 excellent auxiliary work: Ibid., p.63
121 The indomitable 'Mrs B': Titmuss (1950), pp.262–3
122 two hundred people: M-OA FR 431, p.59
122 the real government: *Times Literary Supplement*, 6 August 1971
122 a Socialist of a very: Lambeth Palace Library, Groser Papers, Ms.3562, Letter from Reverend John Groser to the Bishop of Hereford, 14 May 1928
122 When the blitz came: Groser Papers, Ms.3433, 'John Groser – some memories', Mary Giddey, Jack Boggis, Canon C.E. Young, Rector of Liverpool
123 The Reverend Lex Miller: Calder, *Carry on London*, pp.53, 54, 157
123 Jimmy Hall: M-OA FR 431, p.73
123 Gradually, the machinery: Ibid., p.iii
124 Citizens' Kitchens: LCC, 'Important – Blitz Feeding', 9 April 1941, pp.1–3; Calder, *Carry on London*, pp.79–92; Titmuss (1950), pp.266–7
124 Blitz meals: LCC, 'Blitz Feeding', p.2
125 278,623 Londoners: TNA HO 186/952/2352, 26 February 1941
125 a morass of confusion: Titmuss (1950), pp.280–1
125 people are still living: Reckitt, pp.12–13

126 The East End people: Nicolson, 18 September 1940, p.115
126 Fifty homeless Jewish people: *Daily Herald*, 23 September 1940
127 action was taken: M-OA FR 451, 'Reception Areas: Refugees from Blitzed Areas', 11 November 1940
127 far too busy: Frank R. Lewey, *Cockney Campaign*, p.22
128 kept busy all day: Reckitt, pp.16–17, 18–19
128 Yet only 20,500: *Daily Herald*, 26 September 1940
128 760 unaccompanied children: Titmuss (1950), p.285
129 with no questions asked: Reckitt, p.14
130 You can get: Ian McLaine, *Ministry of Morale: Home Front Morale and the Ministry of Information in World War II* (Allen & Unwin, 1979), p.133
130 over a thousand: Titmuss (1950), p.292
132 The big problem: Reckitt, p.19
132 To leave local officials: Calder, *The Lesson of London*, p.37
132 a wartime measure only: Robin Woolven, 'The London Experience of Regional Government, 1938–1945', *London Journal*, Vol. 25 (2), 2000, pp.59–78
133 sixteen Town Clerks: A.D. Harvey, 'Local Authorities and the Blitz', *Contemporary Review*, 1990, p.197
133 dingy Weights and Measures office: Woolven (2000), p.64
133 Bloody lot of matchboxes: M-OA FR 431, p.75
134 Morrison refused: Woolven (2000), p.66; Geoffrey Alderman, 'M.H. Davis: The Rise and Fall of a Communal Upstart', *Jewish Historical Studies*, Vol. XXXI (1990), pp.249–68
134 quite novel: Dr H.J. Eysenck quoted in E. Doreen Idle, *War Over West Ham: A Study of Community Adjustment* (Faber & Faber, 1943), p.61
135 £4,400 a year: Ibid., pp.62–3
135 The task of getting: TNA HO 186/2352, London Region Intelligence Branch Monthly Report, 16 August 1941, quoted in Woolven (2000), p.67
135 a joke: Harvey, pp.199–200
136 a wide-awake unit: Tom Harrisson, 'War Adjustment', *New Statesman and Nation*, 28 September 1940, pp.300–1
136 a party of his colleagues: Harvey, p.200
137 several Labour men: Euan Wallace Papers, 24 May 1940. Further information from Dr Robin Woolven.
137 a sensible food-economy: Calder, *The Lesson of London*, pp.125, 126, 127

138 Far too many people: Nixon, pp.158–70
138 Regional Government has been: W.A. Robson, 'Reform Our Local Government', *Picture Post*, Vol. 10, no. 7, 15 February 1941, pp.24–6; 'Regionaliter' (W.A. Robson), 'The Regional Commissioners', *Political Quarterly*, Vol. 12 (1941), pp.144–53
138 functions were wound up: On 2 May 1945 the powers of the Regional Controllers were transferred to the appropriate ministries; the Ministry of Home Security was abolished on 31 May 1945, and on 10 June 1945 the King reviewed civil defences for the final time.
138 could see no case: Woolven (2000), pp.74–5

Chapter 7: Guernicaed
139 Well, workers: Quoted in Norman Longmate, *Air Raid: The Bombing of Coventry, 1940* (Hutchinson, 1976), p.213
139 Coventry casualty figures: Adrian Smith, *The City of Coventry: Twentieth Century Icon* (I.B. Tauris, 2006), p.149
140 free the town: Longmate, p.13
140 one of the largest: Reverend R.T. Howard, *Ruined and Rebuilt: The Story of Coventry Cathedral, 1939–1962* (Council of Coventry Cathedral, 1962), p.7. The cathedral was started in 1373 and completed in 1460.
141 The Rolls-Royce factory: Longmate, pp.26–7
141 Our task is to repay: Notes written up by a journalist employed by Goebbels' Ministry of Propaganda, quoted in ibid., pp.63–4
142 valiant efforts: Carl Chinn, *Brum Undaunted: Birmingham During the Blitz* (Birmingham Library Services, 1996), p.100
143 flames already lighting: Donoughue and Jones, p.219
143 Looks Coventry way: Marchant, p.128
143 excellently and in great comfort: Colville, p.295
143 Coventry appeared to be: Longmate, p.104
143 the whole wall: Dr Harry Winter, 'The Man in White' in Allen A. Michie and Walter Graebner, *Lights of Freedom* (Allen & Unwin, 1941), pp.97–9
144 carried down a large: Mrs A. Zebrzuski, writing in the *Coventry Evening Telegraph*, quoted in Waller and Vaughan-Rees, pp.102–3; Tim Lewis, *Moonlight Sonata: The Coventry Blitz* (Tim Lewis and Coventry City Council, 1990), pp.124–5
145 The beds began: Quoted in Longmate, p.106
145 although it was November: Ibid., p.127
145 Any calls that did get through: Lewis, p.100
146 a bitter cold wind: Winter, in Michie and Graebner, p.101
147 more than a thousand people: Longmate, p.139

147 Hardly a building remained: BBC Home Service 1.15 p.m., Sunday, 24 November 1940
147 It was like: TNA HO 186/626 and 556
147 picturesque and fine: Marchant, p.141
147 A third of the city centre: Eric L. Bird, *Air Raid on Coventry 14/15 November 1940*, 18 November 1940, TNA HO 199/178 X/J 5467
147 shattered cherubs: Marchant, p.134
148 very rough estimate: Bird, *Air Raid on Coventry*
148 picking up bits: Madge Faulkner quoted in Lewis, p.130
148 a city of the dead: Unknown writer quoted in ibid., pp.157–8
148 The dead included: Ibid., p.128
149 even if it meant: Ibid., p.144
151 Morrison was reasonably satisfied: Donoughue and Jones, pp.291–2; *Herbert Morrison: An Autobiography of Lord Morrison of Lambeth* (Odhams Press, 1960), p.185
151 80 per cent of the workforce: Adrian Smith, p.13
152 Calder was particularly impressed: *New Statesman and Nation*, 23 November 1940, p.510
152 no signs of any official: M-O FR 495, 'Coventry: The Effects of the Bombing', 18 November 1940
153 violent bombardment: Colville, 15 November 1940, p.295
153 in a very sorry state: John W. Wheeler-Bennett, *King George VI: His Life and Reign* (Macmillan, 1958), pp.477–9
153 almost sobbing reference: Nicolson, letter to Vita Sackville-West, 20 November 1940, p.128
154 it was gruesome work: Quoted in Longmate, p.223. A similar procedure was adopted at Dresden in February 1945.
155 Let us vow: Reverend Leslie Cook in *The City We Loved* (Three Spires Publishing, 1942), p.42

Chapter 8: Britain Can (Probably) Take It
156 James [Pope-Hennessy]: *Self-Portrait With Friends: The Selected Diaries of Cecil Beaton, 1926–1974*, (ed.) Richard Buckle (Weidenfeld & Nicolson, 1979), p.75
156 Bombing stiffens people's morale: IWM 67/262/1, Jill Craigie
156 voiceless symbol: Louise Campbell, *Coventry Cathedral: Art and Architecture in Post-War Britain* (Oxford: Clarendon Press, 1996), pp.8–9
157 the ideal recorder: Kenneth Clark, *The Other Half: A Self-Portrait* (John Murray, 1977), p.24
157 a thin fog: John Piper, 'The Architecture of Destruction', *Architectural Review*, July 1941, p.25

157 He stood around: David Fraser Jenkins, *John Piper: The Forties* (Philip Wilson/Imperial War Museum, 2000), p.33

157 for Britain what Picasso's: Frances Spalding, *John Piper, Myfanwy Piper: Lives in Art* (Oxford University Press, 2009), p.183

157 of course I did not: Clark, p.22: 'In this I was not altogether successful, as two distinguished artists, Eric Ravilious and Thomas Hennell, were killed while carrying out WAAC commissions.'

157 transferred his feelings: Ibid., p.24

158 the group sense: John Rothenstein, *Modern English Painters, Vol. II* (Macdonald, 1984), p.68

158 The tube shelters gave: Clark, p.24

158 understandable, that: Keith Vaughan, quoted in Adrian Lewis, 'Henry Moore's "Shelter Drawings": Memory and Myth' in Pat Kirkham and David Thoms (eds), *War Culture, Social Change and Changing Experience in World War Two* (Lawrence & Wishart, 1995), p.118

158 a steaming human throng: Ibid., p.198

158 a white-grub race: Eric Newton in the *Sunday Times*, 18 May 1941, quoted in ibid., p.120

158 was not the human ordeal: Spalding, p.182

159 Hush, hush: Francis Williams, *Press, Parliament and People* (William Heinemann,1946), p.10

159 Duds at the top: *Harold Nicolson: Diaries and Letters 1939–1945*

160 5,000 in all: Angus Calder, *The People's War: Britain 1939–1945* (Jonathan Cape, 1969), p.505

160 frequently scored through: Rear Admiral George P. Thomson, *Blue Pencil Admiral: The Inside Story of Press Censorship* (Sampson Low, Marston & Co., n.d.)

161 by 55 per cent: Quoted in Robert MacKay, *Half the Battle: Civilian Morale in Britain During the Second World War* (Manchester University Press, 2002), p.145

161 Harold Nicolson noted: Nicolson, p.114

161 Details kill: Quoted in McLaine, p.125

162 irritated by propaganda: Ibid., p.64

xxx This is a people's war: Memorandum to the War Cabinet, 24 April 1942. TNA INF 1/679

162 vetoed by the Cabinet: McLaine, p.65

162 It was equally important: Thomson, pp.79, 82

163 the information was removed: TNA INF 1/845, Ministry of Information

163 To have told: Thomson, p.79

163 If clients of: Ibid., pp.79–80

164 this implied threat: Longmate, pp.208–9, 214–15, 218

164 great care must be taken: TNA INF 1/845, Ministry of Information

166 The Minister of Home Security: Ibid.

166 263 people were killed: Chinn, pp.112, 121

167 'leaderless' that night: Ibid., p.103

167 the General Manager: TNA INF 1/845, Ministry of Information

167 People in Bristol: M-OA FR 626, FR 706

167 The woolliest concept: Quoted in Paul Addison, *The Road to 1945: British Politics and the Second World War* (Pimlico, 1994), p.121

168 Ultimately morale: Quoted in MacKay, p.2

168 throwing the shadow: M-OA FR 325, 'Report on "Cooper's Snoopers" Press Campaign', 5 August 1940

169 partly by discussions: TNA INF 1/290, 'The Work of the Home Intelligence Division, 1939–1944', quoted in Addison and Crang, p.xiv

169 Special Branch reports: Ibid.

169 initially it wondered: McLaine, p.23

169 What does one mean: TNA INF 1/848, 12 March 1940

169 the determination to: M-OA FR 606, 'Portsmouth: Reaction to the Blitz'

170 Morale should never: Quoted in McLaine, pp.129–30

170 The first and most: *The Listener*, 7 September 1939, p.464

171 Thirty per cent: Siân Nicholas, *The Echo of War: Home Front Propaganda and the Wartime BBC, 1939–45* (Manchester University Press, 1999), p.53

172 90 per cent of British homes: Tim O'Sullivan, 'Listening Through: The Wireless and World War Two' in *War Culture: Social Change and Changing Experience in World War Two*, (eds) Pat Kirkham and David Thoms, p.179

172 a fixed feature: The BBC's Listener Research Panel estimated that on a typical day, 30 to 50 per cent of the population would listen to the evening news, and this would rise to over 60 per cent if it were known that Churchill would be broadcasting. On the evening of D-Day, 6 June 1944, 80 per cent listened to the 9 o'clock news. (Lewis, p.181)

172 The BBC was regarded: Nicholas, p.71

172 a land mine exploded: Ibid., pp.127, 237

172 most depressing broadcast: TNA INF 1/174A, 28 February 1941

173 likely to be accused: Nicholas, p.126

174 A new Britain: *New York Herald Tribune*, 23, 25, 27 September 1940, quoted in Nicholas John Cull, *Selling War: The British Propaganda Campaign Against American 'Neutrality' in*

World War II (Oxford University Press, 1995), p.100

174 Britain is still: Edward Bliss, Jnr (ed.), *In Search of Light: The Broadcasts of Edward R. Murrow, 1938–61* (New York: Alfred Knopf, 1967), pp.30–1

174 impinge on the American: Cull, p.101

175 James Reston: Ibid., p.106

175 the Committee to Defend America by Aiding the Allies: Ibid., p.73. It was known as the White Committee after its chairman William Allen White, a Kansas Republican.

175 We have begun work: *The Humphrey Jennings Film Reader*, (ed.) Kevin Jackson (Carcanet, 1993), pp.7–8

175 a success: Ibid., p.8, 3 November 1940

176 sixty million Americans: Cull, p.108

176 There is no reason: Harry Watt, *Don't Look at the Camera* (Elek, 1974), p.145. Watt co-directed the film with Jennings; *Britain and the Cinema in the Second World War*, (ed.) Philip M. Taylor (Macmillan, 1988), p.124

176 You burned the city: Archibald MacLeish, *In Honor of an Ideal and a Man: Three Talks on Freedom* (New York: CBS, 1942), pp.5–7, quoted in Cull, p.109

176 almost miraculous change: Ibid.

Chapter 9: The Fear of Fear

177 It wasn't the raids: IWM 67/262/1, Thomas Tapfield

177 How's trade: Quoted in *Our Longest Days: A People's History of the Second World War*, (ed.) Sandra Koa Wing (Profile Books, 2008), pp.49–50

178 strung out in: Edward Glover, 'Notes on the Psychological Effects of War Conditions on the Civilian Population: (I)', *International Journal of Psycho-Analysis*, Vol. XXII, 1941, pp.132–46

178 an impotent fretfulness: *The Neuroses of War*, (ed.) Emmanuel Miller (Macmillan, 1940), p.195

178 not enough trained: Titmuss (1950), pp.19–20

179 in the hope that: Edgar Jones, Robin Woolven, Bill Durodié and Simon Wessely, 'Civilian Morale During the Second World War: Responses to Air Raids Re-examined', *Social History of Medicine*, Vol. 17, no. 3 (2004), pp.467–8. I am most grateful to Professor Edgar Jones for his help with this chapter.

179 The blitz, when it: Edward Glover, 'Notes on the Psychological Effects of War Conditions on the Civilian Population: (III) The "Blitz" – 1939–41', *International Journal of Psycho-Analysis*, Vol. XXIII (1942), p.17

179 rejected without ceremony: Glover (I), p.133

179 it had no patients: Jones et al., p.474; Lyndsey Stonebridge, 'Anxiety at a Time of Crisis', *History Workshop Journal*, no. 45 (1998), p.172

179 in large part: C.P. Blacker, *Neurosis and the Mental Health Services* (Oxford University Press, 1948), pp.xiv, 22

179 After intensive raids: Aubrey Lewis, 'Incidence of Neurosis in England Under War Conditions', *Lancet*, 2 (1942), pp.175–83, quoted in Jones et al., p.474

179 only one case: Lyndsey Stonebridge, *The Writing of Anxiety: Imagining Wartime in Mid-Century British Culture* (Palgrave Macmillan, 2007), p.17

180 the case of Mrs A: Glover (III), pp.24–5

180 a 'war neurotic': Ibid., p.18

181 At the beginning: Quoted in Ben Shephard, *A War of Nerves: Soldiers and Psychiatrists, 1914–1994* (Jonathan Cape, 2000), p.176

182 Melitta Schmideberg: Stonebridge (2007), p.16

182 Life took on: Melitta Schmideberg, 'Some Observations on Individual Reactions to Air Raids', *International Journal of Psycho-Analysis*, Vol. XXII (1942), p.158

182 Neighbours became: Ibid.

183 one would have: Ibid., pp.158, 163–4

183 I see the decorator's: Eileen Agar, *A Look at My Life* (with Andrew Lambirth) (Methuen, 1988), p.153

184 defence through defiance: Glover (III), p.19

184 Apparently normal people: Schmideberg, p.174

184 Marghanita Laski: 'Sarah Russell', *To Bed With Grand Music* (1946; Persephone Books, 2009)

184 I have met many: *Daily Herald*, 11 October 1940

185 No Neurosis Myth: Glover (III), pp.29–30, 36–7

185 Doctors in wartime: Orwell reviewing Emmanuel Miller's *The Neuroses in War* for the *New Statesman and Nation*, 14 September 1940, *My Country Right or Left*, p.269

185 You were just going: IWM 67/262/1, Emily Eary

186 I've not heard: IWM 91/5/1, Miss V. Bawtree diary

186 We started talking: M-OA Diary 5244, November 1940

186 people spoke of: Amy Bell, 'Landscapes of Fear: Wartime London 1939–1945', *Journal of British Studies*, 48 (January 2009), pp.160–1

186 in an incident: IWM 04/40/1, 'The Blitz on London', Mrs I. Haslewood, pp.41–2

187 the school playground shed: IWM 88/10/1, W.B. Regan, diaries and diary fragments, Ms.1, pp.5, 18; Ms.3, p.2

189 a physical injury: *Lancet*, 26 July 1941, p.106

189 The shock troops: Letter to *The Times*, 15 October 1940. I am most grateful to Robin Woolven for drawing my attention to this.

189 A voluntary part-time ARP worker: Letter to *The Times* from Mildred Bosanquet, 18 October 1940

190 blissfully quiet spot: *The Times*, 16 May 1941

190 recuperative rest: *The Times*, 17 September 1942, 18 March 1944

190 exceptional facilities: *British Medical Journal*, 12 April 1941, p.573

191 Too many generalisations: *British Medical Journal*, 31 May 1941, p.832

192 shelter slug: Glover (III), p.28

192 require training: Hansard, 9 October 1940

192 the importance of sleep: M-OA FR 415, 21 September 1940

192 a weekend in Oxford: Warner, 'Journal Under the Terror'

193 First there is: *Housewife*, October 1940, pp.46–7

193 either with their school: In Scotland all evacuees were evacuated with their mother or a carer, rather than with their schools.

194 Keep calm and cheerful: Lifebuoy toilet soap, *Daily Herald*, 10 September 1940

194 Air raids will only: *Housewife*, October 1940, pp.46–7

195 Mummy told Jessica: M-OA FR 253, 'Air Raids', July 1940, p.27

195 Children stand up: H. Crichton-Miller, 'Some Factors Conditioning Air Raid Reactions', *Lancet*, 12 July 1941, p.32

195 Small children are not: Schmideberg, p.166

195 rose in a long: M-OA, 'Living Through the Blitz', Box 230, pp.2–3, 10–11, 12

196 early in 1941: Although the American Foster Parents' Plan became the chief funding agency, there were also contributions from the Red Cross and various British philanthropists, including the Duchess of Kent, the niece of one of Sigmund Freud's analysands, Princess Marie Bonaparte. Elisabeth Young-Bruehl, *Anna Freud* (Macmillan, 1988), pp.246–7

197 a 'glorious': *Lancet*, 23 March 1940

197 Anna Freud made a point: Young-Bruehl, pp.252–3

197 our big girls: *The Writings of Anna Freud: Vol. II, 1939–1945. Infants Without Families: Reports on the Hampstead Nurseries* (New York: International Universities Press, 1973), p.8

197 The children remained stable: This confirmed Freud's understanding of separation anxieties, gained by her work in Vienna, in the circumstances of war.

197 So long as bombing: Glover (III), p.33

197 For these children: Freud, p.172

198 One five-year-old: Ibid., p.8

198 afraid of fantasies: Glover (III), p.33

198 The war crisis is: Charles Berg, *War in the Mind: The Case Book of a Medical Psychologist* (Macaulay Press, 1941), p.182, and review by S.M. Coleman

198 the longest case history: Anna Freud, *Narrative of a Child Analysis* (Hogarth Press, 1961); Stonebridge (2007), pp.23–4, 25–6

198 One three-and-a-half-year-old boy: Young-Bruehl, p.253

198 sat for several days: Glover (III), quoting Freud, p.84

198 Long-drawn-out states: Ibid.

Chapter 10: The 1940 Provincial Tour

200 Naomi Mitchison, 'Siren Night': M-OA, 'Living Through the Blitz', Box 231

200 Tom Harrisson, *Living Through the Blitz* (William Collins, 1976), pp.144–5

200 saving no end: Heap diaries, 7 December 1940

201 Southampton seems: Ibid., 23 December 1940

202 magnificent in her: Brian Perrett, *Liverpool: A City at War* (Robert Hale, 1990), pp.86–7; Richard Whittington-Egan, *The Great Liverpool Blitz* (Gallery Press, 1987), pp.38–9

202 The trauma of: Joe Lucas quoted in the 'Spirit of the Blitz' exhibition, Liverpool Maritime Museum, July 2003–August 2004

203 probably the most: Perrett, pp.87–9; Whittington-Egan, pp.40–2; Arthur Johnson, *Merseyside's Secret Blitz Diary* (Trinity Mirror, Merseyside, 2005), pp.55–91

204 a blazing furnace: Quoted in Adrian Smith, 'Remembering the Blitz: Coventry and Southampton Over Sixty Years on', www.soton.ac.uk/history/docs/blitz

204 severely hit and: Harrisson, *Living Through the Blitz*, p.148

205 perhaps the most ambitious: Nikolaus Pevsner, *The Buildings of England: Hampshire and the Isle of Wight* (Penguin, 1967), p.526

205 A group of RAF: Harrisson, p.153

205 dead town: M-OA FR 517, 'Southampton: Further Reports on Raids', December 1940

206 broken in spirit: Charles Smyth, *Cyril Forster Garbett, Archbishop of York* (Hodder & Stoughton, 1959), p.241

206 The civic organisation: TNA HO 199/322 9, HSI 125/3

207 a proud cross section: Bernard Knowles, *Southampton: The English Gateway* (Hutchinson, 1951), p.167

207 the wintry streets: Harrisson, p.165

207 Morale has deteriorated: M-OA FR 603,

'Southampton: Raids and Morale', March 1941

208 it was estimated: *A City at War: Birmingham 1939–1945*, (ed.) Phyllida Ballard (Birmingham Museums and Art Gallery, 1985), pp.9–12

209 Exeter stew: Chinn, pp.87, 110–12

209 2,241 people killed: *Front Line*, p.96

209 some by-elections: Andrew Thorpe, *Parties at War: Political Organization in Second World War Britain* (Oxford University Press, 209), p.1

210 people were blasé: James Belsey and Helen Reid, *The West at War* (Redcliffe Press, 1990), p.46

210 175 UXBs: *The Blitz: Then and Now, Vol. II*, pp.294–5; John Penny, *Bristol at War* (Breedon Books, 2002), pp.68, 70

210 much of the city's architectural heritage: Alderman T.H. Underdown, *Bristol Under Blitz* (Lord Mayor's War Services Council, 1942), pp.6–7

211 little firm evidence: Alistair Lofthouse, *Then and Now: The Sheffield Blitz* (Alistair Lofthouse, 2001), p.52

211 There is more depression: M-OA FR 529, 'The Aftermath of Town Blitzes: Summary of Research in Bristol, Southampton and Cheltenham'

213 by November 28: Helen Reid, *Bristol Under Siege: Surviving the Wartime Blitz* (Redcliffe Press, 2005), pp.62–3

213 a body blow: Lofthouse, p.3

214 Sheffield's most famous: *Sheffield Star*, quoted in Waller and Vaughan-Rees, p.128

214 realised how bad: Waller and Vaughan-Rees, p.127

214 750 civilians: James S. Abrahams, *Sheffield Blitz* (Pawson & Brailsford, 1941), p.21

215 Bombing is a messy: Cyril Dunn, Notebook XIV, 'War Period', November 1940–April 1941, 26 December 1940

215 Mancunians were amazed: Harrisson, p.247

Chapter 11: Peace on Earth?

216 This evening I: Warner, 'Journal Under the Terror'

217 No bombs fell: *The Blitz: Then and Now, Vol. II*, pp.32, 354

218 10,500 had arrived: O'Brien, p.361

218 This will be a brave: Guy Fletcher, 'Christmas Miscellany', *Radio Times*, 20 December 1940, p.3

219 a crowded and: Warner, 'Journal Under the Terror'

219 Now let's get: *Daily Express*, 23 December 1940

220 reached Brum: Hodgson, pp.97–8

220 afraid we won't: *Our Longest Days*, p.62

220 even if it is a travesty: *Daily Worker*, 24 December 1940

221 Christmas shopping a bit: Chave, p.230, 19 December 1940

221 spent the best part: *Our Longest Days*, pp.61–2

221 Have you seen: M-OA 537, Christmas 1940

221 rather dingy: IWM 86/46/1 (P), 'The War Diary of Gwladys Cox', 22 December 1940

221 Lots of people: M-OA 537, Christmas 1940

221 Like many other people: *Daily Express*, 24 December 1940

222 Lee [his wife Eileen]: Chave, pp.233–4

222 where a good number: Don diary, 25 December 1940

223 Everything was perfect: *Nella Last's War: A Mother's Diary 1939–45*, (eds) Richard Broad and Suzie Fleming (Falling Wall Press, 1981); reissued as *Nella Last's War: The Second World War Diaries of 'Housewife 49'* (Profile, 2006), p.96

223 had Christmas at home: Dunn, Notebook XIV, 26 December 1940

223 It was the first: IWM, Baltrop, pp.25–6

224 No such luck: IWM 07/20/1, The Papers of Private Wilkinson, pp.15–16

224 Though there was little: *Mrs Milburn's Diaries: An Englishwoman's Day-to-Day Reflections, 1939–45*, (ed.) Peter Donnelly (Harrap, 1979), p.76

225 Food rationing was tight: Doris Pierce, *Memories of the Civilians' War* (Temple Publishing, 1996), pp.32–3

225 There was a programme: Chave, pp.233–4

225 Remember this: *The Listener*, 2 January 1941, p.7

226 no over-the-top 'blitz spirit': Nicholas, p.127

226 *Children's Hour* at 5.15 p.m.: *Radio Times*, 20 December 1940, pp.19–21

226 Despite the small attendance: Heap diaries, 24, 25 December 1940

227 it was undesirable: TNA CAB 75/3, Executive Sub-Committee, 36th meeting, 19 December 1940

227 Xmas 1940 was spent: Gregg, p.72

227 £4.10s had been collected: *Swiss Cottager*, Bulletin 5, December 1940, pp.1, 2

227 All the stations: IWM 99/66/1, Florence Mary ('Flo') Rollinson, ' "Blitz and Pieces". My Life During the Second World War', p.14

227 decorated with holly: 'Londoner's Diary', *Evening Standard*, 26 December 1940

228 took no Christmas holiday: Ibid.

228 I don't think we had: IWM 67/262/1, Leonard Jeacocke, p.23

228 A working Boxing Day: Heap diaries, 26, 28 December 1940

Chapter 12: Long Shall Men Mourn the Burning of the City

230 Gone are the churches: *New Statesman and Nation*, 25 January 1941, p.83

230 After three blissful nights: Warner, 30 December 1940; Chave, p.253

231 like apples falling: Eddie Edbrooke, quoted in Richard Trench, *London Before the Blitz* (Weidenfeld & Nicolson, 1989), p.51

231 With its warehouses: Trench, p.5

231 On Sunday night: *The Diary of Virginia Woolf: Vol. V*, p.351

232 That night, all: IWM 67/262/1, Emily Eary, p.28

232 The high wind: Aylmer Firebrace, *Fire Service Memoirs* (Melrose, 1949)

233 The whole of London: IWM P129, Papers of B.J. Rogers

233 The block bounded: David Johnson, *The London Blitz: The City Ablaze* (William Kimber, 1980), p.123

233 fallen to around 5,000: Trench, p.2

234 The four walls stood: Ibid., p.125

234 often been overvalued: *Architectural Review*, July 1941, p.9

235 home to the book trade: Valerie Holman, *Print for Victory: Book Publishing in England 1939–1945* (The British Library, 2008), pp.30–1

235 As I picked: 'Petrel', *Bookseller*, 2 January 1941

236 madrigal in stone: Trench, p.51

236 carpeted in hose pipes: *The Blitz: Then and Now, Vol. II*, p.359

236 see that this night: Ibid.

236 silhouetted against: IWM 67/262/1, Stan Hook, p.87

237 he wanted to make sure: IWM 67/262/2, James (J.M.) Richards, p.25

238 The Cathedral is really: IWM 67/262/2, Ralph Tubbs, pp.1–2

238 After the first weeks: J.M. Richards, *Memoirs of an Unjust Fella* (Weidenfeld & Nicolson, 1980), pp.141, 148–57

239 with a head: The Very Reverend W.R. Matthews, *St Paul's Cathedral in Wartime* (Hutchinson, 1946), p.46

239 The All Clear went: IWM 67/262/2, Louise Savage, pp.29–30

240 You could pick: IWM, Baltrop, pp.30–1

240 used its ruins: Trench, p.117

240 St Paul's was meant: IWM 67/262/1, J.M. Richards, pp.31–2

241 from a splintered Bank: Leo Townsend, 'The Morning After' in Ian Norrie (ed.), *The Book of the City* (High Hill Books, 1961), p.191

241 which was still: Beaton, p.79

242 had suffered a disgusting: James Pope-Hennessy, *History Under Fire* (Batsford, 1941), pp.45, 65; John Betjeman, 'Domine Dirige Nos', *The Listener*, 9 January 1941, pp.37–9

243 Quite spontaneously: Quoted in Juliet Gardiner, *Wartime: Britain 1939–1945* (Headline, 2004), p.364

243 sentimental and superficial: Alan Ross, *The Colours of War: War Art 1939–1945* (Jonathan Cape, 1983), p.167; Meirion and Susie Harries, *The War Artists: British Official Art of the Twentieth Century* (Michael Joseph in association with the Imperial War Museum and the Tate Gallery, 1983), pp.180–1

243 Frank Hurd: M.J. Gaskin, *Blitz: The Story of 29th December 1940* (Faber & Faber, 2005), pp.290, 310

243 Throughout Greater London: Figures from the Commonwealth War Graves Commission, cited in ibid., pp.329–50

244 a fireside chat: Printed as 'Appendix B' to Gaskin, pp.351–7

245 no wild bells: Warner, 30 and 31 December 1930

245 an informal party: Heap diaries, 31 December 1940

245 poor old London: Nicolson, 25, 31 December 1940, p.132

Chapter 13: Standing Firm

247 God is our refuge: Quoted in Mass-Observation, *Puzzled People: A Study in Popular Attitudes to Religion, Ethics, Progress and Politics in a London Borough, Prepared for the Ethical Union* (Victor Gollancz, 1947), p.59

247 all the ledgers: Hodgson, 31 December 1940, 2 January 1941, pp.101–2, 108

248 Some of you: *The Times*, 1 January 1941

248 to spend two or three: Charles Graves, *Off the Record* (Hutchinson, n.d. – probably January 1942), p.78

248 The papers are full: Heap diaries, 5 January 1941

249 compulsion will apply: *The Times*, 1, 4 January 1941

249 it was estimated: Dennis Hayes, *Challenge of Conscience: The Story of the Conscientious Objectors of 1939–1945* (Allen & Unwin, 1949), pp.297–8. Hayes's work, now more than sixty years old, remains an invaluable source.

249 a huge furore: Donoughue and Jones, pp.293–4

249 made some concessions: *The Times*, 10 September 1940

250 Women admitted: M-OA FR 536, 'Fire Spotters and Compulsory ARP', 3 January 1941, pp.1–11

250 other personnel: Helen Jones, *British Civilians in the Front Line: Air Raids, Productivity and Wartime Culture, 1939–45* (Manchester University Press, 2006), p.101

250 Churchill suggested: 'Roof-Watchers', *Picture Post*, 28 September 1940

251 any needlessly stopping: *The Times*, 23 September 1940

251 Bethnal Green Council: Jones, p.79

251 'Jim Crows': *Yorkshire Post*, 18 September 1940, quoted in ibid., p.32

251 perfected a system: 'Roof-Watchers', *Picture Post*, 28 September 1940, pp.27–9

251 The men in these: Rollinson, p.17

252 magnificent underground shelters: Jennie Lee, *This Great Journey: A Volume of Autobiography, 1904–45* (MacGibbon & Kee, 1963), pp.202–3

252 take cover warnings: Cited in Jones, pp.113, 115

253 'Look Out and Work On!': *Daily Express*, 11 September 1940

253 as they were by Churchill: Winston S. Churchill, *The Second World War, Vol. II: Their Finest Hour* (Cassell, 1949), p.311

253 Keep up your morale: *Daily Herald*, 18 September 1940

253 The time has long gone: *The Times*, 1, 4 January 1941

254 assembled most of: Chave, pp.255, 260, 262, 303

254 had unravelled themselves: IWM 95/13/1, Mrs H. Cobb, 'Memoir', pp.6–7

255 involved in the handling: Cited in Peter Brock and Nigel Young, *Pacifism in the Twentieth Century* (Syracuse University Press, 1999), p.157

256 Occasionally there were problems: Hayes, pp.126–7

257 two companies of the NCC: Ibid., p.128

257 that we were prepared: Quoted in Jappy, pp.92–3

257 All you could do: Ibid., pp.93, 97

257 It was doing something: Quoted in Felicity Goodall, *A Question of Conscience: Conscientious Objection in the Two World Wars* (Sutton Publishing, 1997), pp.130, 132

259 the grave question: Ernest Shipp, 'Letters to the Editor', *The Friend*, 4 April 1941, p.170

259 there is a conscientious: Elizabeth F. Howard, 'Letters to the Editor', *The Friend*, 25 April 1941, p.210

259 One is getting: Elizabeth M. Cadbury, 'Letters to the Editor', *The Friend*, 2 May 1941, p.221

259 Friends are already: Mabel A. Reynolds, 'Letters to the Editor', *The Friend*, 25 April 1941, p.210

259 Do not let us: Carl Heath, 'Concerning Compulsion', *The Friend*, 14 March 1941

260 on the ground that: Regulation 27A of the Defence (General) Regulations, 1939, quoted in Hayes, p.296

261 a fine of £5: Hayes, pp.292–306

261 In the serious condition: *Towards Tomorrow: The Autobiography of Fenner Brockway* (Hart-Davis MacGibbon, 1977), pp.139–40

262 The Peace Pledge Union: Hayes, p.74

262 Bryan Richards: Quoted in Jappy, p.98

263 his real flock: 'The Life of an East End Parson', *Picture Post*, 23 November 1940, pp.9–13

263 in the case of Groser: *John Groser: East London Priest*, (ed.) Kenneth Brill (Mowbrays, 1975), p.153

263 we just carried on: 'The Churches Served the People', Groser Papers, Ms.3562

263 'In Westminster Abbey': *John Betjeman's Collected Poems* (John Murray, 1958), p.91

264 I realise that: Quoted in Dianne Kirby, 'The Church of England and "Religious Division" During the Second World War: Church–State Relations and the Anglo–Soviet Alliance', *Journal of International History*, 2000

264 You cannot spread: TNA INF1/251, 'Religious Propaganda at Home'

264 A joint declaration: *The Times*, 21 December 1940

264 one in five English people: Robin Gill, *The 'Empty Church' Revisited* (Ashgate, 2003), p.143

265 'a harmless hobby': M-O, *Puzzled People*, pp.122–4, 143

265 The bombings put: Quoted in Harrisson, *Living Through the Blitz*, p.160

265 The clergy hoped: Cited in Field, p.464

265 did turn a lot: IWM 67/267/II, Ivor Leverton, p.17

266 belief in spiritualism: M-OA FR 769, 'Mass Astrology: Public Beliefs in the Supernatural', July 1941

Chapter 14: Spring Offensive

267 Until the beginning: Hugh Trevor-Roper (ed.), *Hitler's War Directives, 1939–45* (Sidgwick & Jackson, 1964), p.57

267 Many of those here: Quoted in C.M. MacInnes, *Bristol at War* (Museum Press, 1962), pp.89–90

268 the most important: Directive no. 23, 'Directions for Operations Against the English War Economy', 6 February 1941, cited in Trevor-Roper, pp.102–4

269 singing and singing: *Front Line*, p.111

270 scene of utter: *The Times*, 3 January 1941

270 not far in space: *Front Line*, p.110

270 very crowded: *Among You Taking Notes: The Wartime Diaries of Naomi Mitchison, 1939–1945*, (ed.) Dorothy Sheridan (Victor Gollancz, 1985), pp.110–11

271 To complete the destruction: Trevor-Roper, p.57

271 only one German plane: Penny, *Bristol at War*, pp.107–8; Helen Reid, *Bristol Under Siege: Surviving the Wartime Blitz* (Redcliffe, 2005), p.52

271 Two houses might: Quoted in Penny, p.109

272 Annie Caroline Robins: Underdown, p.17

272 killing thirty-four people: Penny, p.113

272 The aeroplanes come back: Orwell, *Partisan Review*, March–April 1941, *My Country Right or Left*, p.55

273 Everything is a shell: Hodgson, p.109

273 It is no exaggeration: Heap diaries, 4 January 1941

273 I went to London Bridge: *The Diary of Virginia Woolf: Vol. V, 1936–41*, p.353

273 the short, intense raid: Graves, *London Transport Carried On*, p.71

273 as far north as Aberdeen: Ibid., pp.57–8

276 a clerihew: Quoted in Andrew Brown, *J.D. Bernal: The Sage of Science* (Oxford University Press, 2005), p.182

278 by the time they reported: *From Apes to Warlords: The Autobiography (1904–1946) of Solly Zuckerman* (Hamish Hamilton, 1978), pp.120–7, 131–9; John Peyton, *Solly Zuckerman: A Scientist out of the Ordinary* (John Murray, 2001), passim; Brown, pp.165–84 passim.

278 the Royal Beach Hotel: Andrew Whitmarsh, *Portsmouth at War* (Tempus, 2007), p.76

278 HMS Vernon: *The Blitz: Then and Now, Vol. II*, p.392

280 The effect on war production: Quoted in Gilbert, p.1056

280 Easter is a very: Nicolson, 9 April 1941, p.161

280 a welcome contrast: Colville, p.773

281 He is not an isolationist: Quoted in Terry Charman, ' "A Bit of Campaign Oratory": Wendell Willkie's Visit to Britain, January 1941, and the Fight for Lend-Lease', *Imperial War Museum Review*, no. 9, pp.75–83

281 he took the country: Cooper, p.72

281 prayed God he would: Ibid.

281 We might not have had: Quoted in Charman, p.82

282 led by the Lord Mayor: Colville, 12 April 1941, p.373

282 It was quite extraordinary: Quoted in Gilbert, p.1059

282 The previous night: MacInnes, p.89

282 for an indefinite time: Ibid., p.87

282 257 dead: Penny, pp.122–9

283 the 'Good Friday Raid': John Dike, *Bristol Blitz Diary* (Redcliffe, 1982), p.71

284 there was nothing: Quoted in *The Blitz: Then and Now, Vol. II*, p.603

285 on average each V-1: Figures, *Beyond the Blitz, Vol. II*, p.441

Chapter 15: The Far Reach

286 Hitler is 52 today: Chave, p.300

286 Things have been: Glasgow City Archive, Mitchell Library, TD 646/14, Colin Ferguson

286 During the past financial year: IWM 89/17/1, Audrey Hawkins, pp.53, 54

286 I am all out: Quoted in Charles Loch Mowat, *Britain Between the Wars* (University of Chicago Press, 1955), p.147

287 engineering apprentices: Brian D. Osborne and Ronald Armstrong, *Glasgow: A City at War* (Birlinn, 2003), p.74

288 Clydebank fell into line: I.M.M. MacPhail, *The Clydebank Blitz* (West Dunbartonshire Libraries and Museums, 1974), p.3

288 It's England they're: Quoted in Seona Robertson and Les Wilson, *Scotland's War* (Mainstream Publishing, 1995), p.54

288 visibility was so perfect: Stuart McAllister, 'The Clydebank Blitz', dissertation for the University of Glasgow School of History and Archaeology, January 1998, p.18

289 as effective as shooting: Quoted in ibid., p.22

290 Which street?: Glasgow *Herald*, 2 April 1941

290 Glasgow houses are: Quoted in Edwin Webb and John Duncan, *Blitz Over Britain* (Spellmount, 1990), p.110

290 bombs carpeted the residential areas: Paul Harris, *Glasgow at War* (Archive Publications, 1986), p.52

291 There is a part: Scottish Record Office HH 50/95, 'Some Impressions of Clydebank'

291 No fire master: Quoted in McAllister, p.28

292 Deciding that operations: MacPhail, p.23

293 This method soon found: Ibid., pp.43–4

294 The success of [the billeting]: Osborne and Armstrong, p.75; MacPhail, p.55

295 Nearly 5,000 meat sandwiches: Scottish Record Office HH 50/91, 'WVS Report on Clydebank, 295 March 1941', p.4

295 It was one of the worst: IWM Department of Documents, P151, The Papers of J.P. Hutchinson. This section is dependent on the Scottish Record Office H 50/90–5 series; M-OA FR 607, 'Preliminary Report on Clydebank', 17 March 1941; McAllister, MacPhail, Osborne and Armstrong, Robertson and Wilson, and

Margaret Bennett, 'See, When You Look Back': Clydeside Reminiscences of the Home Front, 1939–1945 (The Mitchell Library, Glasgow, 2005), passim.

295 Our patch: Shea, p.147

295 We are unbombed: Quoted in Brian Barton, The Blitz: Belfast in the War Years (Blackstaff Press, 1989), p.58

295 the most distant city: Ibid., p.73

296 if there isn't some: Quoted in Clair Wills, That Neutral Island: A Cultural History of Ireland During the Second World War (Faber & Faber, 2007), p.214

296 De Valera indicated: M-OA Diarist 5462 (Moya Woodside), 23 August 1940

297 only 750 shelters: John W. Blake, Northern Ireland in the Second World War (HMSO, 1956; Blackstaff Press, 2000), p.218

297 less well-defended: Quoted in Barton, p.72

297 the powerful headlights: Quoted in ibid., p.106

298 where the poor: Ibid., p.108

299 had the sky to themselves: Robert Fisk, In Time of War: Ireland, Ulster and the Price of Neutrality, 1939–1945 (André Deutsch, 1983), pp.487, 488–90

299 Patrick Finlay: Quoted in ibid., p.498

299 An action like this: M-OA Diarist 5462 (Moya Woodside), 17 April 1941

300 a scene of utter desolation: Belfast Telegraph, quoted in Barton, p.133

300 stream of corpses: Brian Moore, The Emperor of Ice Cream (André Deutsch, 1966), p.231

301 there is absolutely no: M-OA Diarist 5462 (Moya Woodside), 16 April 1941

301 Public opinion is: Ibid., 17 April 1941

302 tears streaming down: Northern Whig, 21 April 1941; Belfast Telegraph, quoted in Barton, p.176

302 Women splashed: Barton, p.200

302 listened to the frightening: Shea, p.149

303 compensation claim: Barton, pp.214–15

303 In the past: Quoted in Wills, p.216

304 Bigotry is rampant: M-OA Diarist 5462 (Moya Woodside), 15 August 1941

305 unsuccessful invasion attempt: Gerald Wasley, Plymouth, A Shattered City: The Story of Hitler's Attack on Plymouth and its People, 1939–45 (Halsgrove, 1991: new edition 2004), p.16

305 more warning: Government communiqué to the Admiralty, 4 December 1939, quoted in Wasley, p.61

307 a bit of a mess: IWM 89/17/1, 'The Second World War Diaries of Mrs A.D. Deacon (née Hawkins) MBE', p.48

308 no subsequent court martial: Wasley, p.106

308 to buy as much: John Bedford, 'Plymouth', Plymouth Record Office, pp.2–3

309 No-one in Whitehall: Quoted in Frank Wintle, The Plymouth Blitz (Bossiney Books, 1981), p.24

311 The oldest killed: W.P. Johns, A Town in the South-West: Schwerpunct [sic] – Pinie . . . Target Plymouth (privately published, 2001), p.173

311 Forty churches: W. Best Harris, Plymouth (The Plymouth Council of Social Services, n.d. ?1958)

313 449 bombers: TNA HO 186/1603; Johns, pp.177, 178, 180, 181. These figures show the number of bombs loaded into German planes: not all landed on target and not all exploded.

314 strong local pride: M-OA FR 683, 'Third Report on Plymouth', 4 May 1941, pp.1–4, 6, 9–11, 17–19, 22

315 I think it is most: TNA HO 199/1442, 18 January 1941

315 only a small proportion: M-OA FR 683, 'Third Report on Plymouth', pp.36–7

Chapter 16: Attrition

316 The street was as flat: Quoted in Calder, The People's War, pp.226–7

316 There was a little woman: Faviell, p.245

317 We've only had: Dunn, Notebook XIV, pp.46, 57, 58, 59

318 The ARP HQ was hit: Tony Geraghty, A North-East Coast Town: Ordeal and Triumph – The Story of Kingston upon Hull in the 1939–1945 Great War (1951; Hull Academic Press, 2002), p.20

318 very grim: Dunn, Notebook XIV, pp.76–7

318 The night before: Dunn, Notebook XV, p, 8

319 They must have got: Ibid., pp.14–17

321 nearly half a million: Reverend Philip Graystone, The Blitz on Hull (Lampada Press, 1991), p.21

321 On 3 May: Bombers Over Merseyside (Liverpool Daily Post and Echo, 1943), p.15

322 too easily satisfied: TNA INF 1/292, 'Report on Merseyside'

324 young men in uniform: IWM 91/5/1, Barbara Roose, 'Got Any Gum, Chum?', p.23

324 a gory incident: Nixon, p.103

324 I lost more: Quoted in Todd Gray, Looting in Wartime Britain (The Mint Press, 2009), p.5

324 nothing helps the recovery: Markham, pp.29–30

326 we wandered: IWM 86/46/1(P), 'The War Diary of Gwladys Cox'

326 The figure rose: Quoted in Gray, p.10

326 Director of Anti-Looting: Donald Thomas, An Underworld at War: Spivs, Deserters, Racketeers and Civilians in the Second World War (John Murray, 2003), pp.84–5

326 the Legislature has: Ibid., p.77

326 When a great city: Ibid., p.76
327 the number of cases: Mortimer, pp.122–3
328 a looting ringleader: *Daily Mirror*, 22 May 1942
328 I'm beginning to wonder: Gray, p.34
328 130 pairs of ladies' gloves: Ibid., p.29
329 They're not doin': M-OA FR 783, Home Intelligence (New Series), Sixth Weekly Report
329 the evil is at: TNA INF 34.187, quoted in Gray, p.67
329 Several Portsmouth policemen: *The Times*, 9 December 1940
330 Each of you was: *The Times*, 23 November 1940
330 A Bristol man: *Bristol Evening Post*, 15 May 1941, quoted in Gray, pp.86–7
330 A seaman whose ship: *Manchester Guardian*, 8 July 1941, quoted in ibid., p.103
330 Leonard Watson: Thomas, p.83
331 'All Clear' didn't sound: Heap diaries, 19, 20 March 1941
331 latest rationing joke: Ibid., 23, 28 March 1941
331 About the worst: Ibid., 17 April 1941
332 There is a hot: Nicolson, 16 April 1941, p.163
333 to find Piccadilly: *Here is Chelsea: Reflections from the Chelsea Society*, (ed.) Jane Dorrell (Elliot & Thompson, 2004), p.61
333 four HE bombs: Don diary, 21 April 1941
333 there was a thud: Theodora Fitzgibbon, *With Love: An Autobiography 1938–46* (Century, 1982), pp.88–91
334 that rare thing: *Architectural Review*, July 1941, p.10
336 dug for victory: IWM 99/91, The Papers of Mrs Yvonne Green
337 taking stock: Doris Pierce, *Memoirs of the Civilian War* (Temple Publishing, 1996), pp.42–3, 45–6
338 the ruins of: Heap diaries, 17, 18 April 1941
338 St Andrew's: Rebuilt in 1971 as the Crédit Lyonnaise bank
339 We called and listened: Markham, pp.29–30
340 London looks bleary-eyed: Colville, p.375
340 Piccadilly resembled: James Lees-Milne, *Another Self* (Hamish Hamilton, 1970), pp.150–1
341 London is definitely: Graves, *Off the Record*, pp.138–9
342 nothing worse for morale: Euan O'Halpin, *Head of the Civil Service: A Study of Sir Warren Fisher* (Routledge, 1989), pp.276–7
342 Travelling by bus: Heap diaries, 1 May 1941
343 Bricks and rubble: Ziegler, pp.153–4
343 a splendid idea: Heap diaries, 4 May 1941
343 no killjoy: Quoted in Gavin Mortimer, *The Longest Night, 10–11 May 1941: Voices from the London Blitz* (Weidenfeld & Nicolson, 2005), p.93

344 awful warbling-like: IWM, Veazey
345 The smoke was such: Cecil King, *With Malice Towards None: A War Diary*, (ed.) William Armstrong (Sidgwick & Jackson, 1970), pp.124–5
345 removed and hidden: *A House of Kings: A History of Westminster Abbey*, (ed.) Edward Carpenter (John Baker, 1966), p.365
346 crevices, ledges: William Sansom, *The Blitz: Westminster at War* (Oxford University Press, 1947), p.90
347 St Thomas's Hospital: St Thomas's suffered six major and countless minor and incendiary attacks during the blitz
347 quite the noisiest: An account by Annie Beale, Casualty Sister at St Thomas's Hospital for thirty-six years, in *The War Diary of St Thomas's Hospital, 1939–1945*, (ed.) Frank and Dorothy Cockett (Friends of St Thomas's Hospital, 1991), p.33
347 We had an unbelievable: IWM 67/262/11, Ralph Tubbs
348 two of the key exhibits: Roy Harrison, *Blitz Over Westminster* (City of Westminster Libraries, 1990), p.26
348 Gray's Inn burned: Mortimer, p.201
348 There were moments: Quoted in ibid., p.207
348 In the early hours: Ibid., p.144
348 the British Museum: Ibid., pp, 146–7
349 London's transport system: Ibid., pp.22–3
349 The whole night sky: *The London Observer: The Journal of General Raymond E. Lee, 1940–1941*, (ed.) James Leutze (Hutchinson, 1972), p.271
350 Carr's Hotel: *Blitz Over Westminster*, pp.25, 27, 28, 29, 31, 32
350 St Silas church: Mortimer, p.241
351 So at the age of 27: Kenneth Sinclair-Loutit, *Very Little Luggage* (unpublished autobiography, http://www.spartacus.schoolnet.co.uk)
352 London was in flames: Quentin Reynolds, *The Wounded Don't Cry* (Cassell, 1941), p.29
353 stood on Westminster Bridge: Colville, pp.376, 386–7, 388; Mitchison, p.146
354 the evening papers: Dunn, Notebook XV, p.19
354 We must not make: Nicolson, p.166
355 from the East End: IWM 95/8/1, M.E.A. Allan, pp.1068–9
355 various shops burnt out: Heap diaries, 11 May 1941
356 Lunched at the Savoy: Graves, pp.154–5
356 cascades of glass: Quoted in Waller and Vaughan-Rees, pp.288–9
356 Park Lane is blocked: *The London Observer*, p.273
357 a very nice letter: Mitchison, p.146
357 ran into an enormous: Chave, pp.311–12

357 I go to see: Nicolson, p.166

358 Don't be distressed: Quoted in Gilbert, p.1086 n. 4

358 worrying about London: Mitchison, p.146

359 The Nazis have given: Dunn, Notebook XV, p.35

359 We got hit: IWM 67/262/11, Cyril Demarne

360 It was not until: Titmuss (1950), p.336

360 Of course we knew: IWM 67/262/11, Herr Hajo Hermann

After

361 It was an extraordinary: IWM 67/262/1, Jill Craigie

361 the past bombed out: Quoted in Vera Brittain, *England's Hour: An Autobiography 1939–1941* (Macmillan, 1941), p.215

362 fewer than 5,000: Shane Ewan, 'Preparing the British Fire Service for War: Local Government, Nationalisation and Evolutionary Reform, 1935–41', *Contemporary British History*, Vol. 20, no. 2, June 2006, p.217

362 In a national emergency: Editorial in *Fire*, October 1935, p.111, quoted in ibid., p.213

362 the brightest jewel: Donoughue and Jones, p.294

362 how totally inadequate: *The Times*, 4 April 1941

363 The task of coordinating: O'Brien, pp.468–95; Wallington, pp.172–9; Michael Wassey, *Ordeal by Fire: The Story and Lesson of Fire Over Britain and the Battle of the Flames* (Secker & Warburg, 1941), pp.146–87

366 There'll Always be an England: Lee, p.195

368 Your courage: Quoted in Anthony Julius, *Trials of the Diaspora: A History of Anti-Semitism in England* (Oxford University Press, 2010), p.324

369 parasites who live: 'Lillian Rogers', quoted in James Hinton, *Nine Wartime Lives: Mass-Observation and the Making of the Modern Self* (Oxford University Press, 2010), p.113

369 If there was any: IWM, Baltrop, p.33

369 talked to several: TNA HO 199/324, Winifred

Holmes, 'Personal Visit to Stoke Newington – October 14th 1940', p.2

369 from personal observations: 21 October 1940, quoted in Julius, p.324

369 *not* all Jews: 25 October 1940, *My Country Right or Left*, p.377

369 With reference to: 21 October 1940, ibid., p.377

370 In those districts: Selig Brodetsky, *Memoirs: From Ghetto to Israel* (Weidenfeld & Nicolson, 1960), pp.202–3

370 wants actually to *do*: George Orwell, 'London Letter to the *Partisan Review*', 1 January 1942, *My Country Right or Left*, p.178

370 London looked merry: Woolf, *Leave the Letters Till We're Dead*, 25 September 1940, pp.434–5

371 people were heroic: IWM, Baltrop, p.31

371 Business as usual: IWM Department of Documents 04/13/1, Jean Crossley, 'A Middle-Class War, 1939–1947', p.35

371 I didn't personally: IWM, Baltrop, p.33

372 It is relevant: Brittain, p.215

372 If Wren's most: Quoted in Trench, p.181

373 not something outside: *Picture Post*, 4 January 1941, p.4

373 Given the will: Maxwell Fry, 'The New Britain Must be Planned', ibid., p.16

373 I do not trust: J.B. Priestley, 'The Future Begins Today', *Horizon*, March 1941, pp.17–18

374 plan boldly: Stephen Essex and Mark Brayshaw, 'Boldness Diminished? The Post-War Battle to Replan a Bomb-Damaged Provincial City', *Urban History*, 35, 3 (2008), p.439

374 National Health Service: The Act was passed in 1946

374 blood transfusions: Richard M. Titmuss, *The Gift Relationship: From Human Blood to Social Policy* (Allen & Unwin, 1970)

375 some of which persisted: There were still prefabs on an estate on the A4 along the Avon Gorge outside Bristol in 2005

375 The ruin, looked on: 'The Architecture of Destruction', *Architectural Review*, July 1941, p.25

BIBLIOGRAPHY

Published Sources

Abrahams, James S., *Then and Now: The Sheffield Blitz* (Pawson & Brailsford, 1941)

Addison, Paul, *The Road to 1945: British Politics and the Second World War* (Jonathan Cape, 1975)

Addison, Paul and Crang, Jeremy (eds), *The Burning Blue: A New History of the Battle of Britain* (Pimlico, 2000)

Agar, Eileen (with Andrew Lambirth), *A Look at My Life* (Methuen, 1988)

Alderman, Geoffrey, 'M.H. Davis: The Rise and Fall of a Communal Upstart', *Jewish Historical Studies*, vol. xxxi, 1990

Allan, John, *Lubetkin: Architecture and the Tradition of Progress* (RIBA Publications, 1992)

Ballard, Phyllida (ed.), *A City at War: Birmingham 1939–1945* (Birmingham Museum and Art Gallery, 1985)

Barton, Brian, *The Blitz: Belfast in the War Years* (Blackstaff Press, 1989)

Beaton, Cecil, *Self-Portrait With Friends: The Selected Diaries of Cecil Beaton*, (ed.) Richard Buckle (Weidenfeld & Nicolson, 1979)

Bell, Amy, 'Landscapes of Fear: Wartime London, 1939–1945', *Journal of British Studies*, 48, January 2009

— *London Was Ours: Diaries and Memoirs of the London Blitz* (I.B. Tauris, 2008)

Belsey, James and Reid, Helen, *The West at War* (Redcliffe Press, 1990)

Bennett, Margaret, 'See, When You Look Back': Clydeside Reminiscences of the Home Front, 1939–1945* (The Mitchell Library, Glasgow, 2005)

Berg, Charles, *War in the Mind: The Case Book of a Medical Psychologist* (Macaulay Press, 1941)

Betjeman, John, *John Betjeman's Collected Poems* (John Murray, 1958)

Blacker, C.P., *Neurosis and the Mental Health Services* (Oxford University Press, 1948)

Blackmore, Peter, 'Early Days' in *Fire and Water: An NFS Anthology* (Lindsay Drummond, 1942)

397

Blake, John W., *Northern Ireland in the Second World War* (HMSO, 1956)

Bliss, Edward Jnr (ed.), *In Search of Light: The Broadcasts of Edward R. Murrow, 1938–61* (New York: Alfred A. Knopf, 1967)

The Blitz: Then and Now, Vol. II, (ed.) Winston G. Ramsey (Battle of Britain Prints International, 1988)

Boog, Horst, 'The Luftwaffe's Assault' in Addison and Crang (eds), *The Burning Blue: A New History of the Battle of Britain* (Pimlico, 2000)

Bowen, Elizabeth, *The Demon Lover and Other Stories* (Jonathan Cape, 1945)

— *The Heat of the Day* (Jonathan Cape, 1949)

Bradford, Sarah, *George VI* (Weidenfeld & Nicolson, 1989)

Brendon, Piers and Whitehead, Philip, *The Windsors: A Dynasty Revealed* (Hodder & Stoughton, 1994)

Brittain, Vera, *England's Hour: An Autobiography, 1939–1941* (Macmillan, 1941)

Brock, Peter and Young, Nigel, *Pacifism in the Twentieth Century* (Syracuse University Press, 1999)

Brockway, Fenner, *Towards Tomorrow: The Autobiography of Fenner Brockway* (Hart-Davis MacGibbon, 1977)

Brode, Tony, *The Southampton Blitz* (Barry Shurlock, 1977)

Brown, Andrew, *J.D. Bernal: The Sage of Science* (Oxford University Press, 2005)

Buggins, Joanne, 'An Appreciation of the Shelter Photographs Taken by Bill Brandt in November 1940', *Imperial War Museum Review*, 1989

Calder, Angus, *The People's War: Britain 1939–1945* (Jonathan Cape, 1969)

— *The Myth of the Blitz* (Jonathan Cape, 1991)

Calder, Ritchie, *Carry on London* (The English Universities Press, 1941)

— *The Lesson of London* (Secker & Warburg, 1941)

Campbell, Louise, *Coventry Cathedral: Art and Architecture in Post-War Britain* (Oxford: Clarendon Press, 1996)

Carpenter, Edward (ed.), *A House of Kings: A History of Westminster Abbey* (John Baker, 1966)

Castle, Barbara, *Fighting All the Way* (Macmillan, 1993)

Charman, Terry, ' "A Bit of Campaign Oratory": Wendell Willkie's Visit to Britain, January 1941, and the Fight for Lend-Lease', *Imperial War Museum Review*, no. 9

Chinn, Carl, *Brum Undaunted: Birmingham During the Blitz* (Birmingham Library Services, 1996)

Churchill, Winston S., *The Second World War, Vol. II: Their Finest Hour* (Cassell, 1949)

Clark, Kenneth, *The Other Half: A Self Portrait* (John Murray, 1977)

Clark, Ronald, *The Life and Work of J.B.S. Haldane* (Hodder & Stoughton, 1968)

Cockett, Frank and Dorothy (eds), *The War Diary of St Thomas's Hospital* (Friends of St Thomas's Hospital/Starling Press, 1991)

Collier, Basil, *History of the Second World War: The Defence of the United Kingdom* (HMSO, 1957)

Colville, John, *The Fringes of Power: 10 Downing Street Diaries, 1939–1955* (Hodder & Stoughton, 1985)

Connelly, Mark, *Britain in the Second World War* (Routledge, 1999)

— *We Can Take It: Britain and the Memory of the Second World War* (Pearson Longman, 2004)

Cook, Reverend Leslie, *The City We Loved* (Three Spires Publishing, 1942)

Cooper, Diana, *Trumpets from the Steep* (Rupert Hart-Davis, 1960)

Cooper, Duff, *The Duff Cooper Diaries*, (ed.) John Julius Norwich (Weidenfeld & Nicolson, 2005)

Cowen, Rhoda, *The Gold and Silver Threads: A Memoir of Life in the Twentieth Century* (Sutton Publishing, 1994)

Cowles, Virginia, *Looking for Trouble* (Hamish Hamilton, 1941)

Crichton-Miller, H., 'Some Factors Conditioning Air Raid Reactions', *Lancet*, 12, July 1941

Crossland, John, 'Black Saturday' in 'Blitz', *Sunday Times*, 2 September 1990

Cull, Nicholas John, *Selling War: The British Propaganda Campaign Against American 'Neutrality' in World War II* (Oxford University Press, 1995)

Devastated London: The Bombed City as Seen From a Barrage Balloon (drawn by Cecil Brown, with notes by Ralph Hyde) (The London Topographical Society, 1990)

Dike, John, *Bristol Blitz Diary* (Redcliffe Press, 1982)

Donoughue, Bernard and Jones, G.W., *Herbert Morrison: Portrait of a Politician* (Weidenfeld & Nicolson, 1973)

Dorrell, Jane (ed.), *Here is Chelsea: Reflections from the Chelsea Society* (Elliot & Thompson, 2004)

Essex, Stephen and Brayshaw, Mark, 'Boldness Diminished? The Post-War Battle to Replan a Bomb-Damaged Provincial City', *Urban History*, 35, 3, 2008

Ewan, Shane, 'Preparing the British Fire Service for War: Local Government, Nationalisation and Evolutionary Reform, 1935–41', *Contemporary British History*, Vol. 20, no. 2, June 2006

Faviell, Frances, *Chelsea Concerto* (Cassell, 1959)

Fire Over London: The Story of the London Fire Service, 1940–41 (Hutchinson for the LCC, 1941)

Firebrace, Aylmer, *Fire Service Memoirs* (Melrose, 1949)

Fisk, Robert, *In Time of War: Ireland, Ulster and the Price of Neutrality, 1939–1945* (André Deutsch, 1983)

FitzGibbon, Constantine, *The Blitz* (Allan Wingate, 1957)

Fitzgibbon, Theodora, *With Love: An Autobiography, 1938–46* (Century, 1982)

Flannery, Harry W., *Assignment to Berlin* (Michael Joseph, 1942)

Foss, Brian, *War Paint: Art, War, State and Identity in Britain, 1939–1945* (Yale University Press, 2007)

Freud, Anna, *The Writings of Anna Freud: Vol. II, 1939–1945. Infants Without Families: Reports on the Hampstead Nurseries* (New York: International Universities Press, 1973)

Front Line (Ministry of Information/HMSO, 1942)

Gannon, Franklin Reid, *The British Press and Germany, 1936–39* (Oxford: Clarendon Press, 1971)

Gardiner, Juliet, *Wartime: Britain 1939–1945* (Headline, 2004)

Garfield, Simon, *Private Battles: How the War Almost Defeated Us* (Ebury Press, 2007)

Gaskin, M.J., *Blitz: The Story of 29th December 1940* (Faber & Faber, 2005)

Geraghty, Tony, *A North-East Coast Town: Ordeal and Triumph – The Story of Kingston upon Hull in the 1939–1945 Great War* (1951; Hull Academic Press, 2002)

Gilbert, Martin, *Finest Hour: Winston S. Churchill, 1939–41* (Heinemann, 1983)

Gill, Robin, *The 'Empty' Church Revisited* (Ashgate, 2003)

Glover, Edward, 'Notes on the Psychological Effects of War Conditions on the Civilian Population (II)', *International Journal of Psycho-Analysis*, vol. xxii, 1941

— 'Notes on the Psychological Effects of War Conditions on the Civilian Population: The Blitz, 1939–41 (III)', *International Journal of Psycho-Analysis*, vol. xxiii, 1942

Golden, Jennifer, *Hackney at War* (Sutton Publishing, 1995)

Goodall, Felicity, *A Question of Conscience: Conscientious Objectors in the Two World Wars* (Sutton Publishing, 1997)

Graves, Charles, *Off the Record* (Hutchinson, n.d., probably 1947)

— *London Transport Carried On: 1939–1945* (London Transport, 1947)

— *Champagne and Chandeliers: The Story of the Café de Paris* (Odhams Press, 1958)

Gray, Todd, *Looting in Wartime Britain* (The Mint Press, 2009)

Graystone, Reverend Philip, *The Blitz on Hull* (Lampada Press, 1991)

Green, Henry, *Caught* (Hogarth Press, 1943)

Greene, Graham, *The Ministry of Fear* (Heinemann, 1943)

Gregg, John, *The Shelter of the Tubes: Tube Sheltering in Wartime London* (Capital Transport Publishing, 2001)

John Groser: East London Priest, (ed.) Kenneth Brill (Mowbrays, 1975)

Haldane, J.B.S., *ARP* (Victor Gollancz, 1938)

Hampstead at War, 1939–1945 (Alden Press, n.d.)

Hanley, James, *No Direction* (Faber & Faber, 1943)

Harries, Meirion and Susie, *The War Artists: British Official Art of the Twentieth Century* (Michael Joseph, in association with the Imperial War Museum and the Tate Gallery, 1983)

Harris, Clive, *Walking the London Blitz* (Leo Cooper, 2003)

Harris, Paul, *Glasgow at War* (Archive Publications, 1986)

Harrison, Roy, *Blitz Over Westminster* (City of Westminster Libraries, 1990)

Harrisson, Tom, *Living Through the Blitz* (William Collins, 1976)

Hartley, Major A.B., *Unexploded Bomb: A History of Bomb Disposal* (Cassell, 1958)

Hartnell, Norman, *Silver and Gold* (Evans Bros, 1955)

Harvey, A.D., 'Local Authorities and the Blitz', *Contemporary Review*, 1990

Hayes, Dennis, *Challenge of Conscience: The Story of the Conscientious Objectors of 1939–1945* (Allen & Unwin, 1949)

Heimann, Judith M., *The Most Offending Soul Alive: Tom Harrisson and his Remarkable Life* (Aurum, 2002)

Herbert, A.P., *Independent Member* (Methuen, 1950)

Hinton, James (ed.), *Nine Wartime Lives: Mass-Observation and the Making of the Modern Self* (Oxford University Press, 2010)

Hodgson, Vere, *Few Eggs and No Oranges: The Diaries of Vere Hodgson 1940–1945* (Persephone Books, 1999)

Holman, Valerie, *Print for Victory: Book Publishing in England, 1939–1945* (British Library, 2008)

Holmes, Richard, *Churchill's Bunker: The Secret Headquarters at the Heart of Britain's Victory* (Profile Books, in association with the Imperial War Museum, 2009)

Howard, Reverend R.T., *Ruined and Rebuilt: The Story of Coventry Cathedral, 1939–1962* (Council of Coventry Cathedral, 1962)

Idle, Doreen, *War Over West Ham: A Study of Community Adjustment* (Faber & Faber, 1943)

Ingersoll, Ralph, *Report on England* (The Right Bookclub, 1941)

Ismay, General Hastings, *The Memoirs of General the Lord Ismay* (Heinemann, 1960)

Jackson, Kevin, *Humphrey Jennings* (Picador, 2004)

Jappy, M.J., *Danger UXB* (Channel Four Books, 2001)

Jenkins, David Fraser, *John Piper: The Forties* (Philip Wilson/Imperial War Museum, 2000)

Jennings, Humphrey, *The Humphrey Jennings Film Reader*, (ed.) Kevin Jackson (Carcanet, 1993)

Johns, W.P., *A Town in the South-West: Schwerpunct [sic]- Pinie . . . Target Plymouth* (privately published, 2001)

Johnson, Arthur, *Merseyside's Secret Blitz Diary* (Trinity Mirror, Merseyside, 2005)

Jones, Edgar, Woolven, Robin, Durodié, Bill and Wessely, Simon, 'Civilian Morale During the Second World War: Responses to Air Raids Re-Examined', *Social History of Medicine*, vol. 17, no. 3, 2004

Jones, Helen, *British Civilians in the Front Line: Air Raids, Productivity and Wartime Culture* (Manchester University Press, 2006)

Julius, Anthony, *Trials of the Diaspora: A History of Anti-Semitism in England* (Oxford University Press, 2010)

King, Cecil, *With Malice Towards None: A War Diary*, (ed.) William Armstrong (Sidgwick & Jackson, 1970)

Kirby, Dianne, 'The Church of England and "Religious Division" During the Second World War: Church–State Relations and the Anglo–Soviet Alliance', *Journal of International History*, 2000

Knowles, Bernard, *Southampton: The English Gateway* (Hutchinson, 1951)

Kops, Bernard, *The World is a Wedding* (MacGibbon & Kee, 1963)

Last, Nella, *Nella Last's War: A Mother's Diary, 1939–1945*, (eds) Richard Broad and Suzie Fleming (Falling Wall Press, 1981); reissued as *Nella Last's War: The Second World War Diaries of 'Housewife 49'* (Profile Books, 2006)

Lee, Jennie, *This Great Journey: A Volume of Autobiography, 1904–45* (MacGibbon & Kee, 1963)

Lee, General Raymond E., *London Observed: The Journal of Raymond E. Lee, 1940–1*, (ed.) James Leutze (Hutchinson, 1972)

Lewey, Frank, *Cockney Campaign* (Stanley Paul, n.d., probably 1941–42)

Lewis, Adrian, 'Henry Moore's "Shelter Drawings": Memory and Myth' in Pat Kirkham and David Thoms (eds), *War Culture: Social Change and Changing Experience in World War Two* (Lawrence & Wishart, 1995)

Lewis, Aubrey, 'Incidence of Neuroses in England Under War Conditions', *Lancet*, 12, 1942

Lewis, Tim, *Moonlight Sonata: The Coventry Blitz* (Tim Lewis and Coventry City Council, 1990)

Lofthouse, Alistair, *Then and Now: The Sheffield Blitz* (Alistair Lofthouse, 1991)

Longmate, Norman, *Air Raid: The Bombing of Coventry, 1940* (Hutchinson, 1976)

Macaulay, Rose, *The World My Wilderness* (William Collins, 1950)

McGrory, David, *Coventry at War* (The History Press, 1997)

MacInnes, C.M., *Bristol at War* (Museum Press, 1962)

MacKay, Robert, *Half the Battle: Civilian Morale in Britain During the Second World War* (Manchester University Press, 2002)

McLaine, Ian, *Ministry of Morale: Home Front Morale and the Ministry of Information in World War II* (Allen & Unwin, 1979)

MacPhail, I.M.M., *The Clydebank Blitz* (West Dunbartonshire Libraries and Museums, 1974)

Mack, Joanna and Humphries, Steve, *The Making of Modern London, 1939–1945: London at War* (Sidgwick & Jackson, 1985)

Manchester Wartime Memories: An Illustrated Collection of Oral History Memories of Manchester in the Second World War (Manchester Library and Information Service, 2006)

Marchant, Hilde, *Women and Children Last: A Woman Reporter's Account of the Battle of Britain* (Victor Gollancz, 1941)

Mass-Observation, *Puzzled People: A Study in Popular Attitudes to Religion, Ethics, Progress and Politics in a London Borough Prepared for the Ethical Union* (Victor Gollancz, 1947)

Matthews, The Very Reverend W.R., *St Paul's Cathedral in Wartime* (Hutchinson, 1946)

Milburn, Clara, *Mrs Milburn's Diaries: An Englishwoman's Day-to-Day Reflections, 1939–45*, (ed.) Peter Donnelly (Harrap, 1979)

Miller, Emmanuel (ed.), *The Neuroses of War* (Macmillan, 1940)

Miller, Kristine A., *British Literature of the Blitz: Fighting the People's War* (Palgrave Macmillan, 2009)

Miller, Les and Bloch, Howard, *Black Saturday, The First Day of the Blitz: East London Memories of September 7th 1940* (T.H.A.P. Books, 1984)

Mitchison, Naomi, *Among You Taking Notes: The Wartime Diaries of Naomi Mitchison, 1939–1945*, (ed.) Dorothy Sheridan (Victor Gollancz, 1985)

Moore, Brian, *The Emperor of Ice Cream* (André Deutsch, 1966)

Morrison, Herbert, *Herbert Morrison: An Autobiography of Lord Morrison of Lambeth* (Odhams Press, 1960)

Mortimer, Gavin, *The Longest Night: 10–11 May 1941, Voices from the London Blitz* (Weidenfeld & Nicolson, 2005)

Mowat, Charles Loch, *Britain Between the Wars* (University of Chicago Press, 1955)

Murray, Williamson, *Strategy for Defeat* (Brassey's, 1996)

Newbery, Charles Allen, *Wartime St Pancras: A London Borough Defends Itself* (compiled in November 1945, published, with an introduction by Robin Woolven, by Camden History Society, 2006)

Nicholas, Siân, *The Echo of War: Home Front Propaganda and the Wartime BBC, 1939–45* (Manchester University Press, 1999)

Nicolson, Harold, *Diaries and Letters, 1939–1945*, (ed.) Nigel Nicolson (William Collins, 1967)

Nixon, Barbara, *Raiders Overhead: A Diary of the London Blitz* (1943; Scolar/Gulliver, 1980)

O'Brien, Terence H., *History of the Second World War: Civil Defence* (HMSO, 1955)

O'Halpin, Euan, *Head of the Civil Service: A Study of Sir Warren Fisher* (Routledge, 1989)

Orwell, George, *The Lion and the Unicorn: Socialism and English Genius* (Secker & Warburg, 1941)

— *The Collected Essays of George Orwell, Vol. II: My Country Right or Left* (Secker & Warburg, 1968)

Osborne, Brian D. and Armstrong, Ronald, *Glasgow: A City at War* (Birlinn, 2003)

O'Sullivan, Tim, 'Listening Through the Wireless and World War Two' in Pat Kirkwood and David Thoms (eds), *War Culture: Social Change and Changing Experience in World War Two* (Lawrence & Wishart, 1995)

Overy, Richard, 'How Significant Was the Battle?' in Addison and Crang (eds), *The Burning Blue: A New History of the Battle of Britain* (Pimlico, 2000)

— *The Battle* (Penguin, 2000)

Pennick, Nigel, *Bunkers Under London* (privately printed, 1985)

Penny, John, *Bristol at War* (Breedon Books, 2002)

Perrett, Brian, *Liverpool: A City at War* (Robert Hale, 1990)

Peyton, John, *Solly Zuckerman: A Scientist Out of the Ordinary* (John Murray, 2001)

Pierce, Doris, *Memories of the Civilian's War* (Temple Publishing, 1996)

Pile, General Sir Frederick, *Ack-Ack: Britain's Defences Against Air Attack During the Second World War* (Harrap, 1949)

Piper, John, 'The Architecture of Destruction', *Architectural Review*, 14, 535, July 1941

Piratin, Phil, *Our Flag Stays Red* (Thames Publications, 1948)

Pope-Hennessy, James, *History Under Fire* (B.T. Batsford, 1941)

Protection of Your Home Against Air Raids (HMSO, 1938)

Ramsey, Winston G. (ed.), *The Blitz: Then and Now, Vol. II* (Battle of Britain Prints International, 1988)

Reckitt, Rachel, *Stepney Letters: Extracts from Letters Written by Rachel Reckitt from Stepney During the 'Blitz'* (privately published, Milthorpe, Cumbria, 1991)

Reid, Helen, *Bristol Under Siege: Surviving the Wartime Blitz* (Redcliffe Press, 2005)

Reynolds, Quentin, *The Wounded Don't Cry* (Cassell, 1941)

— *Only the Stars are Neutral* (Cassell, 1942)

Richards, J.M., *Memoirs of an Unjust Fella* (Weidenfeld & Nicolson, 1980)

Robertson, Seona and Wilson, Les, *Scotland's War* (Mainstream Publishing, 1995)

Robson, W.A. ('Regionaliter'), 'The Regional Commissioners', *Political Quarterly*, vol. 12, 1941

Ross, Alan, *The Colours of War: War Art, 1939–1945* (Jonathan Cape, 1983)

Rothenstein, John, *Modern English Painters, Vol. II* (Macdonald, 1984)

Rothwell, Stanley, *Lambeth at War* (SE1 People's History Project, Morley College, 1981)

'Russell, Sarah' (Marghanita Laski), *To Bed With Grand Music* (1946; Persephone Books, 2009)

Sansom, William, *The Blitz: Westminster at War* (Oxford University Press, 1947)

Saunders, Ann (ed.), *The London County Council Bomb Damage Maps, 1939–1945* (Introduction by Robin Woolven; London Topographical Society, 2005)

Schmideberg, Melitta, 'Some Observations on Individual Reactions to Air Raids', *International Journal of Pyscho-Analysis*, vol. xxii, 1942

Shawcross, William, *Queen Elizabeth, the Queen Mother: The Official Biography* (Macmillan, 2009)

Shea, Patrick, *Voices and the Sound of Drums: An Irish Autobiography* (Blackstaff Press, 1981)

Shephard, Ben, *A War of Nerves: Soldiers and Psychiatrists, 1914–1994* (Jonathan Cape, 2000)

Shirer, William L., *Berlin Diary, 1939–1941: The Rise of the Third Reich* (Hamish Hamilton, 1942)

Smith, Adrian, *The City of Coventry: Twentieth-Century Icon* (I.B. Tauris, 2006)

Smith, Malcolm, *Britain and 1940: History, Myth and Popular Memory* (Routledge, 2000)

Smyth, Charles, *Cyril Forster Garbett, Archbishop of York* (Hodder & Stoughton, 1959)

Southwark at War (compiled and edited by Rib Davies and Pamela Schweitzer) (Southwark Council Local Studies Library, 1969)

Spalding, Frances, *John Piper, Myfanwy Piper: Lives in Art* (Oxford University Press, 2009)

Stansky, Peter, 'Henry Moore and the Blitz' in *The Political Culture of Modern Britain: Studies in Memory of Stephen Koss*, (ed.) J.M.W. Bean (Hamish Hamilton, 1987)

— *The First Day of the Blitz* (Yale University Press, 2007)

Stedman, Henry W., *Battle of the Flames* (Jarrolds, n.d.)

Stonebridge, Lyndsey, 'Anxiety at a Time of Crisis', *History Workshop Journal*, no. 45, 1998

— *The Writing of Anxiety: Imagining Wartime in Mid-Century British Culture* (Palgrave Macmillan, 2007)

Strachey, John, *Post D* (Victor Gollancz, 1941)

Symonds, Julian (ed.), *An Anthology of War Poetry* (Penguin, 1942)

The Terrible Rain: The War Poets 1939–1945 (selected and arranged by Brian Gardner) (Methuen, 1966)

Thomas, Donald, *An Underworld at War: Spivs, Deserters, Racketeers and Civilians in the Second World War* (John Murray, 2003)

Thomson, Rear-Admiral George P., *Blue Pencil Admiral: The Inside Story of Press Censorship* (Sampson Low, Marston & Co., n.d.)

Thorpe, Andrew, *Parties at War: Political Organization in the Second World War* (Oxford University Press, 2009)

Titmuss, Richard M., *History of the Second World War: Problems of Social Policy* (HMSO, 1950)

Townsend, Leo, 'The Morning After' in Ian Norrie (ed.), *The Book of the City* (High Hill Books, 1961)

Trench, Richard, *London Before the Blitz* (Weidenfeld & Nicolson, 1989)

Trevor-Roper, Hugh (ed.), *Hitler's War Directives, 1939–45* (Sidgwick & Jackson, 1964)

Triggs, Anthony, *Portsmouth: A Shattered City* (Halsgrove, 2003)

Twyford, H.P., *It Came to Our Door: The Story of Plymouth Throughout the Second World War* (Underhill (Plymouth) Ltd, 1945)

Underdown, Alderman T.H., *Bristol Under Blitz: The Record of an Ancient City and Her People During the Battle of Britain* (J.W. Arrowsmith for the Lord Mayor War Services Council, 1942)

Vernon, Betty, *Ellen Wilkinson, 1891–1947* (Croom Helm, 1982)

Waller, Jane and Vaughan-Rees, Michael, *Blitz: The Civilian War 1940–45* (Optima, 1990)

Wallington, Neil, *Firemen at War: The Work of London's Fire-Fighters in the Second World War* (David & Charles, 1981)

Wartime Camden: Life in Camden Town During the First and Second World War (compiled by Valerie Hart and Lesley Marshall) (London Borough of Camden Libraries and Arts Department, 1983)

Wasley, Gerald, *Plymouth, A Shattered City: The Story of Hitler's Attack on Plymouth and its People, 1939–45* (Halsgrove, 1991; new edition, 2004)

Wassey, Michael, *Ordeal by Fire: The Story and Lessons of Fire Over Britain and the Battle of the Flames* (Secker & Warburg, 1941)

Webb, Edwin and Duncan, John, *Blitz Over Britain* (Spellmount, 1990)

Weymouth, Anthony, *Plague Year, March 1940–February 1941: Being the Diary of Anthony Weymouth* (George G. Harrap, 1942)

Wheeler-Bennett, Sir John, *King George VI: His Life and Reign* (Macmillan, 1958)

Whitmarsh, Andrew, *Portsmouth at War* (Tempus, 2007)

Whittington-Egan, Richard, *The Great Liverpool Blitz* (Gallery Press, 1987)

Williams, Francis, *Press, Parliament and People* (Heinemann, 1946)

Wills, Clair, *That Neutral Island: A Cultural History of Ireland During the Second World War* (Faber & Faber, 2007)

Wilson, H.A., *Death Over Haggerston* (A.W. Mowbray, 1941)

Wing, Sandra Koa (ed.), *Our Longest Days: A People's History of the Second World War* (Profile Books, 2008)

Winter, Dr Harry, 'The Man in White' in Allen A. Michie and Walter Graebner, *Lights of Freedom* (Allen & Unwin, 1941)

Wintle, Frank, *The Plymouth Blitz* (Bossiney Books, 1981)

Woolf, Virginia, *The Diary of Virginia Woolf. Vol. V, 1936–41*, (ed.) Anne Olivier Bell (Chatto & Windus, 1984)

— *The Letters of Virginia Woolf. Vol. VI, Leave the Letters Till We're Dead, 1936–41*, (ed.) Nigel Nicolson (The Hogarth Press, 1980)

Woolven, Robin, '"Playing Hitler's Game" from Fitzroy Road NW1: JBS Haldane in Controversy in WWII', *Camden History Review*, vol. 23, 1999

— 'First in the Country: Dr Richard Tee and Air Raid Precautions', *Hackney History*, vol. 6, 2000

— 'The London Experience of Regional Government, 1938–1945', *London Journal*, vol. 25 (2), 2000

Young-Bruehl, Elisabeth, *Anna Freud* (Macmillan, 1988)

Ziegler, Philip, *London at War 1939–1945* (Sinclair-Stevenson, 1995)

Zuckerman, Solly, *From Apes to Warlords: The Autobiography (1904–1946) of Solly Zuckerman* (Hamish Hamilton, 1978)

Unpublished Sources

The War Notebooks of Cyril Dunn, nos XIV and XV (reproduced by courtesy of Peter Dunn)

Sinclair-Louitt, Kenneth, *Very Little Luggage* (unpublished autobiography, http:/www.spartacus.schoolnet.co.uk)

Woolven, Robin, 'Civil Defence in London, 1935–1945' (unpublished PhD thesis, King's College, London, 2001)

Bodleian Library, Oxford

GB 161 Mss Eng. Hist. c.495–8 The Diaries of Euan Wallace

Camden Local History Archive

H 355.23 '*Swiss Cottager* Bulletins' 1–4

Churchill College, Cambridge
GBR/0014 ARUP The Papers of Ove Arup

Glasgow City Archive, The Mitchell Library
TD 646/14 The Papers of Colin Ferguson

Imperial War Museum Department of Documents
67/262/1/2. Transcripts of Thames Television interviews:
Robert Baltrop
Jill Craigie
Cyril Demarne
Stan Durling
Emily Eary
Hajo Hermann
Stan Hook
Leonard Jeacocke
Ivor Leverton
Irene Moseley
J.M. Richards
Louise Savage
Ralph Tubbs
Margaret Turpin
Conservation Shelf: The Papers of Veronica Goddard, The Papers of Violet Regan
95/8/1 The Papers of M.E.A. Allan
91/51 The Papers of V. Bawtree
09/37/1 'ARPing on it'. The Papers of Frederick R. Bodley
79/27/1 'War Diary. A Chronicle of events, personal and political. Which took place during three years of War against Oppression which commenced in September 1939 recorded by Sidney Chave'
95/13/1 'Memoir'. The Papers of Mrs H. Cobb
86/46/1 (P) 'The War Diary of Gwladys Cox'
04/31/1 Jean Crossley, 'A Middle-Class War'
89/17/1 'The Second World War Diaries of Mrs A.D. Deacon (*née* Hawkins) MBE
01/31/1 The Papers of Mrs M. Fenlon
99/9/1 The Papers of Mrs Yvonne Green
04/40/1 'The Blitz on London'. The Papers of Mrs I. Haslewood
80/30/1 The Papers of F.W. Hurd
P151 The Papers of J.P. Hutchinson

88/49/1 The Papers of P. Lambah

91/5/1 The Papers of the Reverend J.G. Markham

99/66/1 The Papers of Miss I. Naish

88/10/01 The Papers of W.B. Regan

P129 The Papers of B.J. Rogers

99/66/1 ' "Blitz and Pieces". My Life During the Second World War'. The Papers of Florence Mary ('Flo') Rollinson

89/14/1 Barbara Roose, 'Got Any Gum, Chum?'

PPMCR/199 The Papers of Joan Veazey

95/14/1 'Journal Under the Terror'. The Papers of Phyllis Warner

07/20/1 The Papers of Private Stanley Wilkinson

Lambeth Palace Library

Mss. 2686 The Diaries of the Reverend Alan C. Don

Mss. 3433 The Papers of Father John Groser

London Metropolitan Archive

Acc. 2243/14/1/2 The Diaries of Anthony Heap

Mass-Observation Archive

'Living Through the Blitz' Box 233, 230

File Reports:

A24 ARP: Fulham April–July 1939

253 Air Raids; Reactions to air raid alarms (London): Taking shelter (24–25 June); feelings during raids; reports from Bolton, Romford and London ARP post

325 'Cooper's Snoopers' press campaign against MoI and Duff Cooper

415 Notes on Morale: reactions to air raid damage

425 Young Men in Tubes: behaviour in the underground

431 Survey of voluntary and official bodies during the bombing of the East End

436 Shelter in London: consideration of types and availability of shelters; how people behave in shelters; the psychology of shelters

451 Reception areas: refugees from blitzed areas

465 How the press treated the Blitz

495 Coventry: the effects of bombing

516 Southampton: effects of recent raids

517 Southampton: further reports on raids

529 The aftermath of town blitzes: summary of research in Bristol, Southampton and Cheltenham

536 Fire spotters and compulsory ARP
537 Christmas 1940
538 Liverpool and Manchester: effects of the blitz
601 Bristol: raids and morale
602 Cardiff: raids and morale
603 Southampton: raids and morale
607 Clydebank
626 Plymouth: reaction to raids
640 Hull: effects of air raids
706 Liverpool: effects of the raids
883 Plymouth: raid reactions
Diarist 5462 (Moya Woodside)

The National Archive
CAB 753HO 45/18540
HO 186/626 & 556
HO 186/952/2352
HO 186/1603
HO 186/2352
HO 199/324
HO 199/178/X/J 5467
HO 199/324
HO 199/1442
INF 1/174A
INF 1/251
INF 1/290
INF 1/292
INF 1/679
INF 1/845
INF 1/848
PRO 207/1101

People's History Museum, Manchester
The Papers of Alan Hutt

Scottish Record Office
HH 50/91 'WVS Report on Clydebank
HH 50/95 'Some Impressions of Clydebank'

INDEX